Turbulent Transformations

Turbulent Transformations

Non-Brahmin Śrīvaiṣṇavas on Religion, Caste and Politics in Tamil Nadu

Katherine Young

Orient BlackSwan

TURBULENT TRANSFORMATIONS: NON-BRAHMIN ŚRĪVAIṢṆAVAS ON RELIGION, CASTE AND POLITICS IN TAMIL NADU

ORIENT BLACKSWAN PRIVATE LIMITED

Registered Office
3-6-752 Himayatnagar, Hyderabad 500 029 (Telangana), India
e-mail: centraloffice@orientblackswan.com

Other Offices
Bengaluru, Chennai, Guwahati, Hyderabad,
Kolkata, Mumbai, New Delhi, Noida,
Patna, Visakhapatnam

First published by Orient Blackswan Private Limited 2021

ISBN 978-81-949258-8-0

The responsibility for the correctness of internal details rests with the publisher.
The territorial waters of India extend into the sea to a distance of 12 nautical miles measured from the appropriate base line.
The interstate boundaries amongst Arunachal Pradesh, Assam and Meghalaya shown on this map are as interpreted from the 'North-Eastern Areas (Reorganisation) Act. 1971', but have yet to be verified.
The external boundaries and coastlines of India agree with the Record/ Master Copy certified by Survey of India.
The state boundaries between Uttarakhand & Uttar Pradesh, Bihar & Jharkhand and Chhattisgarh & Madhya Pradesh have not been verified by the Governments concerned.
The spelling of names in this map have been taken from various sources.

Typeset in
Palatino LT Std 10.5/12.4
by Le Studio Graphique, Gurgaon 122 007

032697

Printed in India at
Akash Press, New Delhi 110 020

Published by
Orient Blackswan Private Limited
3-6-752, Himayatnagar, Hyderabad 500 029
e-mail: info@orientblackswan.com

In memory of Dr K. K. A. Venkatachari (1930–2016), who bridged the worlds of traditional learning and modern scholarship, and who inspired and facilitated this book.

Contents

Images and Map

Images

Map

Acknowledgements

My gratitude goes to the Social Sciences and Research Council of Canada, which supported my fieldwork in India; to McGill University for making me a James McGill Professor with funding that contributed to this project over a decade; and to the Centre for Studies in Religion and Society at the University of Victoria, where I have been an Associate Fellow.

I am especially grateful to all the people whom I interviewed in Tamil Nadu, who so generously shared their experiences, memories and insights. In addition, I thank A. Pandurangan, B. M. Sundaram, Davesh Soneji and T. Janaguiraman, who travelled with me to villages and temples; Robert Inkster, who provided photographic and logistical support on one research trip; Paige Zarazun and Nicola Hayward, who typed up my field notes; Raymond B. Williams, who shared his field notes, which are now located in Wabash College Lilly Library Archives; and Srilata Raman, Paul Bramadat, and Ramesh Bairy for their astute comments on the draft. In addition, I appreciate the diligent care of the various teams at Orient BlackSwan.

Finally, I take responsibility for the interpretations offered here, unless attributed specifically to others.

Conventions

Traditional Śrīvaiṣṇava works are written not only in Sanskrit, Tamil, Maṇipravāḷam and Telugu, but they have also been printed in various scripts (for instance, the Telugu script with its *grantha* letters has been used for Maṇipravāḷam texts). To facilitate access to Śrīvaiṣṇavism for those who have only a general knowledge about Hinduism, I have favoured Sanskrit spellings for words that are Tamilised Sanskrit (thus, Rāmānuja instead of Rāmānujar or Irāmānujar, or *sabhā* instead of *sabhai*, or *maṭha* instead of *maṭam* [Tamil]). I give Sanskrit and Tamil equivalents on first use for key terms.

In general, I have used standard Sanskrit and Tamil diacritical marks for words that appear in historical sources, such as names of deities, technical theological and philosophical terms, and people's names (unless there is another standard spelling in the scholarly literature). After the first citation of a name, I have offered shortened versions of many long names and eliminated titles to make it easier for those not familiar with these languages and subjects to read the book. I have used English spellings of names that appear in English-language sources in Tamil Nadu. In some cases where an English equivalent exists, I have used the English word. In addition, I have added an 's' to Tamil plurals to Anglicise the word. Moreover, I have used the spellings of my informants' names provided by them.

Because place names have changed over time, I generally use the name appropriate to the historical context, for example, Madras Presidency in the early twentieth century but Tamil Nadu after Indian independence, or in general comments. Because my interviewees alternated between the names of Madras or Chennai and Puducherry or Pondicherry, both appear.

I do not use diacritical marks for caste names; rather, I use the version common in English language works, but have given Tamil, Telugu or Sanskrit variants in a note. Nor do I use diacritical marks for names of villages, towns and cities; for these names, I follow the spellings of place names on current Tamil Nadu maps with one exception. I use 'T' and not 'Th' in names such as Tanjavur or Tiruchirappalli. However, in Appendix 1 on the location of places, I provide variant spellings.

For the discerning eye, there will be anomalies in the use or non-use of diacritical marks (for instance, the names of some organisations (*sabhā*s) will appear with diacritical marks but others will not, depending on my source. Words and names that are a combination of Sanskrit and Tamil may have features of both languages, as in Ekāṅgi Svāmikaḷ, where Ekāṅgi is Sanskrit and Svāmikaḷ is a Sanskrit word with a Tamil suffix. It is impossible to be absolutely systematic with the linguistic complexity of this subject matter.

The *Nāmam*: A Note

The book cover features a Śrīvaiṣṇava mark worn by men that sanctifies the body in twelve places or just the forehead. It is called the *tirunāmam* (sacred name) or simply *nāmam* (name) because one utters the name of God when applying it. It is also called the *ūrdhva-puṇḍra*, which means a mark (*puṇḍra*) that rises upward (*ūrdhva*) and thereby signifies the spiritual upward path. The two vertical white lines symbolise the two feet of God, which means the way and the goal, but also purity, because they are white in colour. The central red mark between them, made of turmeric and vermillion (*kuṁkum*), signifies the Goddess (Śrī-Lakṣmī) and her compassionate grace.

By extension, the *nāmam* is used to sacralise any place and identify its association with Śrīvaiṣṇavism. The shape of the *nāmam* with a pedestal is that of the Teṉkalai subsect; when the bottom is rounded, it signifies the Vaṭakalai subsect. Most non-Brahmin Śrīvaiṣṇavas are Teṉkalais, although some are Vaṭakalais.

one

Introduction: Setting the Stage

The past two centuries have been a period of momentous religious, social, and political changes in southern India. These include the Tamil Renaissance, late colonialism in the Madras Presidency,[1] Dravidian nationalism, Dalit mobilisation, the Indian struggle for Independence, and then the new political entity Tamil Nadu.[2]

At the epicentre of these changes has been an awakening to injustices—those created by colonialism, but also for non-Brahmins, those long-standing ones created by the caste system. Non-Brahmins have dreamed that equality would create better futures for them. They have refashioned the past into new stories through recuperation, retrospection, and images of reform, revolution and utopia. With power shifting, hierarchies re-aligning and caste identities merging or colliding, they have re-imagined their own identities.

This book is about the turbulent transformations in modern Tamil Nadu from the perspective of non-Brahmin Śrīvaiṣṇavas. Vaiṣṇavism is a pan-Indian umbrella term for the tradition that understands the supreme to be the one God with various names, such as Viṣṇu, Nārāyaṇa, Kṛṣṇa and Rāma, a cluster of deities with historical and regional overlaps and variations. Although some devotees, especially villagers, simply think of themselves as Vaiṣṇavas (Vaiṇavas in Tamil), others identify with a particular regional Vaiṣṇava tradition. In Tamil Nadu, this most likely would be Śrīvaiṣṇavism—the community of those who worship Viṣṇu and his consort Śrī, with its philosophical tradition known as Viśiṣṭādvaita passed down through a lineage of preceptors—although other Vaiṣṇava communities such as Mādhvas and Maharashtrian Vaiṣṇavas also exist.

Most of my interviews were with non-Brahmins who self-identify as Śrīvaiṣṇavas. They were from many castes or caste clusters, including Chettiyar, Dalit, Icai Velala, Naidu, Pillai, Reddiyar, Sattada, Vanniyar, Yadava, and Vellalar. I found a fluid use of the terms Śrīvaiṣṇava and Vaiṣṇava by non-Brahmins belonging to this sect today.[3] Non-Brahmin Śrīvaiṣṇavas most often refer to themselves as Bhāgavatas (devotees).[4] One can sometimes identify non-Brahmins who have been initiated[5] by the common suffix to their names: 'Rāmānuja Dāsar', servant of Rāmānuja. (Rāmānuja, who lived in the twelfth century, was the most important thinker—later considered a salvific figure—in this tradition.)

During my interviews, I never heard my informants (whether they were Dalits themselves or belonged to another caste) use the word 'Dalit',[6] which has pan-Indian currency today as the name used by former outcastes. Moreover, my Dalit informants did not self-identify as an oppositional group outside the non-Brahmin or Śrīvaiṣṇava nomenclature, although they spoke with concern of the special problems that their community faced, or spoke with pride about their roles in Dalit organisations. Still, I am well aware that many things might have been left unsaid because I was a Western researcher. Nor did I hear the Śrīvaiṣṇava circumlocution 'Tirukkulattār', which literally means 'those of the auspicious clan or caste', a Śrīvaiṣṇava euphemism for those once called outcastes.[7] However, I did commonly hear the term Harijans, those born of [god] Hari/Viṣṇu, especially if they were followers of Gandhi. People also used the term Adidravidas, the original Dravidians, in a positive or neutral way, to refer to those once called outcastes. When writing about outcastes in the past, I have used this pejorative term to be accountable to historical realities. Otherwise, I have maintained the term used by informants, such as Harijan or Adidravida. In general discussions, however, I have used the word Dalit. Despite the fact that Dalit voices in Tamil Nadu today have rightly drawn attention to how the term 'non-Brahmin' has been glossed in order to incorporate all those who are not Brahmins and how this has had a negative and even subversive effect on the emergence of Dalit articulation, I have often included Dalit Śrīvaiṣṇavas under non-Brahmin as an umbrella term, unless the context suggests otherwise.

I focus on the sect Śrīvaiṣṇavism, because far more has been written on Tamil non-Brahmin Śaivas than on non-Brahmin Vaiṣṇavas. This is partly because Śaivism (the tradition that reveres Śiva as supreme god) has been the dominant sect in Tamil-speaking regions and has attracted the interest of Orientalists and other scholars.[8] More specifically, I focus on the Teṉkalai sub-sect of Śrīvaiṣṇavism, because its theology is one of radical caste and outcaste inclusiveness, although this has rarely been the sociological reality. Nevertheless, this theology remains for Teṉkalai non-Brahmins today a spiritual inspiration, as they aspire to justice and assume new religious roles.

Finally, I focus on Teṉkalai Śrīvaiṣṇavism, because that is my own area of scholarly expertise. I have made many research trips to Tamil Nadu and have had the privilege of studying with several hereditary religious leaders, and knowing their families over decades. This has facilitated my entry into the existential thoughts and feelings of my informants between 2006 and 2016, the period of my more than twenty interviews that took place mainly in eastern and central Tamil Nadu (in and around Chennai, Sriperumbudur, Puducherry, Tanjavur, and Tiruchirappalli).

Little is known about Śrīvaiṣṇava non-Brahmin history. We often hear about how history disappears, especially in the absence of institutions (which can include lineages of chanters or storytellers). Even manuscripts and books crumble from seaside humidity, or get eaten by ants. And temple renovators are notorious for covering over ancient inscriptions. Śrīvaiṣṇava non-Brahmin histories, which families try to maintain informally as their oral traditions, have disappeared over the centuries, and can be recovered today only by reading between the lines of Brahmin-authored texts or by studying inscriptions that have somehow survived the ravages of time. This is not unlike the loss and partial recovery of women's history, which has preoccupied so many scholars for the past half-century and more.

Śrīvaiṣṇavism has a long tradition of commenting on its key scriptures and writing works on its theological system. Asking questions about this tradition from non-Brahmin perspectives can provide clues to not only its religious ideals, but also its history of caste relations, and about what happened under Brahmin religious domination. And that helps us understand the interface of religious, social and political identities today.

But even modern non-Brahmin Śrīvaiṣṇava history is disappearing because of a lack of non-Brahmin memoirs and scholarship on this tradition. This brings me to my task: to capture Śrīvaiṣṇava non-Brahmin oral histories. Oral history

> is the collection and recording of personal memoires as historical documentation. ... it emphasizes the significance of human experience. ... Oral history is the best method to use ... to get an idea not only of what happened, but what past times meant to people and how it felt to be a part of those times.[9]

This characterisation of oral history is helpful but inadequate in the case of non-Brahmin Śrīvaiṣṇavism. The fact that many of my informants were very knowledgeable about their religious tradition means that they also offered important historical information. I complemented what my interviewees said with my own textual knowledge of Śrīvaiṣṇavism, as well as general historical and political background based on inscriptions, gazetteers during the Raj, court cases, hagiographies, published works by non-Brahmins and newspaper articles.

When I found a conflict between informant and scholarly accounts, I presented only the voice of my interviewee in that section, but sometimes offered a scholarly version elsewhere. I have not presented the textual origins of all the religious stories I was told. Tracing these through many hagiographies and other sources from the fifteenth century—some are even found in modern films—is a large research project in itself, which I must leave for others to do.

Sometimes I interviewed a person only once for several hours; other times I followed that up with one or more additional interviews. All interviews followed ethical principles regarding informed consent based on a discussion of what the project was about—that they could end the interview at any time they wanted, that they could request that some information remain off the record, and that they could choose whether to be identified and photographed. Because I was dealing with delicate topics, I used the most non-invasive interviewing methods possible. I took notes, I did not use recorders or video cameras, and I allowed the interviews to turn into conversations. Most people spoke English. When they did not, my travelling companions who understood the local Tamil or Telugu dialect became translators. My informants decided how much they wanted to reveal. Some willingly told me everything that they could think of; others were reticent and sometimes left their tales hanging. One informant asked me not to reveal his family's caste identity. My research looks somewhat uneven, therefore, but is, I hope, valuable testimony nonetheless.

One of the topics on which my research is uneven is that of gender. I did many more interviews with men than women. One reader has rightly commented that there is a lack of gender equality and analysis in this book. To my chagrin, as someone who has published a great deal about Hinduism and women, I agree.

Why did this happen? In part, because the public religious leadership of Śrīvaiṣṇavism is still heavily male-oriented—*ācāryas*, *jīyars*, *arcakas*, *sabhā* leaders, publishers, trust officials, village elders, and so forth. I was in these male networks to locate informants and was therefore passed on from one man to another as the network extended. The interviews often took place in public places, such as *sabhā* offices and temple *maṇṭapams*. Only when the interviews were in homes did I encounter women, but even there, some women were 'traditionally' behind the scenes, and I could not break out of the interview process, which had been pre-arranged—usually with a time-limit related to the availability of my contact person and transportation—to develop an in-depth conversation with them, away from male ears. I unsuccessfully tried to set up appointments with several prominent Śrīvaiṣṇava women active in religious circles.

As a result of these problems, I decided that I would need another ethnographic project[10] just on Śrīvaiṣṇava women's religion, especially their views on access to religious leadership, caste and politics. Nevertheless, some of my interviews with women gave me insights into women's lives and their changing roles. I set the stage for understanding these changes by providing a summary of the history of Śrīvaiṣṇava views on the roles of women in a section of this chapter, and the changes that I found reflected in the interviews in the concluding chapter.

In short, because my research was focussed on the relation of religion, caste and politics, it was based mainly on the male world of religious leadership in the public realm. I do not think being a woman and an academic had much influence on what men decided to tell me. For this research, I was an honorary male, as it were. Most were delighted that I was interested in non-Brahmins.

By way of introduction, further comment on the word 'non-Brahmin' is necessary. To those unfamiliar with the modern history of Tamil Nadu, non-Brahmin sounds derivative, negative and patronising. Although the word non-Brahmin had occurred occasionally since the late nineteenth century in the Madras Presidency, the Justice Party's 'Non-Brahmin Manifesto' of 1916 used it thirty times, transforming it into a powerful statement of political goals. After the storm of protest subsided—the Manifesto had argued against the British giving self-rule to Indians, because that would simply re-entrench the power of Brahmins over other castes—the term non-Brahmin gained currency. It came to function as an invitation, as it were, to mobilise over the formation of a new identity, one that opposed the hegemony of Brahmins.

In caste associations and new non-Brahmin organisations, non-Brahmins articulated their experiences of humiliation and deprivation. In almost all non-Brahmin communities, according to V. Geetha and S. V. Rajadurai, there were teachers, lawyers and other educated people who introduced to their communities '... a discourse of rights with which caste ranking could be questioned, privileges of higher castes criticised and a corporate caste identity established. Thus, supra-local sodalities emerged; an imagined fraternity of disparate sub-castes was forged.'[11] The imaged fraternity was sufficiently flexible to engage local groups, yet could appeal evocatively to many groups.

The terms Brahmin and non-Brahmin remain deeply lodged in Tamil consciousness and will continue to frame its discourse as long as there is mutual opposition or a memory of times when that famed the landscape of religion, caste and politics. Indeed, my informants freely used the word 'non-Brahmin' to describe themselves, but not always and not always in a context of anti-Brahmanism. Even so, people wanted to tell their stories of discrimination and of hopes for the future.

For many, such as Śrīvaiṣṇavas and those who live in Tamil Nadu, the information in this chapter will be very familiar, and they may move quickly on. Others, however, will need some background to understand the interviews, and so I begin by introducing the religious orientation of this tradition. I continue with the examination of Śrīvaiṣṇavism's position on women, followed by a discussion of caste conundrums found in this tradition and the impact of modern politics, including an analysis of one of modern Tamil Nadu's most famous leaders, Periyar, who came from a Śrīvaiṣṇava family but denounced it and was a central figure in the non-Brahmin movement.

A Sectarian Primer

One etymology of the English word 'sect' goes back to the Latin *secta*, which means a way or path, and by extension a following or school of thought from the proto-Indo-European *sekw*, to follow.[12] We find sects in Indian religious history, defined as a school of thought or religious community with an established path to salvation, usually established by a founder. Śrīvaiṣṇavism is such a way or path. Its concept of founder, however, is traced back through a lineage of teachers and poets to the supreme God himself. The other etymology of sect is from the Latin *secta* from the Proto-European root *sek*, to cut.[13] In this sense, a tradition is cut apart in the sense of being divided to form subsects or new sects. In the case of Śrīvaiṣṇavism, that would be the Teṉkalai and Vaṭakalai sub-sects.

Here, I offer a primer on mainstream Teṉkalai Śrīvaiṣṇava views found in Brahmin-authored texts about the supreme deity, scripture, sacred places, religious leadership, initiation, service and temples. This will help us to understand non-Brahmin engagement with these ideas and gauge how their views are similar to or different from Brahmin ones on these topics. This will also help us to understand what has changed today.

The Supreme Deity

The supreme deity for Śrīvaiṣṇavas has many names and forms. His most common names are Perumāḷ, Nārāyaṇa, Bālāji, Viṣṇu and Kṛṣṇa, although he is said to have 1,000 names, many of which are the Tamil names of temple towns.[14] He has many forms, too, which are classified in the Pañcarātra texts[15] as five types: supreme, cosmic emanation, incarnation in the distant past, incarnation in statue-form, and presence within human beings.[16] He is a deity of royal power, yet also of tender grace and beauty. Descriptions of him and the landscapes where he lives draw on the poetic conventions of ancient Tamil Caṅkam poetry as systematised by the *Tolkāppiyam* (ca. fourth to sixth century CE).

Today, Kṛṣṇa, Rāma and Bālāji (Vēṅkaṭeśvara) are the most popular divine names in villages. Tamils were worshipping Kṛṣṇa by the fourth century CE; this tradition is deeply embedded in many village folk traditions. Over the next few centuries, Rāma became part of folk religion, and Bālāji from medieval times attracted devotees throughout Tamil country, especially in its eastern region, and in the Telugu-speaking country to the north. Today, he is an important pan-Indian deity and his temple is the richest in India. Śrī, the goddess, who also has many names and forms, is the supreme deity's consort.

Scripture

Śrīvaiṣṇava scripture includes both Tamil and Sanskrit texts. Tamil scripture consists of the collected works of 12 poet-sages called *āḻvār*s, who lived from the seventh century CE to the ninth (see Appendix 2). Their works were canonised centuries later as the *Nālāyira-divyaprabandham*, the divine collection of 4,000 [verses] or, for short here, the *Divyaprabandham*, also called the Tamil Veda. Sanskrit scripture includes the Vedas and post-Vedic texts. Among these are the Pañcarātra Āgamas, manuals for temple architecture and rituals used by priests in many temples. Śrīvaiṣṇavas refer to these scriptures as *ubhaya-vedānta* (both *vedānta*s)[17] to honour the legacies of Tamil and Sanskrit traditions.[18]

Until modern times, Brahmins generally controlled the ritual and scriptural traditions by teaching only Brahmins Sanskrit, which was necessary for knowledge of the Vedas and the Pañcarātra Āgamas. Moreover, Brahmins controlled the teaching and interpretation of the many Śrīvaiṣṇava texts they wrote in Maṇipravāḷam (literally, that which consists of sapphires and corals; it refers to a mixed language, in this case of Tamil and Sanskrit[19]) because people needed to know Sanskrit to understand this mixed language. Since Śrīvaiṣṇava non-Brahmins (Bhāgavatas) did not have access to Sanskrit and the Vedas, the Tamil *Divyaprabandham* was important for their religious life and path to salvation. One cannot claim that Brahmins are just Sanskrit-oriented, however, because they too give importance to recitation of the Tamil Veda as a key part of many rituals, and over the centuries have written important commentaries on *āḻvār* works.

Sacred Places

There are 108 sacred places (*divyadeśas*),[20] according to a list compiled from the works of the *āḻvār*s, most of them by far in Tamil Nadu, with a few in northern India and Nepal and two beyond the terrestrial sphere altogether (the Milk Ocean and Vaikuṇṭha, the Supreme Heaven).[21] The three most important places in Tamil Nadu, according to works on the 108 places, have been Srirangam, Tirumalai-Tirupati and Kanchipuram.[22] They have been especially important not only as locations of important temples that attract pilgrims, but also as intellectual and institutional centres of the tradition. In addition, the birthplaces of the *āḻvār*s and early *ācārya*s are important sacred places (Sriperumbudur, for instance, is famous as Rāmānuja's birthplace).

Other places of sacred significance are the *maṭha*s (Tamil *maṭam*). These are associated with lineages of Brahmin ascetics, some going back to the fourteenth century. In popular parlance today, *maṭha* might also refer to any Śrīvaiṣṇava building in which devotees meet. This building might function as a *dharmaśālā* or *choultry*, that is, a charitable guesthouse, usually at an important temple, where devotees stay and eat, especially during festivals. A synonym in this sense is *rāmānuja kūṭam* (Rāmānuja's house or hall[23]).

Bhāgavatas have established their own sacred spaces. These range from house shrines (called *kōyil ālvār*) and village or city temples with non-Brahmin priests, to *maṭhas* where non-Brahmin ascetics live, to places called *bhajana* monasteries (*bhajana-maṭhas*) or *bhajana* temples (*bhajana kōyils*). According to Robert Leopold, *bhajanas* consist of '[m]en, women, and children meet[ing] in some structure .... Placed upon the bench is a framed, painted representation of the main deity to be worshipped ... and the objects used for worship.'[24] Sometimes, Bhāgavatas refer to these temple-like places by the term *sabhā* (Ta. *sabhai*), which is a more general term for a place where people meet. They might also be called *rāmānuja kūṭams*.

There are some village temples that have Śrīvaiṣṇava non-Brahmin priests and non-Brahmin worshippers, others that have Brahmin priests but non-Brahmin worshippers, and still others where non-Brahmins function as priests not only for their own deity, but also for other village deities.

Religious Leadership

Śrīvaiṣṇavism is often described as a *sampradāya* in the sense of a tradition, religious school or system, based on teachings that have been transmitted from one teacher to another. Brahmin religious leaders of this *sampradāya* have been of two types: *ācāryas* and *jīyars (cīyars*; jeeyars; jeears). Since the relation of Śrīvaiṣṇava Brahmins (called Ayyangars, Aiyankars, Iyengars) and non-Brahmins has today been informed in part by the concept of Brahmin leadership, I will describe briefly the development of the concepts of *ācārya* and *jīyar*.

Ācāryas are the foremost of Brahmin Śrīvaiṣṇava householders because of their knowledge of the sacred texts, their orthodox conduct, their right to initiate people and their special role in guiding disciples to salvation. As such, *ācāryas* are distinguished from other learned Brahmins who chant and teach the Vedas or *sampradāya* works, those who are temple priests (*arcaka*s), and those who perform the rites of passage such as weddings and funerals (*purohita*s).

The concept of *ācārya* is closely connected to the idea of lineage. Between the eleventh and thirteenth centuries, an intellectual lineage of Brahmins in Tamil Nadu with family or teacher-disciple relations was developing a cohesive identity. The first chronological list of the important figures (Nammāḻvār, Nāthamuni, Yāmuna and especially Rāmānuja, the twelfth-century thinker who enhanced the philosophical dimension of the tradition) appears in the writings of Rāmānuja's disciple Kūreśa.[25] Other important figures were gradually included in the list (see Appendix 2).

By the mid-thirteenth century, some of these early *ācārya*s were represented in statue-form in the temples and worshipped as divine, as were the *āḻvār*s. According to Erin McCann, by the end of that century, Piḷḷai Lokācārya had defined the *ācārya* as 'both divine and human' and 'the tangible manifestation of the Lord's compassion for the soul', but also the *ācārya* as 'always a soul' who is 'subservient and dependent'.[26] Piḷḷai Lokācārya formalised, moreover, the concept of love of the *ācārya* alone as a true and independent means of salvation. Although the Lord and the devotee are eternally linked, this link may remain dormant until the *ācārya* spiritually awakens the individual and takes on his or her sins. The *ācārya* removes the fear of rebirth. Even today, Teṉkalais argue that salvation will occur at the end of this very life, and they should not even contemplate rebirth. Having surrendered completely to God, they should live joyously as if in supreme heaven.[27]

The *Guruparamparā Prabhāvam 6000* and the *Kōyiḻ Oḻuku*, which I date in the seventeenth and eighteenth century, respectively,[28] although they contain some earlier material, mention that the early (*pūrva*) *ācārya* group (which had come to include famous figures such as Vedānta Deśika and Maṇavāḷa Māmuni) had been extended to seventy-four (Brahmin) families whose lineage went back to Rāmānuja, or a figure associated with him.[29]

A tradition developed that the *ācārya* mantle was passed from the *ācārya* to his eldest son. This *ācārya* institution was not lodged in the individual who might have faults; rather, it was lodged in the institution of the lineage of *ācārya*s. Some *ācārya*s had privileges and rights in particular temples and often lived nearby. In some families, younger sons migrated to new locales and became *ācārya*s, thereby creating sub-lineages and spreading the influence of Śrīvaiṣṇavism. This *ācārya* system could function because the relationship between the *ācārya* and his disciple was reciprocal. The *ācārya* looked after the disciple's soul, as it were, by removing fear of rebirth and guiding the disciple toward salvation, and the disciple looked after the *ācārya*'s body (and his family) by providing all the necessities of life.

Even more classifications of *ācārya*s developed. According to one, some *ācārya*s do the initiations only for their own families and others do the initiations for other people. Yet another distinguishes the *ācārya*s who give initiations and introduce the scriptures by reading the first and last stanzas, and those who teach the important works (*grantha*s) of the tradition.

There is also a parallel ascetic system. In the early period of Śrīvaiṣṇavism, some key figures such as Rāmānuja and Nañjīyar were ascetics. The ritual of renouncing the householder's stage of life is called *saṁnyāsa*. According to the Dharmaśāstras, renunciation is a twice-born (in practice, usually a Brahmin) option,[30] generally reserved for the last stage of life, yet allowed earlier as an exception.

The decision of whether to be a Brahmin householder or an ascetic must have been originally fluid; there were many ascetics who had once been married in the early community. Although the early *ācārya*s included both householders and ascetics,[31] from the fourteenth century CE, the Brahmin ascetic option was being formalised as the *jīyar* tradition, ascetics who were initiated members of *maṭha*s or monasteries. (*Maṭha*s were common among Advaitins, Śaivas and other religious communities.) *Jīyar*s or *tridaṇḍi*s (those with a three-pronged staff) were Śrīvaiṣṇava Brahmin ascetics[32] who ministered to the intellectual and spiritual needs of their disciples, with roles very similar to those of the *ācārya*s.

Three important Teṉkalai Brahmin-led *maṭha*s in Tamil country that have had many non-Brahmin disciples have been the Emperumāṉār Maṭha at Tirukkoyilur (in the region west of Puducherry),[33] which combined *jīyar* and *ācārya* traditions; the Vānamāmalai Mutt (in the southern district of Tirunelveli)[34] and the Yadugiri Yatiraja Mutt (at Sriperumbudur, Rāmānuja's birthplace near Kanchipuram).[35]

Other ascetics are called *ekāṅgi*s. *Ekāṅgi*—from one (*eka*) limb (*aṅgi*)—is a special term for any Śrīvaiṣṇava ascetic who carries a one-pronged staff and has not had *saṁnyāsa* (formal initiation into asceticism). He might be a Brahmin bachelor or a non-Brahmin ascetic (who is barred from the ritual of *saṁnyāsa*). Some *ekāṅgi*s have had their own *maṭha*s, and this is true for non-Brahmins as well. Of particular relevance here is the fact that some non-Brahmin *ekāṅgi*s have been religious leaders.

Non-Brahmins have been important patrons and administrators for the temples, moreover, and some have performed non-priestly roles of temple service or have been priests in non-Brahmin temples. Non-Brahmin religious leaders who are householders are generally called *mudaliyars*. Today, they often give discourses on the scriptures or lead the chanting in Bhāgavata groups.

Initiation

In Śrvaiṣṇavism, another kind of initiation is called *samāśrayaṇam*. It includes both the concept of *prapatti*—taking refuge with God and totally surrendering to him[36]—and a ritual called *pañcasaṁskāra*,[37] which consists of five acts: being branded with an image of a conch and discus on the shoulders; marking the forehead with the sectarian emblem, the *nāmam*;[38] assuming a new name; being taught the three mantras;[39] and worshipping an image. During this ritual, the *ācārya* introduces 'the soul to God', teaches the mantras to his disciple and explains them according to Śrīvaiṣṇava interpretations from secret works. Next, the *ācārya* recites the verses (*taṉiyaṉs*) for each of his ancestors back to the family's link to Rāmānuja. The disciple then repeats a verse about his own *ācārya* (which he or she will do from this time on during morning worship). After this ritual, initiates are to be vegetarian, strictly do their daily worship at their household altar and maintain other orthodox practices.[40]

Jīyars also perform *samāśrayaṇam*. There was once a controversy over whether *jīyars* should do this ritual, which involves a sacred fire. Since, as ascetics, *jīyars* were to beg for their food, they should not touch fire, which was associated with the householder's hearth. This controversy suggests that at some point *ācāryas* were resisting the *jīyar* claim on their role. Today, *jīyars* do perform *samāśrayaṇam* (a householder disciple prepares the fire). In any case, initiation by an *ācārya* or *jīyar* is popularly believed to guarantee liberation (although theologically, that is the prerogative of the gracious God).

Based on her interviews with Śrīvaiṣṇava Brahmins today, Srilata Raman found that those Brahmin men and women who knew less about Śrīvaiṣṇava rituals and theology thought that the ritual signified a transition to a more orthodox life defined by dietary restrictions and enhanced daily worship at the household altar. By contrast, knowledgeable Śrīvaiṣṇava orthodox Brahmin men thought that the ritual qualified them for some temple and domestic rituals.[41] My interviews reveal that many Bhāgavatas today share the first view—that the ritual is a transition to a more orthodox life-style—although some think that it is the ritual that makes them a Śrīvaiṣṇava rather than just an ordinary Vaiṣṇava, or that it is a ritual that gurantees salvation.

Service

Serving God and his devotees, called *kaiṅkarya*, is central to Śrīvaiṣṇavism.[42] The *āḻvārs* often mention it. Nammāḻvār, for instance, describes how he approached the Divine Mother as mediator and took refuge at the Lord's sacred feet. With all obstacles now gone, he had desire only to do all loving service.[43] Periyāḻvār calls serving the Lord a great privilege and declares that he will never serve anyone else so that there will be no blot on God's fame.[44] Tirumaṅkai comments that 'out of my great love for you, I am eager to serve you'.[45] *Āḻvār* poems often refer to worship as service: purifying the floor, decorating sacred places with auspicious designs, offering lamps and pots of water, growing, picking and planting flowers, and so on. In addition, they refer to service as humble solidarity with other devotees. Nammāḻvār, for instance, refers to himself as a servant of the servants of the servants.[46]

*Ācārya*s too mention service in their hymns of praise, commentaries, and theological works. Rāmānuja, for instance, uses the analogy of God as Master and his devotees as servants.[47] He links service with subservience or servitude to God as the soul's essential nature. Service includes serving both God and also his community of devotees.

A corollary of service is humility. The *āḻvār*s castigated those who are full of pride and egotism. This implies that to develop a community of devotees, rather than a hierarchy of castes with superior and inferior ranks, devotees must serve others humbly, do acts of humble service themselves, and insist on equal respect.[48]

Temples

Closely related to the concept of service is the concept of the temple as the locus for redistribution of material resources and services. These are culturally recognised and authoritative rights, in Arjun Appadurai's words, 'to offer service (*kaiṅkaryam*) to the deity, either through endowment (*upayam*) or through prescribed ritual function ....'[49] The system coheres, generally, because it is premised on the idea of service to the deity (which, I would add, is anchored in the central idea of salvation), but also the recognition that all groups and individuals must do their services to ensure that the redistributive and ritual process functions.

Services are recognised as honours. All those who serve—such as priests, musicians, gardeners, weavers, those who light the lamps, bring water from the river, carry the palanquin in which the deity rides in processions, even those who are just present in the sanctum with devotion before the deity—are honoured. Some are honoured with special recognition (for instance, the garland that had been offered to the deity or standing closer to the deity, albeit within certain limits), others with just the simple offerings during temple worship of *tīrtha* (sacred water), *prasāda* (sacred food) and *śaṭakōpa* (the metal crown named after Nammāḻvār, which is embossed with the feet of Viṣṇu, symbolising surrender to him, and placed on a worshipper's head). These acts of honour recognise the worshippers' share (*paṅku*) in the process and binds them to the community. They also mark status, but that is certainly not their primary function. Because these rights/honours are to be carefully protected and recognised by the community as a whole, any abrogation is experienced as dishonour, disgrace, or humiliation (*avamāna*).[50]

Temple processions celebrate weekly, monthly, or annual festivals. The paradigmatic procession is the movement of the deity out of his or her shrine around the temple corridors, or beyond to the streets surrounding the temple, or some destination a short distance away. Processions in major temples are accompanied by the auspicious sounds of drums and *nāgasvarams* in temples. Today, official Brahmin chanters of the *Divyaprabandham* lead the procession and official Brahmin chanters of the Veda follow it.

Processions are central to the system of temple honours. Just as in the temple proper there are many people who serve the temple's ritual process with designated rights to do their 'share', so too for processions, although on these occasions, those who serve with special functions extend beyond designated groups of temple servants to include other groups, such as Dalit Śrīvaiṣṇavas who have the honour of carrying the palanquin, say, or those who have the honour of keeping the great temple carts moving safely through the streets, or others who hold lamps. As the procession moves through the streets, it stops to honour particular places, such as *maṭhas* and *rāmānuja kūṭams*. These honours, however, can be withheld by temple authorities to shame that establishment if something is deemed wrong.

Besides processions of deities, there are processions where an image or picture of an *āḻvār, ācārya* (such as Rāmānuja), or *jīyar* (such as the founder of a *maṭha*) is carried about. In addition, there are processions in which a living person—such as an *ācārya* or *jīyar* on his birthday—is carried on a palanquin. During processions, the leader of an important group of temple servants might be honoured by being carried in the palanquin for all to see.

Such processions are replicated on a smaller scale in villages and neighbourhoods where the music is usually *bhajanas* or the songs of Tyāgarāja sung by members of a *sabhā*, accompanied by the harmonium and drums. Because temples are small or non-existent in many villages and neighbourhoods, the expression of religion in outside space is particularly important. These village processions function to make public the sect's identity, often in competition with other sects. They are occasions, moreover, for proselytisation when the group stops for a short lecture. Processions send off pilgrims and honour their return. In fact, processions are central to the very idea of salvation: the final joyous journey to the 'auspicious land', the supreme heaven, is, after all, described as a grand procession.

A Note on Women in Śrīvaiṣṇavism

Since social justice includes justice for women, and reforms to improve the status of women became a major issue from colonial times, it is important to discuss briefly the position of women in Śrīvaiṣṇavism within a broad historical perspective.

Between the sixth century BCE and the third century CE, there was a decline in the status of women from that of the Vedic period. According to the Dharmaśāstras, a large corpus of texts composed between 600 BCE and 600 CE, views on the proper behaviour of women (*strīdharma*) were structured by notions of auspiciousness and inauspiciousness, but also purity and pollution. Common norms for elite women included *pativrata* (fidelity to husband), pre-pubertal marriage, denial of education, segregation, no divorce, no widow remarriage and, in some contexts, *sati* (self-immolation of a wife on the funeral pyre of her husband). These texts also include misogynistic statements related to women's ignorance, impurity and infidelity. These norms, although by no means universal even in Brahmanical contexts, influenced those of other castes. Women, moreover, were often placed in the same low category as *śūdra*s in many texts. Women and *śūdra*s did not have access to salvation in this life because they could not study the prerequisite, the Vedas, which was for Brahmin men only.

With the growing influence of the *bhakti* movements from the fifth century CE, however, the position of women improved. Descriptions of women in the Tamil *bhakti* poetry of the *āḻvār*s from the seventh century is a case in point. One of the *āḻvār*s, for instance, was a woman, Āṇṭāḷ, and the verses of the other *āḻvār*s view women positively. By the time that this tradition was institutionalised as the Śrīvaiṣṇava sect, we find in the writings an inclusive salvific theology. Rāmānuja, for instance, in his commentary on *Bhagavad Gītā* 9:32, says: 'also women, *vaiśya*s and *śūdra*s shall attain the supreme goal'.[51] Moreover, other *ācārya*s used metaphors to express the feminine aspect of God, drew on the relation of (female) lover and (male) beloved to express the devotee's relation to God, and repeated the *Mahābhārata's* story of how God saved Draupadī when she was menstruating in order to show that woman's periodic 'impurity' was no bar to salvation.

In the sixteenth century, Piḷḷailokam Jīyar describes Śrīvaiṣṇava views on *sati* and widowhood in the *Śrīvaiṣṇava Samayācāra Niṣkarṣa* (*The Essence of Śrīvaiṣṇava Normative*

Behaviour).[52] He argues against *sati*, for instance, saying that the commandments for it pertain only to women who are rebirth-oriented, that this custom is against scripture, that it will prevent the woman's husband from attaining heaven, and that it will turn the woman into a non-Vaiṣṇava—all ideas that Śrīvaiṣṇavism denies.

Nevertheless, in the nineteenth and twentieth centuries, under colonial rule, the general position of women was again declining. As I have argued elsewhere,

> During this period, the British contributed to brahmanical conservatism by codifying its family law and applying it to everyone, not just Brahmins. Throughout India we find texts being written that enshrine conservative norms for women. In the *Śrīvaiṣṇava Tīpikai*,[53] for instance, we see this social conservatism. It prescribes the proper behavior for a woman in her daily activities, domestic roles, relation to her husband such as prostrating to him when awakening, strict observance of purity laws, eating only the remains of food that had been offered to God, husband and other devotees, staying in a 'hidden place' during menstruation and observing orthodox norms for widowhood.[54]

Despite the growing conservatism, the *Śrīvaiṣṇava Tīpikai* remains supportive of women's access to Śrīvaiṣṇava knowledge: they should know the lineage of teachers, the secret mantras, the 4,000 verses (the Divyaprabandham), and theological and philosophical treatises. Like Śrīvaiṣṇava men, women are to be devout, self-controlled, compassionate, egoless, and indifferent to wealth and material objects.

By 1930, the *Śrīśaṇḍīlya Viśiṣṭa Parama Dharmaśāstra*,[55] which has been influential in modern Śrīvaiṣṇava circles, shows that marriage and family life are to be situated within the larger framework of devotion to God. A husband's responsibility is to turn his whole household toward the supreme Lord rather than to demand that his wife treat him as god, that a woman's worth is defined by her religious behaviour, not her fertility, and that it is not incumbent on her to bear sons for the eventual performance of her husband's death rituals and passage to heaven. If she is infertile or bears only daughters, she is not to be abandoned. A widow, moreover, is not to shave her head, a common practice at that time in Brahmin circles, and a widow is not to be considered an inauspicious ogress or witch who had caused her husband's untimely death, because death for all Śrīvaiṣṇavas is categorically auspicious.

In short, although Śrīvaiṣṇavism sometimes embraced the conservative norms for women found in many Brahmin circles in Tamil Nadu and elsewhere, it was more liberal, at least in theory, regarding questions of salvation, education, norms for widowhood and *sati*. It did not overrule, however, the norm of marriage and at least nominal subservience to the husband. On these matters, Teṉkalais and Vaṭakalais had minor differences. Those thirteenth and fourteenth-century *ācārya*s later considered Teṉkalai, such as Piḷḷai Lokācārya, Aḻakiya Maṇavāḷa Perumāḷ Nāyaṉār and Maṇavāḷa Māmuni, argued, for instance, that the sacred syllable OM could be uttered by women, whereas Vedānta Deśika and those *ācārya*s later considered Vaṭakalai did not allow that.[56]

Caste Conundrums

The classic model of social organisation found in many Dharmaśāstras posits four *varṇa*s (groups or classes based on common characteristics). The first three, the 'twice-born' who are ritually superior to the fourth, include Brahmins (priests and scholars), *kṣatriya*s (rulers and warriors) and *vaiśya*s (traders). Below them are *śūdra*s (servants of the higher *varṇa*s). And below even *śūdra*s are *caṇḍāla*s ('untouchables' who are technically outside the 'system' altogether). According to M. N. Srinivas, caste is a 'hereditary, endogamous, usually localized group, having a traditional association with an occupation and a particular position in the hierarchy of castes'.[57] Although this definition has been debated and revised, it is still useful as a working definition. (For a brief history of definitions of caste and debates from colonial times to today, see Appendix 3.) For some groups today, community is a euphemism for caste, but for Śrīvaiṣṇavas it is located in its ancient idea of the 'family' (*kula*), that is, the community of devotees.

In this book, I generally use the word 'caste' in the sense of caste clusters such as Chettiyar, Dalit, Icai Velala, Naidu, Pillai, Reddiyar, Sattada, Vanniyar, Yadava, Vellalar, and Brahmin.[58] As a result, I do not refer to specific *jāti* (sub-caste) identities and only occasionally, in discussions of texts, to the four *varṇa*s (*brāhmaṇa, kṣatriya, vaiśya* and *śūdra*). Sometimes I do use governmental administrative labels such as Scheduled Castes (SCs), Scheduled Tribes (STs), Other Backward Castes (OBCs) and Forward Castes when citing government documents, or media reports that use them. Occasionally, I use the term 'Sanskritisation', a process, according to M. N. Srinivas, by which middle and lower castes that desire upward mobility imitate the behaviour and customs (being vegetarian, say, or wearing the sacred thread) of those who have high ritual status, such as Brahmins and Ksatriyas.[59]

Although Srinivas suggests that Sanskritisation refers to those with high ritual status, who are usually Brahmins or Ksatriyas, I prefer to use Sanskritisation for imitation of Brahmins, and the term Ksatriyasation for imitation of Ksatriyas. In my interviews, I found some castes practising Ksatriyasation by claiming they had ancestors associated with Pallava, Cola, Pandya, Viyayanagara, or Nayaka royal families. For instance, although the Vanniyars worship various deities, some sub-groups are exclusively Vaiṣṇava and connect themselves with Kulacēkara Āḻvār who, according to tradition, had been a Cera king. Edgar Thurston (1855–1935) notes that at the Parthasarathy (Pārtasārati) temple in Chennai, Pallis (Vanniyars) celebrate Kulacēkara's birthday with great éclat.[60]

The Śrīvaiṣṇava Concept of Inclusiveness

Already by the time of the *Mahābhārata*, worshippers of Nārāyaṇa-Viṣṇu-Kṛṣṇa in the north had reacted against the disrespect and loss of dignity caused by the hierarchical social order. They carried their protest with them as migrants to the south (and elsewhere).[61] In the verses of the *āḻvār*s (which became the Śrīvaiṣṇava Tamil scripture, the *Divyaprabandham*), we discover clues, for instance, that they came from different castes. We do not know the caste/occupational identities of the first four *āḻvār*s (Poykai, Pūta, Pēy and Tirumaḻicai). From descriptions in their verses, Tirumaṅkai Āḻvār seems to be a chieftain and perhaps Kulacēkara; Nammāḻvār a landlord or administrator, and Toṇṭaratippoṭi and Periyāḻvār, Brahmins.[62] Because Āṇṭāḷ is the daughter of Periyāḻvār, she would be a Brahmin. The later tradition considered Madhurakavi a Brahmin too. In *sampradāya* works, Tiruppāṇ is described as an outcaste, but there is nothing internal to his own verses to suggest this.

The theme of inclusiveness, I will argue, is about including everyone in the opportunity for salvation in this life and deep respect for those who worship Nārāyaṇa-Kṛṣna-Viṣṇu as the supreme God. That said, Śrīvaiṣṇava inclusiveness might have had economic motivations as well. The *Divyaprabandham* verses often refer to the landscapes of agricultural villages. Even though they do not mention irrigation, we can surmise that the religious orientation emphasised communal solidarity, mutual respect and economic cooperation, in part to facilitate the process of rice cultivation, which required village collaborative efforts and action to prevent agricultural workers from becoming disgruntled and moving elsewhere. Local temples and sectarian networks provided identity until some kings recognised their importance for making connections at the local level, which helped secure their powers. After that, kings occasionally became patrons, contributing monumental architecture, lands and other resources. Gradually, in the Tamil region, these temples became dramatic features of the landscape, as they grew in size with tall *gopuram*s (gateways) that could be seen from a distance.[63]

The *āḻvār*s and those who came after them certainly knew about the north Indian *varṇa* model of society, as it appears in many Dharmaśāstras. The *āḻvārs*' castigation of those Brahmins who are arrogant alludes to the idea of *varṇa* as hierarchical.[64] Epigraphers have noticed, for instance, the lack of Brahmanical and royal domination at many early temples; rather, merchants, weavers, craftsmen and others were patrons.

Through subsequent history, some hierarchically-oriented Brahmins joined the temple milieu, sometimes at the request of local rulers, whose patronage transformed them into wealthy landowners. Customs and gifts, which defined who received temple honours and allowed some groups to approach temple images of God more closely than others, indicate the incursion of northern forms of hierarchy and their increasing hold on identity and status. These developments led to controversies between those who followed the *āḻvārs*' view of the *community* of devotees and those who supported the *varṇa* system.

For the *āḻvārs*, respect for other devotees and a sense of the equality of all devotees did not mean *elimination* of caste. At least, there are no statements to that effect. The same must be said for the *ācāryas*. They defended ideas of respect and argued that non-Brahmins could attain salvation in this life. Periyavāccāṉ Piḷḷai, for instance, insists on deep and humble respect of other devotees, no matter what their caste. In his *Arthapancakam*, Piḷḷai Lokācārya says that insult to any devotee is a sin (*bhagavatāpacāra*).[65] In fact, 'to think of a devotee in terms of caste (*varṇa*) is said to be a heinous act, comparable to examining the genitals of one's own mother; such a devotee becomes an outcaste (*caṇṭāḷa*)'.[66]

Aḻakiya Maṇavāḷa Perumāḷ Nāyaṉār in his *Ācārya Hṛdayam*[67] advocates respect for all devotees, also with strong words. He writes that ignorant people are confused about *varṇa*, stage of life (*āśrama*) and amount of knowledge, thinking that these define people as superior and inferior, even though this is not so. A Brahmin might study all the four Vedas, but without the knowledge of God, he is a donkey. A person who is born in a good family and who appears like a sage (*muni*) but has no god in his heart is worse than a person who eats dog meat. One who is master of all learning that does not help one obtain salvation, moreover, is master only of that which is equal to repairing sandals. In spite of having all knowledge, not understanding the supremacy of Lord Nārāyaṇa, and taking his feet into one's heart (that is, taking God as refuge) is a waste, like offering something into ashes instead of into the sacred fire. The author certainly puts emphasis on devotion to God and suggests that this mandates equal respect.

Despite this strong stance upholding inclusiveness and respect, some Śrīvaiṣṇavas were more conservative. In the fourteenth century, Vedānta Deśika was reinforcing the orthodox Brahmanical stance on some issues, drawing on Dharmaśāstra and Pañcarātra passages. In his works, he argues, for instance, that only Brahmin men may utter the sacred syllable *Om*.[68] In his commentary on Tiruppāṉ's *Amalanātippirāṉ*, moreover, he avoids the controversy over worshipping an outcaste (all *āḻvār*s were worshipped as images in temples) by saying that Tiruppāṇ had been born to a Brahmin family, even though he was brought up by non-Brahmins, and is therefore not really an outcaste. That said, Vedānta Deśika does support the importance of the Tamil Veda, because it provides easy accessibility to the essence of the Vedas for everyone, including women and *śūdra*s.

Maṇavāḷa Māmuni in the late fourteenth and early fifteenth century once again defends caste inclusivity in no uncertain terms. In his commentary on Aḻakiya Maṇavāḷa Perumāḷ Nāyaṉār's *Ācārya Hṛdayam*, he insists that in order to remove pollution caused by pride, knowers of the Veda of lofty birth should serve and teach low-caste devotees. In fact, they should worship the low-castes

> ... as a family deity, equal to the Lord .... The Lord has revealed that the water in which [a Bhāgavata's] feet are washed is excellent *tirtha* [holy water], his leftover food is the best purifier. Therefore, if those who are unclean and drunk with egoism partake of this *tīrtha* or *prasāda*, their essential natures (*svarūpa*) will be purified.[69]

In this way, Maṇavāḷa Māmuni used extreme rhetoric to underscore the importance of utmost respect for all Śrīvaiṣṇavas, of whatever caste.

In support of this view of inclusiveness, many *ācāryas*—Rāmānuja, Periyavāccān̲ Piḷḷai, Piḷḷai Lokācārya, Aḻakiya Māṇavāḷa Perumāḷ Nāyan̲ār, and even Vedānta Deśika, despite his conservatism—had explained how low-caste or outcaste figures such as Vidhura, Dharmavyādha, Pāduvān̲ and Vibhīṣaṇa, mentioned in the epics and *purāṇas*, were righteous, devout, wise, and learned. As such, they were not only included in the religion, but were exemplary figures.

This rhetoric of caste inclusiveness, a key strategy for proselytism, attracted many non-Brahmins over the centuries, which can be detected in the inscriptions. In the fifteenth century, for instance, we have the famous figure of Kantāṭai Rāmānuja Ayyaṅkar,[70] a disciple of Aḻakiya-maṇavāḷa-cīyar, the head of the Paravastu Maṭha (Vādhikēsari Aḻakiya-maṇavāḷa-cīyar Maṭha) in Kanchipuram, supposedly founded by Maṇavāḷa Māmuni. He also managed projects for the Vijayanagara emperors Saluva-nara-simha-deva-raya I (r. 1486–91) and then Saluva-nara-simha-deva-raya II (r. 1491–1505). Kantāṭai Rāmānuja Ayyaṅkar is best described as a non-Brahmin entrepreneur at Tirupati and Tirumalai who organised irrigation works on land that donors had gifted to the temples, the income of which was used for the support of various religious activities such as temple rituals, festivals, and feeding and housing pilgrims in the *rāmānuja kūṭams* (choultries), which he managed.

All this made Kantāṭai Rāmānuja Ayyaṅkar a wealthy and powerful man in the area. Of interest here is the likelihood that he enhanced the profile of the *āḻvārs* at Tirumalai by instituting directly or indirectly an annual cycle of festivals on their birth star (*nakṣatra*) and having their verses chanted by Sattada (non-Brahmin) chanters along with Sattina (Brahmin) chanters.[71] From inscriptions, we know that his son, who went by the same name, and disciples[72] also had influence at Kanchipuram and Srirangam. The chanting of the verses of the *āḻvārs* in temple rituals no doubt attracted other non-Brahmins, who identified with the fact that the *āḻvār*s came from many castes.

Francis Clooney warns scholars today, who are predisposed to think that caste is evil, not to read into this literature the idea that the *āḻvār*s and *ācārya*s wanted to eliminate the caste system altogether.[73]

Patricia Mumme makes much the same point.[74] She sees in Victor Turner's theory of *communitas*—a religious modality of role reversals to glorify 'the lowly, the liminal, and the subservient while castigating the privileged, the dominant, and the authoritative'[75]—a way to understand the Teṉkalai mention of eating the leftover food or drinking the foot-washing water of low-caste devotees. Whether or not these were ever practised, the very rhetoric instigates *communitas*. Following Turner, she notes that *communitas* exists dialectically with structure, a structure in Śrīvaiṣṇavism that is best represented by Vedānta Deśika's insistence on the duties of caste and stage of life. Mumme argues that it is highly unlikely that modern Teṉkalai Brahmins even read books by Bhāgavata authors or trained them in the commentaries, much less prostrated to them or had them as preceptors, as the *sampradāya* texts advocate. In other words, Teṉkalai Brahmins did not treat Bhāgavatas in their own community much differently than other non-Brahmins, aside from *communitas* in devotional contexts, initiating them when requested, or allowing them to chant *Om*.

There is some truth to this comment, I think, but Rāmānuja and other *ācārya*s certainly differed from many orthodox Hindus by arguing that women and *śūdra*s could attain salvation in this very life, whereas orthodox Brahmins often held that being reborn was a minimum requirement. I would add that despite criticism from some orthodox Brahmins that Śrīvaiṣṇavas were, in fact, advocating destruction of the caste system, virtually all *ācārya*s up to today never advocated abandonment of caste, only expressions of superiority and inferiority, which were often its byproduct. By the eighteenth century, with general Brahmanical reinforcement of caste norms to provide a buttress against change and an escalation of tensions between Vaṭakalais and Teṉkalais over temple control, some Vaṭakalais were also accusing Teṉkalais of advocating abandonment of caste, which could be read into scriptural and *sampradāya* passages.

Even though Teṉkalai Brahmins tried to finesse the ostensible contradiction between denying caste and yet living by it by arguing that it was unnecessary to observe caste norms, *although it was permissible to do so for the sake of convention*, in point of fact they continued to observe Brahmanical norms unless there was a direct conflict with a Śrīvaiṣṇava one.[76] Otherwise, they would have lost their status as Brahmins. Therefore, there was a tacit acceptance of many caste norms for pragmatic reasons, despite the inclusive rhetoric.[77] An underlying problem, which Teṉkalais recognised, was that the arduous Brahmanical tradition of memorising the Vedas and other scriptures would most likely be maintained only if Brahmins themselves maintained the duties of caste and stage of life. To attract patrons, these Brahmins would need religious authority. And that relied both on their knowledge and their distinctive, orthodox Brahmin way of life.[78]

In the final analysis, even when Śrīvaiṣṇavism had managed to create an ethos of respect, there were many structural aspects of discrimination that must have festered resentment in non-Brahmins, and especially in outcastes who, by the sixteenth century, if not much earlier, were not allowed to enter Hindu temples, including Śrīvaiṣṇava ones. Although Nammāḻvār in *Tiruvāymoḻi* 3.7.9 (discussed in Chapter 3) had proclaimed that the lowest of the low, the outcastes (Caṇḍālas) of the outcastes, are our lords, a verse often quoted by *ācārya*s (even today), the irony of this rhetoric would not have gone unnoticed. The Caṇḍāla as the key symbol of Śrīvaiṣṇava inclusiveness could not even enter God's temple, so impure was he or she. No wonder Dalit anger was real and mobilisation was already occurring in the colonial period. And no wonder many Teṉkalais struggled from that time to make sense of their tradition.

The Politics of Religion

Religion became highly politicised in the colonial period, on account of criticism by missionaries, new concepts of Dravidian languages and culture, Dalit mobilisation, competition with Śaivas, tensions between Brahmins and non-Brahmins, and actions by the colonial government, such as the secularisation of space and alliances with elite non-Brahmin landowners (see Appendix 4.). This culminated in the non-Brahmin movement of the late colonial period and political populism after Independence.

Caste conflict between Brahmins and elite non-Brahmins as well as between elite non-Brahmins and the lower castes spiralled, in the early twentieth century, over issues of precedent and respect, triggered in part by the census, which tried to document the hierarchy but had the effect of hardening it.[79] The turbulence of Tamil politics during the early twentieth century and the dramatic political and economic changes, especially after Independence, which offered many non-Brahmins new opportunities, become the catalysts for social justice movements.

As a window on these changes, I focus on a key political figure. He interests us not only because of his role in the non-Brahmin movement and his positions on caste and women, but also because he came from a Śrīvaiṣṇava family.

Periyar, a Śrīvaiṣṇava Renegade

Of great significance for non-Brahmins in general and Śrīvaiṣṇava non-Brahmins in particular was the figure popularly known as Periyar or E. V. R. (1879–1973). He was born as Raghav Erode Venkata Ramasami Naicker in the town Erode (Coimbatore district), to a wealthy non-Brahmin (Balija Naidu) business family that spoke three languages: Kannada, Telugu and Tamil. A pious Teṉkalai Śrīvaiṣṇava, Ramasami's father, whose ancestors had given an image of Lord Nārāyaṇa to the Tirukkottiyur temple, would invite Śrīvaiṣṇavas to give religious discourses in the family house. Nonetheless, his son, who managed only a few years of primary school, delighted in being a prankster and broke taboos to disturb the orthodox household. He began to criticise religion.

Even as a child, Periyar was disturbed by Hindu mythology's many contradictions. A few years after his marriage, according to his biographer,[80] he had a fight with his father and left home to don the garb of a holy man. With two Tamil Brahmins, he headed off to Hyderabad. The three became famous for their entertaining religious talks. These included stories, jokes, puns, irreverent questions and harangues. Periyar, the pseudo-ascetic, travelled as far as Calcutta and then the holy city of Varanasi, where he assisted the priest of a Śaiva temple. Eventually, the priest dismissed him for refusing to bathe.

Meanwhile, his dislike of Hinduism developed into revulsion at the sight of corpses in the Ganges and beggars in the streets. His dislike grew when a Brahmin charitable guesthouse refused to give him the free meals that it gave Brahmin pilgrims. (Very hungry, he tried to gain entry again by dressing up as a Brahmin; his moustache, which Brahmins never wore, gave him away.) Fuelling his rage was the fact that a non-Brahmin from south India had founded this guesthouse. These experiences reinforced his antipathy to religion, turning him into an avowed atheist and rationalist.

In 1919, Periyar joined the Indian National Congress, becoming vice-president of the Tamil Nadu Congress Committee.[81] He trained volunteers for strikes and pickets to protest British rule and championed various Congress activities, such as wearing homespun cotton cloth, prohibiting alcohol and participating in *satyāgraha*s, such as the one that agitated in 1924 for the right of Dalits to enter Hindu temples, an event that led to both he and his wife being imprisoned.

Two pivotal episodes transformed him into an anti-Gandhian. The first took place at a Congress-sponsored school near Madras. It became mired in a conflict over separate eating places for Brahmins and non-Brahmins. The second took place at a Gandhi *ashram* in Tirunelveli district that was linked directly with some Congress leaders. Once again, Periyar was shocked that Brahmins and non-Brahmins could not eat together. These events probably reminded him of his own rejection in the Varanasi 'Brahmin' guesthouse, and cemented his contempt for Brahmins and their religion.

After these episodes, Periyar left the Congress Party, pointing out Gandhi's short-comings: deference to Brahmins and their Sanskrit texts, the *varṇa* system, caste rules forbidding inter-marriage or inter-dining, non-allowing Dalits to enter temples, and so on. All this led Periyar's followers to argue that he offered Dalits more support than Gandhi did.

Periyar launched the Self-Respect Movement in 1925 for non-Brahmins. It promoted reason over religion and real social equality over hierarchy as a way to destroy caste and orthodox gender norms. In the final decades of the Raj, Periyar became the key proponent of Dravidianism. The latter's goals were an independent country for the South, to eliminate Brahmin domination through the caste system, and northern domination through Hindi, should it become the national language.

Of interest here, though, are Periyar's views on caste and religion. In 1929, he decided to drop his caste name, Naicker, in order to promote a casteless society. He became known, therefore, as E. V. Ramasami, E. V. R. for short. His followers knew him affectionately as Periyar (the great or elder one).

His views on religion tell us much about him. Periyar was vehemently against all religions, especially Hinduism, ridiculing its myths and urging people to break images of deities, put the cherished *Rāmāyaṇa* in bonfires, and mock the gurus. Periyar, who had Communist connections and had visited the Soviet Union (along with many other European countries), argued that 'people used religion only as a mask to deceive innocent people and therefore took it as one of his duties to life to warn people against superstitions and priests'.[82] For him, the only necessary scripture was the *Tirukkuṟal*, which he considered a secular work. (Scholars have identified it as a cosmopolitan Jain text, in the sense that its author was a Jain who celebrated religious diversity.) He was active, moreover, in helping Dalits gain entry to Hindu temples; this contributed to the Temple Entry Acts of 1924, 1931 and 1950.

As a propagandist, Periyar wanted to make atheism the new dogma through public campaigns, and remove ritualism by advocating secular marriages without mantras and priests. Periyar's greatest ire had been directed at the Brahmins. He sometimes incited people to kill Brahmins and burn down their homes. Despite the fact that such dire acts never occurred, Periyar lost a court case in Tiruchirappalli and was jailed for his extreme rhetoric (he spent his jail time in hospital). He 'has not often called for the killing of Brahmins, but he has for many years called for their expulsion from Tamilnad'.[83]

The Justice Party, which began in 1917, advocated reservations based on caste and educational reforms. But it favoured high-ranking non-Brahmins, a position criticised by the Dalits. Initially, there was hostility between Periyar's Self-Respect Movement and the Justice Party. This was partly because of Justice Party's views on Brahmins. It was not so harsh on them, unlike members of the Self-Respect Movement, who attacked the Brahmins as missionaries of a northern religion brought to the south, enslaving Tamils and destroying their indigenous culture.

Members of the Justice Party were often devout Hindus. They imitated Brahmanical ways. Members of Self-Respect, though, were severe critics of this orientation. The parties found support, moreover, from different castes. Justice drew support from 'forward' non-Brahmins who owned land, had businesses, or practised professions. These non-Brahmins included Mudaliyars, Pillais and Reddiyars, about 19 per cent of the population. They mobilised partly to gain good government jobs for themselves and did little for the Backward Castes (49 per cent) and Scheduled Castes (17 per cent), even refusing to support a law against untouchability in 1922.[84] In other words, the Justice Party sided with those who were only somewhat less privileged than the twice-born, whereas the

Self-Respect members supported Dalits and other 'low' castes as well.

Aside from changes advocated by the Self-Respect Movement and the Justice Party, the Raj too was instigating change. 'The management of temple trusts, the abolition of *devadāsī*s (temple dancers), and the legislative efforts to promote temple entry for untouchable groups,' says Nicholas Dirks, 'were all pitched in terms of principles having to do with fundamental human rights.'[85] Ironically, the government's attempts to reform Hindu institutions and control Brahmin power by setting up new agencies, such as the Hindu Religious and Charitable Endowment Board (1927),[86] not only drew on Sanskritic interpretations and rituals, but it also placed Brahmins on temple-managing boards that had been under the control of non-Brahmin castes groups.[87]

By the late 1930s, Periyar was becoming less radical and the Justice Party was soliciting his support in order to stem its waning political influence. The two became more closely allied in their common cause of avoiding Brahmin and Hindi domination after Indian independence. According to V. Geetha and S. V. Rajadurai, non-Brahmins did not want independence before the British could destroy Brahmin domination and the hierarchical caste system. They opposed the Congress Party, which advocated Home Rule[88] and had many Brahmin leaders. Some who opposed the platform were Śrīvaiṣṇava Brahmins themselves.[89] Others, such as Periyar and P. Varadarajulu Naidu, had been born into Śrīvaiṣṇava non-Brahmin families.

And then, in 1939, Periyar became head of the Justice Party. This was after it had lost mass support. In 1944, he renamed the party the Dravidar Kazhagam (DK), which means the Dravidian Association. It attracted students with its demand for social justice; villagers with its demands for better education, communication and transportation; women with its demands for women's education and reforms of customs governing marriage and widowhood; along with Dalits with its demand for the abolition of untouchability. 'Its flag is black above to designate the injustice in society, and red below, to show the revolutionary fervor with which the party tries to overthrow injustice.'[90]

After Independence, the party split in 1949 over the issue of whether Tamil Nadu should be a separate country, or whether it should join the new country of India. Periyar stayed with his long-standing demand for separation, whereas C. N. Annadurai, who then formed the Dravida Munnetra Kazhagam (DMK, the Dravidian Progress Federation), accepted the idea of union, albeit with increased rights for Tamil Nadu. Periyar and Annadurai also differed on whether they should just be social reformers, or whether they should try to form a government by gaining power through the vote. Periyar opted for the former and Annadurai the latter.

The issue of separation was finally laid to rest after Independence by a 1957 law that banned public agitation for it, although Periyar periodically spoke about his dream. The DMK went on to become a well-organised party with a democratic constitution, moderate propaganda, and fewer attacks on religion in general and Brahmins in particular.

Political Populism

From the middle of the twentieth century, Tamil political power was being defined largely in terms of populism. Populism helps account for the politics of reservations in Tamil Nadu. Reservation policies had been first introduced by the Raj in the middle of the nineteenth century, and in earnest in the first half of the twentieth, thanks in part to the Justice Party, which introduced reservation of seats in educational institutions.

A big change occurred after Indian independence in 1947 with the introduction of democracy and the vote in 1950. In 1954, Tamil lower castes succeeded in ousting C. Rajagopalachari,[91] the Brahmin Chief Minister from the Congress Party, and replaced him with Kamaraj Nadar—a Congress member from the once low-status Nadar caste (see Appendix 6)—who then held power for the next decade and did much for the lower castes. Over time, the Backward and Scheduled Castes, which together constituted about 66 per cent of the population, exerted great influence on all the political parties with their large vote banks[92] and astute political organisation.

The DMK had come to power in 1967 with considerable support from Dalits, despite the latter's stronghold in Congress. When Annadurai died in 1969, Muthuvel Karunanidhi (1924–2018), a politician, playwright and screenwriter, became leader of the party and was elected thirteen times to the Tamil Nadu Assembly, and was Chief Minister of Tamil Nadu five times between 1969 and 2011.[93] Together with relatives who have held other important positions in the Tamil Nadu and Central governments, not to mention the DMK party, he has wielded enormous wealth and power. His influence radiates out to the media and business, which has led to many allegations and some convictions of corruption, especially nepotism. Despite this strength, the DMK did not always hold power in the second half of the twentieth century and beginning of the twenty-first. Nevertheless, it has influenced many people. As we will see, some of my informants had brief flirtations with the DMK, one was the propagandist for the party and one is connected to Karunanidhi by caste and family.

One of the keys to Karunanidhi's success was his unabashed populism: various welfare schemes, besides reservations that touched many households and included food subsidies, midday meals for school children (which had begun under MGR), reduction in the price of rice, a health insurance scheme, and free electricity to farmers. His critics considered these crass attempts to secure votes; others saw them not as patronage politics, but as serious contributions to social development and social justice. Karunanidhi was especially attentive to addressing women's needs with schemes such as securing property rights, free graduate education for girls, and support for inter-caste marriages and widow remarriage.

Another split in the Dravidian parties occurred in 1972, when M. G. Ramachandran (1917–87), a popular film star, broke away from the DMK to form the Anna Dravida Munnetra

Kazhagam (ADMK), which would later be renamed as the All India Anna Dravida Munnetra Kazhagam (AIADMK) when it established itself in other states. With his massive popularity and a platform that was not so anti-Brahmin and anti-Hindi as the DK and DMK had been, M.G.R. mustered political power, which led to his becoming the Chief Minister in the elections of 1977, 1980, and 1984.

After M. G. R.'s death in 1987 (followed by the very brief rule of his wife), J. Jayalalithaa—a Tamil Śrīvaiṣṇava Vaṭakalai Brahmin originally from Melkote, Mysore (now Karnataka), who had become a Chennai-based actress—led the party. It was only after Karunanidhi's government was dismissed in 1990 by Prime Minister Chandra Shekhar (an ally of Jayalalithaa) that Jayalalithaa came to power. She stayed in power in Tamil Nadu through much of the next two decades,[94] thanks to populism in the form of various welfare schemes, free bicycles, colour televisions, mobile phones and cheap broadband Internet, and laptops to certain constituencies. Jayalalithaa also had influence in the Central government, thanks to Congress or Bharatiya Janata Party (BJP) alliances.

Jayalalithaa was accused, eventually convicted (September 2014) and forced to step down, in a case that went on for eighteen years, over her amassing a large amount of properties, jewellery, luxury cars, cash and investments while she was Chief Minister during 1991–96.[95] Nevertheless, by 2015, an appeals court overturned the judgment of the lower court. After her acquittal, she again became Chief Minister of Tamil Nadu on 23 May 2015. The saga was not yet over. There again was an appeal on the corruption charge, which went to the Supreme Court. The Court heard the appeal; however, there was no verdict in May 2016, when the Court went into recess.

Then Jayalalithaa died on 5 December 2016, followed eight months later by the death of Karunanidhi. We will return to this turbulent period, the changing of the guard as it were, in the last chapter.

* * *

As this Introduction suggests, religion, caste and politics have been deeply intertwined in Tamil society. Sectarian temples—and there have been many besides the Śrīvaiṣṇava ones studied here—have been important focal points for the organisation of society at multiple levels. With our focus on Śrīvaiṣṇavism, several topics introduced here must be tracked carefully in the following chapters. For example, we need to track how the Śrīvaiṣṇava ideas of inclusiveness and community have been understood by Brahmins and non-Brahmins, as politics and economics shifted ground from late colonialism to the non-Brahmin movement, Indian Independence, and then political populism.

More specifically, we must watch for whether sectarian identity—as shaped by the system of temple honours—was seriously threatened by Periyar's Self-Respect Movement and subsequent political parties upholding a message of equality, or whether the temple system still exerted a stronghold on devotees, which one day might be tapped by Hindutva parties. Another point of special interest is whether non-Brahmin Śrīvaiṣṇavas, emboldened by the non-Brahmin movement of the past century, their sizeable numbers and their new intellectual prowess, are shaping Śrīvaiṣṇavism in a new way or whether the courts are not allowing changes—at least in the major temples—on the basis of precedence.

But before we enter the world of the interviews, we have one other preparatory task to set the stage: taking a closer look at what some Śrīvaiṣṇava non-Brahmin leaders were doing after the middle of the nineteenth century. This takes us to the next chapter.

Notes

1. Madras Presidency, which the British established in 1801 for administrative and tax purposes, included most of what became Andhra Pradesh (which was subsequently divided in 2014 into Andhra and Telangana), the Malabar part of the present Kerala, and several districts that are now in Odisha and Karnataka.

2. This occurred in stages: the creation of Madras State in 1950 after Indian Independence and then, in 1969—after divisions on linguistic and other grounds—the modern state of Tamil Nadu.

3. Some people argue that the word Śrīvaiṣṇava should be used only for Brahmins; others were simply Vaiṣṇavas. I do not think such a hard boundary should be generalised, however, because this sect, from its very beginnings, included people of all castes in this sense of a community of devotees.

4. The word *bhāgavata* has a long history of referring to those who worship the intertwined gods Vāsudeva, Nārāyaṇa and Kṛṣṇa. After appearing in the *Mahābhārata*, the word *bhāgavata* appeared in inscriptions all over India. It was also common in what is sometimes called *bhāgavata-sampradāya* or *bhāgavata-śāstra*, and in the *Bhāgavata Purāṇa*. In his *Āgama Prāmānyam*, Yāmuna (an eleventh-century Śrīvaiṣṇava thinker) refers to *bhāgavata brāhmaṇas*, which suggests that the word *bhāgavata* was once an umbrella term for both Brahmins and non-Brahmins. According to K. K. A. Venkatachari (personal communication, 2005), *bhāgavata* came to connote only non-Brahmin devotees about a century or two ago; no census, however, has referred to a community called Bhāgavata. I found that Śrīvaiṣṇava non-Brahmins accept *bhāgavata* as a positive designation.

5. For a discussion of initiation, see the section in this chapter.

6. Dalit is Sanskrit for suppressed or crushed. The fact that this name did not occur in my interviews might not mean anything, or it might indicate that Śrīvaiṣṇavas who were once called 'outcastes' consider their religious identity more important than a pan-Indian, politicised identity (at least when talking to me).

7. There is a story about how the name *tirukkulattār*—those of the auspicious (*tiru*) caste (*kula*)—was given to outcastes. They had helped Rāmānuja (in the twelfth century) at Melkote (Tirunarayanapuram). The hagiographies and the local history about that place (*sthala-purāṇa*) describe how Rāmānuja carries the image of Lord Sampatkumāra from Delhi. One night, the local outcastes protect him. To recognise their service, Rāmānuja gives them the privilege of entering the temple three times a year and worshipping Lord Sampatkumāra at Melkote (Seshadri, *Social Change*, 43).

8. See, for example, Vaithees, *Religion, Caste and Nation in South India*.

9. See 'Fundamentals of Oral History: Texas Preservation Guidelines'.

10. Over the past decades, the ethnography of Tamil women's religious lives has been growing. In a seminal chapter on 'Devotional Experience Among Urban Smārta Women', for instance, Mary Hancock shows that Smārta women in middle-class business and professional families in Chennai in the 1980s did not exemplify the two prevailing models of female devotees as either conforming to normative caste and domestic values, or radically renouncing them, as had the woman saints. Rather, the reality of *bhakti* for these Smārta women was more polyvalent; they transgressed some boundaries to negotiate power relations, but nonetheless still maintained their status as wives and mothers (see Hancock, 'The Dilemmas of Domesticity', 66–91). This is probably true of most Śrīvaiṣṇava women as well. A good ethnographic study focussed on Śrīvaiṣṇava women, both non-Brahmins and Brahmins, and how they negotiate the two paradigms of domestic devotional religion and female renunciation represented by women (such as Āṇṭāḷ, who refused to marry a mere man but only Lord Raṅganātha himself), awaits further study.

11. Geetha and Rajadurai, *Non-Brahmin Millennium*, 89.

12. Online Etymology Dictionary, available at https://www.etymonline.com/word/sect (accessed 9 June 2019).

13. In Western religions, sect is often understood as that which is cut apart from a dominant group, which makes it a heretical or deviant one. Religion in India does not operate within such strong institutional structures that would define a division as the creation of a heretical sect, although the term *nāstika* (not [knowing] that which exists) was sometimes applied pejoratively to Buddhism and Jainism when the competition became particularly strong.

14. Young, 'Āḻvārs' Supreme God'. In the *āḻvār*s' verses, Tirumāl, Māl and Māyōṉ are the most common names. In Tamil, they refer to the deity's dark colour and therefore the black god Kṛṣṇa or Nārāyaṇa who has the dark colour of the sea.

15. Pañcarātra is a strand of northern Vaiṣṇavism with a large corpus of Sanskrit texts that are mainly about temple rituals and architecture. Priests from this tradition became prominent in temples in the Tamil world under Śrīvaiṣṇava control by the thirteenth century CE.

16. These are *para* (supreme), *vyūha* (four cosmic emanations), *avatāra* (past incarnations such as Rāma), *arcā* (present incarnations in statue-form in temples and home shrines), and *antaryāmin* (the inner

dweller). This is a Pāñcarātra Āgama formulation that the *ācāryas* integrated into their concept of God.

17. The word *vedānta* is understood very loosely in this context. Sometimes it refers to the Vedas, sometimes the Upaniṣads, and sometimes the entire Sanskrit sacred corpus. Even the Tamil Veda may be understood as Nammāḻvār's *Tiruvāymoḻi*, his four works, or the entire corpus of 4,000 verses by the twelve *āḻvārs*.

18. Seeds for the concept of the Tamil Veda are found in the *āḻvārs*. Nammāḻvār, for instance, describes how God speaks through him (*Tiruvāymoḻi* 7.9.1). Whereas the Sanskrit Veda is considered beginningless and authorless, an eternal revelation, the *āḻvārs* identified themselves as poets (*kavi*) who expressed and transmitted this God-inspired truth. Later commentators describe the Tamil Veda as the essence of the Sanskrit Veda.

19. In Maṇipravāḷam, most Tamil words are verbs, pronouns, adverbs and particles, and most Sanskrit words are nouns and adjectives, albeit inflected with Tamil case, number, and gender/rationality. See McCann, 'Defining Identity: Language, Religion and Caste', 143–49. For instance, *Nālāyira-divya-prabandham* (*Nālāyira-tivyap-pirapantam*) is a Maṇipravāḷam term. It means 'the collection of divine works [that have] four thousand verses'. In this compound, we find the Tamil word *nālāyira*, which means 4,000, the Sanskrit adjective *divya*, which means divine, and the Sanskrit noun *prabandha*, which means a work or collection of works.

20. See Young, 'Beloved Places', and Young, 'Śrīvaiṣṇava Topoi', 335–64. There are minor differences in the number of places associated with each region.

21. The tradition refers to two supreme celestial places, the Milk Ocean (Kṣīrābdhi) and Vaikuṇṭha, because it associates the former with the cosmogonic myth of Nārāyaṇa, and the latter with Viṣṇu's supreme heaven. The merger of these two gods with overlapping yet distinguishable histories accounts for separate supreme places for creation and salvation, respectively. The Milk Ocean and Vaikuṇṭha are sometimes included in the northern regions, in texts that enumerate the 108 *divyadeśas*.

22. Srirangam is where Lord Raṅganātha lives on an island in the middle of the Kaveri river, a mirror reflection, we are told, of the place where the cosmogonic supreme god reclines on his serpent couch in the Milk Ocean. Tirumalai, now in the state of Andhra, is located high

on the Ghat mountain range with Tirupati at the foot of the mountain. Kanchipuram is a city of many temples in eastern Tamil Nadu.

23. According to tradition, Rāmānuja established the *rāmānuja kūṭams*, although it is likely that these places date mainly from the Vijayanagara period. Their antecedent was the ancient *dharmaśala* tradition, an expression of charity that builds on the concept that 'the guest is god'. Rulers and wealthy people built these shelters to provide lodging, food, bathing facilities, and even medical help for pilgrims and traders who were guests travelling through their country.

24. Leopold, *Spiritual Aspects of Indian Music*, 51.

25. Rāmānuja's most famous work is the *Śrī Bhāṣya*, a commentary on the *Brahma Sūtras*. The philosophical tradition became known as Viśiṣṭādvaita Vedānta (the Vedānta which is the non-duality of that which is differentiated). Another important figure in the Teṉkalai tradition, our focus here, is Piḷḷai Lokācārya (ca. 1270–1330), who wrote eighteen works collectively called the Rahasya Granthas. For background on Piḷḷai Lokācārya, see McCann, 'Defining Identity: Language, Religion and Caste'. Yet another key figure in the tradition is Maṇavāḷa Māmuni (ca. 1350–1410), who gave lectures and wrote commentaries on some of the works of the *āḻvār*s and early *ācārya*s, popularising the tradition with help from eight disciples. For a discussion of Maṇavāḷa Māmuni's life and works, see Mumme, *The Srivaisnava Theological Dispute*, 15 ff.

26. McCann, 'Defining Identity: Language, Religion and Caste', 89.

27. See Young, 'Dying for *Bhukti* and *Mukti*: The Śrīvaiṣṇava Theology of Liberation as a Triumph Over Death', 389–96.

28. My arguments for the dates of these two works are forthcoming in my book, *Development of the Divyaprabandham: A New Approach to Śrīvaiṣṇava History*.

29. The idea of seventy-four *ācārya* families is attributed to Rāmānuja, but I have found no references to the seventy-four in Rāmānuja's works, or in *sampradāya* works until the *Guruparamparā Prabhāvam 6000*, and the *Kōyiḷ Oḻuku*.

30. In the *varṇa* system, there are four groups—brāhmaṇas, kṣatriyas, vaiśyas and śūdras. The first three are twice-born (in the sense that they are eligible for the *upanayana* ritual and study of the Vedas), the sūdras once born, and the outcastes are beyond the *varṇa* system altogether.

31. There are some hints that originally, the tradition was mainly a householder Brahmin one. The thirteenth-century author Periyavāccāṉ Piḷḷai, in his *Māṇikkamālai*, states that an *ācārya* 'has no interest in wealth or desire yet lives within the world and follows *dharma*, *artha*, and *kāma*' (in other words, adheres to an ascetic version of householder life). See Venkatachari, *The Maṇipravāḷa Literature*, 120.

32. For additional information on the topic of Śrīvaiṣṇava asceticism, see Olivelle, *Rules and Regulations of Brahmanical Asceticism* and *Ascetics and Brahmins*, and Narayanan, 'Renunciation in Saffron and White Roles', 161–90.

33. The first *jīyar* of the Emperumāṉār Mutt at Tirukkoyilur was Emperumāṉār (1521–69), who was originally from Andhra. According to the *maṭha*'s history, he reduced Śaiva influence in the area, renovated and established rituals in local Vaiṣṇava temples, and even renovated temples in such remote places as Alvartirunagari and Srirangam. Because some Vijayanagara rulers supported Andhra migrants and Vaiṣṇavism, it is possible that Emperumāṉār was connected with them. What started out as a *jīyar* tradition—albeit one with family connections, because in each generation at least one person in the family became a *jīyar* who headed the monastery—turned into an *ācārya* or householder tradition. This happened when the sons no longer became ascetics, even though the connection of other *jīyars* to the *maṭha* continued, as did the title *jīyar* (for the *ācārya*).

34. The Vānamāmalai Mutt is in the southern district of Tirunelveli at Nanguneri, near the Tirukkurunkuti *divyadeśa*. Its history goes back to the time of Maṇavāḷa Māmuni's disciples. It has had Telugu connections, too, and has attracted non-Brahmin Naidus from Telugu-speaking families. Today, this Mutt has more than 200 subsidiary *maṭhas* (called Totādri) throughout India. For a history of this Mutt, see Tatachar (1937), *The Vanamamalai Temple and Mutt*. The current head is H. H. Vanamamalai Madhurakavi Ramanuja Jeeyar Swamy.

35. According to K. K. A. Venkatachari (personal communication, December 2008), the first Etirāja *Jīyar* was Doddācārya. He was a great Sanskrit scholar and wrote a commentary on Vedānta Deśika's *Śatadūṣaṇī*, which argues against Advaita. His commentary is known as *Chanda Marutam*. (This means a kind of heavy wind; it implies that no one could have a counter-reply to his text.) His disciple came to Sriperumbudur from Andhra and established a *maṭha*. Because of his scholarship, he was accepted by the local people as an *ācārya* at the

Sriperumbudur temple. Since then, Teṉkalais have been heads of this *maṭha*. This is the *maṭha* of Varataa Ethiraja Jeeyar, mentioned to me many times, and who will be discussed in Chapter 6.

36. It is also known as *śaraṇāgati*. Srilata Raman traces the history of the concept of *prapatti* in *Self-Surrender (Prapatti) to God in Śrīvaiṣṇavism: Tamil Cats and Sanskrit Monkeys*. See also her article '*Samāśrayaṇam* in Śrīvaiṣṇavism'.

37. Srilata Raman thinks that the underlying text for the *pañcasaṁskāra* ritual, which does not appear in the early Pañcarātra texts—they mention only *dīkṣā*—is the *Parāśara Viṣṭa Paramadharmaśātra*. It is an appendage to the *Parāśara Smṛti* (also found in Chapter 107 of the *Garuḍa Purāṇa*), and is dated sometime after the twelfth century. The ritual is next mentioned in eight stories found in the *Guruparamparā Prabhāvam 6000*, in the context of defining Brahmin Śrīvaiṣṇava male identity, more specifically as a mandatory ritual connected to initiation into Vedic study (*upanāyana*), or for conversion of Brahmin householders and ascetics from Śaivism or Advaita to Śrīvaiṣṇavism. There is a brief mention that it could be done for women and *śūdra*s (Raman, '*Samāśrayaṇam*', 109), and could be performed at any stage of life. The lack of specific examples of women and *śūdra*s in this text raises the question whether the brief allusion to them is just to appear inclusive, or whether it reflects reality. Because aspects of the *pañcasaṁskāra*, such as branding on the shoulders, are ancient, there was surely some kind of initiatory ritual for women and *śūdra*s over the centuries. Inscriptions from the fifteenth century, for instance, mention non-Brahmin disciples with initiatory names. It is reasonable to assume that there were two versions, one for twice-born men and one for others.

As for women, the *Śrīvaiṣṇava Tīpikai*, which I discuss in the section of this chapter entitled 'A Note on Women in Śrīvaiṣṇavism', says that women should know the lineage of teachers, the secret mantras, and the theological and philosophical treatises. Because *samāśrayaṇam* is the initiation ritual into a connection with an *ācārya* or *jīyar*, and study of the tradition's treatises, the mention of such a connection in the *Śrīvaiṣṇava Tīpikai* implies that women, at least Brahmin women, by the time this text was written, routinely performed *samāśrayaṇam*.

The history of Śrīvaiṣṇavism in the seventeenth and eighteenth centuries is very poorly understood. At some point, there must have been major attempts by the *ācārya*s to recruit non-Brahmins to Śrīvaiṣṇavism, to counter the power of the Śaiva non-Brahmin *maṭha*s that were actively recruiting non-Brahmin elites as patronage from kings waned. Given the new Teṉkalai-Vaṭakalai competition over control of the temples, moreover, it would have been important to attract wealthy and powerful non-Brahmins to the Teṉkalai community, and have them wear the Teṉkalai *nāmam*, a move that was likely extended over time to other non-Brahmins.

Samāśrayaṇam might have been extended from a Brahmanical context to a more general one that included non-Brahmins as a formal entry of Vaiṣṇava non-Brahmins into a 'Brahmin-style' Śrīvaiṣṇavism to consolidate their allegiance. This was not a conversion per se, even for Brahmins, over hard sectarian boundaries (see Raman 'Initiation and Conversion', 281–89, for a discussion of hard and soft boundaries in this sect). Rather, it was a re-orientation of a Vaiṣṇava identity over soft boundaries within the Vaiṣṇava world itself, to a new orientation modelled on Brahmanical orthodoxy including vegetarianism, elaborate daily *pūjā*s, and so forth. I would argue that when this ritual was extended to non-Brahmins, it served some purposes, but it created problems for Brahmin religious leaders because an important part of the ritual was to initiate the person into a study of the *sampradāya* texts, the knowledge of which had been carefully protected by the Brahmins. In Chapter 2, I trace the struggles by non-Brahmins to obtain access to this knowledge.

38. It is also called the *ūrdhvapuṇḍram*, an emblem with white clay and turmeric. Kandadai Seshadri quotes archaeologist I. K. Sharma on this topic: 'It is from the 10th or 11th century onwards that the *urdhva pundrika*, both single or three (*eka* or *tri-pundrika*), becomes an exclusive vaishnavitic cult-mark and sub-sects grew based on the manner and composition of this symbol' (Seshadri, *Srivaishnavism and Social Change*, 36).

39. These are the *tirumantra*, *dvaya mantra* and *caramaślokas*. See Mumme, *Theological Dispute*, Appendix II, for the mantras and their role in the tradition. The *tirumantra* (*om namo nārāyaṇāya*) is important here because it begins with the sacred syllable *om*. For a history of *om*, see Young, 'Om, the Vedas, and the Status of Women with Special Reference to Srivaisnavism'. According to K. K. A. Venkatachari (personal communication, 2011), Teṉkalai women now recite it silently because of the general tradition against women chanting Vedic mantras.

40. There are various understandings of this ritual or what aspects are important. Some think that repeating mantras during

samāśrayaṇam itself is the act of surrender. For Vaṭakalais, *samāśrayaṇam* is an additional ritual done by the *ācārya* immediately following the five acts. Others think that because Rāmānuja had already done *prapatti* for all his followers, no ritual is necessary as long as one takes refuge with a bona fide *ācārya* or *jīyar* in one's own life (Mumme, *The Srivaisnava Theological Dispute*, 226). Srilata Raman discusses the Teṉkalai and Vaṭakalai understandings of *samāśrayaṇam* at length and concludes that the ritual has become important for both traditions (Raman, '*Samāśrayaṇam*', 110).

41. Raman, '*Samāśrayaṇam*', 109.

42. The word *kaiṅkarya* is a Sanskrit abstract noun, which is first found in *Bhāgavata Purāṇa* 3.2.22 (Monier-Williams, *Dictionary*, 311). The word derives from *kiṁkāra* (service) and that from *kim karomi* referring to the servant's question, 'What may I do?'). A Tamil synonym is *aṭimai*. Related to the word *aṭi* (foot), it too means being subservient. A common form of address, even today, is *aṭiyēṉ*, 'I am [your humble] servant'. Another Tamil synonym for service is *paṇi* (meaning shortness, submissiveness, inferiority, and by extension, work and service. Yet another word for service is *kuṟṟeval*, which means menial service). It is derived from the word *kuṟumai*, meaning shortness and defectiveness.

43. Nammāḻvār, *Tiruvāymoḻi* 6.10.10.

44. Periyāḻvār, *Periyāḻvārtirumoḻi* 5.3.3. For more Nammāḻvār stanzas expressing service (*kaiṅkarya*), see Carman and Narayanan (1989), *The Tamil Veda: Piḷḷaṉ's Interpretation of the Tiruvāymoḻi*, 210, 228, 240.

45. Tirumaṅkai Āḻvār, *Periyatirumoḻi* 8.10.1.

46. *toṇṭar toṇṭar toṇṭaṉ cāṭakōpaṉ* (Nammāḻvār, *Tiruvāymōḻi* 6.9.11).

47. Carman, *The Theology of Rāmānuja*, 222.

48. Humble service is important for everyone, at least in theory; however, there is an interesting twist. According to the texts, the *essential nature* of non-Brahmins, that is, *śūdra*s and outcastes, is to serve others. This implies that birth defines their essential nature, not behaviour. Despite the fact that it is meant to be words of praise—because Brahmins have to overcome their pride to be able to serve others, whereas non-Brahmins are humble by nature—the idea of essential nature as service still alludes to the *varṇa* hierarchy, in which *śūdra*s and outcastes were to serve the elite.

49. Appadurai, *Worship and Conflict under Colonial Rule*, 36.

50. Ibid., 46.

51. Rāmānuja says that 'I remain the same (*samo`aham*) to everyone, whatever their caste (*jāti*), degree of knowledge, form and innate nature'. Unlike Bhāskara but like Abhinavagupta, he refuses to describe women and *śūdras* as those of evil wombs (*pāpayonayaḥ*); that is another category. I translate the particle *api* in *Bhagavadgītā* 9:32 as 'also' rather than 'even' to capture his inclusive theology. See Young (2009), 'Fate Hangs on a Particle: The Hermeneutics of *Bhagavadgītā* 9:32–33', 229–41.

52. I have not located the details of this publication.

53. See Aḻakiyamaṇavāḷa Rāmānuja Ekaṅki Svāmikaḷ, *Śrīvaiṣṇava Tīpikai*. For my translation of the section on women, see Young, 'Theology Does Help Women's Liberation: Śrīvaiṣṇavism, A Hindu Case Study', 210–13. The author's name is the same as two mid-nineteenth to early twentieth-century figures whom I discuss in Chapter 2: (Bhuvanagiri) Aḻakīya Maṇavāḷa Rāmānuja Ekāṅgi Svāmikaḷ and (Kōyiḷ) Aḻakiya Maṇavāḷa Rāmānuja Ekāṅgi Svāmikaḷ. Unfortunately, I cannot find the title of this work in the sources that I have for these figures, although that might simply be because I did not find all of them. There is another problem. The *Śrīvaiṣṇava Tīpikai*'s description of women follows orthodox Brahmin norms, although they are adjusted to the *Śrīvaiṣṇava* sectarian context. The two authors with this name whom I discuss in Chapter 2, however, are not only non-Brahmins, they are also radical ones who publicly argue that non-Brahmins can be *ācāryas* and *jīyars*, roles that had been exclusively for Brahmins. One of them even argues that women can be *ācāryas*, a very radical stance indeed.

The author of the *Śrīvaiṣṇava Tīpikai* does support the sectarian education of women, as do the two non-Brahmins just mentioned. It is conceivable that if the author is one of these two figures, he simply held to orthodox Brahmin norms for women, as was common in elite non-Brahmin households of the time, and also supported their sectarian learning. Or, it is possible that there are two authors by this name, one a Brahmin and one a non-Brahmin. The fact that this book was published by a non-Brahmin (K. Nārāyaṇa Reṭṭiyar) makes me think that the work was probably a translation of a Brahmin-authored Sanskrit text by the non-Brahmin Bhuvanagiri Aḻakīya Maṇavāḷa Rāmānuja Ekāṅgi Svāmikaḷ. Perhaps a Brahmin *ācārya* or *jīyar* instigated him to take up this work.

54. Young, 'Women's Liberation', 209.

55. See *Śrīśaṇḍīlya-viśiṣṭa-parama-dharma-śāstra*.

56. See Young, 'Om', 84–122.

57. Srinivas, *Caste in Modern India*, 3.

58. There are many variations of spelling, use of diacritical marks and variant names in the literature of academic disciplines and in modern use. Here are some of them: Dalit (Adidravida, Ādidrāviḍa; Āttirāviṭar), Chettiyar (Chettiar, Ceṭṭi), Icai Velala (Icai Veḷāḷa), Nadar (Nāṭār), Naidu (Nāyuḍu, Nāyuṭu), Pillai (Piḷḷai), Reddiyar (Reṭṭiyar, Reḍḍiar), Sattada (Sāttāta, Cāttatavar, *Chāttāda*), Vanniyar (Vaṉṉiyar, Nāyakama, Palli, Padayachi/Padayātchī/Padāyacī), Paraiyar (Paṟaiyar), Yadava (Yādava), Vellalar (Veḷḷāḷar).

59. See Satish Deshpande, 'Srinivas, M. N. (1916–99)', and Upadhyay, 'Sanskritization at Large', 1–44, for discussion of this concept developed by Srinivas in 1956, and an update on the usefulness of the concept today. David Shulman rejects this concept, because he thinks that Tamil and Sanskrit were so intertwined in the past that one cannot make Sanskrit represented by Brahmins normative and worthy of emulation: 'the term "Sanskritization,"' he says, 'creates an unnecessary, stark dualism, itself foreign to the Tamil tradition, with implications of mutual exclusivity; it also reduces our descriptive capacity to impoverished notions of influence and assimilation' (Shulman, *Tamil: A Biography*, 182). Whereas that might be the case in *pulavar* (poet) culture, I would argue that it certainly was not the case in Śrīvaiṣṇava communities, where status was defined by Brahmanical norms of behaviour, and members of many other castes imitated them.

60. Thurston, *Castes and Tribes*, 1–2.

61. See Young, 'Who is the Āḻvārs' Supreme God?'

62. Hardy, *Viraha-Bhakti*, 253–56.

63. Dirks tries to correct the colonial emphasis on Brahmins by reasserting the medieval roles of kings, chiefs, and village headmen in the power dynamics of Tamil Nadu. See Dirks, *Castes of Mind*, as summarised in Appendix 3. Other scholars have argued that political figures were often not involved in temples.

64. Ibid., 437–38.

65. *Artha Pañcakam* 5.1-5. See Venkatachari (1978), *The Maṇipravāḷa Literature*, 133.

66. Piḷḷai Lokācārya, *Śrīvacana Bhūṣaṇam* (*sūtras* 196–200). (See Young, 'Theology Does Help Women's Liberation', 177).

67. *Ācārya Hṛdayam* 86.

68. Although the chanting of *om* by women and śūdras in some Vaiṣṇava circles probably goes back to the *Nārāyaṇa Upaniṣad* (ca. 500–300 BCE), it became a matter of dispute in Śrīvaiṣṇavism when Vedānta Deśika rejected the tradition and Maṇavāḷa Māmuni reaffirmed it. The *Guruparamarā Prabhāvam 6000* reinforced the legitimacy of chanting *om* by all Vaiṣṇavas, through a story about how Rāmānuja revealed its secret meaning by shouting it from the temple tower at Tirukottiyur (Young, 'Oṁ, the Vedas, and the Status of Women with Special Reference to Śrīvaiṣṇavism', 106).

69. Mumme, 'Rules and Rhetoric', 117–18.

70. His name originally had *dāsar* as the final component. *Dāsar* today signifies a non-Brahmin, but was once used for any devotee. According to Eugene Irschick, in Tamil Nadu *ayyaṅgar* referred exclusively to a Śrīvaiṣṇava Brahmin. The variant *ayyaṅgaru* referred to all Śrīvaiṣṇavas in Andhra. It is possible, he thinks, that those non-Brahmins who originally came from Andhra had traditions or links that did not hold such a strong distinction between non-Brahmin and Brahmin Śrīvaiṣṇavas. Still, because 'only a few non-Brahman groups in the districts, such as the Velamas, were permitted to study Sanskrit, the Brahmans exercised almost complete control over the body of Hindu religious works written in Sanskrit' (Irschick, *Politics and Social Conflict*, 5).

71. TTDES (Tirumalai-Tirupati Devasthanam Epigraphical Series) 2.68. The fact that here, non-Brahmins are officially recognised chanters with remuneration counters the later claim by Śrīvaiṣṇava Brahmins that only they have been official temple chanters.

72. There are clues that KRA had some followers for a generation or two at Kanchipuram and Srirangam, but this was never formalised as a lineage or institution.

73. Clooney, 'Fierce Words', 418.

74. Mumme, 'Rules and Rhetoric', 118. See pp. 113–20 for important proof texts on caste in Śrīvaiṣṇava works.

75. Ibid., 118.

76. This was explained to me by K. K. A. Venkatachari, January 2011.

77. By contrast, following Vedānta Deśika, Vaṭakalais say that caste norms must be maintained until death, even by those who have surrendered to God. Caste does not prevent liberation, which is virtually guaranteed by one's surrender to God. In other words, this is a controversy over whether surrender to a gracious God is sufficient,

or whether devotees must also maintain the duties of caste and stage of life (*varṇa-āśrama-dharma*). Rhetoric aside, evidence suggests that the practice was mandatory for Vaṭakalais, and only customary (nevertheless done) for Teṉkalais, unless there was a conflict whence the Teṉkalai tradition took precedence.

78. According to B. K. Rangachari, both sects hold that anyone of any caste is qualified for *prapatti*. Teṉkalais go a step further, however, and say that all *prapannas* are equal, which means that Brahmins are not superior to any other group (Rangachari 2000, *Sri Vaishnava Brahmins*: 45–46).

79. Dirks, *Castes of Mind*, 239–40.

80. Geetha and Rajadurai, *Towards a Non-Brahmin Millennium*, 305, reporting on Sami Sitambaranar's account in *Thamizhar Talaivar Periyar E Ve Ra Vazhkai Varalaru*.

81. Congress was very active in Tiruchirappalli district, which was a major centre of agitation against British rule. That was because the Tiruchirappalli fort had been a British stronghold.

82. Veeramani, *Periyar on Women's Rights*, xi.

83. Spratt, *D.M.K.*, 22.

84. Ibid., 24, 19.

85. Dirks, *Castes of Mind*, 257.

86. See Appadurai, *Worship and Conflict*, 52, for a history of the Hindu Religious and Charitable Endowments Board.

87. Dirks, *Castes of Mind*, 257.

88. Geetha and Rajadurai, *Towards a Non-Brahmin Millennium*, 140 ff.

89. These included R. Narayana Iyengar, a lawyer and leader of the non-cooperation movement; P. Narayana Ayyengar, a lawyer, leader of the Vedaranyam Salt Sathyagraha, and organiser of a Sathyagraha Ashram; R. Krishnasamy Ayyengar, who took over the Ashram when Narayana Ayyengar was arrested at Mannargudi; and N. Ramasamy Ayyengar, who organised volunteers for the movement.

90. Spratt, *D.M.K.*, 38.

91. See Waghorne, *Images of Dharma*.

92. Spratt, *D.M.K.*, 19.

93. Karunanidhi was Chief Minister 1969–71, 1971–76, 1989–91, 1996–2001, and 2006–11.

94. Jayalalithaa was in power 1991–1996, 2002–06, 2011–14 and 2015–16.

95. The judgment was pronounced on 27 September 2014, sentencing her to four years in prison. This disqualified her as Chief Minister of the state and as an MLA, with the additional proviso that she could not contest elections for ten years. With this verdict, violence by her supporters erupted across Tamil Nadu, including several self-immolations. M. Karunanidhi, leader of the DMK, requested the President and Prime Minister of India to help restore peace. The AIADMK chose O. Panneerselvam to replace her as Chief Minister of Tamil Nadu. In October, the Supreme Court granted her request for bail.

two

Traces of Non-Brahmin Śrīvaiṣṇava Leaders

My study of Śrīvaiṣṇava non-Brahmins was to be about recent changes in Tamil society. Perhaps it was fortuitous that I wanted to interview some elderly Śrīvaiṣṇavas, because their stories would soon be lost to history. My questions about memories of grandparents and parents took me back into late colonial times.

This chapter is about the traces of some Bhāgavata leaders, ones that I discovered just in time—that is, before they are erased forever from the historical record. I searched for more details. Sometimes this took me to village shrines and tombs or memorial temples (*samādhis*), to photographs near descendants' household altars, to pamphlets forgotten in personal libraries, and occasionally to a court case. One trace sometimes led to another, such as a booklet containing a short biography. Other vestiges led nowhere. These included many references to published books that no longer exist, even in the libraries of Tamil Nadu.

I am surprised that only traces remain, especially because the past century has been a time of non-Brahmin political awakening, 'subaltern' studies and robust scholarship on the colonial period in general and religions such as Tamil

Christianity and Śaivism in particular. Given all the changes surveyed in the Introduction, how were Śrīvaiṣṇava Bhāgavatas affected by these changes during the nineteenth century? And why do only traces remain?

Turning first to traces of seven non-Brahmin leaders, I analyse how they tried to make Śrīvaiṣṇava theological claims of inclusiveness more substantive than rhetorical, and therefore offer Bhāgavatas more support than before. At the heart of this Bhāgavata chutzpah were the ostensibly subversive acts of lecturing on the meaning of the *Divyaprapandham* verses and Śrīvaiṣṇava theology, as well as performing the initiation ritual (*samāśrayaṇam*), which only Brahmin *ācāryas* and *jīyars* performed. With these traces recovered, I discuss how the road to recognition for non-Brahmins was oddly connected to Dalit mobilisation, how they became part of *pulavar* (poet) culture, and how they eventually achieved recognition. After comparing Śaivism and Vaiṣṇavism on the topic of non-Brahmin leadership, I conclude the chapter by comparing the trajectories of Śrīvaiṣṇavism and Śaivism under late colonial rule, and offer reasons for why Śrīvaiṣṇavas were slower to awaken to possibilities for leadership.

A Forgotten Colonial History

The seven pivotal non-Brahmin leaders are Rāmānuja Nāvalar, Bhuvanagiri Ekāṅgi Svāmikaḷ, Nārāyaṇa Dāsar, (Kōyiḷ) Ekāṅgi Svāmikaḷ, Gōpāla Kṛṣṇa Piḷḷai, Appāvu Mudaliyār and B. R. Purushottama Naidu. Some of the following descriptions of their lives are based on booklets that their followers wrote about them. These combine the modern genre of biography with the traditional one of hagiography to emphasise the special status of these Bhāgavatas. Little is written about the last two leaders, however, and my information is garnered from remarks in the introductions to their own books.

Rāmānuja Nāvalar

A. V. Rāmānuja Nāvalar (1829–91), also known as Putuvai Navalar, was first known as Muttu Ramanuja. According to the brief biography on Ramanuja Navalar,[1] he was born in 1829 to a Balija Naidu couple[2] at Eppakkam, which is north of Puducherry. After receiving *samāśrayaṇam* from the *jīyar* at Emperumāṉār Mutt in Tirukkoyilur, he went to Bhaṭṭarpirāṉ *jīyar* of the Vānamāmalai Mutt in the southern district of Tirunelveli. Mastering Tamil, Sanskrit and Telugu, he studied philosophical and other works about Śrīvaiṣṇavism. He strongly supported Teṉkalai views. Because of the high standard of his scholarship and his status as a poet, orator and philosopher, Śrīvaiṣṇava scholars gave him the title Rāmānuja Nāvalar (one who is the master of his tongue, that is, a learned person).

Nāvalar's biography describes how Poṉṉuraṅkam Piḷḷai, a devotee belonging to the Yadava caste, learned about the greatness of Nāvalar and asked him to live in Putuvai (Puducherry). After moving there, Nāvalar resided on Perumāḷ Kōyil Street, where the Śrī Varadarāja Perumāḷ temple was (and still is) located, until the end of his life. He married and had one son, Śaṭakōpa Rāmānuja Naidu, who was also a good scholar and poet.

Once, when Nāvalar visited his *jīyar* at Tirukkoyilur, the *jīyar* gave him a copy of the Sanskrit *Padmottara-purāṇa* and instructed him to translate its 4,123 verses into Tamil and popularise it. When it was finished in 1869, Nāvalar presented it to a public gathering of Śrīvaiṣṇavas[3] in Kanchipuram, which was customary for new works. It was then printed with the addition of 55 praise-poems in honour of the author and distributed by Poṉṉuraṅkam Piḷḷai. Because only Brahmins knew Sanskrit works, says the biographer, when Nāvalar translated some into Tamil, people began to think that he was an incarnation of God.

According to the biography, sometime later Nāvalar dreamed that the Lord of Srimushnam temple had appeared to him and asked him to translate the *Śrīmuṣṇa-purāṇa* from Sanskrit into Tamil. He did that too, and then presented it to scholars in the presence of his *jīyar*. When Nāvalar was reciting the work, his disciples were surprised that a verse had forecast his birth: 'though an eternal being (*nityasūri*), by the grace of God, Nāvalar was born on earth'.

This translation was followed by translations of two more *purāṇas*.[4] In addition to these, he wrote forty-six prose works on Śrīvaiṣṇavism,[5] and composed some devotional songs[6] in Carnatic musical style about God and his divine places. The biography points out that these are sung in *bhajana maṭhas* in many towns and villages, because singing songs is the easiest way to pray during the Kaliyūga. Nāvalar himself travelled to many places where he taught about the tradition, gave lectures and led *kīrtana*-style songs for learned and ordinary people alike, just as Nampiḷḷai (1210–70) had done centuries earlier.[7]

Next, the biography describes how Somasundara Nāyakar[8] (1846–1901), a Śaiva, mocked Vaiṣṇavism, the *ācāryas*, the *āḻvārs* and especially the sectarian symbol, the *nāmam*, in his *Śaiva Cūtāmaṇi*. Nāvalar wrote a rejoinder to this, which he called the *Hari Darśana*. He filed a suit in the magistrate court, moreover, stating that he had been abused by Somasundara Nāyakar. After learning about the legal proceedings, Somasundara Nāyakar offered him 100 rupees, a written commitment that he would not abuse a Vaiṣṇava again, and an apology that appeared in a popular journal.[9]

Describing some miracles, the biography tells the following stories. One time, when Nāvalar was young and sleeping under a tree, his parents saw a serpent protecting his face from the sun's heat by spreading its hood. Another time, when climbing Tirumalai hill, he became thirsty and lay down under a tree for a short nap. When he opened his eyes, he found a water pond and *tulasī* plant, an incident that he mentions in his *Bhāgavatam Nāma-saṅkīrtana*. On yet another occasion, when Nāvalar was giving a series of discourses on the *Bhāgavata-purāṇa*, a parrot used to sit on his lap and then fly away when he was done.

In 1891, Nāvalar died. He was remembered for decades. A dictionary of Tamil literature,[10] published in 1904, contains references to several of his books. Another work[11] includes his 1914 *Pañcaratnamālā* about Nammāḻvār. Several poets composed works about him.[12] In 1925, a scholar, K. Rāmānuja Svāmi, established an organisation in Pannurutti,[13] west of Cuddalore, called Śrīmad Rāmānuja Nāvalar Svāmikaḷ Sabhai. This organisation celebrated his birthday every year, and also honoured him at an annual conference.

The biography says that his portrait, which was painted in Srirangam, was under worship in the house of the secretary, and that Nāvalar presided in this form over the annual conference. In Koyampalli village, where another image was established and daily *pūjā* performed on his birthday, people reported that a snake used to come and open its hood over Nāvalar's image, staying for a week and not hurting anyone. There was yet another image in Vilakkoli Sannidhi, a *rāmānuja kūṭam* in Kanchipuram that had been built by a woman named Āṇṭāḷ-ammāḷ. There, daily and annual *pūjā*s were conducted.

I visited a temple dedicated to Rāmānuja Nāvalar in the village of Eppakkam, on the outskirts of Puducherry, where he had been born. Although this was once a Naidu village, most inhabitants today are Vanniyars and Yadavas. Śrīnivāsiṉ Piḷḷai, a wealthy merchant in Pannurutti, built the temple. He was an erudite scholar in the *Divyaprabandham* and would sing it with the melodic modes or *pāṇ*s, not the Brahmin style of chanting.[14] He would also conduct an annual Śrīvaiṣṇava conference in Pannurutti and invite important Bhāgavatas to lecture.

The Eppakkam temple, which Śrīnivāsiṉ Piḷḷai's family still maintains, has Lord Śrīnivāsa for its presiding image. When facing the image, one sees in Image 2.1 a statue of Rāmānuja Nāvalar on the right.

He wears a turban like that found on the image of Maṇavāḷa Māmuni. The shrine's external roof is adorned with images of Rāmānuja Nāvalar and famous historical figures of the Teṉkalai tradition: Nammāḻvār, Maṇavāḷa Māmuni and Rāmānuja. There is a monthly festival on Kārtikā (Ta. Kārttikai)

IMAGE 2.1: Non-Brahmin priest at shrine north of Puducherry with image of the non-Brahmin scholar Rāmānuja Nāvalar (1829–91).

Image credit: Author's collection.

star,[15] paid for by the Piḷḷai family. The non-Brahmin priest told me that hundreds come on that day, mainly the local Vanniyars and Yadavas who are agriculturalists in the area.

Bhuvanagiri Ekāṅgi Svāmikaḷ

Bhuvanagiri Ekāṅgi Svāmikaḷ (1860–1927) is formally known as Aḻakiya Maṇavāḷa Rāmānuja Ekāṅgi Svāmikaḷ (a name that overlaps with another figure from Srirangam whom I discuss shortly) and Aḻakiya Maṇavāḷa Dāsar.[16] According to his biography,[17] he was born in Bhuvanagiri, a village near Cuddalore, which was a centre of Śaivism and Christianity, to a Naidu family.[18] His biography says that his original name was Raṅgasvāmi, the name of the God of Srirangam. Here, I will call him Bhuvanagiri. After marriage, he became a farmer and weaver to support his wife and daughter. Following his family's tradition, he was initiated by Emperumāṉar Jīyar of Tirukkoyilur.

One day, continues the biography, Rāmānuja Nāvalar visited this family at Bhuvanagiri. Cinnaiyya Naidu and his son, the future Bhuvanagiri, prostrated themselves before him. Nāvalar selected a verse and asked Bhuvanagiri to read it. As if already familiar with it, he read it loudly and interpreted it. Impressed, Nāvalar decided that he should become a leader for the Śrīvaiṣṇava *sampradāya* and instructed his father to provide a good teacher, saying that his son would become a very important person.

Cinnaiyya Naidu sent Bhuvanagiri to study with Nāvalar himself, who was teaching other students. Besides Tamil works, Bhuvanagiri studied Telugu and Sanskrit. He so distinguished himself with his excellent memory, says the biography, that Nāvalar named him after Aḻakiya Maṇavāḷa Dāsar (Piḷḷai Perumāḷ Ayyaṅgar), author of the famous *Aṣṭa Prapandham* (Eight Books).[19]

Bhuvanagiri became very popular because of his teaching,[20] composition of verses on particular temples, singing and rhetorical power. A number of people were jealous of him, says the biography, and challenged him to a debate. After he answered all their questions (which were later published as a small book called *Kaṭāviṭai Cattai*), his defeated rivals started verbally abusing him, and even physically assaulting him.

Vēnugōpāḷa Naidu, chairman of the Cuddalore municipality, intervened and struck a compromise. On another occasion, according to the biography, someone in Chidambaram composed a poem with the following line: 'O god of death, be compassionate by ending the life of Bhuvanagiri'. Surprisingly, the person who composed that line became very sick. The doctors lost hope for him. Fearing that the bad karma created by insulting Bhuvanagiri caused his illness, he wanted to go to Bhuvanagiri and apologise, even though his condition prevented that. When he learned of Bhuvanagiri's visit to Chidambaram, however, he waited at his house until Bhuvanagiri passed by and then prostrated himself, requesting forgiveness. Bhuvanagiri replied that the Lord would forgive him.

Bhuvanagiri decided to work full-time for the Śrīvaiṣṇava *sampradāya*. His wife went to stay with their daughter, who was now married. He travelled from town to town giving discourses in a style of mixed prose and music with percussive rhythm (the *harikathā* style of *bhajana*). Arguing that all religions have truth, Bhvanagiri said that one should follow one's own strictly. In an age when Christian missionaries claimed that Christianity was the only truth, this was an attempt to keep Hindus within their own tradition.

Having heard about Bhuvanagiri's discourses, Damodharaṉ Naidu, the sub-magistrate of Bhuvanagiri village, invited him home to lecture on *Kampaṉ Rāmāyaṇam*. After Bhuvanagiri did this, the man was pleased and offered him a gift. Bhuvanagiri refused it, suggesting instead that he arrange for daily *pūjā* at the Rāmaṉ temple—presumably the Pattabi Rāmaṉ temple in Bhuvanagiri village that I refer to below. The sub-magistrate not only did that, but he also endowed the temple with 2 acres of land, a small tank and a grove of trees.

Once, the Vānamāmalai *jīyar*, by name Śaṭhakōpa Rāmānuja Jīyar, visited the town of Bhuvanagiri. After Bhuvanagiri prostrated himself, the *jīyar*, who was familiar with the work of Bhuvanagiri, advised him that he could not find liberation merely by *harikathā* and discourses on *purāṇa*s. He would need to learn the basic principles of reality (*tattva-jñāna*) and customary norms (*ācāra*). The *jīyar* instructed him to study with Amarāvati Tiruvēṅkaṭācāriya and Chinna Kaliyaṉ Rāmānuja Jīyar, the twenty-fifth head of the Vānamāmalai Mutt. Both asked Bhuvanagiri to lecture and found his knowledge impressive.

In 1908, Bhuvanagiri went to Sriperumbudur during the festival celebrating Rāmānuja's birthday and gave lectures.

After listening to one, a young man named Gōpāla composed two poetic works about Bhuvanagiri: *A̱lakiya Maṉavāḷa Mālai* and *A̱lakiya Maṉavāḷa Antāti*. (The works were never published and disappeared.) That same year, Bhuvanagiri decided to become an ascetic (*ekāṅgi*). Śrīnāth Bālakṛṣṇa Ekāṅgi at Sriperumbudur did the ritual and renamed him after his birthplace: Bhuvanagiri Ekāṅgi Svāmikaḷ.

To counter Śaiva critics of the *Divyaprabandham*, Bhuvanagiri wrote and published the *Drāviḍaveda Vaibhava Prakāśika* (1906),[21] which explains the glory of the *Divyaprabandham*. In 1908, he wrote the *Nālāyira Divyaprabandham Ābhāsa Darpaṇa* to argue against a Śaiva work[22] that interprets the *āḻvār*'s hymns as if they were about the glory of Śiva. He established that one cannot interpret Vaiṣṇava works by relying on Śaiva ones, or vice versa.

In Kallakurichi, Bhuvanagiri's followers constructed an *ashram* and provided a cook for him. When Bhuvanagiri was writing the *Tirucitrakūṭa Mahātmyam*, he appointed one Devarājulu to help him, yet when Bhuvanagiri gave discourses on the *rahasya grantha*s (secret works), he would send him away, saying that he could not reveal the secrets to anyone except a Śrīvaiṣṇava who had completed the initiation ritual (*samāśrayaṇam*). Therefore, Devarājulu should go to the Emperumāṉār *jīyar* at Tirukkoyilur for initiation. After doing so, Devarājulu joined the group.

A member of the Tirukkulam (the sacred clan, a euphemism for the outcaste community) wanted to study with Bhuvanagiri, so Bhuvanagiri took him to Tirukkoyilur and asked the *jīyar* to initiate him. Instead, the *jīyar* gave Bhuvanagiri his own ritual utensils for branding, a key part of the ritual, and asked him to perform the ritual. Bhuvanagiri complied, and the outcaste was renamed Nārāyaṇa Dāsar. (This implies that by having a non-Brahmin initiate an outcaste, the Brahmin *jīyar* thinks he will not be caste-ist or polluted.) Nārāyaṇa Dāsar then studied about Śrīvaiṣṇavism. (I will discuss his biography in the next section.) To counteract the propagation of Śaivism in the area, Bhuvanagiri proselytised among the outcastes and initiated them into Śrīvaiṣṇavism. This activity generated enormous controversy, according to the biography.

Bhuvanagiri became famous for his recitations of devotional songs and talks on Śrīvaiṣṇavism. Even so, he provoked criticism within Śrīvaiṣṇavism for arguing against Brahmanical positions. When he gave lectures at Nammāḻvār's birthplace (Alvartirunagari) in Tirunelveli district, for instance, the local Brahmin leaders refused to give him accommodation or organise the events.[23] In response, Bhuvanagiri's disciples raised funds and built a *rāmānuja kūṭam*, where he stayed and lectured.[24]

Since the Śrīvaiṣṇava schools (*pāṭhaśālās*)—which taught both the Vedas and the *Divyaprabandham*—were for Brahmins only, Bhuvanagiri founded his own school in 1912 in Srirangam. Called Rāmānuja Darśana Vidyāśālā, it taught Bhāgavatas the *Divyaprabandham*, Śrīvaiṣṇava theology, and Tamil literature. Negamam Zaimindar Ramakrishna Naidu rented a house for the school.[25] The first year, it admitted ten students with full board and lodging. Many students attended, including B. R. Purushotamma Naidu (whom I will discuss). Brahmins vociferously criticised it. Presumably this was because Bhāgavatas were receiving knowledge that customarily belonged to Brahmins alone. When students dwindled and costs rose, the Zamindar closed the school. Bhuvanagiri moved it to Chidambaram, where it continues to this day, only as an elementary school.

In 1914, in Tuttukkuti village, the Śrīvaiṣṇava Mahāsabhā was organised. When Bhuvanagiri gave a lecture, the Brahmin president Rāghava Ayyaṅgar, an authority on Tamil literature, found a mistake. At the end of the meeting, Bhuvanagiri stood up and said that there 'was no mistake. I can support everything.' The next day, in the Mahāsabhā, Bhuvanagiri refuted the president's critique by quoting the relevant authorities. After listening to Bhuvanagiri, Rāghava realised his mistake and met him privately. Nevertheless, from that day on, Bhuvanagiri resolved not to give lectures in the presence of Brahmins.

When Bhuvanagiri went away on pilgrimage,[26] Brahmins continued to criticise his views for threatening the duties of caste and stages of life (*varṇa-āśrama-dharma*) in general, and Brahmin control of Śrīvaiṣṇavism in particular. In fact, they complained to the Vānamāmalai *jīyar*. However, the *jīyar*, after scrutinising Bhuvanagiri's activities, told him to continue his good work.[27]

A Srirangam *jīyar*, Ayodhyā Rāma Svāmi, sided with the opposing Brahmins. In 1918, he published *Tattvatraya Vyākhyāna* and *Tātparya Dīpikā* to argue that only Brahmin *ācārya*s had the right to perform initiations. Bhuvanagiri travelled around Tamil Nadu to counter the Srirangam *jīyar*'s attacks. His *Tattvatraya Vyākhyāna Tātparya Tīpikā Vicāram* (1918)[28] and *Samāśrayaṇam Sarvatikaram* (1921) defend the idea that both non-Brahmins and women can perform *samāśrayaṇam*.[29]

One of the Brahmins with whom Bhuvanagiri debated was Śrīraṅga Rāmānuja Jīyar, who had argued in a book that because the ritual for initiation involved a sacred fire, the ritual was Vedic and therefore could be performed only by Brahmins. In 1919, at Tiruvahindrapuram, Bhuvanagiri countered this by arguing that the fire used for branding was a Vaiṣṇava fire, not a Vedic one, and so non-Brahmins could perform *samāśrayaṇam*.[30]

That same year, Bhuvanagiri gave a public lecture in Cuddalore on the Brahmins' monopoly on initiation. Quoting elaborately from the *Divyaprabandham* and *sampradāya* works, he argued once again that initiation is not the exclusive right of Brahmins. Rather, anyone who has expertise in these works, is devoted to God, and follows the behavioural norms of the scriptures, has a right to perform it. That includes women.[31] Although Brahmin scholars from several communities were invited to debate him, they requested a postponement and failed to show up even at the later date.

After meeting Govindarājulu from Manakkuppam (Cuddalore), who had become a government servant at Tirukkoyilur, Bhuvanagiri asked him to teach deserving devotees about Śrīvaiṣṇavism. On a later occasion, Bhuvanagiri asked him to initiate them and gave him the required conch and wheel-branding tools.

In 1926, Bhuvanagiri established his own *maṭha* in Sriperumbudur. He called it Maṇavāḷa Māmunikaḷ Maṭam, after the famous *ācārya* Maṇavāḷa Māmunikaḷ (whom I date 1370–1443), and lived there until his death the following year (11 June 1927). In his will, he instructed that his *samādhi* should be built in the corner of a garden that belonged to his devotee Lakṣmiprapanna. Bhuvanagiri's *samādhi* is now in an open field on the outskirts of Sriperumbudur, along with the *samādhi* of his disciple Prabandhasvāmi.

A *maṭha* called Emmidi Maṭam, which a disciple established during Bhuvanagiri's lifetime, exists in Sriperumbudur. Today, its head is a single man who is an ordinary devotee. When I interviewed him, he said that on every anniversary of Bhuvanagiri's death, his descendants come from the Puducherry area and perform *pūjā* at the *samādhi*s that his grandsons fixed up in 2005.

There is also a temple in Bhuvanagiri's birthplace dedicated to the presiding deity Pattabi Rāmaṉ. Besides the main shrine, there are three smaller ones on the right, to Bhuvanagiri, Rāmānuja and Nammāḻvār.[32]

Nārāyaṇa Dāsar

Nārāyaṇa Dāsar (1872–1912) was born to Rāmadāsar, a staunch outcaste devotee of Lord Viṣṇu and Periyammā in the year 1872; they named him Nārāyaṇaṉ. The family lived in Kottaimedu, now known as Karunapuram. Rāmadāsar was a farmer, owned land, and had a kiln. According to Nārāyaṇa Dāsar's biography,[33] which often reads like a hagiography, Nārāyaṇaṉ helped his father. Rather than playing with other boys, he spent his time praying to the Lord.

Nārāyaṇaṉ went to Madras for teacher training. He lived in the Kontittoppu area, which was a stronghold of Vaiṣṇavism. Elsewhere, when hooligans mocked the Vaiṣṇava mark (*nāmam*) on his forehead, says the biography, he 'conquered' them by patience. After marrying the daughter of a staunch Vaiṣṇava Dalit couple of his village, Nārāyaṇaṉ decided that he did not like married life. He wanted to be an ascetic, and so he left home and went by foot all the way south to the Vānamāmalai Mutt. On his way there, he met a group of yogis and learned astrology, medicine, and yoga from them.

Nārāyaṇaṉ stayed one year at the *maṭha* to learn the works of Śrīvaiṣṇavism and asked the *jīyar* to initiate him into asceticism. By this time, his wife had figured out where her husband had gone and came to the *maṭha* to bring him home. The *jīyar*, learning that the young man was married, refused to initiate him, commanding him to remain married and serve the Lord that way. Nārāyaṇaṉ returned home and lived devoutly with his wife. As I mentioned, Bhuvanagiri gave him *samāśrayaṇam* and the initiation name Nārāyaṇa Dāsar. Nārāyaṇa Dāsar used to send one-third of his salary to Bhuvanagiri every month, until his retirement. During holidays, he went on pilgrimage to sacred shrines.

Nārāyaṇa Dāsar was the headmaster of the government elementary school for outcastes in Virapandi, near Tirukkoyilur. The village had a separate government school for the upper castes too. Gradually, the villagers recognised Nārāyaṇa Dāsar as an able teacher and a man of noble qualities. Even high-caste students wanted to attend his school.

The biography describes a miracle. Learning that Nārāyaṇa Dāsar was bedridden, Sundararāja Bhāgavatar, Bhuvanagiri's son-in-law, went to see him. On his way, he stopped at the Chidambaram temple. While worshipping Lord Govindarāja there, he prayed for the early recovery of Nārāyaṇa Dāsar. Sundararāja was sitting on the edge of the sacred tank when a priest handed him a basket full of *prasāda* (sacred food) and a garland. The priest said that Nārāyaṇa Dāsar had come there in the early morning and worshipped the Lord, but had left the temple without taking the sacred food. When the priest went away, Sundararāja wondered how Nārāyaṇa Dāsar could have visited the temple when he was far away and bedridden. Not only was this a miracle, Sundararāja decided, so was the fact that the Lord himself in the guise of a priest had given Nārāyaṇa Dāsar the *prasāda*.

Sundararāja Bhāgavatar finally reached the house of Nārāyaṇa Dāsar, where he lay in a semi-conscious state. Nārāyaṇa Dāsar woke up and sat on his cot. His guest gave him the *prasāda* and the garland of Lord Govindarāja in Chidambaram. Nārāyaṇa Dāsar was in trance. Uttering the Lord's name, Nārāyaṇa, he died and attained liberation.[34]

After the news spread to surrounding villages, people came and placed garlands on his body. There was a funeral procession with chanting of the *Divyaprabandham* and Vedic mantras. On the way to the cremation ground, people worshipped him with lighted camphor. Finally, he was cremated with sandalwood. When the fire cooled, they created the *samādhi* (the memorial temple to honour him). This was followed by a thirteen-day funeral ceremony, during which people chanted the *Divyaprabandham* and *Rāmānuja-nūṟṟantāti* (a work in praise of Rāmānuja). The funeral was to conclude with a ritual, except there was no rice for it. Nārāyana Dāsar's chief disciple (Āṟumuka Bhāgavatar) gave some paddy that he had saved for seedlings. Later, his seedling supply miraculously replenished itself and the paddy overflowed.

People believed that Nārāyaṇa Dāsar had performed many miracles and honoured him, especially during the month of Mārkaḻi. At his *samādhi*, devotees of many castes, especially the Vanniyars, worship him even today. Because he had forbidden his followers to place images of him in the shrine, there is only a *nāmam* image there, with the discus and conch on either side.

(Kōyiḻ) Ekāṅgi Svāmikaḷ

(Kōyiḻ) Ekāṅgi Svāmikaḷ (1850–1907) is also called Ekāṅgi Rāmānuja Dāsar, Aḻakiya Maṇavāḷa Ekāṅgi Svāmikaḷ and Kōyiḷ Aḻakiya Maṇavāḷa Rāmānuja Ekāṅgi. Given his many names and the overlap of one name with one of Bhuvanagiri's, I will call him here simply Ekāṅgi Svāmikaḷ. Although we do not know his birth name, his biography[35] notes that he was born in Srirangam to parents of a family 'related to the Lord' (*bhagavat-sambandha*). This, along with the presence of the word *kōyil* (meaning temple, specifically Srirangam) in one of his names, likely alludes to a Sattada family identity, that is, a non-Brahmin family, which had the hereditary right to serve in the temple by protecting the deity and treasury, as well as by carrying processional torches and making special garlands for the *pūjā*.

The biography points out that during his school years, Ekāṅgi Svāmikaḷ preferred the company of Śrīvaiṣṇava elders who gave religious lectures. Very orthodox and pious, he was always keen to worship Lord Raṅganātha. With another Bhāgavata, Kōyil Rāmānuja Dāsar, he visited many sacred places mentioned by the *āḻvār*s (*divyadeśa*s) and then returned to Srirangam.

Following hagiographic precedent, the account describes several supernatural events. On one occasion, the pious boy was walking through the paddy fields and, like Nammāḻvār, fell down unconscious because of his eagerness to receive God's vision.[36] A Bhāgavata devotee helped him get up and return to the temple. Then the devotee revealed that he was God himself.

On another occasion, the Lord appeared in a dream and instructed him to become a disciple of the Brahmin Ciṟupuliyūr Jīyar (see Chapter 6). As usual, the future *ekāṅgi* went to the Kaveri, had his bath, put on his *nāmam* and worshipped Lord Raṅganātha in the temple. As he was returning, a *jīyar* came out of the temple tank. The future *ekāṅgi* saw that this was the same person who had appeared in his dream. He prostrated to the *jīyar* and requested *samāśrayaṇam* along with Śrīvaiṣṇava teachings. After he narrated his dream to the *jīyar*, the latter told him about having a similar dream. 'I am pleased,' the *jīyar* said, that 'you are the one who appeared in my dream'. Then the *jīyar* initiated him and taught him verses from the *Divyaprabandham*.

The fact that the *jīyar* does not mention the name of his own preceptor might allude to the *jīyar's* self-initiation because the name (and lineage) of one's preceptor is very important to an initiate, who must chant a verse about him daily. Of course, it might simply mean that the author of the biography did not know this detail.

The biography continues with a story about how the *ekāṅgi*-to-be wanted to learn the Sanskrit Veda but was unable to produce the correct intonation (*svara*). (Perhaps the real situation was that the Brahmins would not teach him Sanskrit and the Vedas in their schools.) Extremely disappointed, he tried to commit suicide on the banks of the Kaveri. Although he was seriously wounded, another non-Brahmin devotee got him treatment, and he lived.

The future *ekāṅgi* then went to Ciṟupuliyūr Jīyar and asked for initiation into asceticism. The *jīyar* did so, blessed him and gave him a Krishna image for daily worship (a very unusual act for a Brahmin). Now also known as Aḻakiya Maṇavāḷa Ekāṅgi Svāmikaḷ, he built a small *maṭha* for himself on the banks of the Kaveri river.

Ekāṅgi Svāmikaḷ gave *samāśrayaṇam* to everyone who wanted it and, as had Rāmānuja Nāvalar and Bhuvanagiri, lectured on the Śrīvaiṣṇnava tradition, even though only Brahmins had done these things. He had hundreds of followers.[37] When he went on pilgrimages to Srivilliputur, Alvartirunagari, Tirukkottiyur, Chidambaram and elsewhere, he gave lectures, performed initiations and defeated opponents in debate, which established his scholarly credentials. After a while, at the invitation of two pious Bhāgavatas, Rāghava Dāsar and Ceṅkalvarāya Nāyakar, he moved to an *ashram* that the latter had built for him in his own garden in Madras. From that time, Ekāngi Svāmikaḷ gave religious lectures all over Madras. They were so popular that many people became Śrīvaiṣṇava devotees. His lectures on Āṇṭāḷ's *Tiruppāvai* were especially popular.

The more famous he became, the more some Brahmins tried to prevent his radical behaviour. A Brahmin at Sriperumbudur, for instance, told him that he could not give *samāśrayaṇam*. That was only for Brahmins to do. Ekāṅgi Svāmikaḷ refuted his arguments. When the Brahmins approached Empār Jīyar there and informed him about these arguments, Empār, though a Brahmin himself, replied that Ekāṅgi Svāmikaḷ was correct.[38]

As Ekāṅgi Svāmikaḷ continued his lectures and teaching of the *Divyaprabandham*,[39] controversy flared again. One Brahmin, Cittākāra Śrīnivāsa Ācārya, told him that only Brahmin Śrīvaiṣṇavas give initiation and call themselves *ācārya*s. Ekāṅgi Svāmikaḷ convinced the Brahmin that others could do so by using the same arguments that he had used at Sriperumbudur. Later, Ekāṅgi Svāmikaḷ went to Tiruchirappalli and many other Śrīvaiṣṇava sacred places to debate the matter of who could do initiations.

The biography concludes by reaffirming Ekāṅgi Swāmikaḷ's teaching: that anyone may give initiation and recite the *Divyaprabandham*.[40] Even though he was abused, he was a religious leader, an *ācārya* like Bhaṭṭar (twelfth century) and Nampiḷḷai (thirteenth century), two famous *ācārya*s. When he died in 1907, his body was placed in a *samādhi* in a western suburb of Madras.[41] His disciple, Appaṉ Rāmānuja Swāmi, was persuaded to take over his role.[42]

I visited Ekāṅgi Svāmikaḷ's *samādhi* in 2007 and 2008 (see Chapter 3), in what is now the neighbourhood of Ekangipuram. The *samādhi* looked like a small temple. The focal point was a painting of Ekāṅgi Swāmikaḷ, which was probably painted from a photograph.[43] Beside his staff and sandals, the shrine had photographs of some disciples such as Appaṉ,[44] along with a picture of Āṇṭāḷ.

Gōpāla Kṛṣṇa Piḷḷai

Gōpāla Kṛṣṇa Piḷḷai (end of the nineteenth century) came from a Yadava (cowherd) family and was a disciple of the Brahmin *ācārya* Kōyiḻ Āṇṭāṉ Swāmi of Srirangam.[45] We know almost nothing about Gōpāla Kṛṣṇa Piḷḷai's life, because no one wrote his biography. We do know that he was the president of the Varavaramunendra Sabhā near Triplicane, a section of central Chennai that borders the sea and is the location of the

Parthasarathy temple.[46] And we know that he published the *Ācārya Hṛdaya Sāra Saṅgraham*[47] in 1892.

In his Foreword, he says that he wrote this work in simple Tamil so that everyone could understand Nammāḻvār's *Tiruvāymoḻi* and the views of commentators. He then discusses the essence of the *Ācārya Hṛdayam*[48] and provides several appendices that list major topics, supporting them with quotations from the commentaries about what *ācārya*s such as Rāmānuja had said, justifications for their interpretations, unusual interpretations of Nammāḻvār, his own contribution to the interpretations, the meaning of important Sanskrit words in the commentary, and a list of corrections.

How did Gōpāla Kṛṣṇa Piḷḷai learn all this? He might have listened to discourses by various *ācārya*s, taken notes and collated them. There were other opportunities, which I have already mentioned. He might have studied with the *jīyar*s at Emperumāṉār Mutt in Tirukkoyilur, or at Vānamāmalai Mutt in Nanguneri (Tirunelveli district), for instance, or studied with Rāmānuja Nāvalar or Bhuvanagiri.

Appāvu Mudaliyār

Appāvu Mudaliyār (end of the nineteenth century) was the first to publish the *Divyaprabandham*,[49] thereby defying the attempt by Brahmins to control the Tamil scripture by not allowing its publication. The Brahmins had feared that non-Brahmins would read it and claim the right to chant it and lecture about it, which is exactly what happened.

B. R. Purushottama Naidu

The tradition of scholarship continued in Bhuvanagiri's family. His brother Rājagopāla's son was B. R. Purushottama Naidu (1901– ?). Purushottama was initiated by Bhuvanagiri and considered him his *ācārya*. He spent three years in the Śrīvaiṣṇava school (*pāṭhaśala*) in Srirangam, sponsored by the non-Brahmin Negamam Zamindar and run by Bhuvanagiri. After that, he studied with well-known scholars, some Brahmins and others non-Brahmins.[50]

His scholarship attracted attention. He became a professor of Tamil in 1935 at Government Tamil College, Tanjavur, and joined the University of Madras Tamil Department as a Reader in 1948. Editing important classics of Śrīvaiṣṇavism,[51] he simplified the language of these works by translating the Maṇipravāḷam into Tamil. (In fact, this process of Tamilisation had been occurring for some time in Brahmin scholarship, too, and many scholarly aids had been prepared to make the works more easily understood.) At the beginning of his edition of Aḻakiya-maṇavāḷa-perumāḷ-nāyaṉār's *Ācārya Hṛdayam*, he comments that his father's elder brother Bhuvanagiri had prepared the notes for this work. Because he is using these notes, the entire work is really that of Bhuvanagiri. In his introduction to his edition of Piḷḷai Lokācārya's *Śrīvacana Bhūṣaṇam*, he mentions that when 'writing this book, I received the assistance of the University Grants Commission'.[52] This indicates that the modern university system was now recognising the scholarship of non-Brahmins, and they no longer had to rely on the praise of other scholars who were generally Brahmins.

The Road to Recognition

It was difficult for Bhāgavatas to become religious leaders when Brahmins controlled the teaching of Sanskrit and the basic doctrines of the tradition, which were only taught orally by Brahmins. Oddly, non-Brahmin entry into this realm was facilitated by the need to address Dalit mobilisation and the attraction of people to other sects or even other religions. In other words, what started out as leadership by default for elite non-Brahmin Śrīvaiṣṇavas turned into serious activism. Here is how that happened.

Gaining Esoteric Knowledge

The Śrīvaiṣṇava non-Brahmin challenge to Brahmin roles had several basic components. One was gaining access to esoteric learning in order to qualify as scholars of the tradition. This happened in several ways. Ekāṅgi Svāmikaḷ, for instance, learned much by listening to lectures by Brahmins and learning from his Brahmin *jīyar*, Ciṟupuliyūr (he would not have attended the school started by Bhuvanagiri, which taught Sanskrit to both Brahmins and non-Brahmins; it started only in 1912). We are told that he had difficulty chanting Sanskrit and therefore could not learn that language in the traditional Brahmanical manner. Perhaps this was a circumlocution to avoid saying directly that no Brahmin would teach him. Whatever the case, he did not learn Sanskrit. The fact that the commentaries on the *āḻvār*s' verses and many of the formative works about Śrīvaiṣṇavism were written in Maṇipravāḷam (a combination of Tamil and Sanskrit) meant that, without Sanskrit, he also could not read these works, and had to rely on oral sources.

By contrast, Rāmānuja Nāvalar learned Sanskrit from the Vānamāmalai *jīyar* and thus also had access to Sanskrit commentaries and treatises, as well as Maṇipravāḷa ones. His contribution, therefore, was showing that non-Brahmins were capable translators and interpreters of texts. Bhuvanagiri too had the advantage of learning Sanskrit from both Rāmānuja Nāvalar and the Vānamāmalai *jīyar*, which gave him access to all the *sampradāya* literature.

Therefore, a few Brahmin *maṭha*s were willing to help Bhāgavatas become educated in the tradition. This means that they deviated from traditional Śrīvaiṣṇava Brahmanical control of the intellectual tradition through Sanskrit, Maṇipravāḷam, and schools only for Brahmins. No doubt the theology of inclusiveness in Śrīvaiṣṇava works, especially those of Maṇavāḷa-māmuni, was pressed into service to support the non-Brahmins, and counter the proselytism of other religions.

Why the *maṭhas*? Maybe these *jīyars* were more entrepreneurial in recruiting new disciples because the lineage in *maṭhas* did not pass down through a family, with generational links to the families of their disciples. Because these *maṭhas* had strong Telugu and non-Brahmin connections, they might have been more relaxed about maintaining convention and took the inclusive theology to heart. They were also in remote agricultural areas, where non-Brahmin landlords such as Naidus were important patrons, and where it was important to attract agricultural workers so that they would not move elsewhere.

In any case, those non-Brahmins who had learned Sanskrit, Maṇipravāḷam, and the sectarian texts then began to teach other non-Brahmins. Bhāgavata support for these students and scholars helped extend non-Brahmin expertise. So did the use of the printing press to publish their works. (The printing press had arrived in Goa in 1556 and was used by Tranquebar missionaries in Tamil Nadu in 1714. Until 1835, Indians were not allowed to license printing presses from the Europeans. The latter, however, began themselves to publish Tamil texts.)

Besides, the fact that some non-Brahmins translated Sanskrit and Maṇipravāḷa works into Tamil dramatically democratised access to knowledge, as did Appāvu Mudaliyār's publication of the *Divyaprabandham*—the key Tamil scripture.

Becoming *Ācāryas* by Default and then Revolt

Harder to understand is why the Brahmin *maṭhas* encouraged non-Brahmin leaders to perform the initiation ritual, which had been an exclusive Brahmin ritual role that ostensibly provided access to salvation itself (ultimately, salvation comes from God). This takes me to the next topic. Should initiation be extended to Dalits?

In this context, it is important to remember that Dalits were mobilising. As Rupa Viswanath has documented in *The Pariah Problem: Caste, Religion, and the Social in Modern India*

(2014), Dalits in the nineteenth century provided slave labour and were segregated in ghettos, but were virtually ignored by the colonial government despite agitation in Britain to do something about slavery. Only when Pariahs began to convert to Christianity *en masse* from the late 1870s did their plight begin to be addressed with more education, the right to own property, and by 1910, their own representation of their communities in governmental bodies.[53]

This period is exactly when our Bhāgavatas, with the blessings of some *jīyar*s with *maṭha*s in agricultural areas, began to initiate Dalits. It is highly likely that there was a link between the desire to stop Dalit conversions, pressure to improve their conditions and Bhāgavata performance of initiations.

We know that Bhuvanagiri had connections with Dalits. According to his biography, on one occasion, some Śrīvaiṣṇava outcastes who had built an Āṇṭāḷ temple asked for his help. They were being harassed by someone who did not want Śrīvaiṣṇavism to be practised by outcastes. To protect their worship, Bhuvanagiri not only went there immediately and drove the harasser away, but he also stayed a while to teach them more about Śrīvaiṣṇavism.[54]

The biography describes how Bhuvanagiri preached about Śrīvaiṣṇavism to the Dalits of a Tamil village[55] in order to counter the propagation of Śaivism there. After that, the Dalits wanted him to initiate them. He asked them to have the Vānamāmalai *jīyar* perform the ritual. The *jīyar* insisted, however, that Bhuvanagiri do it instead. After teaching Dalits about the importance of *tāpa* (branding the shoulders with conch and discus), Bhuvanagiri performed the initiation ritual.

Among the Dalits who became Bhuvanagiri's disciples, as I have already said, was Nārāyaṇa Dāsar from near Tirukkoyilur. This time, Bhuvanagiri asked the *jīyar* at Tirukkoyilur to perform the initiation. Like the Vānamāmalai *jīyar*, however, he refused. Instead, he gave his conch and discus-branding tool to Bhuvanagiri and asked him to do it.

Although I found nothing about Dalits directly in Ekāṅgi Svāmikaḷ's biography, I have found indirect evidence that he too had a special interest in them. His *samādhi*, for example, was located in a *paṟaiccēri*, that is, an outcaste neighbourhood, in what is now a suburb of northwest Chennai. There, he used to give lectures to the Dalits. This area is now called Ekangipuram after him.[56]

How do we explain the reluctance of Brahmin *jīyar*s and *ācārya*s in the Teṉkalai tradition to initiate Dalits? After all, one *āḻvār*, Tiruppāṇ, was an outcaste. Between a rock (the inclusive theology of Śrīvaiṣṇavism and not wanting outcastes to convert to another religion such as Śaivism, Christianity, or Buddhism when Vaiṣṇavism was already a minority religion) and a hard place (Teṉkalai Brahmins' loss of status in the eyes of orthodox Brahmins), Teṉkalai *ācārya*s or *jīyar*s probably thought it best to encourage disciples such as Bhuvanagiri to initiate the Dalits. There was one Brahmin, and possibly two, however, who did initiate outcastes (Sāttvika Ācārya, whom I discuss in Chapter 6), and possibly others.

Furthermore, it is likely that non-Brahmins such as Bhuvanagiri and Ekāṅgi Svāmikaḷ saw an opportunity for higher status and more disciples for themselves, because they now would have ritual roles that had once been exclusively Brahmin. So, Bhāgavatas gained the right to perform initiations initially by default, it seems, and not by design. The Brahmins needed the job done for outcastes, yet did not want to do it themselves, so they turned it over to a few learned non-Brahmins. Nevertheless, once these non-Brahmins had the expertise and the legitimation, they began to argue their right to do it for everyone, and thereby began to usurp what had been a carefully protected Brahmanical role.

Struggling into the *Pulavar* World

As described in early Tamil poetry, poets (*pulavar*s) praised rulers in oral performances to broadcast their fame and thereby increase their status in return for gifts, including economic support, food, and sometimes items of conspicuous consumption. By medieval times, patrons were not just rulers, they were also temples, *maṭha*s, or wealthy individuals.

In *Colonizing the Realm of Words*,[57] Sascha Ebeling (2010) gives us insight into the transformations of the *pulavar* 'economy of praise' as the poets adapted to colonial power and the transformation of an oral performance culture to one of print and a reading public. Although Ebeling discusses this *pulavar* world in the context of Śaivism, his analysis helps us understand the quandaries faced by non-Brahmin Śrīvaiṣṇavas.

From the medieval period, Śaiva *maṭha*s were patrons of *pulavar* culture. On the model of royal and temple processions, monastic heads toured the countryside in ostentatious processions with other dignitaries, elephants, musicians and dancing girls. The birthdays of *maṭha* founders were celebrated with grand festivals, moreover, with poets performing their works, chanters reciting Vedic and Tēvāram verses (the Śaiva *bhakti* verses of Campantar, Appar and Cuntarar), learned men giving discourses, and musicians entertaining the crowd with concerts.

The fact that there were major non-Brahmin Śaiva *maṭha*s meant that non-Brahmins participated in this transactional *pulavar* culture as patrons and poets. According to Ebeling, this ostentatious *pulavar* culture became even more important at the beginning of the nineteenth century as the Madras Presidency consolidated its power by turning independent rulers into subordinates, through curtailing warfare and therefore the status of military men, especially those who were victorious.

Some Śrīvaiṣṇava Brahmins participated in *pulavar* cosmopolitan culture, both in their own *maṭha*s as centres of learning and also in royal courts, if the hagiographic stories of poetic competitions there reflect historical reality. In this context, poetic works such as Garuḍavāhana's *Divyasūricaritam* might have been creations in a *pulavar* milieu.

A booklet[58] published by the Bysani-Madhava Chetty Charity (1820–1900) provides an insight into Brahmin and non-Brahmin status in relation to *sampradāya* knowledge in the nineteenth century. This charity reflects the perspective of twice-born (Vaiśya) non-Brahmins, such as the founder Madhava Chetty Garu.

The booklet mentions the kinds of lecturer that are funded. These may be learned Brahmins or Bhāgavatas who have been initiated into the mantras by *ācārya puruṣa*s (those belonging to one of the 74 *ācārya* families), more specifically, those who have had *samāśrayaṇam* in the Teṉkalai tradition.

In addition, the booklet offers support to Bhāgavatas who know Piḷḷai Lokācārya's 18 Rahasya (secret) works and commentaries, and who can recite the 4,000 verses of the *Divyaprabandham*, poems on the lives of the *āḻvār*s and various praise-poems (*stotrams*). (These were demanding prerequisites for anyone!) The booklet mentions non-Brahmins in a separate section after the Brahmins, although it recognises their learning and supports them, whether as lecturers or students.

Śaivism and Vaiṣṇavism Compared

Unlike the Vellalar Śaiva Siddhāntins who had wealthy non-Brahmin *maṭha*s that were involved in *pulavar* culture, Śrīvaiṣṇava non-Brahmin *maṭha*s—there were a few—were very modest affairs, without libraries, and more like the *rāmānuja-kūṭams*, the charitable feeding houses. It was probably more an exception than a rule that the birthdays of their founders or leaders were celebrated on the same scale as the Śaiva ones, although we do have the case of the fifteenth-century figure Kaṇṭāṭai Rāmānuja Ayyaṅkar, the manager of many *rāmānuja kūṭams* in Tirupati and Tirumalai, who celebrated his birthday with processions of musicians, dancing girls, and others.

Influence from Āṟumuka Nāvalar?

In this context of *pulavar* culture, it is useful to think about the possible influence on Śrīvaiṣṇava non-Brahmins of the Sri Lankan Āṟumuka Nāvalar (1822–79), who came to live in

Tamil Nadu. After learning Tamil literature from his father, a poet, Āṟumuka attended a missionary school to learn English. An excellent student, he eventually found work at the school as a teacher of English and Tamil, and then as an assistant to the missionary and orientalist Peter Percival, helping him to translate the Book of Common Prayer, the Bible, and other Christian works.

Āṟumuka Nāvalar turned his attention next to editing and publishing Tamil works, for which he founded a press, the Preservation of Knowledge Press. In 1852, Āṟumuka brought out a Tamil prose version of the *Periya-purāṇam* (a medieval text in verse about the lives of the Śaiva saints), which he hoped would inspire Śaivas to maintain their traditions. He followed that with polemical tracts against Christianity, including *The Abolition of the Abuse of Śaivism* (1854). That same year (he was then thirty-two), he took an advanced initiation in Śaiva Siddhānta, which made him an ascetic.

Āṟumuka spent the next twenty-five years in both Sri Lanka and Tamil Nadu publishing books (he himself brought out about ninety-seven works of various kinds), establishing more schools (eleven in Sri Lanka and one in Chidambaram), and battling against Christian missionary polemics.

Dennis Hudson puts his accomplishments this way:

> Āṟumuka Nāvalar changed Śaiva Orthodoxy by creating a new Śaiva school system that fused modern knowledge with sectarian ideas and by revitalizing Śaiva culture through temple reform, preaching, and the printing press. He created an "evangelical" Śaivism by stressing scripture over custom and by seeking an individually motivated spiritual regeneration of culture.[59]

Āṟumuka fell into no conventional category of Śaiva scholar, comments Hudson;[60] he was an independent, celibate scholar.[61]

I see intriguing similarities between Rāmānuja Nāvalar and Āṟumuka Nāvalar. Both belonged to elite non-Brahmin castes (Naidu and Vellala, respectively), both published many works (Rāmānuja Nāvalar about forty-six and Āṟumuka approximately double that number). Both were called Nāvalar because of their erudition, both knew Tamil and Sanskrit, and both resorted to the British legal system to fight their opponents.

I see parallels too between Āṟumuka and Bhuvanagiri. Āṟumuka became upset over Christian conversions of Śaiva youth. In 1848, he helped to found a school that would teach not only Western subjects with a Western pedagogy, but also Hindu ones such as the Vedas, Āgamas and Śaiva Siddhānta. Like Āṟumuka, Bhuvanagiri started a school in Srirangam and then Chidambaram that included religious subjects, but to my knowledge no English or Western subjects. Although the Srirangam school soon collapsed for lack of funding, it set a precedent. Like Āṟumuka, moreover, Bhuvanagiri travelled around the countryside, preaching. Bhuvanagiri lived a bit later than Āṟumuka (he would have been nineteen when Āṟumuka died); however, he probably knew of him. Chidambaram, where Āṟumuka spent considerable time, was not far from Cuddalore, near where Bhuvanagiri lived.

Here is another similarity. Āṟumuka had built a small temple in Chidambaram.[62] Soon after, the temple acquired an image of Āṟumuka.[63] According to Hudson, elsewhere, images of him were likely worshipped. From 1910, Āṟumuka's birthday was celebrated like those of the early medieval Śaiva saints, the *nāyaṉmār*, who were worshipped in image-form.[64] As I have noted, images or portraits were also made for Rāmānuja Nāvalar, Bhuvanagiri and Ekāṅgi Swāmikaḷ, to be worshipped in household shrines, temples, *rāmānuja kūṭam*s, or *samādhi* shrines.

There are differences, too, between Āṟumuka and the Śrīvaiṣṇava non-Brahmin leaders I have discussed here. For instance, I can find no direct links between the latter and the missionary orientalists who promoted Dravidian nationalism or provided access to Western learning, even though Bhuvanagiri lived near Cuddalore, an important trade centre for the East Indian Company, and a Christian mission centre. Another difference was about caste. Āṟumuka argued that *śūdra*s (including Vellalars) may not recite the Vedas or perform Vedic rituals. In the nineteenth century, Śrīvaiṣṇava non-Brahmins (to my knowledge) did not take such an explicit stand; they simply seemed more interested in access to Śrīvaiṣṇava *sampradāya* knowledge, and the right to perform *samāśrayaṇam*, a specific Śrīvaiṣṇava ritual.

Even though Śrīvaiṣṇavism had an Āgamic tradition—the Pañcarātra Āgamas—knowledge of this literature was of interest mainly to Brahmin temple priests. At that time, Bhāgavatas were not interested in becoming Āgamic priests, even if they had been allowed.

Āṟumuka states that Śaiva non-Brahmins who have had the Āgamic ritual of *dīkṣā* (which involves becoming vegetarian) become twice-born, indeed Brahmins, if they practice the way of life appropriate to their *varṇa* and Āgamic status. They have the authority to recite the Āgamas, though not the Vedas, and to be *ācārya*s.

Like the Śaiva *dīkṣā*, Śrīvaiṣṇava *samāśrayaṇam* involves becoming vegetarian; however, the ritual per se does not transform a Śrīvaiṣṇava into a twice-born or Brahmin. Rather, the ritual ostensibly provides access to salvation (indirectly, it probably provides access to social or religious status as well). If we understand an *ācārya* as a teacher and interpreter of the tradition, then Bhāgavatas certainly wanted to be *ācāryas*. The Śrīvaiṣṇava understanding of *ācārya* was more specific, however, than just being a teacher and exegete; it also meant belonging to one of the seventy-four Brahmin families supposedly appointed by Rāmānuja.

Finally, Āṟumuka had quite a different position on Dalits than did the Śrīvaiṣṇava non-Brahmin leaders of his time. He thought that they were so innately impure that they could never have *dīkṣā* in the Āgamic tradition. Although they could worship God and attain salvation, they could not enter the temples. By contrast, the nineteenth-century Śrīvaiṣṇava Bhāgavata leaders considered Dalits worthy not only of *samāśrayaṇam*, but also of deep respect and honour. Yet, even the Śrīvaiṣṇava non-Brahmins did not do much about temple entry until the mid-twentieth century.

The major difference between the non-Brahmin Śaivas and Śrīvaiṣṇavas was that the former had an important institutional base. Many Śaiva *maṭhas*, after all, were the exclusive domain of non-Brahmins. Bhāgavatas controlled no major *maṭhas* and thus had no established centres of learning, libraries, or formal leadership roles, although they did have *Rāmānuja kūṭams*.

Influence from Maṟaimalai Aṭikaḷ?

A comparison of the Śrīvaiṣṇava non-Brahmin leaders mentioned here with Maṟaimalai Aṭikaḷ (1876–1950), who was Āṟumuka's disciple, is somewhat different. According to Ravi Vaithess, Maṟaimalai promoted reform from within the religion, and a neo-Śaivism that was pro-Dravidian, pro-Tamil, and anti-caste in the tradition of Rāmaliṅga.[65] Sometimes Aṭikaḷ aligned with Periyar and sometimes he differed from him. Vaithees argues that nevertheless, we can see religious roots of the secular Self-Respect movement in Aṭikaḷ's thought.[66]

Like Maṟaimalai Aṭikaḷ, Śrīvaiṣṇava non-Brahmins were against caste discrimination, which made some of them join the Self-Respect movement (although others did not, because of its avowed atheism). Nonetheless, most elite Śrīvaiṣṇava non-Brahmins of the time were not as anti-Sanskrit as Maṟaimalai. They wanted access to the world of Sanskrit learning, not its destruction.

Finally, the fact that these non-Brahmin Śrīvaiṣṇava leaders did not claim that their religion could be found in Tamil origins, or that it was central to the nineteenth-century Tamil Renaissance, meant that their message was marginal to the great identity narratives of the day, which Śaivas had successfully appropriated.

Why Śrīvaiṣṇava Marginalisation?

It is fair to say that non-Brahmin Śrīvaiṣṇavas in the late nineteenth and early twentieth century were not yet trendsetters, despite their inclusive religious position on caste and women and their growing self-confidence under British rule that broke down some traditional barriers to status. They were also out of the Tamil mainstream, in part because many had ancestors who had come from what became Andhra after independence, but was then part of Madras Presidency.

In the late nineteenth and early twentieth century, all these 'Andhra' connections were alive and well. In this context, remember that the ancestors of Rāmānuja Nāvalar and Bhuvanagiri were Naidus whose families had originally migrated from the Andhra region as warrior-cultivators.[67] Ekāṅgi Svāmikaḷ's family was possibly Sattada (many Sattadas were originally from Andhra or Karnataka). The *jīyar* at the *maṭha* in Tirukkoyilur, who performed initiation for Rāmānuja Nāvalar and Bhuvanagiri, belonged to a lineage that had originated in Andhra. The *jīyar* there sometimes sent his disciples to study with the *jīyar* of the Vānamāmalai Mutt in Nanguneri, which had Andhra connections as well. Both the *maṭha* in Tirukkoyilur and the *maṭha* in Nanguneri were located, moreover, in major cotton-growing regions, where many Telugus had migrated in Vijayanagara times to work as cotton-growers. Vijayanagara kings had been partial to Vaiṣṇavism and to Telugu-speaking warriors and other migrants, such as the Naidus, Reddiyars and Vanniyars, who accompanied them into the south.

Non-Brahmin Śrīvaiṣṇavism was important in the Telugu-speaking northern parts of Madras Presidency too. I remember discovering in Salarjung Museum (Hyderabad) a set of miniature wooden figures with *nāmams* painted on their foreheads. They were obviously from colonial times, given their dress. What intrigued me the most was the representation of Śrīvaiṣṇavas across a range of occupations and roles; the figures included policemen, house servants, ascetics, musicians in a band, learned Brahmins, women, labourers, farmers, and others.

The fact that most Bhāgavata leaders were Telugu speakers, not Tamil, helps explain why they were not in the intellectual and literary mainstream, even though there had been Telugu Brahmin literati in the established cosmopolitan *pulavar* culture, including Carnatic music culture, in Tamil Nadu. Besides, for Śaiva non-Brahmins, Śrīvaiṣṇavism represented a Sanskritised Tamil tradition under Brahmin domination. This might have made it more difficult initially for Śrīvaiṣṇava Bhāgavatas to be part of a Dravidian movement, which came to champion Tamil as central to identity. Finally, with the Tamil Renaissance and Madras as a new colonial centre of Tamil learning, Telugus were being further marginalised, and had little Telugu nationalism as a counterpoint. At the risk of digression, it is important to understand why.

According to Peter Schmitthenner, before the nineteenth century, Telugus had little sense of a common literary tradition, or even common identity, given their migrations and lack of a common caste, patron-client network, or religious sect.[68] This began to change in the nineteenth century with the consolidation of the East India Company rule, and interest in Indian languages and literatures by Company officials and missionaries who collaborated with local scholars and brought Telugu literature into the public eye.

Schmitthenner speaks of a Telugu resurgence developing at this time. One of its leaders was C. P. Brown (1798–1884). A British civil servant and private scholar, he wrote Telugu grammars and dictionaries. In addition, he collected, edited, and published Telugu literature and translated Christian literature into Telugu.[69] Brown encouraged the appreciation of Telugu literature in Madras and elsewhere. He often drew on non-Brahmin informants to help gather and understand colloquial Telugu. He was especially fond of the seventeenth-century peasant poet Vemana, who adhered to Vīraśaivism, a Hindu sect mainly found in Karnataka that emphasised humility, tolerance, compassion, vegetarianism, and a casteless society that honoured women as well as men.

Brown's interest in non-Brahmin language and literature created tensions with Brahmin scholars who wanted to control Telugu literature. Eventually, it would be non-Brahmins who broke this control, although Schmitthenner thinks that they never became as anti-Brahmin as the Tamil non-Brahmins.[70] In any case, although the foundations for a broad-based Telugu identity were being formulated in the nineteenth century, and a new mentality was emerging, it had yet to become the focus for Telugu-speaking non-Brahmins in Tamil Nadu.

In addition, Madras had become the intellectual centre of Tamil Nadu, but as Eugene Irschick has said, educated Telugus considered Madras 'a hostile city in which Telugu interests were not looked on kindly. This is not to say that Madras city did not contain many Telugus [but] .... It was the Tamils who tended to monopolize the educational facilities and the administrative and political opportunities in Madras.'[71] (Even Telugu Brahmins were marginal. According to C. J. Fuller and Haripriya Narasimhan, the reason Telugu Brahmins lagged behind Tamil Brahmins was because 'they did not pursue medicine, engineering and administration to the same degree and because they did not have as large patronage networks and organization'.[72])

So Śrīvaiṣṇava non-Brahmins lost out on several fronts. They were not part of the mainstream *pulavar* and missionary cultures, for the reasons already discussed. As Telugu speakers, they had neither deep identification with the Tamil Renaissance (focussed on Caṅkam literature) and incipient Tamil nationalism (focussed on Tamil), nor did they have a vibrant Telugu identity with an institutional base in Madras as counterpoint. In other words, as Telugu speakers, the Śrīvaiṣṇava non-Brahmin leaders discussed in this chapter were once-removed Dravidians, notwithstanding many Telugu *pulavar*s in courts and Śaiva *maṭha*s.[73] However, even though Telugu was their mother tongue, they did speak Tamil and identified deeply with the Tamil poems of the *āḻvār*s, their scriptural canon. This would pave the way for their eventual participation in the Dravidian parties to challenge old social hierarchies.

Despite their marginal status, the leaders discussed in this chapter were on the verge of creating a new orientation.

Since we cannot characterise it as reform without evidence that Bhāgavatas ever functioned as *ācārya*s or *jīyar*s in previous centuries, we must call this development a revolt, or at least the seeds of a revolt. Perhaps the participants were even on the verge of creating a new sub-sect. The description of miracles in the biographies of leaders such as Rāmānuja Nāvalar, Bhuvanagiri and Ekāṅgi Svāmikaḷ, and the existence of temples and *samādhi*s that enshrined their presence, are signs of sainthood in the making.

Even so, they did not attain the kind of sainthood or prophetic stature that Rāmaliṅga[74] or Ayya Vaikuṇṭar did (see Appendix 6). Perhaps this was because they did not have what psychologists of religion call Credibility Enhancing Displays (CREDS), such as dramatic or costly rituals that attract attention, become memorable, and induce group cohesiveness. Neither did they have extreme messianic messages from someone believed to have the power to change the world,[75] nor did they create an intellectual *sampradāya* for lack of institutionalisation; although it appears that the mantle was passed on for a generation or so in several cases. Nevertheless, a few Śrīvaiṣṇava Bhāgavatas developed major scholarly skills, the power of oratory, and a message of justice, which paved the way for identification with Dravidian nationalism.

As for Teṉkalai Brahmins, they had become moribund and could hardly lead the way to social justice. Because they had been put on the defensive to prove that they were real Brahmins, for instance, most were not willing to risk their reputations to adjust to social change, preferring to stay with 'convention', despite their caste-inclusive theology. Besides, there were conflicts within Śrīvaiṣṇavism that had been simmering for several centuries, and that led, by the eighteenth century, to a division of the tradition into the Teṉkalai and Vaṭakalai sub-sects, as well as to fierce fights over control of major temples, battles that often ended up in court.[76]

Śrīvaiṣṇava Brahmins had little inclination to become involved in caste politics or issues of social justice. Many aligned themselves with other Brahmins to fight for independence from the British. They were open to a few reforms, such as improving the lives of Dalits and women, or shoring up the Śrīvaiṣṇava identity of non-Brahmins to prevent conversions. However, nothing too radical was advocated.

* * *

This chapter has recovered a forgotten history of seven non-Brahmin Śrīvaiṣṇava leaders in the colonial period. Although some of them had followers, who kept their memory alive for a while with pamphlets, memorial shrines and discourses about them, almost all knowledge about these leaders has disappeared from historical memory, even many of their books from libraries. Still, through the memories of non-Brahmins involved in this study, pamphlets they provided and visits to their temples and *samādhis*, we have found traces of a remarkable moment in the history of non-Brahmin Śrīvaiṣṇavism.

By reading between the lines of more general discussions of colonial history, it becomes possible to situate their life histories and what little is known about them in the larger social, economic, and political currents of the late-colonial period. We know that this was a time of Dalit awakening, which led to the desire to redress past acts of discrimination at a time when the colonial government was addressing the need to abolish slavery and improve the appalling situation of the outcastes. It was also a time of growing literacy and demand by non-Brahmins for education.

For most of the Bhāgavatas discussed here, their greatest grievance was lack of access to knowledge about their religion, because Brahmins had always had that firmly in control by allowing only Brahmins to learn Sanskrit and Maṇipravāḷam, the languages of the sect's many erudite works, despite claims that the sect was inclusive of all castes. Once Bhāgavata leaders had access to Sanskrit and *sampradāya* works, and had opportunities to perform *samāśrayaṇam* for Dalits—because even the liberal *ācārya*s and *jīyar*s did not want to do this—they decided that they too could be *ācārya*s or *jīyar*s, and so they took on this role for other non-Brahmins and Dalits. More than that, they argued that anyone with the requisite knowledge and initiation, *śūdra*s and women, too, could be such religious leaders.

Despite the fact that they travelled about Tamil Nadu preaching about the sect, converting people and debating with Śrīvaiṣṇava Brahmins on the one hand, and with Śaivas on the other, the lasting impact of their activism, it seems, was the creation of access to Śrīvaiṣṇava literature for non-Brahmins. This led to roles as translators, commentators, and above all, teachers, about the religion, all of which paved the way to modern scholarship on the religion by non-Brahmins and the confident religious leadership that non-Brahmins practise today. The second major contribution was alerting the Śrīvaiṣṇava community to the fact that they must take Dalits seriously, not as mere symbols of inclusiveness, but as bona fide devotees. That change, however, has been much slower in coming.

I turn now to the interviews, beginning in Chapter 3 with those in the area of Chennai and its surrounding districts, followed in Chapter 4 with those in greater Puducherry, and in Chapter 5 with those from Tiruchirappalli and Tanjavur.

Notes

1. *Tivya Vaipava Caṅkrakam* (*Divya Vaibhava Saṅgraha*) about Putuvai Vilakṣaṇa Kavi, A. V. Irāmānuja Nāvalar Svāmikaḷ, collected by K. Nārāyaṇa Reṭṭiyar. See Reṭṭiyar, *Tivya Vaipava Caṅkrakam*.

2. Vēṅkaṭarāmaṉ was his father and Alarmēlmaṅkai Ammāḷ his mother.

3. This was the Bhāgavata Vidvat Sabhā, at the Vaikuṇṭhaperumāḷ temple in Kanchipuram.

4. These were the *Tirucitrakūṭa-purāṇam* and *Sudarśanagiri-purāṇam*. I found a reference to A. V. Irāmānuja Nāvalar, *Tirucitrakūṭa-purāṇam* (Chennai: Sriniketana Mutraksaracalai, 1891) in K. R. Sundaram

Iyer, Memorial Library. See https://www.yur/user/musicademy (accessed 23 January 2015).

5. His 43 works as listed in *Tivya Vaipava Caṅkrakam* (1972) include: 1) Śrīpātmottara Purāṇam, 2) Pālacaṁvāta Vi<u>n</u>viṭai, 3) Varata<u>n</u> Pati<u>r</u><u>r</u>uppattantāti, 4) Varata<u>n</u> Tirumālai, 5) Pōrrit Tiruppātikam, 6) Peruntēvittāyār Pātikam, 7) Nammāḻvār Pañcaratti<u>n</u>am, 8) Maṇavāḷamāmu<u>n</u>ikaḷ Tiruppātikam, 9) Tecika<u>n</u> Tiruppātikam, 10) Pātmōttara Purāṇa Vaca<u>n</u>am, 11) Tirukkōvalūr Purāṇam, 12) Tiruvayintira Purāṇam, 13) Tirumu<u>r</u>aippāmālai,14) Tiruccitrakuṭa Purāṇam, 15) Tirumuṭṭa Purāṇam, 16) Cutarica<u>n</u>akiri Purāṇam, 17) Tiruvēṅkaṭa Kōvai, 18) Ti<u>n</u>acaryāmirutataṭākam, 19) Arītūkṣaṇa Kapālacapēṭikai, 20) Śrīvaiṇava Kumpīrajōti, 21) Śrī Vaiṣṇava Tatvam, 22) Vairākkiya Cūriyōtayam, 23) Tirukkōvalūr Tekaḷīca<u>n</u> Kalaṁpakam, 24) Tirukkōvalūr Āyanār Piḷḷaittamiḻ, 25) Caṅka<u>r</u>pa Cūriyātayam,26) Vikkirakārāta<u>n</u>a Viḷakkam,27) Cāntapuṣ Caṁpuṭam, 28) Jīva<u>n</u>a Cintāmaṇi, 29) Avirōtacanattōtayam, 30) Śrīcūrṇa Viḷakkam, 31) Tiruvaraṅka<u>n</u> Tirumu<u>r</u>ai, 32) Tēkaḷīca<u>n</u> Antāti, 33) Emperumā<u>n</u>ār Vijayam, 34) Emperumā<u>n</u>ar Pātikam, 35) Etirāja Caṭakam, 36) Vilaimātar Viḷakkam, 37) Pakavannāma Cantīrttaṇam, 38) Vaiṇavamaṅkaiyar Vaḻkkaippāṭu, 39) Catcaṁparatāyattāḷ, 40) Pō<u>n</u> Cūrattāḻvā<u>n</u>carittiram, 41) Jeyatēvar Cirittiram, 42) Śrīmat Toṇṭāṭipoṭiyāḻvār Carittiram, 43) Āṇṭāḷ Viṣayam.

I have been unable to trace most of these and was told that some exist only in manuscript form. Their recovery and cataloguing are an important research project beyond the scope of this book. The *Vairāgya Sūryodayam* (reprinted in 1968 by the Rāmānuja Nāvalar Svāmigal Sabhai in Pannurutti in Tamil script) was also translated into Telugu and published in West Godavari. Two more books were the *Dīnācariya-amṛta tatākam* and *Vaiṇava-maṅgalya-vaḻkai Pāṭu*, which are about Śrīvaiṣṇava daily rituals. The Classified Catalogue of Tamil Printed Books by John Murdoch refers only to Rāmānuja Nāvalar's *Varatāraca Perumāḷ Pati<u>r</u><u>r</u>uppattāntāti*, which is about a Viṣṇu temple near Puducherry. On the Internet, I found *Patmottara Purāṇam* tr. Rāmānuja Nāvalar (Madras, 1869; http://books.google.ca/books?id). *Vairakkiya Curiyotayam* (Pannurutti: Ramanuja Navalar Svamigal Sabhai, 1968). See http://nationallibrary.gov.in/showdetails.php[?id=376178 (accessed 9 June 2016).

6. These are called *bhagavat-nāma-saṅkīrtana*s.

7. The hagiographies tell us that Nampiḷḷai gave popular lectures filled with stories, but not *kīrtana*s.

8. A well-known Śaiva Siddhāntin scholar, Somasundara Nāyakar, was famous for his polemics not only against Vaiṣṇavism, but also against Vedānta. His disciple Maṟaimalai Aṭikaḷ wrote a biography about him. For general information about Somasundara Nāyakar, see Steinschneider, 'Beyond Warring Sects'.

9. This settlement was reported in a journal called *Śrīlokarañjani*, 8 January 1891 (p. 47 of Rāmānuja Nāvalar's biography gives the Śaiva's letter of apology, which was submitted to the magistrate).

10. This dictionary is *Tamiḻ Ilakkiya Akarādi* by Selva Keśavarāya Mudaliar. I have not been able to locate publication details.

11. This book, entitled *Vaiṇava*, compiled by A.M. Keśava of Madras and published by P. V. Kannappa Mudaliar, included Maṇavāḷa Māmuni's verses that honour important figures in the tradition (*taṉiyaṉ*s), some of Āṇṭāḷ's verses, Maturakavi Āḻvār's *Kaṇṇinuṇciṟuttāmpu* and Rāmānuja Nāvalar's works. Only after Rāmānuja Nāvalar's works were presented were those by Brahmins mentioned.

12. P. V. Vakuḷābharaṇa Rāmānuja Dāsar composed eleven verses about his life. In 1936, V. Putūr Vidvaṉ Veṅkaṭa Svāmi composed the *Pukalpa Mālai* (the Garland of Fame) about him. I do not have the publication details.

13. In the nineteenth century, Pannurutti was a station on the railway and an important junction on roads that led to Tiruchirappalli, Mannargudi, Tirukkoyilur and Cuddalore. As a transportation hub, it was an important centre of trade.

14. This was told to me by Dr A. Pandurangan, who personally knew him.

15. A person's birth date is aligned with one of the twenty-seven constellations (*nakṣatra*s) along the ecliptic and has astrological significance for a person's life; the Western equivalent of Kārttikai is the constellation Pleiades.

16. These are the names that I found in several libraries.

17. See Nāyuṭu, '*Puvaṇakiri*'. See also Pāṇḍuraṅgaṉ, 'Nālaikku Śrīvaiṣṇava', 19–34.

18. Although this is not mentioned directly in the biography, I have deduced his caste from the fact that his nephew, B. R. Purushottama, was a Naidu, as was his teacher Rāmānuja Nāvalar and his biographer.

19. Pāṇḍuraṅgaṉ, 'Nālaikku Śrīvaiṣṇava', 5.

20. According to the biography, one Chettiyar who established the Śrīvaiṣṇava Grantha Mudrāpaka Sabhā and published many

sampradāya works conducted an exam on Maṇavāḷa's commentary on Piḷḷai Lokācārya's *Tāttvatrāya*. In that exam, those who did very well were Bhuvanagiri's disciples.

21. For this, he had the help of Vidvān̲ Muttu Kṛṣṇa Naidu.

22. This work was Pamban̲ Kumāraguru Dāsar's *Nālāyīra Prapanta Vicāra Āpāsa Tarppanam* (1905). I do not have the publication details.

23. The biography does not give any indication when these events occurred, but it must have been in the first decade of the twentieth century.

24. Pāṇḍuraṅgan̲, 'Nālaikku Śrīvaiṣṇava', 7.

25. For more on the Nigamam Zaimindar charity, see Chapter 5, section: 'Gardeners for the Lord's Garlands' (this volume).

26. According to the biography, around 1915, Bhuvanagiri and his followers went on a pilgrimage to the north—Nasik, Pancavati, Gujarat, Dvaraka, Brndavan, Mathura, Kuruksetra, and so forth. Similarly, he travelled to *divyadeśa*s in Kerala and then to Kanchipuram, also worshipping at *divyadeśa*s along the way.

27. The biography says that in 1915, Śrīmath Puruṣottara Jīyar of the Śrīraṅga Nārāyaṇa Jīyar Maṭha was impressed by Bhuvanagiri's scholarship and discussed many topics with him. Bhuvanagiri had become very popular because of his association with Rāmānuja Nāvalar, the twenty-third and twenty-fifth *jīyar*s of the Vānamāmalai Mutt and Amarāvati Tiruvēṅkaṭa Ācārya.

28. This was a reply to the *Tattvatraya Vyākhyāna Tātparya Tīpikā* by Ayodhya-Rāma Svāmi, who claimed that women and *śūdra*s were not eligible to perform the ritual.

29. I learned that Bhuvanagiri's speeches were published by the Vellore Śrīvaiṣṇava Siddhānta Mahā Saṅgam. I have no details, however, of this work. Another work by Bhuvanagiri was *Arthapañcaka Sāram*, in which he explains the five basic teachings of Śrīvaiṣṇavism in a question and answer format, based on Piḷḷai Lokācārya's book by the same name. On his *samādhi* stone at Sriperumbudur, I found the following works mentioned: *Tirāviṭa Veta Vaipava Prakācikai; Nālāyirappirapanta Vicāra Apāt Tarppaṇam; Arthapañcaka Sāram; Śrīvaiṣṇava Vināviṭai; Śrī Vacana Puṣaṇa Mālai; Irāmānuca Nān̲maṇi Mālai* and *Patika Mañcari Mutaliyan̲*. In the Roja Muthiah Research Library, Chennai, I found Aḻakiya Maṇavāḷa Rāmānuja Ekāṅgi Svāmikaḷ, *Tiruppati Kamañcari* (1914), and Aḻakiya Maṇavāḷa Rāmānuja Tācar Avarkaḷāḷ, *Tiruppātikam* (1933).

30. See Aḻakiyamaṇavāḷa Rāmānuja Ekaṅki Svāmikaḷ, *Śrīvaiṣṇava Tīpikai*.

31. See Young, 'Women's Liberation', 173–98.

32. According to the biography, after Bhuvanagiri's death, his image was placed in the temple *maṇṭapam*. However, I did not see this, only the image of him in the small shrine to the right of the temple, when facing it. Of course, the one in the *maṇṭapam* could have been moved there. At Bhuvanagiri, I met Satyā, his descendant, who oversees the shrine at his birthplace. The Brahmin priest could not tell me about this shrine's past. The temple was in poor condition.

33. See Aṟumukaṉ, *Tirunārāyaṇatāca*.

34. This is expressed idiomatically as 'attaining the holy feet' of the *ācārya*.

35. Followers published Ekāṅgi Svāmikaḷ's biography in 1930. The booklet says that Lokanātha Rāmānuja Dāsar from Kalati, who was close to him, gathered the information and wrote the biography. Lokanātha obtained the approval for the biography from Rāghava Rāmānuja Dāsar, who was a disciple of Ekāṅgi Svāmikaḷ. The biography concludes that it relies on information from pious people; if others know more, they should make that information available. A reprint was brought out in 2007 through the instigation of K. K. A. Venkatachari. I no longer have the details for the biography.

36. Friedhelm Hardy points out that some hagiographies describe how Nammāḻvār repeatedly swooned when he heard the stories about Krishna's stealing butter, etc. (Hardy, 'Śūdra Saint', 41).

37. One day, according to the biography, Ekāṅgi Svāmikaḷ learned that his guru, Ciṟupuliyūr Jīyar, was ill. He went to Ciṟupuliyūr's *maṭha* to serve him. After some time, Ciṟupuliyūr, realising that his end was near, gave away his images and books to Ekāṅgi Svāmikaḷ. Ekāṅgi Svāmikaḷ prepared for the funeral by creating a *samādhi* for the body, arranging for the recitation of the *Tiruvāymoḻi* and *iyal caṟṟu* (a selection of *āḻvār* stanzas), and organising the feeding of devotees.

38. I have not been able to verify this point made by Ekāṅgi's disciples and recorded in the biography.

39. For instance, in 1886, he addressed the Jana Anukūlami Sabhā of Vellore and after that the Viśiṣṭādvaita Siddhānta Pramodhara Sabhā in a Chennai suburb, and a group at the Parthasarathy temple.

40. Although Ekāṅgi Svāmikaḷ did unorthodox things, such as initiating non-Brahmins and probably outcastes, he also imitated some orthodox customs. After he went to Sriperumbudur for

Rāmānuja's birthday festival, for instance, he put a yellow vertical line in his *nāmam* instead of red (very orthodox Brahmins use yellow tumeric, as do many Vaṭakalais).

41. The *ekāṅgi* died elsewhere and was brought here. He was buried close to the *samādhi* of someone who was a trustee of the Śrīnivāsa temple. One of his close disciples, Appa<u>n</u> Rāmānuja<u>n</u> Svāmi, performed the last rites according to the tradition of Vaiṣṇava *saṃnyāsis*. A local oral tradition refers to the *ekāṅgi* as 'coconut-headed'. The biography does not refer to this tradition, although it does refer to 'iron-headed' as a metaphor for 'strong-willed'. The coconut-headed reference must be an oral tradition related to the fact that *ekāṅgis*, after death, are placed in pits, and their skulls are broken with coconuts so that the soul can escape (K. K. A. Venkatachari; personal communication, November 2009). According to the biography, a sign of Ekāṅgi Svāmikaḷ's influence is that M. C. Mathurai Piḷḷai, later called Vāsudeva Rāmānuja Dāsar—a member of the Upper Council—built a house at Kolar and performed the daily *pūjā*, and other festivals connected with the *ekāṅgi*.

42. After Appa<u>n</u>'s death, his picture was hung at the *samādhi* near the *ekāṅgi*'s picture.

43. This was probably from the photograph of Ekāṅgi Svāmikaḷ that appears in the booklet about him.

44. There is a large photo in the shrine that could be him.

45. K. K. A. Venkatachari (personal communication, December 2008).

46. For a history and analysis of the administration of this temple, see Appadurai, *Worship and Conflict*.

47. Gōpāla Kṛṣṇa Piḷḷai, *Ācārya-hṛdaya-sāra-saṅgraham*. The contents were summarised by K. K. A. Venkatachari (personal communication, 2011). Gōpāla Kṛṣṇa Piḷḷai also wrote a very similar work, *Discourses on the Tiruvāymoḻi*, as well as *Viṣṇu Tattuva Viḷakkam*, *Teṇṇosāriya Pirabāva Tipikai*, and other works. I was unable to locate the publication details for these.

48. This was written by Aḻakiya Maṇavāḷa Perumāḷ Nāya<u>n</u>ār in the late thirteenth or early fourteenth century. According to K. K. A. Venkatachari, the *Ācārya Hṛdayam* is

> the largest and most important of the author's works [and] uses a special style in Maṇipravāḷam, for it is composed of verbatim phrases borrowed mainly from the Āḻvārs and Ācāryas. Only new suffixes are provided. Such a style,

> while clever, is also abstruse, for the average reader needs a commentary for comprehension of this magnum opus .... *Ācāryahṛdayam* is devoted to expounding the greatness of Nammāḻvār ... let us recall the author's statement that Nammāḻvār was born in a lower *varṇa* to raise the status of that caste by his efforts, and so any man from a lower *varṇa* who through knowledge and devotion rises above the limitations of his birth should be honoured (Venkatachari, *The Maṇipravāḷa Literature*, 156–57).

49. Also, A. Pandurangan told me about a student's dissertation on the history of getting the *Divyaprapandham* published for the first time. I have not been able to obtain the details.

50. B. R. Purushottama Naidu studied, for instance, with Tirunārāyaṇa Ayyaṅkar of the Tamil Sangam in Madurai and Veṅkaṭarājulu Reddiyar of Madras.

51. B. R. Purushottama Naidu is famous as editor of *Tiruvāymoḻi Īṭiṉ Tamiḻ Ākkam*, 10 vols (Madras: University of Madras, 1951–59); *Acharya Hridayam (with Manavala Mamunigal's commentary)* 2 vols (Madras: University of Madras, 1965), and *Śrī Vacana Bhūshaṇa (with the commentary of Maṇavāla Māmuni)* (Cuddalore 1970). He also wrote *Śrīrāmāyaṇam Pācurappaṭi* (*Rāmāyaṇa* as found in the [*āḻvārs*'] verses) (Chennai: Manavar Manram, n.d.); in this work, he takes a few words or a phrase from an *āḻvār* and composes a verse.

52. Purushothama Naidu, *Śrī Vacana Bhūshaṇa*, 6.

53. See also Appendix 4 here.

54. For more about this community, see Narayanan, *Vernacular Veda*, 66–79.

55. The village is Nallan Pillai Perral.

56. A Dalit (J. J. Thiruanarayana Ramanujar Dasar), who lived as a child in a house that adjoined the *samādhi*, had gone to court to have the name of the neighbourhood changed from Paṟaiccēri to Ekangipuram. This would eliminate the stigma attached to the name Paṟaiccēri (which means an outcaste hamlet). He, his sons, and then their descendants, became important Śrīvaiṣṇava leaders among the Dalits in the immediate locale and at Sriperumbudur. See Chapter 3 (this volume).

57. Ebeling, *Colonizing the Realm of Words*.

58. *The Rules and Regulations of Bysani Madhava Chetty's Charity Fund* (Madras, 1977) (no other details provided). Madhava Chetty Garu, p. 64, mentions that he is of Vysia (Vaiśya) caste and Viṣṇu

sect. The booklet also mentions Srimath Paramahamsa Embar Jeeyar Swami of Sriperumbudur, and the Embarswami Devastanam.

59. Hudson, 'Hindu Responses', 117. See also Ambalavanar, 'Arumuga Navalar'.

60. Hudson, 'Winning Souls', 30.

61. An independent spirit can be seen in the way that Āṟumuka countered both the missionary orientalists and other Hindus, such as fellow Śaiva Rāmaliṅga Piḷḷai (1823–74), who had claimed that his poems were scripture which could replace the *Tēvāram* hymns in temples, and that his own path to enlightenment was the right one. Āṟumuka used the British legal system to prevent the emergence of what amounted to a new Śaiva cult by Rāmaliṅga.

62. Its main image (*mūrti*) was that of Cēkkilār, the author of the *Periya-purāṇam*. Āṟumuka had established this temple because the Chidambaram priests, who were Vedic rather than Āgamic, did not want anyone to worship the image of a *śūdra* Vellalar.

63. Hudson, 'Winning Souls', 43.

64. Ibid., 45–46.

65. See Chapter 4, section: 'The Poet from Seliyamedu Village' for a discussion of Rāmaliṅga.

66. See Vaitless, *Religion, Caste and Nation*.

67. See Stein, 'Coromandel Trade'.

68. Schmitthenner, *Telugu Resurgence*, 26.

69. See also Mitchell, *Language, Emotion, and Politics*. Although her study is focussed on Telugu identity in the post-Independence period, she locates the roots of these seemingly new sensibilities in nineteenth-century shifts, such as patronage practices, new narrative conventions, print and lithograph technologies, the relation among language, place, and person, 'the relation between languages and the meaning of translation, and corresponding shifts in the organization of pedagogical content, historical narrative, and literary canon formation' (ibid., 213).

70. Schmitthenner, *Telugu Resurgence*, 282–85.

71. Irschick, *Politics and Social Conflict*, 23. Still, the context was complex. Shulman points out that some Telugu merchants were 'among the first politically oriented "Dravidanists" in Madras' (Shulman, *Tamil: A Biography*, 309).

72. Fuller and Narasimhan, *Tamil Brahmins*.

73. According to Irschick, as Tamil came to be considered the original Dravidian language known to India, Dravidianism

was initially identified with those who spoke Tamil. By contrast, Dravidianism was usually not identified with Telugu speakers because of Telugu's many Sanskrit loan words pointing to an Aryan connection. 'Partly also,' says Irschick, 'the Telugu area did not exhibit the same polarities between Brahman and non-Brahman, such as between the Kapus and the Kammas on one side and the Brahmans on the other, as compared with the feelings of competition and hostility between the Vellalas and the Tamil Brahmans' (Irschick, *Politics and Social Conflict*, 275).

74. See Chapter 4, section: 'The Poet from Seliyamedu Village'.

75. See Hinde, *Why Gods Persist*.

76. For an account of one such conflict that occurred at Tiruventipuram, which was litigated in several court cases from the mid-seventeenth to late-nineteenth centuries, see Francis, *Gazetteers: South Arcot*, 96.

three

Stories from Chennai and Beyond

These oral histories emerged from the heart of Chennai, its surrounding suburbs, nearby towns such as Sriperumbudur, and villages between the hubs. They represent several generations—from 'seniors' to students—many castes, and both men and women. Each story expresses a lived experience, which is the raw material from which narratives are fashioned.

The Grandson and the Outcaste Hamlet

The old Ambassador car lurched through yet another pothole. The monsoon had reminded the city once again that natural forces can halt human progress. The pock-marked road wound to the northwestern edge of Chennai's sprawling suburbs, relentlessly intruding on the paddy fields. Endless storefronts stacked with stainless-steel pots, tires or saris—this is the land of the small businessman—made it impossible to know where one municipality ended and another began. Occasionally, our driver stopped for directions. In a staccato voice, someone listed the turns and gesticulated toward the horizon. Again, we bumped along for what must have been an hour in heavy traffic. As we neared our destination[1] and entered a maze of alleys, we stopped for instructions more often.

And then, miraculously, we were there in what had once been a *paṟaiccēri* (outcaste hamlet),[2] now called Ekangipuram, adjacent to a huge cloth mill, the oldest and largest in the area near a major train station. Suburbanisation had engulfed the area with roads, schools and hospitals. Land in this once-despised hamlet was fetching a good price and many owners were selling out. Some Dalits had moved into suburban neighborhoods with a mix of castes, hoping to hide their identity and take advantage of new opportunities. Others took what little they had into the city core to start new lives, only to find themselves stuck in slums, their search for justice ending in the terrifying struggle for survival.

A man directed us down a tiny alley, almost impassable because of motorcycles parked on the edge. At that moment, something caught our attention: a Śrīvaiṣṇava emblem on a house wall, the ubiquitous conch, *nāmam* and discus[3] that adorn, sanctify and protect place or person. We had arrived. Our host ran forward to greet us, bowing with hands folded, uttering *vaṇakkam* (welcome).

This handsome young man is J. N. B. Chakravarthi Ramanuja Dasar (Chakra for short). In his household also live his wife Mahalakshmi (who is pregnant with their first child; she had a son later that year), his mother Lokanayaki. and his maternal grandmother Kumbhavalai Nacciyar. Chakra works in an automobile engineering business on Mount Road in Chennai. Several years later, he worked in the accounts department of Surya TV. Mahalakshmi has a B.Com. degree. She is a medical transcriptionist. The transcripts are sent from London and the United States; when they arrive in oral form, she writes them into formal medical records on the computer, and then she sends the computer files back.

The family's religious identity has been defined by formal initiation (*samāśrayaṇam*) into Śrīvaiṣṇavism. The male members of the family had been the first to be initiated. Their names include the initiation name Ramanuja Dasar. According to Mahalakshmi, the women were initiated only after marriage.

> When Chakra's mother, Lokanayaki, married, she did this ritual and began to worship Perumāḷ whom her husband's family considered to be the supreme god.[4] And then, so did her mother and her father but not her brother. My own family worshipped Perumāḷ, although only I have had initiation. This was after my marriage to Chakra. A Brahmin *ācārya* initiated us.

We entered their home. A large house-shrine dominates the main room. Chakra prostrated himself before it and then honoured K. K. A. Venkatachari and me with ceremonial shawls. Photos of deities include Vēṅkaṭeśvara, Krishna, Rāma, Varadarāja, Perumāḷ, and also Āṇṭāḷ, the female poetess who is also considered a goddess, the consort of Lord Raṅganātha. There is a small image of Rāmānuja, too. Chakra said, 'The family does daily *pūjā*, chanting together short poetic works of the *āḻvārs*[5] or a selection of Nammāḻvār's verses.'[6] I asked about other rituals that require the chanting of *āḻvār* hymns. 'We chant some at weddings,' Chakra said, 'and during a wife's pregnancy.'[7]

My attention turned to the wall next to that shrine. As in many Hindu household shrines, it displays pictures of earlier generations: deceased parents, grandparents, aunts and uncles. The conversation focussed on a picture of one of Chakra's grandfathers, J. J. Thirunarayana Ramanuja Dasar (1901–83), a very distinguished looking man.

Thirunarayana, as I will call him here, came from a poor family. Chakra told me the following: 'My grandparents[8] had a piece of agricultural land near Vellore, in a village called Kilamanavur. The village had a small Krishna temple. My great grandfather, Jaganathan, taught my grandfather with the help of local pandits.'

I later discovered that one Hindu non-Brahmin ascetic (*ekāṅgi*) from Srirangam had lectured in Vellore. He was probably (Kōyiḻ) Ekāṅgi Svāmikaḷ, whom I discussed in Chapter 1 and discuss in this chapter as well. The area of

IMAGE 3.1: J. N. B. Chakravarthi Ramanuja Dasar (Chakra) and his wife Mahalakshmi holding a picture of Chakra's grandfather J. J. Thirunarayana Ramanujar Dasar (1901–83), a Śrīvaiṣṇava Dalit leader.

Image credit: Author's collection.

Vellore produced considerable Dalit mobilisation. Vellore had absorbed Christian influence too, which explains its famous Christian Medical College and the fact that many Dalits had converted to Christianity. Other Dalits had turned to neo-Buddhism. Krishnaswamy (1916–73), for instance, studied in Madras, then returned to Vellore and, as a follower of Ambedkar's neo-Buddhism, worked his entire life to improve Dalit well-being.[9]

Chakra told me more about the family's history in Chennai.

> My grandfather married Godai Nacciyar. They had three sons and two daughters.[10] The family lived outside Chennai in this outcaste hamlet.[11] My grandfather had a good job. He was employed as a diesel-engine examiner

> for the southern railway; his second son, my uncle J. N. Devaperumal Ramanuja Dasar, was a manager for the southern railway.

The British often argued that the railway, which they gradually introduced after 1853, would usher in capitalist modernity; it would create a work ethic, moreover, and dissolve caste. Even Marx claimed that it would bring progress to India by eliminating the hereditary divisions of labour. Nevertheless, it took over a century to achieve some progress. Dissolving caste was not part of this. In the meantime, railways created new hierarchies with Europeans and Eurasians at the top, Brahmins in choice 'native positions', such as stationmaster, and other castes in lower jobs, such as ironworkers. The obvious contradiction between the British rhetoric on equality and this workplace inequality[12]—status, pay, access to education, and other opportunities—contributed to agitation by Indian railway employees. By the 1920s, with a growing number of strikes, railway workers were becoming a dangerous force both for the Raj, which needed trains to transport goods and soldiers, and for Indian political parties.

For instance, to be successful, the Congress Party had to compete with the Communist Party and other parties for the loyalty of these railway workers who daily experienced indignity. Mahatma Gandhi visited railway unions in order to win their support for Indian nationalism in general and for the Congress Party in particular. Many railway workers became Congress Party stalwarts, although they remained potential threats to any party in power even after Independence. Gradually, however, fair wages, good working conditions and democratic principles prevailed.

With that in mind, let us return to the interview. The conversation turned to the family's political affiliations. Chakra informed me about his family's connection with the Congress Party.

> My grandfather was a staunch member of the Congress party, and his family had personal connections with

> Mahatma Gandhi. When Gandhi came to Chennai, he stayed with a Śrīvaiṣṇava family. The couple named their daughter after Gandhi's wife Kasturba. Later, this daughter became the wife of J. N. Arangaram Ramanuja Dasar, my uncle. The Congress connection has continued into my generation.

Thirunarayana's job in the railways and his political connection to Gandhi might have been related to Gandhi's interest in winning support from railway workers. Now I understood the presence of a three-foot statue of Gandhi in Chakra's home.

Chakra made it clear that his family has had additional political connections:

> My grandfather was close friends with Kamaraj. Known for his honesty, Kamaraj worked in the Congress party and went from the lowest level to the highest. He was from the Nadar caste, which was prevalent in Ramanathapuram, the southernmost district of Tamil Nadu. Nadars were traditionally toddy tappers.[13] Their status was not high; they used to fight with outcastes over who had the right to pull the festival chariot (on which the deity rides) through the streets surrounding the temple. Kamaraj became the Tamil Nadu Congress president and later president of the National Congress Party. He had close relations with Vaiṣṇavas because Nadar religion has some Vaiṣṇava roots (see Appendix 6), but he also had good relations with all religions.
>
> C. Rajagopalachari—a Brahmin Śrīvaiṣṇava whose daughter had married Mahatma Gandhi's son—had been Chief Minister in Tamil Nadu, Governor of Bengal and the Governor-General of India. Then he became Chief Minister in Tamil Nadu for a second time. People thought that with his admirable statesmanship and good governance, he was the only one who could handle the DMK, which was becoming powerful. Kamaraj and other Congress non-Brahmins protested his appointment on the basis that he was a Brahmin. As a result, C. Rajagopalachari resigned as Chief Minister, and Kamaraj became Chief Minister in 1954.

The family showed me a picture of Indira Gandhi with Kamaraj, who had just died and was lying in state (1975). Thirunarayana was there (even though he could barely be seen at the edge of the picture). 'Ekangipuram still has some Congress party influence,' Chakra said, 'even though the DMK and AIDMK are also active in this area.'

Chakra remarked that his grandfather Thirunarayana was also known as a very learned Śrīvaiṣṇava. 'My grandfather was called a *nityasūri* (an eternal being) because of his exemplary behaviour, and an *ubhayavedāntin* because of his knowledge of both Tamil and Sanskrit scripture. He established a Vedic school where he and then later his sons taught Vedic hymns.'

As an *ubhayavedāntin*, Thirunarayana would have known Tamil and some Sanskrit. There is another example of this phenomenon: members of a Dalit community learning and chanting Vedic hymns. Vasudha Narayanan describes one of these communities in Melkote. This group recites selections from the Vedas, including the *Puruṣasūkta*, and the *Taittirīya Upaniṣad*. I was told by others that Thirunarayana was in communication with this Melkote community, perhaps because the Melkote community's spiritual advisor was Sri Govinda Ramanuja Dasar, who was from Ganesapuram in Madras,[14] and Thirunarayana knew him. Aside from his religious knowledge, Thirunarayana knew several languages. His sons were also known for their linguistic skills: the first son was a scholar in Tamil, the second was good in English, and the third was proficient in Hindi.[15]

Thirunarayana was a leader in his neighbourhood. According to Chakra, government documents show that Thirunarayana and one of his three sons fought with the municipality to change the name of the locale from the pejorative *paṟaiccēri* (outcaste hamlet) to Ekangipuram. After all, it contained the *samādhi* of (Kōyil̲) Ekāṅgi Svāmikaḷ, whom we have already encountered.[16] Perhaps because Ekāṅgi Swāmikaḷ gave lectures and initiations in this *paṟaiccēri* to Dalits, he was buried here.

When the American scholar Raymond Williams[17] visited Ekangipuram in 1991, he interviewed two of Thirunarayana's sons (who have since died). They told him that there were 15 Śrīvaiṣṇava Harijan families living there. They were strictly vegetarian, and, like orthodox Brahmins, did not even eat onions or garlic. They led *bhajanas* (devotional songs). One brother did the rituals for new temples in the area. The family, Williams wrote, took care of the burial place of the Ekāṅgi and his shrine in the adjacent building.

On the day of his visit, Williams witnessed a procession of Śrīvaiṣṇavas at Ekangipuram. The people who gathered at the shrine were almost all Dalits, except for a few Brahmin visitors. They went through the colony with a group chanting some *āḻvār* verses at the beginning of the procession (the lead person was holding a copy of the *Divyaprabandham*, the Tamil Śrīvaiṣṇava scripture), and another group chanting *bhajanas* at the end of the procession and dancing. That day, the procession had two drummers, a person who played the cymbals and a harmonium player. The procession stopped at many houses and received honours: sacred water, sandal paste and *kumkum* on the feet. Women of the households prostrated themselves before those in the procession. By the time they returned to the *samādhi*, the group had grown to about 100 people. There was more chanting and dancing, followed by a lecture by a Brahmin about Āṇṭāḷ.

Now back to the present. As we walked to the *samādhi* a short distance away, Chakra said,

> Ekāṅgi Svāmikaḷ's disciple Appaṉ cared for the *samādhi* after his death. After Appaṉ's own expiry, his picture was also hung in the shrine, near his master's. My grandfather and his family lived in a building adjacent to the *samādhi*, caring for the shrine and tending to the daily worship of the images. Members of my family continue to do this.'[18]

When we returned to Ekangipuram, a few weeks later, Śrīvaiṣṇavas had gathered in Chakra's house for our visit. Chakra commented on the changes in this neighbourhood.

> Previously, there were 25 to 30 outcaste Śrīvaiṣṇavas in the vicinity; now there is only my family. Once there was an Āṇṭāḷ association in this area; now it is no longer functioning. By contrast, Christianity is growing in popularity. For this reason, we are trying to revive Śrīvaiṣṇavism in the neighbourhood. In 2005, we started a new organisation called Varadaraja Sabhai. Ten people attended; six belonged to my family. We also periodically hold functions and invite honoured guests to speak about Śrīvaiṣṇavism. One, for instance, was when the family offered a stone for building the temple at Ayodhyā in 1987.[19] Another was when two honoured guests—Varataa Ethiraja Jeeyar Swami[20] and Kumaravadi Swamikal—gave talks, which we recorded on video.

The honoured guest on this occasion was K. K. A. Venkatachari. His homily was on Nammāḻvār's *Tiruvāymoḻi* 3.7.9.

> Those whose minds are absorbed [in the Lord] [thinking] [we are] 'the servants of the King who holds a powerful discus, the One of sapphire-hue,'
>
> even though they be outcastes of the
> outcastes who have no goodness
> are inferior to the four castes
> that support the families,
>
> the servants of their servants [are]
> our masters. (Nammāḻvār, *Tiruvāymoḻi* 3.7.9; Young [trans.])
>
> kulaṁ tāṅku cātikaḷ nālilum kīḻ iḻintu
> ettaṉai nalam tāṉ ilāta caṇṭāḷa caṇṭāḷarkaḷ ākilum
> valam tāṅku cakkarattu aṇṇal maṇi vaṇṇaṟku āḷ eṉṟu
> uḷ kalantār aṭiyār taṁ aṭiyār eṁ aṭikaḷē.[21]

This verse was apropos, given its focus on outcastes (here, the word is *caṇṭāḷa*) who are absorbed [in God], and even though they are the lowest of the low, inferior to the four castes (*cāti*; *jāti*)—that is, the four *varṇa*s—that support the families on which society depends, they are our true masters. The implication is that even the Brahmins should serve them with humility. After reciting the verse, Venkatachari elucidated its meaning, drawing from commentaries by *ācārya*s between the thirteenth and fifteenth century. Their basic point is that outcastes are pre-eminently qualified to serve God, because their essential nature is to serve others and therefore they exemplify the ideal of service, which others should imitate. As such, outcastes are the real masters or preceptors. Service to God and his devotees (*kaiṅkarya*) is, of course, a key concept of Śrīvaiṣṇavism. As the homily drew to a close, Chakra presented ceremonial shawls to Venkatachari and me, and performed *pūjā*. Then we examined the many family pictures.

At the end of our visit, we walked to Ekāṅgi Svāmikaḷ's *samādhi*. I learned that there is now a legal dispute.[22] Someone had seized control of the property, which had become valuable as part of metropolitan Chennai. Several weeks later, I returned to Chakra's and found that the entire *samādhi* had been bulldozed. One chapter of local history had disappeared. Now, not only was Chakra's family almost the only Śrīvaiṣṇava one left in the area, but there was also no trace of Ekāṅgi Swāmikaḷ.

The Granddaughter and Rāmānuja's House

N. D. Sabari Natchi is Chakra's first cousin and the granddaughter of J. J. Thirunarayana Ramanuja Dasar. Her father[23] followed in her grandfather's footsteps, working for the southern railways, and eventually became a manager; her mother[24] was a teacher for the Corporation of Madras. One of her brothers is a mechanical engineer and the other is a civil engineer. Her husband Sivagnanan is director of a Central Government department that promotes small enterprises throughout Tamil Nadu and Puducherry. Sabari Natchi works for the Central Government office of the Oil and Natural Gas Corporation as a purchase officer.

I first met Sabari Natchi and her husband at K. K. A. Venkatachari's house in Triplicane. It was the Tamil month of Mārkaḻi (December–January) when Śrīvaiṣṇava Brahmins meet in the early morning to chant Āṇṭāḷ's *Tiruppāvai*, 30 verses about maidens gathering in the early morning to go to the temple to perform a vow.[25] Ostensibly, the maidens do so to find good husbands. On a deeper level, though, they do so to serve the Lord. Sabari Natchi and her husband were invited guests on this occasion. After the recitation, Venkatachari introduced them to me. They invited us to visit them the following weekend.

And there we went. Another long sojourn took us to the even more distant northwestern suburbs of Chennai, this time to a place named Athipet, part of Ambattur. As we neared our destination, the roads were so muddy that we almost gave up for fear that the old car would get stuck. We finally came to Mahatma Gandhi Road and an open field with a palatial new house. Checking the address, we realised that we had reached our destination. As we climbed out of the car, we saw the words 'Rāmānujar Illam' (Rāmānuja's House) on the façade. And there were Sabari Nacchi, Sivagnanam and their two sons: S. Nedumaalavan and S. Shree Saranathaperumal. They greeted us and offered us ceremonial shawls.

Our conversation began with the story of Sabari Natchi's life. 'Until marriage,' she said, 'I lived in Ekangipuram. My brother still lives there. My family could not find a suitable Śrīvaiṣṇava match for me, and so they turned to a Śaiva family that worships Murukaṉ.' Sivagnanam chimed in: 'I made it to the short list and promised to follow Śrīvaiṣṇavism and be a strict vegetarian. When I had *samāśrayaṇam*, I was renamed Srinivasin, but I don't use that name except within the family.'

As we sat down after tea, I asked them: 'What is the best aspect of Śrīvaiṣṇavism?' They eagerly responded.

> Sabari Natchi: 'We are very fond of Rāmānuja. He rejected untouchability; no one is big or small. There is equality. This allows us to live with satisfaction and in a decent way, which is sometimes difficult to do in our community.'
>
> Sivagnanam: 'In the Epics, Krishna describes how to follow values and morals. We find these in Rāmānuja who says, "I can see the Lord in the form of lower caste people." I am impressed, moreover, that Rāmānuja revealed the mantra *om, namo nārāyaṇāya* to everyone.'[26]

(Sabari Natchi, too, brought up this point later in the conversation.)

Nedumaalavan: 'Once, when Rāmānuja went for his sacred bath, he went with an upper-caste person and returned with a lower caste person.'

Sivagnanam: 'If you just whisper the name of God with full devotion, you become a devotee and get what you desire.'

Sabari Natchi: 'Vaiṣṇavas are very strict. The religion helps them to have discipline and get ahead.'

Sivagnanam: 'Dr Venkatachari understands real Vaiṣṇavism. He is very devout. Devotion has been nullified by northerners and others who claim to be true Śrīvaiṣṇavas. By just wearing the *nāmam* without having the morals and good knowledge, discrimination comes in. Therefore, lower castes have to be empowered with knowledge and empowered economically. Education is a must, and we must be educated with values. We are not interested in big rituals, only just the values. The number of Śrīvaiṣṇava Harijans is growing; however, many are ignorant. It would be good if upper castes teach lower castes. The lower castes will listen. Upper castes should take this seriously. In the *Gītā*, Krishna spread the message to everyone. The upper castes don't want to do this. All people are equal; they come without anything into this world and won't take anything with them after death. Naidus and Reddiyars, too, maintain a distance from us. Because of this, we need piety, vegetarianism and ethics. This makes humans full. Śrīvaiṣṇava Brahmins should come forward and educate lower castes in order to transform them into Śrīvaiṣṇavas, although they need to reeducate the Brahmins and caste Hindus too.'

Sabari Natchi: 'Every day, I tell stories about Śrīvaiṣṇavism to my sons. I use the *Tattva Loka*, a monthly magazine,[27] and buy Śrīvaiṣṇava books. Our sons go to an Arya Samaj school, which is near our home. They do *pūjā* and *yajña* rituals there. Both kids want to do Śrīvaiṣṇava service.'

Sabari Natchi: 'There is a lot of politics in the temples. The most important thing is being a good human being and

> only then a Vaiṣṇava. One needs the real culture of being a Śrīvaiṣṇava. Besides K. K. A. Venkatachari, another real Śrīvaiṣṇava is Varataa Ethiraja Jeeyar Swami[28] of Sriperumbudur. We know him well and always get his blessing when we go there.'

Sabari Natchi and Sivagnanam mentioned that they rarely went to Śrīvaiṣṇava lectures, yet did so whenever they had the time. They are intent, however, on doing *kaiṅkarya*. 'The whole family,' said Sabari Natchi,

> goes to Tirupati for the Brahmotsavam festival. Following a tradition started by my father, we distribute beforehand an invitation to poor Śrīvaiṣṇavas. It says, 'If you go to Tirupati, we will feed you. We will also pay for the train and for darshan [sight of and being seen by God].' We spend a week there, cooking and offering food to the devotees at the Tirumalai-Tirupati Devasthanam guesthouse.

Despite successful careers, a happy home, and deep Śrīvaiṣṇava identity, the family occasionally encounters the old outcaste stigma. Sabari Natchi and her sons, for instance, have not yet had *samāśrayaṇam*. Nevertheless, they want it. Sabari Natchi explained:

> When my grandfather was ill, he told his first son to get initiation from the same *ācārya* who had performed the initiation for him. Now that *ācārya*'s son is doing the initiations. However, when I went to him, along with others from my community, he refused to do it. I want to follow the instructions of my grandfather and have an *ācārya* from this family perform the initiation. I want to chant from this lineage during the *pūjā*, moreover, in the traditional way. I do not want to deviate from the family tradition.

Sivagnanam remarked, 'Go to the person who is willing to do the initiation. When driven away, why follow the forefather? Your grandfather would not go to such an *ācārya* if he were alive today!' With the interview concluding, we went on a tour of their new home, 'Rāmānuja's house', including its shrine room with its contemporary pictures of the deities.

For centuries, the entry of Dalits into major Śrīvaiṣṇava temples had been contentious, as the following story of Tiruppāṇ Āḻvār reveals:

> One day a minstrel, duly aware of his outcaste status at the temple, was singing to the Lord from outside the Srirangam temple. A priest who was fetching water from the Kaveri for the ritual tried to chase him away from the river to prevent him from polluting it. The Lord himself intervened and chastised the priest in a dream for his behavior. The next day, the priest himself carried Tiruppāṇ on his shoulder into the temple's sanctum. On seeing the Lord, the *āḻvār* sang the ten verses known as the *Amalanātippirāṉ*.[29]

This story of Tiruppāṇ reveals the desire of some Brahmins in the past to keep outcastes outside the temples. The command of God was to bring them inside. This might well reflect a growing tension in the community at that time, between Brahmanical views on orthodox purity (which considered outcastes impure and therefore not allowed in the sacred temple space) and the inclusive Śrīvaiṣṇava theology (which argued that any devotee of God is to be accepted and honoured). The orthodox eventually won; outcastes could not enter the major temples until the mid-twentieth century.

Sriperumbudur, the birthplace of Rāmānuja, also excluded outcastes from the temple. For this reason, the bronze image of Rāmānuja was taken in procession around the temple in the Tamil month of Tai (mid-January to mid-February), during a three-day festival at Sriperumbudur, which commemorates the installation of Rāmānuja's image there.[30] Śrīvaiṣṇavas have believed, after all, that Rāmānuja is both divine and the mediator between the Supreme God and humans; by surrendering to an *ācārya* or *jīyar*, they are in point of fact surrendering to Rāmānuja himself, which guarantees salvation.

During this festival, outcastes had the right to carry the palanquin. Just as the gracious deity went *outside* his home or temple on special occasions, so that everyone could see him, and he could proffer the opportunity for service, devotion and salvation, so did Rāmānuja. He had (and still has) an iconic body. The Lord going in procession outside the temple, which was common in most temples, was important, because even though outcastes could not go *inside* the temple proper, they could perform service *outside* the temple and have *darśana* of God there. With Dalit political mobilisation in the twentieth century, Dalits no longer accepted their exclusion from the temple and relegation of their *darśana* to the streets. Nonetheless, they have maintained the tradition of carrying the palanquin as an honour that belongs to their community.

'My grandfather was instrumental,' said Sabari Natchi, 'in improving the relation of the Harijans with Śrī Rāmānuja's temple authorities in Sriperumbudur and agitated for their right to enter the temple.' In this activity, I might add, Thirunarayana could have been inspired by Gandhi's visit to Vellore[31] and Pallikonda. When Gandhi visited a temple in Pallikonda in 1934, he was told that the outcastes who had experienced severe discrimination in the area were not allowed to enter. Gandhi declared that he would not enter the temple until the outcastes too could go inside. Caste Hindus denied his request, and so Gandhi went away.[32]

Gandhi agitated for temple entry, not only at this temple but also throughout India, including many places in Tamil Nadu. Thirunarayana had political and family connections with the Mahatma, and if Thirunarayana had been at this attempted temple entry, or at least heard about it or about one of the many other events when Gandhi agitated for temple entry in Tamil Nadu, he might have been inspired to work for the opening of the Sriperumbudur temple to Harijans. According to Sabari Natchi:

> my grandfather had bought land at Sriperumbudur and built a *maṭha* there in 1936, calling it Srimatha Yamunariya Priyar Bhakti Jana Sabha. Since 1939, outcastes have gathered there to celebrate the birthday of Śrī Rāmānuja for ten days in April–May, because Śrī Rāmānuja had

> shown the path to many people. This *maṭha* is meant only for Harijans. It provides food and shelter during festivals. My grandfather preached to Harijans at that time about Śrīvaiṣṇavism and told everyone how to do *pūjā*. After his death, his first son did this.

The government finally granted Dalits temple entry in 1947.[33] It took some time, however, for temples to comply, and even now there are problems sometimes.

Thirunarayana's special connection to Sriperumbudur might be related to his (and his family's) *samāśrayaṇam* by Sāttikva Ācārya from nearby Tirumalicai, one of the few Brahmin *ācāryas* who initiated outcastes at that time (I discuss him in Chapter 6). In 2009, Sabari Natchi described to me the plans to celebrate the fifty-second year of the *maṭha*:

> Five hundred to six hundred Harijans from all over south India will come to this. Funds are collected from the devotees to finance the event. Now we are renovating the *maṭha* at Sriperumbudur, and I am in charge. I continue to do the service of my father and grandfather. I teach people how to do the *pūjās*, *bhajanas* and so forth when Harijans come from all over south India.

Obviously, Sriperumbudur has been a hub of Dalit Śrīvaiṣṇavism since Thirunarayana's time, if not earlier.

The 'Almost Ācārya' and his Cousins

My destination was an *ashram* at Punga Medu, in the town of Minjur located northwest of the huge Ennore port north of Chennai. The road-trip there was an adventure, both because of monsoon damage to the roads and because of the many huge lorries that were parked bumper to bumper in Ennore, awaiting their turn to be loaded, and making the road virtually one-way. Because the trucks had no drivers and therefore seemed to be parked for future action, our driver, uttering a prayer to Lord Vēṅkaṭeśvara, took off down the single lane for several kilometres. I held my breath, hoping that we would not meet an oncoming lorry and have to head for a deep ditch at the side of the road. We made it through and soon came to a village surrounded by verdant fields and then the *ashram*.

IMAGE 3.2: Sudarshana 'Acarya' leading a send-off procession for pilgrims going from his ashram in Minjur (north of Chennai) to Tirupati by foot.

Image credit: Author's collection.

I was about to meet a Telugu family that migrated into this area several generations ago.[34] The grandfather was a farmer who had about 40 acres of land (although only four remain). He did the paddy measurements and solved problems for the village council. 'A very attractive man,' said his grandson Padu, 'he was famous as a singer. One day, when he was husking rice, he looked to the sky and sang. It began to rain everywhere except at that spot. Because this was miraculous, he built a temple there. That was about twenty-five years ago.'

Today, this temple has been enlarged and is part of an *ashram* that is run by the family, which has been Vaiṣṇava for several generations. The key person is Sudarshana 'Acharya', who was forty-two when I first interviewed him.

Besides Sudarshana, I interviewed two of his cousins: M. Dhamodharan, a lawyer at the High Court in Chennai who often returns to his home village, and Padu, who lives with his family next to the *ashram*.

Sudarshana's Saga

> My family is Vaiṣṇava, and so I went with them as a child to Tirumalai-Tirupati. When I was in the seventh grade, I became interested in social work and the religious path of devotion. At that time, I saw in a dream a figure with *nāmam*, crown, flowers and jewels. The next month, when I went to Tirupati, I recognised that same figure as Lord Bālāji (Vēṅkaṭeśvara). Bālāji encouraged me to pursue the way of devotion.
>
> When I was in the tenth grade, I saw Tirupati Bālāji again in a dream. He told me to learn more about the Śrīvaiṣṇava tradition. I began by contacting Varataa Ethiraja Jeeyar Swami of Sriperumbudur, who asked me to go to the Śaṅkara *maṭha* in Kanchipuram for training. Between 1983 and 1986, I studied *yoga, siddha, āyurveda* and naturopathy, as well as how to read the Vedas and give lectures. I lived in Sriperumbudur during my studies. In 1986, at the age of eighteen, I was initiated by Ethiraja. At that time, he gave me a new name, Shriman Sudarshana Acharya.

'Ācārya' is certainly a provocative title, because this role had remained under Brahmin control, notwithstanding the agitation of figures such as Ekāṅgi Svāmikaḷ and Bhuvanagiri in the previous century to open the role to Bhāgavatas. Something else was unusual here. Brahmin *ācārya*s marry and belong to one of the seventy-four families appointed, according to tradition, by Rāmānuja.[35] Sudarshana, who was not married, obviously did not fit this description, and so, as he told me, he was an 'almost *ācārya*'. Because of the unorthodoxy of his title, it came as no surprise to find that Sudarshana also used the Brahmin title *jīyar*. He showed some signs of being an ascetic. He wore an orange *dhoti* and *rudrākṣa* beads, for instance, or sometimes a white *dhoti* and orange upper-cloth. (Ascetics wear orange vestments and *rudrākṣa* beads.) His cousin Padu described Sudarshana as a celibate. When I asked Sudarshana if he was a *saṃnyāsin* (even though, traditionally, only Brahmins can be *saṃnyāsins*), he replied, 'Ethiraja told me that I will have the position of being "almost" a *saṃnyāsin*. I am neither a *saṃnyāsin* nor a married householder, but in between.'

Sudarshana calls himself Chinna Jīyar (little Jīyar), too, in a pamphlet that he wrote. If Sudarshana is the little *jīyar*, who is the big one? Near Sudarshana's office hangs a huge banner with three figures: at the top is Rāmānuja, in the middle Varataa Ethiraja Jeeyar, and at the bottom Sudarshana. Chakra and Sabari Natchi had already mentioned Ethiraja from Sriperumbudur. The banner makes it clear that he is Sudarshana's 'Big Jīyar'.[36]

Sudarshana continued with more stories about his life.

> As a traditional (*siddha*) physician who uses no Western medicine, I treat people on Sundays and give medicines for free. This is one reason the place is so popular. About 100 people come. When I cure people, they want to offer something to me, and I tell them to offer a statue or something else for the temple. I am an astrologer, too. And I give books and pencils to poor students who worship at the temple. However, I don't like doing rites of passage such as naming ceremonies, marriages and

> funerals, although I will bless marriages if I am invited to them and will do *nārāyaṇabali* [the ritual to counter the bad karma of an unusual death] and chant verses from the *Tiruvāymoḻi* after the death of a Vaiṣṇava. Sometimes, I perform Vedic fire rituals or *homa* at temple openings—sixty-three temples have been recently opened—and do blessings at new homes and school functions. And each year, I give *samāśrayaṇam* to about 1,000 people who come from nearby districts in both Tamil Nadu and Andhra. In one hour, they obtain new lives; they become pure vegetarians, wear the *nāmam* and do daily *pūjā*.

Sudarshana gave me a tour of the *ashram*. At the centre of the compound is a temple dedicated to God Śrīnivāsa, who is present as an immovable stone statue and a movable bronze festival image. On the left of the main temple is Sudarshana's office. At the back of the *ashram* are cowsheds and the medical clinic. To the right of the main temple is a smaller temple. Dedicated to Rāmānuja, it contains both immovable and movable images. In addition, we find on the right side of the main temple another shrine with images representing the nine planets.

On another visit to the Minjur *ashram*, a few weeks later, I watched Sudarshana giving a woman *samāśrayaṇam*, branding her with the ritual utensils heated in a sacred fire, and revealing to her the secret mantras. I learned that her husband was waiting in a rickshaw on the street outside, too sick to come into the temple for the ritual. I saw Sudarshana initiate him there.

Padu told me that local people highly respect Sudarshana. Devotees support the temple with their gifts and locals as well as visitors from Chennai and elsewhere visit. Saturday night is the main *pūjā*. On this visit, I saw Sudharshana performing *pūjā* with some Vedic verses. He led *bhajana* singing, too, along with four young men dressed in *lungi*s. Because they were bare-chested, I could see that they all wore sacred threads like those worn by Brahmins.[37] A 94-year-old man was wandering about, touching the feet of devotees. When the *bhajana*s started, he began to hop and dance. After a while, he put on a Hanuman wooden mask and danced with it. As the tempo increased, he stuck out his tongue. Everyone knew that he had dementia and gently joked with him, yet also accepted him as a genuine devotee.

I noticed many visiting devotees. Some were merely Saturday visitors, whereas others were gathering for the biannual pilgrimage by foot to Tirupati, which is about 150 km away. Gradually, men who had been seated on the floor singing *bhajana*s stood up and a procession began. Leading it was a man with a small white horse. The four young *bhajana* leaders now carried the palanquin with the image of God Śrīnivāsa, swaying it back and forth. Then came Sudarshana, walking under a ceremonial parasol. Several young men pulled a big drum, which they beat. The procession moved slowly down a lane to the road. Then, the pilgrims moved on. Along the way, the group stops at various charitable guesthouses for the night. Sudarshana has a connection with a *jīyar* in Tirupati who had made the arrangements.

I visited Sudarshana's *ashram* once more to witness the ritual wedding of Āṇṭāḷ (as goddess) and God. This was a major event with many visitors, processions, and a Vedic-style fire ritual. Sudarshana was the chief ritualist. Occasionally, he consulted a book, even though he knew most of the chants by heart. It was a grand celebration. As Sudarshana's cousin Dhamodharan told me, 'Sudarshana is doing *pūjā*s beautifully. Even the Brahmins can't do it like that.' When interviewing Sudarshana, I mentioned rumours that Ethiraja might appoint him as his successor. He replied, 'I have no idea who the successor will be. What God wants, he will do.'[38]

M. Dhamodharan's Life Story

I met Dhamodharan on several occasions, both at the *ashram* and in Chennai. Gradually, I learned his life story.

> I was born and brought up in Minjur. It is an agricultural village. Both my father and mother were from farming

families. The land where the ashram is located was once my family's land. We gave it to the ashram. Then a devotee purchased some more land next door and gave it to the ashram.

I am the first one in my family to be educated. My first degree was in history: European, Indian and Tamil. I studied at Loganatha Narayanaswamy Government College in Ponneri and graduated in 1976. Then I went to the Law College of the University of Madras now called Dr. Ambedkar Law College. I joined in 1980 and graduated in 1983, after which I enrolled in the Bar Council as a lawyer. I obtained a certificate that allowed me to practice in all courts. I went to the high court. Now, I have a law office there with a typist. My specialisations are labour law, criminal law, employee problems within the government service and real estate. I am currently investigating twenty-five criminal cases of office fraud for the Ministry of Company Affairs, which regulates small businesses regarding problems of trading to relatives, inside deals, and so forth.

I belong to the Indian National Congress. I was the Vice President of its Legal Cell for Tamil Nadu. Through that, I developed many contacts in Tamil Nadu. I was a member of the Free Legal Aid Committee, a Tamil Nadu Government body. Now, I am a senior counsel for them. This is a free service for the poor. The Dalit Sahitiya Academy in Delhi gave me a national award for my service to the community. In my regular job, I have clients from Chennai, Ooty, Coimbatore, and elsewhere.

I have not had *samāśrayaṇam* because I like non-vegetarian food. I have a *pūjā* room in my home. In the morning, after I bathe and don a fresh dhoti, I stand before the photo of Lord Vēṅkateśvara (Bālāji), our family deity. I have not memorised *Divyaprabandham* verses; rather, I offer prayers from my heart.

My wife is a medical doctor. She also serves the poor. Our only child, a daughter, is now in a boarding school near Coimbatore. She wants to be a medical doctor like her mother and will soon take entrance exams.

> We have land in Minjur. Our dream is to start a free medical college and hospital. However, we need money to start. We are looking for an NRI (a non-resident Indian) or someone like you to help.

Padu's Saga

Another of Sudarshana's cousins is Padu. He had quite a different perspective on religion.

> I went to a government school in the village. Later, I went to the government sculpture school in Mahabalipuram, where I learned how to carve stone temple statues. I have not looked for that kind of work, although my brother who studied at the same school has carved some of the statues around the temple here and now acts as a priest assisting Sudarshana. As for me, I dream of having a jewellery shop or becoming an actor, playing villain roles in Tamil films.

He showed me some terrifying faces for his upcoming film audition, then continued:

> I was initiated ten years ago. It was done by Sudarshana. My grandfather, father, brothers, and others had all had it. It didn't really change my life. The real change was when I married at twenty-three and had children. There were more expenses.
>
> I know the *Tiruppāvai*. Every Saturday, Sudarshana and my brother, the priest, sing *Tiruppāvai* and other verses from the *Divyaprabandham*. I wear any kind of dress for ordinary situations and special dress for special religious ones. The family is vegetarian. I eat meat. Because I am now trading in gems and often go into tribal areas, I want to accept tribal hospitality and eat with them. I am following my own life, which is a gift from God. God is in the heart. I go to all temples, mosques and churches.
>
> If you help people, they think God does it. Whether Brahmin or non-Brahmin, everyone will die. People get different opportunities from God. Poor people have bad karma; rich people have good karma. Sadhus go away

> from the family and live in the street. They get respect. Gypsies live with their families. They all have the same quality of life. Life is nothing—our bodies will disappear. At death, our souls will go to Paramapadam (the supreme heaven). One needs to get rid of karma. Brahmins and non-Brahmins—all are going to die. Although Siddhas (holy men) used to live for 500 years, they also now die. Everything comes from God, although we can't see him. Pure people have no jealousy or anger; they are helpful and selfless. Like Sai Baba. Why are the *āḻvārs* famous? Because they had no egos, no buildings. They expected nothing. Both rich and poor are subject to karma. I want to help; however, I also want to live.
>
> Now I am earning just enough to live. Still, I have some rupees or clothes to give others. I now take care of my four kids. Ultimately their lives are in their own hands. I go about with ordinary people, the poor and others. True love is when you don't expect anything. Rich people are selfish. I love the poor. When you get more things, you have more problems. The poor have fresh faces and can laugh. We follow Rāmānuja as our guru. If there was no Rāmānuja, there would be no Śrīvaiṣṇavism. I stay away from politics. And I don't like caste. God is one. In my own family, castes are mixing.

On my final visit to the ashram, Padu told me that a huge highway would be built just behind the ashram. Everyone worried that its beauty and tranquility would soon be gone.

The Music Shrine's Protector

I visited a Naidu Śrīvaiṣṇava family in Triplicane. T. Vijaya Raghavan, who works for Allied Publishers, a company that imports medical books for libraries, was my host and introduced me to his family. His wife is a housewife, and his sister works in an eye hospital as a general nurse. In the past, she was a dancer and performed in Kanchipuram and various *sabhās*. Also, I met Vijaya's two sons Parthasarathi and Venkatakrishnan, and several other relatives. Vijaya began to narrate the family's history. 'My family has been Śrīvaiṣṇava for several generations,' he said. 'The whole family has been initiated. We are disciples of Ramanuja Acarya of Sriperumbudur.' He then told me about his family's musical tradition.

> My great grandfather, Munuswami Naidu (1880–1950), played the clarinet and the music of Tyāgarāja (1767–1847). Tyāgarāja was a Telugu Brahmin born in Tanjavur; he composed classical (Carnatic) music, especially devotional songs praising Lord Rāma. Kuppuswami Naidu, my grandfather, studied in Ambur in Vellore district with a famous *vidvāṉ*,[39] a performer named Sri Chinnaswami. The clarinet is not caste-based. It is a Western instrument used for Carnatic music. Often, Naidus play it.[40]
>
> By contrast, the *nāgasvaram*, a traditional Tamil reed instrument, is played only by one caste and is therefore considered a hereditary instrument. My grandfather learned *mṛdaṅgam*, too, from Sri Umayalpuram K. Sivaraman,[41] another famous performer in Tamil Nadu. Afterwards, my grandfather had his own 'band', a small troupe of about ten relatives who gave concerts in the pillared hall at the Parthasarathy temple and played in processions during Brahmotsavam and other festivals. This was done as service to God, not for pay. There was no tradition of concert performances at that time.
>
> My father, Sri Keshavalu, learned the clarinet, and my younger brother, C. K. Vasudevan, learned it from him. He has played in bands for dance and drama performances around Tamil Nadu and Singapore. He also does *naṭṭuvaṅgam* (a kind of song accompanied by tapping the rhythm on wood or with cymbals) and earns his living now by accompanying Alarmel Valli, a famous Indian dancer, in performances in Europe, America and around the world.[42] My younger brother's two sons play instruments as well. My sons and I play no instrument. I am more interested in devotion and service and hearing lectures about Śrīvaiṣṇavism.

When I asked whether Bhāgavatas face discrimination in the music world, he replied 'I don't think so.' He added: 'Even though Alarmel Valli is a non-Brahmin, she is so famous that her caste is not a problem. If a *vidvāṉ* is really good, there is no problem getting on stage.' Vijaya gave a few more examples of famous non-Brahmin performers, such as A. K. C. Natarajan, who played the clarinet.[43]

Evidence of the family's musical heritage is found in the music shrine next door. It is built very much like a temple, and so it is called a *bhajana kōyil*. Vijaya performs the *pūjā* there every morning and during festivals. We went to see it. Vijaya proudly said that the shrine 'was built about 120 years ago and then was passed to my grandfather Kuppuswami and down through my family. It contains many Tanjavur paintings.'

We circumambulated a very narrow walkway, with walls on either side, all painted with red and white stripes. Outside, along the back walkway, were a storage room and a kitchen. Standing in front of the sanctum, I saw a painting of Lord Nārāyaṇa. There were also small paintings of Rāmānuja and Maṇavāḷa Māmuni on either side of the central image. Just outside the sanctum, in the hall for *bhajana*s, were many more Tanjavur paintings, including ones of Āṇṭāḷ and Tyāgarāja. I saw a palanquin that devotees use to take images around the streets during festival processions. A Telugu inscription on the wall says that this temple is their family's property, that daily *bhajana*s must be done, and that devotees must be fed during the day after Vaikuṇṭha Ekādaśī. The inscription had no date. Vijaya thought that it might belong to the time when the temple was built. Vijaya then explained more about this place.

> *Bhajana*s continue to be held and many festivals are celebrated here, such as Navarātri, Mārkaḻi, Vaikuṇṭha Ekādaśī and the birthdays of Rāma and Krishna. At these times, there are morning *pūjā*s and evening *bhajana*s featuring the music of Tyāgarāja and Annamācārya.[44] And there are concerts with live classical music. This place is not used, however, for religious talks or *sabhā* meetings.

> There is a special upstairs room next door where guests can relax between morning and evening events.

After touring the *bhajana kōyil*, we returned to Vijaya's home. He showed me their house shrine. Besides the sacred *śalagrāma* stones, there are small images. Each is 300–400 years old. There is one of the dancing Krishna, another of Rāma, Sītā and Lakṣmaṇa together, one of Lord Śrīnivāsa Perumāḷ and his consort, as well as ones of Nammāḻvār, Rāmānuja and Maṇavāla Māmuṉi. Vijaya said that he does the daily worship, offering incense, light, cooked rice, and fruits while reciting the *Tiruppāvai*, *Tiruppallāṇṭu*, and *Tirupaḷḷiyeḻucci*.

Every Sunday, the family goes to a Rāmānuja *maṭha* near the Parthasarathy temple. There, they chant selections from the *Divyaprabandam*. Vijaya's sister Hema knows 400 verses, including the *Tiruppāvai* and *Tiruppallāṇṭu*. For the rest, she reads from a book. Vijaya's son Venkatakrishnan knows 1,500 verses out of the 4,000; he needs the help of a book for the rest. In their lane is another *bhajana maṭha*, where seven to eight Bhāgavatas learn *bhajana*s from a Brahmin, Veera Raghavan, who teaches each evening. When I asked if they belonged to any *sabhā*, Hema mentioned one in T. Nagar and a *rāmānuja kūṭam* near the Parthasarathy temple, where they sometimes go to hear lectures.

One young woman commented:

> I like the *Tiruppāvai*, because it is for everyone. We enjoy devotion to God with *bhakta*s who gather for recitation. A group of devotees is key to Vaiṣṇavism. Festivals bring people together. Periyāḻvār comes with us when we say the blessing *pallāṇṭu* ('May you live long') for God.[45] Even the Harijans join in festivals and pull the Lord's chariot.

Later, K. K. A. Venkatachari remarked that Vijaya's father, Sri Keshavalu, used to attend the *Tiruppāvai* recitation at his home, and sat silently with the chanting Brahmins. This man died last year. Now, Vijaya and his uncle come. They chant silently, as the Brahmins chant aloud. Venkatachari says that most Bhāgavatas are not bothered that they should not chant with the Brahmins in a Brahmin's home. Nonetheless, Vijaya is certainly distressed by acts of discrimination at temples. He told me:

> Sixty to seventy years ago, there was a fight in Srirangam over whether Bhāgavatas could chant in the temple. The non-Brahmins lost, and now only the Brahmin *goṣṭhi* (a registered group) has the right to do this. At the Parthasarathy temple, non-Brahmins were given no *tīrtham* and no *prasādam* up to 1961. T. K. Ramanuja Dasar, a strict Śrīvaiṣṇava Bhāgavata from Chidambaram, visited the Parthasarathy temple. Like other Bhāgavatas, he experienced discrimination. He took his case to the Hindu Religious and Charitable Endowments Board. An order was passed on 20 December 1967, which said that no discrimination should be shown while distributing the *tīrtham* and *prasādam* among Śrīvaiṣṇavas at the Parthasarathy temple. Even after the Hindu Charitable Endowments Board took over management of the temple, Brahmins still cause problems for non-Brahmins.

During my visit to his home, Vijaya complained about a current injustice. This involved a clash at the old Yathoktakārī temple in Kanchipuram, between Brahmin and non-Brahmin devotees. He wanted advice from Venkatachari on how Bhāgavatas should handle this.

At the end of the interview, I brought up the topic of political affiliation. Vijaya said that he has none. Rather, he votes for individuals.

The Maker of Village Priests

P. Balakrishnan Swaamy, also known as Necavalar or Kakkalayam, has been a non-Brahmin priest (*arcaka*). I wanted to meet him, because I was told that he had been teaching non-Brahmin boys the *Divyaprabandham* as part of a government programme to train boys, including non-Brahmins, to be priests. The classes are held in a building across the street from a gate to the Parthasarathy temple in Triplicane.

I arrived in the midst of a class. About twenty young men dressed in white *dhoti*s and bare-chested, except for the sacred thread across their shoulders, were sitting at desks. When Balakrishnan called on a student, he stood and chanted a verse. The students sometimes stopped or made mistakes, Balakrishnan gently corrected them, and the class moved on.

After the class, I sat down with Balakrishnan to learn more. 'This school, which has been in operation for about a year,' he told me,

> is run by the Parthasarathy Devasthānam. There is a similar program in Srirangam run by the Srirangam Devasthānam. Most temples are now administrated by non-Brahmins. The Tamil Nadu government initiated this scheme of training non-Brahmin priests. Open to students of all ages and castes, it gives students a 500-rupee stipend, plus food and accommodation. They come from all over Tamil Nadu. This is a three-year course. Students take classes in Veda, Āgama, *Divyaprabandham*, and Tamil. The goal is to become priests in village temples. Of the sixty-five students that attend, 95 per cent are non-Brahmins, even though there are a few Brahmins too. There is also a Śaiva school like this one, except it is located in a different place. Vaiṣṇavas must have *samāśrayaṇam* before joining the school, although there is no such initiation requirement for Śaiva students.

I found the government's insistence on initiation unusual and learned that this requirement is not demanded by the government, but rather by the Śrīvaiṣṇava organisers of this programme.

'I am one of four teachers in the new government school,' continues Balakrishnan.

> My job is to teach the *Divyaprabandham*. I am the only non-Brahmin teacher. The Veda, Āgama and Tamil teachers are all Brahmins. I teach three times a week. So far, the students have memorised about thirty stanzas, how to chant them and how to explain their basic meaning. Because the students are from the villages, sometimes I

> have to explain a verse several times to them. At first, the students were not so interested. Now they are becoming more interested. The young boys must stand up and recite in the traditional way. This is considered polite.
>
> This school has been controversial. Some Brahmins did not want it, and so they took a case to court. The government fought back, arguing 'no caste discrimination'. There is now a Supreme Court case in Delhi [I discuss this in Chapter 7]. Not even 1 per cent of the population is against this government plan. Just a few Brahmins. Because Śrīvaiṣṇavism is caste-inclusive, the government is not against it. There is a lot of public support plus the equality clauses in the Constitution. In March, the government will extend the classes into more parts of Tamil Nadu.

When I met Balakrishnan again, this time outside the school, he told me this.

> I am originally from Nellur in Andhra and belong to a caste of weavers. I am now fifty, married and have two sons. One has a Bachelor's degree in engineering and has a job as an engineer. My second son is still a student in engineering. We have had initiation from the Tirukkoyilur *jīyar*.
>
> I received much of my training in *prabandha sevai* (service related to the *Divyaprabandham*) and *vaidika-kārya* (Vedic rituals) from my father. He was a pure Vaiṣṇava, a trustee of a non-Brahmin temple in Mylapore (a Chennai neighbourhood) called Andal Rangamannar Sannidhi. He was also the priest there. I took Sanskrit as my second language in school. I know the vocabulary, but am not very proficient in the grammar. Most of my Sanskrit knowledge I got from my father. I like the *āḻvār*s and prefer the Tamil *Divyaprabandham* to Sanskrit texts. I became a priest in the same temple where my father was the priest.
>
> I no longer officiate as a priest. Besides teaching at the new government school in Triplicane, I do private chanting and give 'discourses' not for money, rather from the heart. Still, the payment given to me helps provide income for my family. In addition, I perform the last rites,

> annual *śrāddha*s (the rituals for one's deceased ancestors) and weddings. I did them for Vijaya Raghavan's family.[46] I am the last one in my family doing this kind of work. It gives me a lot of respect. I am now doing *prabandha sevai* discourses in many places.

I asked Balakrishnan if Bhāgavatas should perform *samāśrayaṇam* for others. 'No,' he told me, and then explained why:

> Rāmānuja established the seventy-four families for performing the initiation ritual. He selected only these Brahmin families to be *ācārya*s. Moreover, for the initiation ritual, one needs preliminary *adhikāra*, that is, scriptural expertise. Only the *ācārya*s have this qualification because they know Sanskrit well.

Next, I asked: 'Can non-Brahmins join the Brahmin group or *goṣṭhi* chanting the *Divyaprabandham* in the temple?' Balakrishnan began his answer by referring to Nammāḻvār's passage about the Cāṇḍāḷas (*Tiruvāymoḻi* 3.7.9) and said, 'Once Bhāgavatas have had initiation, they too can chant the *Divyaprabandham*.' I remarked that even now, non-Brahmins are not allowed to chant near the sanctum in many temples, and he replied:

> This is wrong; it is against the *sampradāya*. Nammāḻvār, who composed the *Tiruvāymoḻi*, himself is a non-Brahmin. Therefore, Brahmins can't reject non-Brahmins. Some Brahmins are wrong, not the *sampradāya*. To give discourses in the temple twenty years ago was impossible. Then the government ordered that this be allowed in Parthasarathy temple. The government supports non-Brahmins.

Our conversation expanded on the relations of Brahmins and non-Brahmins. Balakrishnan commented:

> Śrīvaiṣṇavism has four classes (*varṇa*s). Each has its own *dharma* (occupation and duties). If a *śūdra* becomes a Śrīvaiṣṇava through initiation, he becomes a Bhāgavata. Once people of any *varṇa* are initiated, they are dependent only on God and become *Rāmānuja*-dāsas (servants of

> Rāmānuja). Therefore, all four classes become Rāmānuja-dāsas, including the Brahmins.
>
> This is the theory, if not the practice. Only with initiation does one become connected to Rāmānuja. Once we belong to the *sampradāya*, we have to act according to Rāmānuja's values and so *varṇa-dharma* applies only to rituals. For example, Brahmins must do certain rituals, whereas others do 'customs' according to the Rāmānuja *sampradāya*. *Śāstra* (Vedic scripture) is the basis for Brahmin rituals. It is *sanātana-dharma*, eternal, and always there. One is a Brahmin only if one knows the Vedas and does Vedic rituals. If a Brahmin does other work, he is not a Brahmin. Character is important too. Viśvamitra was born as a Kṣatriya and became a sage (*ṛṣi*) by character. Birth is not important; occupation and character are.
>
> If a non-Brahmin studies the Vedas and Vedic ritual, he is a Brahmin, even though Brahmins do not accept this idea. Priesthood is becoming a job with a commercial orientation: *varṇa* is eternal, even though defined by occupation and character, not birth. Before, non-Brahmins were subservient. Now that is changing. Why? Because Bhāgavatas are learning everything. Brahmins are becoming office workers and secular teachers; some Brahmins are becoming poor. Therefore, there is equalisation going on. After 500 years, there will be no caste. Or maybe this will take only twenty years. There have been many changes in society. Before, non-Brahmins were prohibited from entering a 1-kilometre area around Brahmin establishments. That no longer occurs.

When I asked Balakrishnan about his political affiliation, he said:

> I don't belong to a political party. Last time, I voted DMK. Even though Karunanidhi is an atheist, which is bad, he believes in no caste. Therefore, I like this party's position. Before that, I had voted twenty years for Congress, because I like Gandhi's philosophy.

The next year, when I visited Triplicane, I enquired about the government school and was told that it was no longer running after a year. No one knew why, although there were speculations. According to one person, the government was just politically motivated and not interested in carrying through its plan. Of course, there was also a case before the Supreme Court; authorities might have decided to await the outcome. I will return to this topic of access to the priesthood in Chapter 7.

The Lawyer and his Service

V. Raza Narayanan started the interview by telling me that he belongs to the Nayaka (that is, the Vanniyar) caste.

> Nayakas were once warriors and therefore are technically Kṣatriyas who descended from Pallava and Cōḻa rulers. Many generations ago, my family had a palace near Chidambaram. I was born into a Vaiṣṇava family. The word 'Hindu' for identification is new. Before, people said that they belonged to a Vaiṣṇava family or a Śaiva one. On the front door of my house is a huge *nāmam*. My grandfather, Mr Sadar Adikesavalu Nayakar, who wore a big *nāmam*, lived in Madurantakam, where Rāmānuja long ago had received *samāśrayaṇam*. My grandparents dressed as traditional Śrīvaiṣṇavas. My grandfather wore a dhoti and had a hair tuft like the Brahmins. Unlike the Brahmins, he wore a turban. My grandfather had initiation at Sriperumbudur.
>
> During the lifetime of Gandhi, my family supported the Congress party. In 1939, my grandfather gave the welcome address to Gandhi when he came to Chennai. My father, a lawyer, was a great orator in both Tamil and English. A freedom fighter and Member of the Legislative Assembly (MLA), he attended the first Indian parliamentary constituent assembly, which was set up in 1946, and was a member of the first parliament after independence in 1947. He wrote about Vaiṣṇavism. After his death, I collected his essays into three books and published them. And I endowed a lecture series in his honour. My mother also studied law. She did not finish, however, because she

> had me. I, too, am a lawyer. My daughter, however, wants to be an engineer.

Our conversation turned to religion. Raza described his daily religious activities and his views on some Śrīvaiṣṇava traditions.

> In the morning, I chant the *Tiruppaḷḷāṇṭu, Tirupaḷḷeḻucci, Tiruppāvai, Kaṇṇinuṇciṟuttāmpu* and twelve songs about Lord Parthasarathy. I do this while going about my work, because I must do my karma and prepare for court. Then, I offer *tulasī* at my home shrine. I don't sit to chant, because that is just to impress others. My life is very hectic. Yesterday alone, I had to appear for three cases in three courts in three parts of the city. My duty is to protect my clients, and so work must take precedence over religion. Still, I manage to read religious books in bed at night and listen to religious cassettes.
>
> I oppose *samāśrayaṇam*, because it is not practical. It makes me leave my own traditions and lifestyle, making me a slave to the Brahmins. Take a Brahmin as an *ācārya*, and you become a slave to him. In *Gītā* 18:66, Lord Krishna says, 'leave all *dharma*s and come to me' [in other words, reject all duties of caste and stage of life, according to some interpretations; there are others]. Āṇṭāḷ's *Tiruppāvai* 5 says, 'We have come to you pure.' This doesn't mean having a sacred bath, rather, having a pure heart. One should bring pure flowers and worship only with love.
>
> People should stand on their own two legs. 'Give them fishing rods, not fish.' It is important to teach skills. For development, there should be no discrimination. Today, according to the government, anyone can be a priest. Even now, many non-Brahmins are priests. Non-Brahmins are better chanters and orators than Brahmins. Brahmins just want money, although they claim that they have better qualifications, including knowledge of the Veda, ability to preach, expertise to perform ritual *yāgam*s, competent teaching and contacts necessary for donations. Show me one Brahmin who has all of these qualifications.
>
> Brahmins are just Brahmins by skin colour. In fact, the one whom they think is their father might not be their real

father, for only a mother knows for sure. Rather, someone who knows Brahman, the supreme reality, is a Brahmin. If you call yourself a doctor, you must know medicine. And so, if you call yourself a Brahmin, you must know the Veda. Wearing a *dhoti* and *nāmam* is not enough. Do the Brahmins at Parthasarathy temple know the *āḻvārs*' names and titles of their works?[47] No. By contrast, I know all the *āḻvārs*' verses by heart.

We must conduct religious camps for Vaiṣṇavas. There is not enough infrastructure. There should be services for children, such as evening schools on each street. Children should memorise the short *āḻvār* works and participate in prayer meetings. Forget the Sanskrit Vedas. The New Testament (the Tamil hymns of the *āḻvārs*) has come, so let the Old Testament (the Veda) go. It is useless, when the Tamil Veda is here.

One should go to Tirupati for devotion, not for bargaining with God, as in 'If I give you X, you give me Y.' When I go to any temple, I go just to chant the *āḻvār* songs about that temple. I don't go to beg. God has given me everything. I need nothing more. We should go to our God to thank him, not to beg. If you ask him for something, this means that you don't believe he will give you that. Just thanking God is true devotion. Tirupati is lots of 'business'.

I want Vaiṣṇavism to be everywhere, because I feel that everyone is a Vaiṣṇava. Viṣṇu is the pervader. He is in everyone. Therefore, I say, 'don't discriminate. When he is in even the non-living, how can you discriminate among living things?' A Vaiṣṇava is for all and in all. Therefore, a Vaiṣṇava should go to all. This is a simple religion with a high philosophy, which everyone can practice. If you feel part of God, there can be no enmity with anyone. There should be no discrimination against anyone. Therefore, this is the only religion that can survive. It is for the people of the world. Even Christians and Muslims are really Vaiṣṇavas, although they might not know this. God is in churches and mosques, too.

Religion has nothing to do with politics. The Bharatiya Janata Party is just using religion. Politicians are only

> interested in religion to gain the votes of the devotees. Because of vote-bank politics, they have little interest at heart in the people. For us, God and service to him are more important than politics.

It was obvious that Raza's religious life was an expression of *kaiṅkarya*. He wanted to communicate his knowledge to others.

> I lecture on the *Tiruppāvai* during the thirty days of Mārkaḻi. Whenever I am invited to lecture, I do. I refuse to accept money for this. It is my donation to the Vaiṣṇava Mahasangam. Nothing can be better than the *āḻvār*s. They wanted to be near the people in a language that the people can understand. They created a Veda in Tamil.

One evening, I went to the Sri Manavala Mamunigal temple (at Alwarpet, a neighbourhood of Chennai), an important non-Brahmin Chennai temple, where Raza was teaching a group of Bhāgavatas how to recite and understand the *āḻvār* hymns. He had told me that this is a temple without discrimination: no class, no gender, and no dress distinctions. His commitment to this temple is strong. Several years later, in October 2015, I noticed on the Internet that he was lecturing there on the first three *āḻvār*s. Raza was also active in a major non-Brahmin organisation.

> I have been the general secretary of the Vaiṣṇava Mahasangam, which is sponsored by the Narayana Dhanam Trust. It began in 1925, when five non-Brahmins were attending a Vaiṣṇava conference in Triplicane. They were asked to leave and told that they had no right to hear these things and no right to sit with the Brahmins. Because Raghava Ramanuja Swami wanted to have a common platform so that all Bhāgavatas could have access to knowledge and discussion, he started the Vaiṣṇava Mahasangam. A women's section began in 1930; it argued for the rights of women to maintenance and property. Every month, we meet to propagate Vaiṣṇavism.
>
> All the *āḻvār*s' birthdays are celebrated. Bhāgavatas sit together and read that *āḻvār*'s hymns. There is no discrimination. All are welcome. Women come as well as

> men. There are no dress rules, no caste restrictions. Even Muslims and Christians have attended for 'knowledge'. Those who come are given a copy of the *Divyaprabandham* and pictures of the *āḻvārs*, first one and eventually all twelve. After that, they receive statues of them. The *pūjā* is done by the devotees, the Rāmānuja Dāsas. It includes chanting from the *Divyaprabandham* and *ārātti*. *Ārātti* merely takes the evil spirits away. For Brahmins, *ārātti* is a custom only to collect money.

I learned that this annual four-day conference of the Vaisnava Mahasangam attracts non-Brahmins (mainly Vanniyars) from all over Tamil Nadu. It takes place during December, in an elegant old colonial building on Govindappa-naicken Street (in the Georgetown area in Chennai), which had once belonged to Vuppattur Alvarchetty (a Vaiśya businessman and philanthropist). He bequeathed it to Vaiṣṇavas for use as a *rāmānuja kūṭam*. Members rent it out for Vaiṣṇava marriages, meetings, and other events.

The main hall is decorated with a collection of old Tanjavur glass paintings that illustrate the *Rāmāyaṇa*. It also has a large picture of P. B. Annangaracariyar (1874–1936) of Kanchipuram. According to K. K. A. Venkatachari, he was a Brahmin Teṉkaḷai Śrīvaiṣṇava, learned scholar, a marvellous orator with a wonderful memory and voice, famous author,[48] and editor of five magazines. He regularly gave discourses here, but would stop them during the conference, which he supported strongly.

The day that I visited was the seventy-fifth anniversary of the women's organisation, and one of the two days of the annual event especially for women. (Another day was for youth.) Because this was the month of Mārkaḻi, there were lectures on Āṇṭāḷ. One woman told me that Āṇṭāḷ is an important model of empowerment, because she had gathered together girls for their ritual bath, and to serve the Lord. 'If women act collectively in the name of the Lord,' she said, 'they will be empowered.'

That day, the organisation was also honouring thirty-eight authors who had written books on Vaiṣṇavism, mainly in Tamil. And it was honouring those over seventy who had dedicated themselves to service in temple kitchens, gardens, and *rāmānuja kūṭams*; they are Śrīvaiṣṇava *selvar*s ('royal' people in the service of God). In addition, there were daily concerts and speeches by Bhāgavatas from all over south India. And there was a communal evening meal.

Raza had a very broad concept of service, which went far beyond his religious activities as *kaiṅkarya*:

> I am also secretary of the Bharat Sewak Samaj. It is a pan-Indian organization, founded by former Prime Minister Nehru. It has chapters all over India. It is intended for social workers and is secular. There is a three-month training programme in social work for college students, which leads to a certificate. Students go to orphanages, schools for the blind, and so forth to see the real world. They are taught about the importance of working actively to benefit society.
>
> The Bharat Sewak Samaj has a students' wing, a youth wing and leadership camps. Funding comes from patrons and friends, not the government, which would make it political and therefore subservient to government bureaucracy. Every month, the organisation celebrates a national leader's birthday. In this way, it provides role models for young people. I am a member of the Humour Club as well. It is open to everyone and teaches people how to criticise others with laughter and politeness. Some go on to have careers in films. As well, I encourage drama and music *sabhās* and studies of contemporary society.

Service was certainly a common orientation for my informants, although the specific activities varied from one person to another.

The Lord's Proselytiser

T. Bhasya Ramanuja Dasar belongs to the Beri Cettiyar,[49] a caste of small businessmen. He grew up in Tirumani, near Chengalpattu. He has lived in Chennai for many years. Varataa

Ethiraja Jeeyar of Sriperumbudur initiated him. When I visited Bhasya, he was in the Sri Nampillai Sabhai, in Chintadripet near Mount Road, the oldest part of Chennai.

> The *sabhā*, founded in 1889 by some Bhāgavatas, is named after the thirteenth-century figure Nampiḷḷai, who had given many learned yet popular discourses on the *Tiruvāymoḻi*, which were recounted by Vaṭakku Tiruvīti Piḷḷai in his commentary known as the *Īṭu*. This *sabhā* used to meet every Saturday in the front yard of the house of a Śrīvaiṣṇava who gave talks on religion.
>
> In 1980, Krishnaswami Reddiyar, a justice in the Madras High Court, was elected president of the *sabhā* and, with his new committee, collected money through donations and loans to construct a new building, which opened in 1990. This building has three shops in it; the income from the rent in addition to donations from devotees make possible the daily *pūjā* to the pictures of God Rāma and others kept on the premises. Ten or fifteen years ago, I took over the maintenance of the *sabhā*'s building and manage it.
>
> Every week, a Bhāgavata lectures on Śrīvaiṣṇava thought and someone else teaches the *Divyaprapandham* in a traditional way: a teacher reads one line from a stanza, and the student repeats it three times. At monthly meetings, members talk about spreading Vaiṣṇavism. Every month, the birth stars, that is, the birthdays, of the *āḻvār*s and *ācārya*s born in that month are celebrated by singing all 4,000 verses.
>
> During the festival that celebrates Rāmānuja's birthday (*brahmotsavam*), the *sabhā* conducts a camp at Sriperumbudur to teach Bhāgavatas the meanings of Amutaṉār's *Rāmānuja Nuṟṟantāti* in praise of Rāmānuja. During November and December (the lunar month of Kārttikai), the *sabhā* conducts its annual festival of Nampiḷḷai for ten days, and Bhāgavatas recite the 4,000 hymns. It gives prizes to students who came first in Tamil in the state and the district. Also, it gives free school uniforms and books for five students in the immediate area, provides medical help for others, serves a free lunch

> for 100 people at a local temple, and provides buttermilk to devotees who pull the temple chariot on festival days at the Sriperumbudur and Triplicane temples.
>
> Bhāgavata leaders have devoted themselves to educating Bhāgavatas about their religious tradition by publishing cheap Tamil pamphlets and books. I myself have brought out many such publications, some of them for free distribution.

Bhasya showed me some of these magazines and booklets, which contain articles by him and others. Many contained basic information and edifying stories about the tradition. One issue of the magazine *Eṇṇāyiramum Irāmānucaruman*, for example, includes the story of Rāmānuja's preference for a poor woman—she is willing to prostitute herself to get money to buy food for him and his entourage—instead of his richer and more egotistical disciples.

Another publication provides a collection of verses from the *Divyaprabandham*, which are often recited together.[50] The booklet *Śrī Kūrattāḻvāṉ* provides a short biography of Kūrattāḻvāṉ (Kūreśa), who was Rāmānuja's scribe. An issue of *Tirumāmakaḷ* comments at length on a stanza of Amutaṉar's *Rāmānuja Nuṟṟantāti*, discusses the importance of two months, Kārttikai and Mārkaḻi, for Vaiṣṇavas, and analyses one stanza from the *Tiruppāvai*.

These publications include discussions about problems that Śrīvaiṣṇavism is facing and what to do about them. *Śrīvaiṇavar: Yesterday, Today, and Tomorrow*, for instance, discusses the future of Vaiṣṇavism and makes the following suggestions: Bhāgavatas should avoid preachers who cannot describe religious matters properly for the common people, and they should criticise those who commercialise Vaiṣṇavism, or claim to be collecting money for local temples, while actually stealing it. In addition, they should criticise those who claim that they are protecting Vaiṣṇavism, despite the fact that they can recite only a few Sanskrit stanzas.

An article by Bhasya in the *Tirumāmakaḷ*[51] says that *ācārya*s and *jīyar*s, in earlier times, discussed the problems of

Śrīvaiṣṇavas. The *ācārya* lineages have virtually disappeared today. The *jīyar*s who head the *maṭha*s come with their disciples in six or seven cars to attend functions with 'pomp and show', and then return to their comfortable *maṭha*s, which are 'like heaven'. Some of these *maṭha*s are accountable to no one, including the government (even though the government partially regulates the big ones). *Maṭha*s now control the lands that had been donated to Śrīvaiṣṇava temples; the *jīyar*s spend the income for display, though, and not for the benefit of religion. Many *maṭha*s do not even have complete records of their own properties and therefore lose an enormous amount of money. Moreover, temples now use 200 litres of milk every month for bathing Rāmānuja's image during the celebration of the birth-star (birthday) of Rāmānuja. The *jīyar*s, however, refrain from criticising this extravagance.

And here is another problem. Temples hide their wealth, so communities do not know how much there is. Recently, in the birthplace of Kūreśa, the priest's son stole the temple's jewels and sold them. Only after a month did the villagers hear about this. Magazines reported very different amounts of what was stolen. With a proper board in control, of course, the true value would have been clear to everyone. In short, *maṭha*s that do not follow the tradition strictly are beneficial to neither devotees nor the public.

Consider the case of the son of a Brahmin priest who had married a Muslim woman. He wanted to be a priest. Because the temple rejected him, he went to court and won the case. No Śrīvaiṣṇava *maṭha* objected. Even though this case occurred outside Tamil Nadu, says the author, it could be used as a precedent in Tamil Nadu (presumably for Muslim control of Hindu temples or government control of religion). The article concludes that these irresponsible *jīyar*s should be relegated to the 'garden', since they cannot return to family life and should not participate in temple life.

In this publication, Bhasya describes other problems that the *jīyar*s ignore. One is connecting Rāmānuja with astrology. About ten years ago, an astrologer announced that anyone affected in his or her horoscope by Rahu (a shadowy planet) should perform the bathing ritual with milk to an image of Rāmānuja. Although there was no precedent for this, no *jīyar* objected. Moreover, someone published an astrological book and claimed that it was a genuine work of Rāmānuja. No *jīyar* objected or bothered to find out the truth. Bhasya tells us that he himself objected in his journal and made the publisher apologise. Then there was the matter of Agnihotra Ramanuja Tattacarya, who wrote in a general magazine about Lord Raṅganātha's sex life with goddess Lakṣmī. Many Śrīvaiṣṇavas found this article disturbing, Bhasya remarked, because it created the 'wrong impression'. Once again, comments Bhasya, the *jīyars* ignored a significant problem.

These discussions of problems in the magazines are interspersed with advice on how to handle them. One is to engage the younger generation in religious affairs. Young people should take responsibility for giving lectures on Vaiṣṇava subjects in a language that everyone can understand. More generally, every village and thickly-populated non-Brahmin district in a city should have a *bhajana maṭha* or *bhajana kōyiḷ*, where people can gather once a week, or even more often, to sing the *Divyaprapandham* or Rāma or Krishna *bhajanas* to the beat of cymbals. More than 10 of these groups meet in Chennai. Moreover, Śrīvaiṣṇavas should use these occasions to promote the *sampradāya* and invite other good Śrīvaiṣṇava scholars to deliver special lectures.

As for the *maṭhas*, Bhasya points out that a board of honest and impartial Vaiṣṇavas should control them and their funds should be available to all Vaiṣṇava temples. On a more political note, Bhasya tells readers to give their votes only to politicians who support their local temples.[52]

These articles by Bhasya provide examples of how the printing press has helped democratise knowledge. It has encouraged Bhāgavatas to educate other Bhāgavatas on their own terms and in their own *sabhā* communities.

Bhasya told me about the Srivainavar Peravai, an organisation that he began in 1998 in his village (Tirumani), and has continued to lead from its subsequent base in Chennai. It now has 1,500 chapters all over Tamil Nadu. Its purpose is to discuss non-Brahmin social problems and to recruit non-Brahmins to Śrīvaiṣṇavism. The chapters, he explained, are established in the following way.

> Members of the Srivainavar Peravai might alert a village that members, usually about twelve, will arrive to tell them about Śrīvaiṣṇavism and its *sabhā* organisations. Or a village might request their visit. The Srivainavar Peravai group travels in a big van, covering fifteen to twenty villages in a day. In the villages, they chant verses from the *Divyaprabandham*, accompanied by drums and harmoniums.[53] They march through the streets carrying pictures of Rāmānuja and Āṇṭāḷ, eventually collecting 100 or 200 people. In the city of Cuddalore, as many as 2,000 joined the procession.
>
> In addition to this *nagara-saṅkīrtana* (singing *saṅkīrtana*s in the city), they do the following: lecture, distribute free copies of the *Tiruppāvai* or the *Divyaprabandham*, and hold *bhajana* competitions for people who come from several villages and compete for prizes such as a harmonium. They also give plates that have been embossed with pictures of Rāmānuja to Śrīvaiṣṇavas who did something special, such as travelling 11,000 kilometres to many of the *divyadeśa*s.
>
> Today, Bhāgavatas' chanting of verses in the *sabhā*s and during visits to villages draws on both the Śrīvaiṣṇava tradition and that of pan-Indian *bhajana*s.

Bhasya described how the ritual called *bhajana paddhati* began during the fifteenth century in Tirupati and took definitive shape during the eighteenth in Tanjavur. This is a sequence of songs by poet-composers. They describe people who seek communion with God.[54] Simon Leopold thinks that the ritualised march of the Śrīvaiṣṇava *nagara-saṅkīrtana*, organised by the urban Bhāgavatas, might have originated in a Smārta procession called *uñcchavṛtti*. Devotees acted out the life of Tyāgarāja (1767–1847) in public processions through villages in the area of Tanjavur. But, I think, one need not turn to a Smārta procession for origin; processions have been ubiquitous in Tamil Nadu and elsewhere.

In 'Aims and Objectives of the Śrīvaiṇavar Peravai', Bhasya comments:

> you can see real Vaiṣṇavism only in villages. This is why we travel to so many of them, now over 6,000, to give lectures. The Peravai also visits schools. In Cuddalore, for instance, we gave *Tiruppāvai*s to 1,200 students and sent circulars to announce that a teacher would be available to prepare the kids for competitions. Later, the students took tests. They had to recite all twenty-nine stanzas and interpret some of them.[55]

A proselytising perspective, I would add, lies at the core of Śrīvaiṣṇavism. Bhasya mentions a hagiographic story about Rāmānuja. When he goes to worship, he holds the hands of his two disciples, Mutaliyāṇṭāṉ and Piḷḷāṉ. One time, Mutaliyāṇṭāṉ says, 'In all *deśa*s, and in whatever time, may the great valor of Rāmānuja grow and grow without any obstruction.' Then Piḷḷāṉ composes a verse, which says that the divine commandments of Rāmānuja should grow every year, reach all the directions and shine. Another pious man holds Rāmānuja's hand and, alluding to him, says: 'May the concept of Śrīman, the wealth of Srirangam, increase'.[56]

In fact, says the scholar Kandadai Seshadri (whose book was published in 1998), until recently the *ācārya*s would visit villages, where they were treated with acts of hospitality. They not only gave religious talks and answered questions about the religion, but they also tried to resolve disputes so that villagers did not have to resort to the feudal courts, and would accept the decision because of its religious sanctity. The *ācārya*s also intervened on behalf of the Vaiṣṇava outcastes 'to lessen their burden'.[57] According to K. K. A. Venkatachari, although Śrīvaiṣṇava *ācārya*s themselves went to the villages by bullock cart to spread Śrīvaiṣṇavism, they stopped doing so in the twentieth century because land-redistribution programmes and secular jobs took too much of their resources and time.[58]

I sensed that there was considerable competition among religious sects. One Bhāgavata told me that for the past sixty years, many non-Brahmins have been attracted to the Ayyapa tradition. Another Bhāgavata said that the Ayyapa religion offered more worldly benefits (he did not say what these were) than worshipping Nārāyaṇa did. As a good Śrīvaiṣṇava, however, he would not go to another deity. Some Sai Baba disciples once asked him to give a lecture to them. He refused to wear their *vibhūti*, however, and thought only of God Nārāyaṇa as they were chanting their mantras.

Vaiṣṇavas compete with Śaivas as well. Another Bhāgavata told me that Śaivism might attract more Bhāgavatas than Vaiṣṇavism because their temples are less strict than Śrīvaiṣṇava ones. If one wants to go to the Śrīvaiṣṇava temple after work and is dressed in Western clothes, one may not enter the sanctum. This is not the case in Śaiva temples. Bhasya noted that Śaivas invite Śrīvaiṣṇavas to recite the *Tiruvempāvai* and *Tiruppāvai*, and both communities now join together to recite these popular poems during the month of Mārkaḻi—but Śaivas do not allow Śrīvaiṣṇavas to distribute *Tiruppāvai*s.

When I asked Bhasya if these non-Brahmin organisations are connected with the national BJP or the RSS, he replied, 'These Śrīvaiṣṇava organisations are purely religious.'

The Business Family's Reflections

I am in a taxi going along Poonamalle High Road in Chennai, looking for Pettukola Towers. And there it is. A grand high-rise, a sign of Chennai's economic boom. It is obviously owned by the family that I am about to interview, the Pettukolas, because I had already learned that they are a very prosperous Vaiśya (non-Brahmin, twice-born) family with businesses in pharmaceuticals, hospital equipment, and many other things. India is known as the pharmacy of the world, and Chennai is one of its hubs. After introductions, my conversation about religion with several family members—Mr Pettukola senior

(Pettukola Sriramulu Bhashyam), his wife (Pettukola Kalavathi Bhashyam), and their son Gnaneshwar Pettukola—begins.

> Mr Pettukola senior: 'We are a Telugu Vaiśya (Arya Vysya) family, originally from Andhra.[59] My parents were Śrīvaiṣṇavas and had *samāśrayaṇam*. My mother was a great devotee. I wear the sacred thread. My son doesn't, saying that it is too hard to keep clean.'
>
> Mrs. Pettukola: 'My father was a Śrīvaiṣṇava scholar, like a Brahmin, and studied the Brahmasūtras. Someone taught him Vedas in his small town. People used to prostrate themselves to him. My father was a lawyer and businessman.'
>
> Mr Pettukola senior: 'Brahmins had a monopoly. Periyar led the non-Brahmins. Now non-Brahmins want to rule rather than the higher castes. That is good. The country is so changed. What is this distinction between Brahmins and non-Brahmins? The Brahmins' memory is well-developed. Because of millennia of discipline, they have become so clever. Despite that, today their children go to parties just like *śūdras*. People should learn the general principles of Śrīvaiṣṇavism, such as total surrender to God, and eliminate the Vedas and the priests who do Āgamic rituals.'
>
> Gnaneshwar Pettukola: 'Every Indian now says this is my country. This was a very distinctive development, because it was done peacefully. I am attracted to Gandhi.' Changing the topic, he recounted an adage: 'The *servant* asks, "why is the master ... doing *pūjās*?" The servant takes jaggery (a form of cane sugar) in his hand and calls [God] Nārāyaṇa ... saying "come". Then Nārāyaṇa comes. Nārāyaṇa eats the jaggery. The *master* says, "I've been doing *pūjā*, but he [God] never came." Then he prostrates himself before the servant and says, "you are a real Nārāyaṇa devotee."'
>
> Mr Pettukola senior: 'I used to do *kuṇḍalinī* yoga and sit for three hours. I would ask Gnaneswar, when he was a small boy, to sit for an hour. *Sādhana* is to purify you for God's grace. Still, there are easier methods. Now, I do

mental *pūjā*, simple yogic postures and *japa*-chanting of the names of many deities. I am a Vaiśya and have learned to get around in this world. Similarly, we need the help of the nine *navagrahas* (planets), the *devatās* (minor deities) and finally Lord Nārāyaṇa. I worship Nārāyaṇa-Viṣṇu because Vēṅkateśvara is our family deity. It is important to get the real principles. *Bhakti* is an emotional approach. I don't accept the literalism of Vaikuṇṭha, supreme heaven, or the Ocean of Milk, the cosmic ocean. They are symbols. We need name and form only for concentration.'

Gnaneshwar Pettukola: 'If I call it a mere symbol, then I won't be devout.'

Mr Pettukola senior: 'The common person requires something concrete. Ramakrishna says, "Kill, the goddess, to go to the next stage." I exercise the mind. I believe in the *arcā* (the image) because it is there in me. It is a means, like it was for the Buddha, not an end. All is *māyā*, illusion. It is my limitation. Ultimately there is only the perception of truth within. The ego creates differences; the higher identity is beyond difference. We reach Nārāyaṇa or Śiva or whatever god. I am secular yet deeply religious. One should meditate with a pure mind and get the nectar of immortality.'

Gnaneshwar Pettukola: 'We are all created through the grace of the Lord. God acts through man. Nothing is good or bad. I am against actions to fulfill desires (*kāmya-karma*).'

Mr Pettukola senior: 'Karma, through parents, is genetically structured. Do you have to submit to it? Man can change and purify himself. When one believes in God, karma is mitigated. Grace comes in; bad things go away. Truth is changeless, eternal. Science is the essence of *dharma* (the order of the universe); it is the essence of the Vedas. This is all true science. Our stories are an allegory of science. The story of churning the milk ocean, for instance, is about evolution; everything started from the ocean. Permanent truths are the expression of the essence of the Vedas. When my wife was pregnant, she listened to auspicious sounds—works such as the *Viṣṇu-sahasranāma*

> and the *Suprabhātam*. Vedic knowledge is subtle science today.'

I sometimes ran into Gnaneshwar at a coffee shop and occasionally met him and his wife Ramā—who runs IND RASAYAN (a large private company) with her husband—for dinner. Our conversations focussed on Śrīvaiṣṇavism, although my summary here draws mainly from Gnaneshwar's three essays, which are now on his blog.[60] They express his own existential involvement with Śrīvaiṣṇavism. This is focussed on the concept of *prapatti* or surrender, and how this should be understood as a universal and not a parochial concept.

Gnaneshwar argues his case by drawing on proof texts from the *āḻvār*s and *ācārya*s. First, there are millions of devotees who visit Viṣṇu temples across the world, even though they do not categorise themselves formally as Vaiṣṇavas. Second, in an egalitarian society, who can deny these devotees their surrender to God? Third, Śrīvaiṣṇavism promises easy accessibility to God through surrender, so there can be no restrictions on access, such as a person's village, family, and caste. Fourth, Śrīvaiṣṇavism says that devotees may worship God in whatever form they want. Fifth, the *nāyaṉmār*s, who lived at the same time as the *āḻvār*s, did *prapatti* to Lord Śiva. So, all people surrender to the one God who is known by different names. Sixth, because Śrīvaiṣṇava theology has been the subject of research by scholars from religions across the world, it is obvious that its teachings hold great appeal to non-Vaiṣṇavas as well. Seventh, Śrīvaiṣṇavism teaches that God dwells within every individual as the *antaryāmi*. A person who is aware of this will strive to uplift society at large, without considering caste or religion.

Because of this universalistic aspect of Śrīvaiṣṇavism, Gnaneshwar thinks that it should be popularised for the benefit of all mankind.

> I wish to state that if I, as a Vaishnavite, live in an illusory denial that these great truths are to be adhered to only by those born into my religion or sect, it would be like

> a Gujarati born into the community to which Mohandas Karamchand Gandhi belonged, declaring that the Mahatma's *satyāgraha* cannot be performed by anyone other than members of his own community.[61]

Gnaneshwar tries to reconcile the idea of Śrīvaiṣṇavism's universalistic teachings with the reality of its division into two rival sects (the Tenkalai and the Vaṭakalai) by locating all their similarities and showing how misinterpretations have arisen over different emphases.

> Therefore, friends, we have seen that in several aspects there is an identity of intention in the minds of the Ācāryas of the Tenkalais and Vadakalais. As in the words of [Vedanta] Desika himself .... The differences therefore lie in the interpretations only ... we can still stand rigid dwelling upon the many differences of opinion on intricate doctrinaire issues. If we imprison our minds thus in prejudice, we do ourselves a great disservice; for the Lord stands beckoning to us all in his limitless grace and I would rather partake in His bliss than allow my distrust and disbelief in one tradition or the other prevent me from partaking in that joy. For as Mao, the Chinese leader, once said, it does not matter whether the cat is black or white as long as it catches the mouse.[62]

In his essay on Nammāḻvār, Gnaneshwar begins by noting that Nammāḻvār praises Nārāyaṇa as the supreme god who is superior to all other gods. Although Gnaneshwar admits that this sounds like parochial dogma, or even bigotry, he argues that it is really a matter of unshakable faith that has completely transformed the person, as does the miraculous healing of a terminal illness or the ability to walk on fire.

Gnaneshwar often turns to modern analogies to elucidate his theological point and to appeal to young people. He makes references to shooting stars, genetic codes, scientists such as Einstein, or technology such as the Hubble telescope. With reference to faith, for instance, he points out that just as a printer will print data only when connected to the central processing unit of the computer, so the soul will find supreme bliss only when utterly dependent on the Lord.[63] Put otherwise, one must reject the idea of independence.

Gnaneshwar's own service, or *kaiṅkarya*, is to help revive the Sriperumbudur Sanskrit College[64] (Ubhaya Vedanta Vardhi), which was established in 1872 by Sri Singam Chetty Ateendrooloo Chetty Garu, a Telugu-speaking man. It has had the patronage of several Chetty caste people, if I judge correctly from its list of past presidents. It has been affiliated with the University of Madras, moreover, for post-graduate studies in Sanskrit grammar and logic. Today, its mission statement is about providing Sanskrit instruction for 'school going children who are eager to imbibe their ancient traditions', because 'it is a fact that Sanskrit, being an important medium towards this end, is becoming a much-demanded subject'.[65] Its website announces a lecture series called Svatantra Chintana (Freedom of Thought) in the Department of Sanskrit at the University of Madras.

My next meeting with Gnaneshwar was in 2016. We discussed whether non-Brahmins should be trained as priests and what that might involve. We also discussed the many social changes occurring in south Indian society, and how challenging arranging marriages and parenting had become as young people became more independent.

The Merchant and his Medium

In Chennai, I visited P. V. Prasad and his 86-year-old uncle in an elegant old house. Prasad first briefed me on the family's history.

> We belong to the Balija (Naidu) Puligar community. Balijas were chieftains in the early sixteenth century under the Vijayanagara ruler Krishnadevaraya. Our mother tongue is Telugu. Our family had land in a village called Arani in north Arcot district. We were camphor and diamond merchants. About 100 years ago, the family came to Chennai.

> The family still has a temple in Walajahpet, north Arcot (now Tiruvallur district). It was built about three or four generations back, because at that time no member of our family had children and hoped that if they built a temple, God would grace them with progeny. It is called Śrīnivāsa Perumāḷ temple. We hire a Brahmin priest, a Pañcarātrin, to do the worship with a mantra ending with *namaḥ*. This is the style of worship in the Telugu communities of this area. It is difficult to get a priest today. We are very lucky, because this priest has worked for us for thirty-five years, and his son might continue because he has had no modern education.
>
> We have not had *samāśrayaṇam*, mainly because we don't want to give up eating meat. Even many Brahmins now are not vegetarian. They are no longer strict in their values and lifestyle and have become Westernised. The *nāmam* is worn mainly by Brahmins; we wear only a red dot.

When I asked about their daily *pūjā*, the old man found a little booklet in Telugu script, containing the Strī Stuti, Viṣṇusahasranāma, Śrī Sūktam, Rāma Stotra and Āditya Stotra, and read a bit from this. Then Prasad told me the following. 'I know no *āḻvār* hymns; rather, I only chant the mantra *oṁ namo nārāyaṇāya*. Sometimes, I visit Viṣṇu, Hari Hara, Śiva and Murukaṉ temples. I go to Tirupati every year and Srirangam once every three or four years.'

Prasad's religious life extends beyond Śrīvaiṣṇavism. This takes us to Agastiya. Hindus believe that Agastiya was one of the seven ancient Vedic sages. In south India, his followers think that he is the transmitter of Siddha medicine from Lord Murukaṉ and also the guru of spiritual adepts called *siddha*s (*cittar*), who have eight supernatural powers. Prasad comments:

> My guru is Agastiya, one of the eighteen *siddha*s. Today, the medium for Agastiya is Subramaniya, a farmer from the Nayakar (Vanniyar) community who lives in the village Walajahpet where our temple is. When renovating the temple, I was told by a gentleman in the village

about Subramaniya and went to meet him. There is a group of about twelve people who follow this medium. I travel about 160 kilometres every month to visit him. However, I talk by phone every day with him. This helps me understand Hindu philosophy and the experiences I have with chanting mantras.

The Sattadas at Sriperumbudur

On the way from Chennai to Sriperumbudur to interview some Sattadas, K. K. A. Venkatachari gave me background information on this endogamous group, which does various jobs in the temple. 'Sattadas go to *ācārya*s and *jīyar*s for *samāśrayaṇam*,' he said. 'Today, my relative Koyil Andan Swami, for instance, does initiation for those at Sriperumbudur.'

Venkatachari remarked, 'I remember one time when the priests brought water from the lake to the Sriperumbudur temple. They did this every morning. Each day, a Sattada followed the procession, entered the temple and prostrated himself before God. One day, he didn't get up for some time. Then everyone realised that he had died.' Venkatachari's reminiscences quickly came to an end as we saw the *gopuram*s of the Sriperumbudur temple on the horizon. Soon, we were at the home of a Sattada named Srinivasin. He narrated the following:

> My family is the only Sattada family left in Sriperumbudur, although there are more in Kanchipuram. My grandfather, Narasimha, who died in 1990, was a Sattada at the Sriperumbudur temple. My father works in the temple, as do I. Devotees may put offerings on a plate, which comes to us. My other brother Raghavan works in the electrical business; his income is an important resource for supporting our family.
>
> The traditional job of Sattadas is temple service. We prepare for the daily temple *pūjā*s, which take place from 7–11 in the morning and 4.30–9 in the evening. We make the garlands, for instance. Only Sattadas make the

> garlands that have the image of a parrot created from leaves and flowers; these are the garlands associated with Āṇṭāḷ. Both men and women make garlands; only men offer them in the temple. Sattada women have no other specific religious jobs. In addition, we keep the temple keys, buy groceries for the temple, carry the images on a palanquin in processions, protect the deities' ornaments, and keep crowds in order at festival times. During processions outside the temple, we protect the image and carry the torch. At Sriperumbudur, Sattadas have a separate trust that feeds Sattadas at festival times.

I interviewed Cakrapani, too, who belongs to another Sattada family. He began by recounting the history of the Sattadas, especially their role of protecting the temple images when they were about to be destroyed by the Muslims. 'The Sattadas are equal to Brahmins,' he said, 'but do not wear the sacred thread, because when they have to do the worship five times a day, it is too much.' He did not tell me why it is too much.

> I'm a fifth-generation Sattada here. One hundred years ago, there were twenty-five Sattada families in Sriperumbudur. Others are at Srirangam, Srivilliputur, Alvartirunagari and Tirukkoyilur. Members of my family still do some service in the temple, although usually not in a formal sense. When they do service, they are paid for their time. Today, many Sattadas, including my own people, are acting as priests in Vaiṣṇava temples, mostly village ones.

Learning about the decline of the Sattada tradition in major temples, I asked him if this was a sign that Hinduism will die out.

> It won't die out. Hinduism survived through Muslim and British rule. The tradition will go on. We have our gurus. Of course, there will be some changes in our way of life. There were periodic reforms in the past and will be today as well. The 1,000-year anniversary of the birth of Kūreśa, Rāmānuja's scribe, is this year.

Back in Chennai, I went to the home of Dr Rajagopalam, a Sattada and former schoolteacher, who had completed his Ph.D. at Bharathiar University in Coimbatore in 1993, and had retired in 1995. His desire for learning was inspired by his father who ran a school, was a scholar in Telugu and Tamil, and read many books. Rajagopalam was initiated by Varataa Ethiraja Jeeyar of Sriperumbudur and has memorised all 4,000 verses of the *āḻvār*s. He recites most often the *Tiruppāvai, Tirupallāṇṭu*, and *Tirupaḷḷiyeḻucci*. Here is his take on Sattada history:

> Sattada is the name of our community in Tamil Nadu; Chāttāda is the name in Andhra. Sattada refers to those without the sacred thread and who are not registered at the temple for the right to recite the *Divyaprabandham* there. This was the result of a legal case at Srirangam about 100 years ago over the Sattadas' right to recite the two lines of an *āḻvār* verse. The court took this right away from the Sattadas and gave it to the Brahmins. Because of lack of finances and will power, the Sattadas could not contest this, and so the Brahmins obtained the right of recitation for the entire verse [for more about this case, see Chapter 7].
>
> However, Sattadas do chant for families in their homes during the ten-day ritual after death and at other private gatherings, and they sing wedding verses such as Periyāḻvār's verse, 'I have only one daughter',[66] and the sixth decade of Āṇṭāḷ's *Nācciyārtirumoḻi*, which is about her dream of marrying Lord Raṅganātha. If they cannot chant because they have not memorised the verses for their own rites of passage, they hire a Śrīvaiṣṇava Brahmin to do so.
>
> There are other differences between the Sattadas and Teṉkalai Brahmins. The old generation, my father's generation, didn't wear a *dhoti* like the Brahmins; they wore only a *lungi*. They did wear their hair in a tuft similar to that of the Brahmins. Although technically Sattadas are those who serve in the temple but don't wear a sacred thread, some Sattadas wear it to do *pūjā*s in village temples. People associate priests with sacred

threads, and so they want their priest to wear one. Unlike the Brahmins who chant the *gāyatrī* mantra after their sacred thread ceremony, Sattadas don't chant it. Neither do Sattadas study the Vedas, recite Vedic *stotras* or chant Vedic mantras.

The Academic Devotee and his Village

K. K. A. Venkatachari introduced me to Dr Parandhaman.

IMAGE 3.3: Dr Parandhaman in front of his home shrine in Tambaram with pictures of God, Āṇṭāḷ, and others, flanked on the side by family photographs.

Image credit: Author's collection.

Knowing that I was interested in non-Brahmin Śrīvaiṣṇavas, Parandhanan started the interview by giving me several examples of Śrīvaiṣṇava caste inclusiveness. The first one is from the Tirukkottiyur *sthala-purāṇa*.

Service (*kaiṅkarya*) is good for everyone. We are born to do service in the world. God has given us body and soul to render service. Those who do so are Bhāgavatas.

Long ago other people, when they came to earth, forgot about God and his disciples. They had interest only in worldly life. When Lord Viṣṇu saw this, he became very sorry for them, and so he introduced the Vedas, Itihāsas, Purāṇas and Śāstras. They did not use these scriptures. Next, he gave the mantra *om namo nārāyaṇāya*, still to no avail. After that, he gave the essence of the Vedas in the Tirumantram, thinking that this would be easy. Because he gave this mantra at Badrinath in the Himalayas yet found no suitable people there to teach it, he himself became a teacher named Nārāyaṇa and also became a disciple named Nara.[67] This, too, was not fruitful, and so he decided to be born on the earth as ten *avatāra*s born in various castes.

This is the main thesis of Śrīvaiṣṇavism: caste inclusiveness shown by God himself. Even after incarnating as *avatāra*s, God had not attained his goal. Next, he sent the *nityasūri*s (eternal beings, in this case, the *āḻvār*s) to be born on earth and sing songs with the meanings of the Vedas. Here, too, there was no caste. Nammāḻvār was in the fourth *varṇa* (*śūdra*); Tiruppāṇ in the last (outcaste); and Periyāḻvār in the first (Brahmin). Tirumaṅkai was a thief. There was no difference.

Next, the *nityasūri*s became twenty-four *ācārya*s to give the meanings of 4,000 hymns to the people. The first *ācārya* was Viṣṇu, the second his consort Mahālakṣmī, and so on up to Rāmānuja. Because the mantras had been kept secret, Rāmānuja wanted to learn them. With great difficulty, he went from Srirangam to Tirukkottiyur eighteen times to learn the meanings, and also fasted for forty days. Only then did the priest at Tirukkottiyur give him the meanings. After that, Rāmānuja thought, 'How can I give these meanings to everyone?' Therefore, he simplified the process, giving them all in public at the Tirukkottiyur temple and then asked the Brahmin *ācārya*s to teach them to everyone. As a cloud gives rain to all, so

> Rāmānuja gave knowledge and salvation to all. Because of these social reformers, Śrīvaiṣṇavism became popular.

Here is another story he told me:

> When Rāmānuja brought the statue of Sampatkumar from Delhi, thieves attacked him. Harijans protected Rāmānuja and the statue. To thank the Harijans, he allowed them into the Lord's temple at Melkote (a tradition that has continued to the modern period) and called them Tirukkulattār (members of the sacred family). Rāmānuja was the first reformer. After that, only Mahatma Gandhi has been a reformer.

Parandhaman then told two more anecdotes. The first was about a wrestler named Villidāsar, who worked as a guard for the Cōḻa king at his Uraiyur capital, next to Srirangam. The second story was about Rāmānuja's belief in equality.

> The wrestler met a beautiful girl. He fell in love and married her. In the summer, he took her with him to guard the king. Because they had to cross the hot sands of the dry Kaveri riverbed, he had his wife walk on his cloth and provided her shade with an umbrella. Because Indian men should not serve ladies, the people who witnessed his behaviour became agitated and told Rāmānuja. However, Rāmānuja understood the wrestler's love and decided that his affection should be directed toward Lord Viṣṇu. Later, Rāmānuja took the wrestler and his wife to worship Lord Raṅganātha in the Srirangam temple. Lord Raṅganātha made them his disciples.
>
> One day at Srirangam, Rāmānuja, along with his disciples, went to the Kaveri to bathe. On the way, Rāmānuja put his hand on the shoulder of a Brahmin. On return, he put his hand on the shoulder of Villidāsar. When the Brahmins became jealous, Rāmānuja explained his behaviour to the Brahmins and tried to eradicate the caste tension.

By now, I had heard the last story many times. The conversation turned to Parandhaman's own life:

The name of my village is Nariyampakkam; it is about 10 kilometres from Sriperumbudur. In the past, when we saw the temple *gopuram*, we would pray. My grandfather had eight sons and three daughters. Ramanuja Acarya, who is now Embar Jiyar, from Sriperumbudur, initiated my grandfather and my parents. Today, only some of their offspring have had *samāśrayaṇam*.

When I was a child, I walked 8 kilometres through a forest to a village school. I studied to the eighth grade there. Then I went by bike 15 kilometres to Tambaram to pre-university. I got married, and we had six children: four daughters and two sons. Five are now married. My wife, my children and I are all vegetarian; we cook vegetarian food and offer it to God. We live in Tambaram, although I often return to my village.

I became a clerk and then the superintendent and deputy registrar in Anna University. In this job, I was known for my efficient administration and integrity. Even on the day of my retirement farewell party, I still worked, giving out the benefit checks. I never accepted bribes for anything. I have also been doing academic degrees. I have done two M.A.s, an M.Phil. and a Ph.D. from the University of Madras with a thesis on the Nayakar (Vanniyar) caste. I wrote that in Tamil. Since retirement, I have been teaching Tamil.

In 1979, when I was forty-five, I was on pilgrimage, visiting temples and doing *maṅgalāśāsana* (chanting the verses about those *divyadeśa*s). At Tirukkurunkudi, I needed a *dhoti* to enter the temple and didn't have one. Tirunarayana Aiyankar, the Brahmin manager and priest, asked me where I was from. I told him near Sriperumbudur. He gave me a silk *dhoti*, so that I could enter the temple. He arranged *tirumantiram* teaching and gave me a book. This inspired me to have *samāśrayaṇam* in Nagerkoyil. I wanted fruitful gains; any religious act multiplies 100 times with initiation. Tirunarayana Aiyankar is still alive. I saw him last month and dedicated my book to him, which was published with special blessing songs at a book-release function.

About 300 years ago, my family built a 10-foot by 10-foot temple in Nariyampakkam. Originally, the temple had both Viṣṇu and Gaṇapati images; now, Gaṇapati has his own temple. In 1984, I collected money for renovations at the Viṣṇu temple, which has a big tank next to it. Varataa Ethiraja Jeeyar came to celebrate. On another occasion, Ramanuja Acarya came to the village as a special guest.

Today, the main image is Lord Śrīnivāsa; there is real gold on it. My brother, called Kulacekara Ramanuja Dasar, is the priest. They are renovating the temple. Every Saturday, the villagers do *bhajana*s in the streets, singing some of the simple *āḻvār* verses from the works of Āṇṭāḷ, Kulacēkara and Tirupāṇ. Nammāḻvār's verses are too difficult. The villagers take only an oil lamp in these processions, although they take images at festival times. Though poor, the villagers have faith. Next to Viṣṇu, Rāmānuja is an important god for them. In this village, Śrīvaiṣṇavas are all *kṣatriya*s (Vanniyars). They all wear the *nāmam*. Only about ten have had *samāśrayaṇam*, because as farmers, they don't have time for the early morning ritual bath followed by prayer and offering food to God.

Now I live in Tambaram. Varataa Ethiraja Jeeyar[68] once lived here. Before becoming a *jīyar*, he came to my house and recited prayers. He has walked 4,000 kilometres throughout Tamil Nadu. Working hard for Bhāgavatas, he founded the Tirumal Atiyar Kulam, of which I am now in charge. We celebrate the birthdays of the *āḻvār*s and *ācārya*s, feed Bhāgavatas, and hold processions on new-moon days. In addition, we hold functions in various places. Before starting one, we go through the streets to celebrate non-Brahmins singing in public. This breaks down the Brahmin monopoly on religion. One Brahmin told me not to sing at all in public. As we go in procession, we might stop at a temple, a tree or a *sabhā* building. Anywhere the event can occur. We sing *bhajana*s and then three or four Bhāgavatas, good orators, will speak about the *āḻvār*s in loud voices. Sometimes Vaiṣṇavas in a village invite us, pay for our bus fare and give *prasādam*. Those who give help might not wear the *nāmam* [that is,

> they may not even be Śrīvaiṣṇavas, or they are modern Śrīvaiṣṇavas who have given up this custom].

The interview drew to a close, and the mood changed. It was the Tamil harvest festival called Pongal, held in January (the Tamil month of Tai), which is when the sun begins its journey northward for the next six months. 'Pongal' means to boil over; it symbolises fertility and abundance. The season's first rice—which is made into a sweet with milk, cardamom, jaggery, raisins, and cashews—is offered to Surya, the sun god. It is cooked outside in the sunlight in a decorated pot. I went with Dr Parandhaman, his wife, and other relatives to the rooftop, which had been decorated. We sat and ate our Pongal on banana leaves. On another occasion, I went with him to his native village Nariyampakkam and met his brothers and other Śrīvaiṣṇavas there.

* * *

Many topics were covered in my interviews in and around Chennai, from sectarian and personal religious beliefs and activities, to views of formal initiation, religious leadership, organisations with religious aspects (such as *sabhā*s), caste (especially regarding Brahmins, but also other castes, including Dalits), and the relation of both religion and caste to politics. Because I found that many of these topics were covered in similar ways in my interviews from other regions of Tamil Nadu, I will save discussion of their similarities and differences for the book's final chapter, and in this chapter and Chapters 3 and 4, I will conclude simply by noting some of the region's highlights.

In the case of greater Chennai, several points stand out. One is the fact that conversations often mentioned Sriperumbudur, the birthplace of Rāmānuja, the key figure of Śrīvaiṣṇavism. In fact, in the area surrounding this temple, including nearby Kanchipuram, were born many key Śrīvaiṣṇava figures: besides Rāmānuja and his family, there were Tirumaḻicai Āḻvār, Tirukkaccinampi, Mutaliyāṇṭāṉ, Empār, and Kūreśa. I found that the people I interviewed from Chennai and beyond had far more connections with Sriperumbudur than with the famous temples in Kanchipuram. In part, this can be explained by the fact that the key organiser for my fieldwork was K. K. A. Venkatachari, whose ancestors go back to Rāmānuja's nephew Mutaliyāṇṭāṉ. Venkatachari's family has had a relationship with the Sriperumbudur temple over generations, including family members still living in Sriperumbudur. Many of the people I met had connections with this family.

There were other *ācārya* families who had their own networks of disciples. A number of *maṭha*s exist in Sriperumbudur, such as the Varada Yadugiri Yatiraja Maṭha[69] and the *maṭha* founded by J. J. Thirunarayana Ramanuja Dasar for Dalits, which his granddaughter N. D. Sabari Natchi was renovating.[70] The *maṭha*s all had their own networks of family members, disciples, or caste associates, which extended into the surrounding villages where the *ācārya*s and *jīyar*s had proselytised.

This certainly explains some of the emphasis on Sriperumbudur that I encountered. Nevertheless, I think that this emphasis was also because of the disputes between Teṉkalais and Vaṭakalais in Kanchipuram at the Varadarajaswami temple. Moreover, the major Vaiṣṇava temple in Chennai, the Parthasarathy temple, has Vaikhānasa Āgama priests, which occasionally has caused conflicts. At Sriperumbudur, by contrast, the Teṉkalai administrative control was aligned with the Pañcarātra Āgama priesthood, and there were no major disputes with the Vaṭakalais, thereby providing a consolidated identity and therefore a hub for Teṉkalai networks in the Chennai region.

Another hub, albeit a remote one, for Teṉkalais has been Tirumalai-Tirupati. The history of this sacred place predates the formation of Śrīvaiṣṇavism as a sect. Today its fame as a pilgrimage destination attracts Teṉkalais from the region around Chennai, such as Sudarshana's disciples (as it attracts other Śrīvaiṣṇavas and Hindus in general). The fact that

Tenkalai *jīyar*s have special privileges and honours at these temples facilitates the Tenkalai pilgrims and the larger Tenkalai networks.

Finally, the fact that Chennai is the major metropolis of Tamil Nadu helps to explain other aspects of the interviews from this region. Many of my interviewees were first-generation or second-generation migrants from the immediate region, although some had come from places across Tamil Nadu for education and job opportunities. They were part of the phenomenon of urbanisation and the growing middle class.

Notes

1. Ekangipuram is near Perambur, now in metropolitan Chennai. Perambur was a railway stop in the nineteenth century. On a satellite map today, one sees that there is still some greenery in the immediate vicinity, but that is surrounded by dense buildings. It is about 10 kilometres to Triplicane by car, a trip that takes a long time, however, with traffic congestion.

2. The origins of this impurity practice are still being debated but, having done research (unpublished) on the history of drummers and their changing social status in Tamil texts from the time of early Tamil poetry, I offer the following explanation. Those who practised non-injury (*ahiṁsā*) (such as Jains and Brahmins) by the fourth century CE considered those who played drums impure, because drumheads were made of the skins of slain animals. This contributed to one name for untouchables: *paṟaiyar*s, from *paṟai*, drum. The category of untouchable came to include tribals assimilating into mainstream society, defeated soldiers of enemy kings, people rejected by society and those, including slaves, who were forced to labour for others. Categorised by caste society as impure, they were forced to live in a segregated place, so that their impurity would not infect other castes. There were other reasons for the ascribed impurity. Outcaste hamlets were located at the edge of agricultural villages, because outcastes worked for the villagers; they tended the rice paddies, made cow-dung 'fuel cakes' and collected firewood.

3. The discus, *nāmam* and conch are key symbols of the deity Nārāyaṇa-Kṛṣṇa-Viṣṇu. The symbolism of the *nāmam* is described on p. xv.

4. That is Nārāyaṇa-Kṛṣṇa-Viṣṇu.

5. These are the *Tiruppaḷḷiyeḻucci, Tiruppallāṇṭu* and *Tiruppāvai.*

6. This is called the *Kōyil Tiruvāymoḻi.*

7. At weddings, they chant Āṇṭāḷ's *Nācciyārtirumoḻi* and *Tiruppāvai.* 'Because my wife is now pregnant,' says Chakra, 'we will do two special rituals.'

8. His parents were Jaganathan and Armelumankai.

9. See Kshirsagar, *Dalit Movement.*

10. J. N. Aranga Ramanuja Dasar was married to R. Kasturibai Ranganayagi; J. N. Devaperumal Ramanuja Dasar to E. O. Govindammal; J. N. Bhoominatha Ramanuja Dasar to Lokanayagi; J. N. Poovirundavalli Natchiyar to Ramudhu; and J. N. Nilamangai Natchiyar to Sanjeevi Ramanuja Dasar.

11. Eventually, the second son moved out, but lived nearby.

12. Hierarchy was a complicated matter. British actions were sometimes a reflection more of practical need than of ideology. They needed literate people in administrative positions, for instance, and it was mainly the Brahmins who were literate. In some contexts, the British sided with the non-Brahmins because they feared the growing Brahmin power in the fight for independence.

13. Toddy tappers are those who climb palm trees to collect sap that would be fermented to create an alcoholic beverage.

14. Carman and Narayanan, *Tamil Veda*, 72.

15. This was pointed out to me by N. D. Sabari Natchi, his granddaughter.

16. See Chapter 2, section: 'A Forgotten Colonial History'.

17. Williams, 'Srivaishnava Handwritten Field Notes'.

18. Ekāṅgi Svāmikaḷ's biography (see Chapter 2, section 'Traces of a Forgotten History') does not mention Thirunarayana's connection with Ekāṅgi Svāmikaḷ. Thirunarayana was born in 1901 and Ekāṅgi Svāmikaḷ died in 1907. Therefore, Thirunarayana could not have known him personally, except as a small boy. The fact that Thirunarayana lived next to the *samādhi* and members of his family did the *pūjā* after the *ekaṅgi*'s death is probably the link.

19. I cannot determine whether there was any direct Hindutva influence in this event. The children of one branch of the family went to an Arya Samaj school, which has had connections with the

Hindu Right and the Ayodhya movement. I saw no other indications of a Hindutva worldview. I suspect the family's connection with the Arya Samaj was due to a desire for a Hindu education open to Dalits, rather than a political orientation per se.

20. See Chapter 6, section: '*Jīyar*s and *Ācārya*s with Non-Brahmin Disciples'.

21. The Tamil text is from *Nālāyira Tivya Prapantam* (Vol. 2), 66, but here with *sandhi*s broken. I thank Dr Eva Wilgen, Centre for the Study of Manuscript Cultures, University of Hamburg, Germany, for insights into the translation of this verse. The commentaries on it are: *Piḷḷāṉ: 6000, Nañjiyar: 9000, Periyavāccāṉ Piḷḷai: 24,000,* and *Vaṭakku Tiruvīti Piḷḷai: 36,000.*

22. I do not know what became of this legal dispute.

23. Her father, J. N. Devaperumal Ramanujar Dasar, was the second son of J. J. Thirunarayana Ramanujar Dasar.

24. Her mother was E. O. Govindammal.

25. See Venkatesan, *The Secret Garland,* for a translation of this work, and Venkatesan and Branfoot, *In Āṇṭāḷ's Garden,* for traditions connected to Āṇṭāḷ.

26. Carman, *Theology of Rāmānuja*, 39.

27. *Tattva Loka* is an international English magazine on Hinduism, especially Advaita Vedanta, published by the Sringeri Sarada Peetham.

28. See Chapter 6, section: '*Jīyar*s and *Ācārya*s with Non-Brahmin Disciples'.

29. This story is found in the *Guruparamparā Prabhāvam 6000*. See Narayanan, 'Tiruppan Alvar', 56–57.

30. According to the hagiographies, this occurred during the last few days of his life. Inscriptions indicate, however, that images of Rāmānuja developed in the thirteenth century.

31. See Ramasamy, *Tamil Nattil Gandhi.*

32. Kshirsagar, *Dalit Movement*, 252. Pallikonda is about 25 kilometres from Vellore.

33. See Chapter 7, section: 'Temple Politics and the Courts'.

34. As narrated by Sudarshana's cousin, Padu.

35. See note 18.

36. See Chapter 6, section: '*Jīyar*s and *Ācārya*s with Non-Brahmin Disciples' for a discussion of my interview with Varataa Etirāja Jeeyar.

37. During the colonial period, the British gazetteers included many pictures of non-Brahmins wearing sacred threads.

38. Etirāja never appointed a successor before his death and someone else, selected by others associated with the *maṭha*, was appointed.

39. The word *vidvāṉ* denotes a learned person, who is sometimes addressed as Dr, and in this context connotes a classical musician.

40. Others have told me that Brahmins seldom play the clarinet, because the saliva that is generated would pollute them.

41. He gave a presentation at the Percussive Arts Centre in Bangalore in 1998. See 'Achievements in the Field of Percussive Arts over 50 Years (1947–97)'.

42. Alarmel Valli (b. 1956) was the winner of many dance awards, including the Padma Bhushan by the Government of India in 2004. She is an exponent of the Pandanallur style of Bhārata Nāṭyam. The BBC made a film about her (Omnibus, producer Michael Macintyre), as have others in the Netherlands, Japan and France. See 'Alarmel Valli'.

43. A. K. C. Natarajan (b. 1931), a Carnatic music clarinetist, has won the Sangeet Natak Akademi Award (1994) and has been given the title Sangeetha Kalanidhi by the Madras Music Academy (2005), and Nadha Sweepa Kalanidhi by the Nadhadweepam Trust, Tiruchirappalli (2008). See 'A. K. C. Natarajan'.

44. T. Annamācārya (1408–1503), a Telugu-speaking Smārta Brahmin devotee of Lord Vēṅkaṭeśvara at Tirupati, introduced the genre of *saṅkīrtana*, a call and response chanting of hymns or mantras accompanied by drums, cymbals or harmonium, which has remained popular in Carnatic music.

45. Periyāḻvār composed verses on this topic, known as the *Pallāṇṭu*, which devotees often chant.

46. See Chapter 3, section: 'The Music Shrine's Protector'.

47. This might be because the priests at this temple are Vaikhānasa, a tradition that is not linked to the *āḻvār*s, unlike the Pañcarātra.

48. According to K. K. A. Venkatachari (personal communication, November 2005), P. B. Annaṅgarācāriyar was responsible for spreading Vaiṣṇava *rahasya-grantha*s (secret works) by giving lectures to Vaiśyas and Bhāgavatas. If anyone asked about any Vedic word, he could instantly provide all references to it in the Vedas. Moreover, he could do the same for any word in the 4,000 hymns of the *Divyaprabandham* (having written a commentary on these in simple Tamil) and other *stotra*s. The Central government honoured him as *Pādma-vibhūsaṇ*. Because of his special interest in Bhāgavatas,

he regularly inaugurated the Vaishnava Mahasabha. Attracting financial support to spread the word, he published cheaply all the works of Rāmānuja, Vedānta Deśika and Maṇavāḷa Māmuni, so that they would be accessible to everyone.

Patricia Mumme comments that as an *ācārya,* Annaṅgarācāriyar gave initiation to hundreds of non-Brahmins and graciously extended hospitality to those who came to hear his lectures, even though he himself did not eat with them and maintained the rules of Brahmin orthodoxy (Mumme, 'Rules and Rhetoric', 132–33).

49. There are three groups of Chettiyārs. One is considered *vaiśya* or twice-born according to the *varṇa* system, and it usually consists of prosperous business people. The other two groups (Berichettiyar and Variya Chettiyar) have smaller businesses and are not twice-born.

50. These are the short works: *Tiruppallāṇṭu, Tiruppaḷḷiyeḻucci* and *Tiruppāvai,* and a decade from Tirumaṅkai's *Periyatirumoḻi* (2.3.1–11) about the Tiruvallikkēṇī (Parthasarathy) temple, and the sixth decade of the *Nācciyārtirumoḻi* (about Āṇṭāḷ's dream of marrying the Lord).

51. T. Bhasya Ramanuja, 'Are the *maṭhas* essential?' *Tirumāmakaḷ,* November 2005.

52. More specifically, the article says that Śrīvaiṣṇavas who live in villages with a Vaiṣṇava temple should vote only for candidates who promise to support these temples. Others call this 'politics of the vote bank', which means that politicians appeal to caste groups for their vote. The government approaches the strongest groups and listens to them. Their suggestions will reach all political parties, including Chief Minister Jayalalithaa, because they are non-Brahmins and are very influential in the villages.

53. Leopold, *Indian Music,* 47, 51, 57, 68.

54. Ibid., 57.

55. The organisers told me that this was an extra-curricular activity, and that they had no problem with school authorities representing the secular state.

56. K. K. A. Ventkatachari, personal communication, January 2011. Seshadri alludes to this incident (Seshadri, *Social Change,* 111).

57. Ibid., 30.

58. K. K. A. Venkatachari, personal communication, January 2011.

59. Vaiśya men could study the Vedas.

60. Pettukola, 'Are We Different', 'Towards Reconciling the Soteriologies of the Tenkalais and the Vadakalais', which was first delivered at the Freedom of Thought-Lecture Series (8 August 2009)

at D. G. Vaishnav College, Chennai; 'Thiruvaimozhiyil Saaranagathi', which was presented at Bharathiar Illam on 10 February 2008. 'Is Sri Vaishnavism for Vaishnavites Only', which was co-sponsored by the Department of Vaishnavism at the University of Madras on 20 January 2007, and was subsequently published in *Symposium on Sri Vaishnavism Tomorrow* (Chennai: published by Byasani Madhavachetty's Charity Fund, 2007, 72–82). See Pettukola, 'Neovaishnavism Blogspot'.

61. See Pettukola, 'Neovaishnavism Blogspot'.
62. Ibid.
63. Ibid.
64. See 'Sriperumbudur Sanskrit College'.
65. Ibid.
66. Periyāḻvār, *Periyāḻvārtirumoḻi* 3.8.4.
67. Nara is the primeval soul and Nārāyaṇa the supreme god. They are sometimes worshipped together.
68. See Chapter 6, section: '*Jīyar*s and *Ācārya*s with Non-Brahmin Disciples'.
69. Ibid.
70. See Chapter 3, section: 'The Granddaughter and Rāmānuja's House'.

four

Oral Histories from Puducherry and Beyond

I refer loosely to the general area around Puducherry. This region includes the former British area of South Arcot and the former French colony of Pondichéri (traditionally known as Putuvai), which then became Pondicherry. Today, India has redefined South Arcot as the districts of Cuddalore and Villupuram, and Pondicherry as a Union Territory (a special status to recognise its French heritage). This general region is significant for my purposes here, because it was for several centuries an area of Śrīvaiṣṇava proselytism and non-Brahmin leadership in the late nineteenth century. When Pondicherry emerged as the cultural and intellectual metropolis of this area, after joining India in 1954 as a Union Territory, Bhāgavata academics from other regions joined local traditional scholars and literary figures to further the strong non-Brahmin presence in the city, with links to the surrounding villages and the *maṭha* in Tirukkoyilur.

The Octogenarian's Flashbacks

In Puducherry, I met M. Radhakrishnan, who is also known as Pāvalar Maṇī Cittaṉ, Visnuchittan or just Chittan. He told me many stories, some about Śrīvaiṣṇavism in Pondicherry in his parents' generation and others about Vaiṣṇava caste inclusiveness, from traditional lore. This elderly yet still energetic man had been a traditional dentist, although he is now more famous as a Tamil poet and a prominent Śrīvaiṣṇava Bhāgavata.

> I am a third-generation Śrīvaiṣṇava. In my father's time, a non-Brahmin called Ramanuja Swami came from Srirangam to Pondicherry, gave public talks and converted many people. Another Bhāgavata leader, Varadarājulu Naidu, also lectured on Vaiṣṇavism. My father, whose name was Mudaliyantan (after Rāmānuja's nephew), was a worker in a government hospital and after his conversion, was also initiated with the *samāśrayaṇam* ritual by Manjakkupam Svamikal, the non-Brahmin swami of Manjakkupam (Cuddalore) and a disciple of Bhuvanagiri.[1]

My father was a staunch Vaiṣṇava. He would not take food from outside, in fact not even from his son or daughter, only his wife. After marriage, his brother's sons lived in Chennai. Once, he visited them. To avoid their food, he went to the Parthasarathy temple instead to take the *prasādam*. The priest said that there was none. Then someone intervened and told the priest to give him food. My father thought that this person was God himself.

My wife was stauncher than I was. When she was dying, Venkataswami Reddiyar, a Bhāgavata who had published the *Divyaprabandham*,[2] took her to a famous *siddha* doctor. He came and gave her medicine. A Murukaṉ devotee, the doctor told her first to wear *vibhūti* (sacred ash) and then take the medicine. She refused, because this was the emblem of another god. She subsequently died in the local hospital. She made no compromises. In fact, she made many sacrifices in her life for her faith.

Recollecting Śrīvaiṣṇava practices in his own family reminded Chittan of other Śrīvaiṣṇavas he had known.

Great Śrīvaiṣṇavas lived here in the past. For instance, there was Manika Kannan, belonging to the Vanniyar caste, who was a constable. He would wear a *nāmam* on his forehead. When the chief opposed this, he resigned his post and lived by begging. Once, when Manika Kannan went on the street where Bharati-dasan,[3] a famous poet who was staunchly atheistic, was living, Bharati asked his wife to fill a pot with rice and give it to him. Bharati later told his followers that he had given rice because this man had a very strong character. Manika Kannan made a garland of flowers and *tulasī* and offered it to the Lord at Varadarāja Perumāḷ temple in Pondicherry daily until his death. He used to do *bhajana*s on important holy days. If people offered money, he said, 'Please put it in my pot', but would not touch it. He would cook rice and offer it to God at his home shrine. Manika Kannan was my father's best friend.

Then there was a pious Śrīvaiṣṇava lady, a Naidu named Etiraja Valli. After her husband died, she refused to remove her *tāli* [the necklace symbolising her status as a married woman], saying, 'my husband is living in Paramapadam [supreme heaven], so why should I remove it?'

Antal Amma, too, was a great Śrīvaiṣṇava. A woman of little education from the Reddiyar community, she would chide her daughter-in-law if she put a pot of very hot milk before the deities in the home shrine, saying, 'Can you drink extremely hot milk? If not, how can the Lord drink it? We must give it at the right temperature.'

I remember being told about a very pious woman who refused to use the vegetables that she had just bought at the market because a male friend of her husband had asked for them, and so she thought that they were polluted. She gave the greens to her own female friend instead. [In other words, as a pious wife, she would not touch anything that had been touched by a man other than her husband.]

More memories surfaced, this time of Śrīvaiṣṇava Harijans.

> My father and his friends converted Harijans in this area to Śrīvaiṣṇavism. The leader of the Harijans who encouraged this was Glovis Varadarajan. He had the French name Glovis because he had French citizenship on account of his military service. He was a well-off grocery merchant and wore a big *nāmam*. Glovis lived in Uppalam in Pondicherry, which is a Harijan colony. He would come on his bullock cart. My father and his friends would eat with this Harijan, invite him to all the functions and give the first *prasādam* to him. Whenever the *sabhā* organised a conference, it would get donations from Glovis. In the Perumāḷ temple, there were many high castes; still they honoured Glovis by asking him for donations, and he would give large ones. After that time, there was a Harijan *sabhā*. The main person is now gone. He maintained a temple and arranged for *bhajana*s, lectures and festivals.
>
> Many Harijans were initiated by Krishna Premi Jīyar near Paranur or Varataa Ethiraja Jeeyar in Sriperumbudur. I have been told that in Ethiraja's will, he has requested that the Dalits should perform the rites after his death.
>
> In Vaiṣṇavaism, there are ten *avatāra*s. Rāma and Krishna are the most important. According to the epics, these two gods don't belong to the Brahmin caste. Rāma is a Kṣatriya and Krishna belongs to the Yadava (cowherd) clan. The majority of the *āḻvār*s are non-Brahmins. They put the Vedas into Tamil. Of the 10, only Periyāḻvār and Toṇṭaraṭippoṭi are Brahmins.

'Now there are no Harijans in the *sabhā*s,' Chittan told me, before narrating the story of Periya Nampi, 'the guru of Rāmānuja, a great person who honoured the "outcastes"'.

> When Periya Nampi built a new house, he had to fix an auspicious date for a 'house-warming'. When an outcaste named Māṟannēri Nampi arrived at the house, Periya Nampi said that there was no need to fix an auspicious date, because Māṟannēri was there, which by itself created an auspicious time and place [in other circles, as an outcaste, he would have had to stay away from the house altogether].

Māraṉṉēri is an important symbol for the *sampradāya*'s concept of an inclusive community. He is remembered as an ascetic outcaste disciple of Yāmuna at Srirangam in the eleventh century. Another story about Māraṉṉēri tells how, when he was dying, he asked Periya Nampi to perform his last rites since his relatives were not Śrīvaiṣṇavas. When Periya Nampi did this, other Śrīvaiṣṇavas complained vociferously to Rāmānuja. Periya Nampi defended his action by citing many prior examples from the scriptures, such as Rāma doing the final rites for the vulture Jaṭāyu in the *Rāmāyaṇa*, or the many *Divyaprabandham* verses such as *Tiruvāymoḻi* 3.7.9 that honour outcastes, which later *ācārya*s in their commentaries linked to the stories of Māraṉṉēri.[4]

Remembering Māraṉṉēri inspired Chittan to tell the tale about what happened when the twelfth-century *ācārya* Parāśara Bhaṭṭar committed a small mistake.

> Regretting it, he bathed and prayed. Still he had no peace of mind. He told his learned mother Āṇṭāḷ (not the *āḻvār* Āṇṭāḷ) his problem and asked her what to do. His mother told him to wash the feet of a pious and learned non-Brahmin and drink that water as sacred water (*tīrtha*). Bhaṭṭar pointed out that a non-Brahmin might not allow this and asked her to prepare him to do this, just as one calms a cow before milking it. After Bhaṭṭar brought a non-Brahmin home, his mother did this, and so a non-Brahmin agreed to have his feet washed by a Brahmin.

Chittan narrated yet another anecdote, this one about Rāmānuja walking on a *bund* (raised path), across a huge irrigated field belonging to the temple.

> An outcaste woman was approaching him. Because the bund was narrow, someone needed to get down so the other could pass. Although Rāmānuja asked the lady to get down, she refused, even though the custom was that the outcaste should do so. She said, 'I cannot move, because outcastes should not put their feet on temple land. If I get down from the bund, I'll have to put my feet there.' Then Rāmānuja realised that she was a great

> lady and asked her to join him and his disciples. After her death, Rāmānuja honoured her and had a statue of her installed under the foot of Lord Perumāḷ. Since then, whoever worships God, worships the outcaste lady.

'This happened at Tirumaṅkai Āḻvār's birthplace,' commented Chittan, 'which is now the Tiruvāli-Tirunagari temple at Cirkali, beyond Chidambaram.'

To illustrate the inclusiveness of the religion, Chittan told me: 'There are four *varṇa*s. Below them are the *cāṇṭāḷa*s (outcastes). They used to eat the meat of dead animals floating in the river, and so they were considered very inferior.' After telling me the etymology of the name Toṇṭaraṭippoṭi—*poṭi* (dust) on the feet (*aṭi*) of the servants (*toṇṭar*)—he pointed out that even a Brahmin *āḻvār* should worship dust on the feet of devotees (including the feet of *cāṇṭāḷa*s). Chittan continued: 'Toṇṭaraṭippoṭi Āḻvār, a Brahmin, said that an upper-caste person may marry an outcaste, if that person is a devotee of Lord Perumāḷ and also good and pure.[5] Even a Brahmin girl may marry a low-caste devotee.'

I asked Chittan whether this was a fact or a story, because I had never encountered this idea in the texts or interviews. Chittan replied that it once was 'fact', although that changed after 'the thirteenth-century Brahmin commentator Periyavāccaṉ Piḷḷai altered the meaning of Toṇṭaraṭippoṭi's poems to eliminate the idea of a Brahmin marrying a pure, albeit low-caste, woman'. 'Although inter-caste marriages were no longer done,' Chittan continued, 'today there is inter-caste marriage; partners might be chosen on the basis of income and education. The Dravidian movement has been against caste and religion.'

After a pause in the conversation, I asked Chittan about his political affiliations.

> I had joined Periyar's Self-Respect movement, as had 99 per cent of the non-Brahmins, when I was twenty-seven. My father protested because Periyar was an atheist and chided me. Once I went as a dentist to a fisherman's colony and saw a man from Periyar's movement at

> a local temple there. I noticed that he was wearing the Śaivite marks of *vibhūti* and *kuṁkuma*. I wanted to know why he did this as an atheist, which followers of Periyar supposedly were. The man said that his son and wife had made him do it. I then decided that Periyar and members of his party were pseudo-atheists. I told my father, and he agreed. That was the end of my attraction to Periyar. Many Vaiṣṇavas and Śaivas who joined Periyar's Self-Respect Movement found out that it was not a true movement. K. M. Balasubramaniam, a populariser of Maṇikkavācakar's *Tiruvācakam*, was with Periyar. Later, he returned to Śaivism, realising that it was right. For forty to sixty years, Vaiṣṇavism declined because of this atheistic movement. Now Dravidian atheism has declined. Vaiṣṇavism is becoming popular once more. Some non-Brahmins even give initiation.

This idea of non-Brahmins giving initiations was nothing new for Chittan. After all, the non-Brahmin Manjakkupam, who was Bhuvanagiri's disciple, had initiated his father.[6]

The Carpenter's Masterful Chanting

Hoping to find some Bhāgavatas to interview, I sat on the steps of a pillared hall in the courtyard of a Perumāḷ temple, which had been built about 100 years ago, on the outskirts of Puducherry. After a while, I noticed a man moving from one sub-shrine to another, bowing deeply. When he had finished praying, I approached him. Ramanuja Nayakar agreed to an interview.

> A carpenter by profession, I live with my family nearby and come to the temple daily. Like so many other non-Brahmin Śrīvaiṣṇavas in this region, I belong to a long-standing Śrīvaiṣṇava family. It had founded the Muthial Manjini Kuppa, a *maṭha* for chanting *bhajana*s. My father was well-versed in chanting the verses of the *Divyaprabandham*, and I learned to chant from him. I have memorised all 4,000 verses.

> I rise at 4:00 am and take my bath. I chant about 200 verses, changing them each day until I have chanted a cycle of all 4,000. Then, I worship the image of Perumāḷ in my home shrine. On weekdays, my children chant with me. Because of all the chanting, my sons and daughters are now educated and getting good jobs. In fact, they receive offers of employment even before completing their courses. Whenever my children wrote their exams, I would sit at home and chant. Or when they went for job interviews. Therefore, they received all the benefits of chanting. I myself have no other goal than to surrender at the Lord's feet. Because I am a daily wage labourer, I have not had formal initiation into Śrīvaiṣṇavism. I cannot maintain the purity of that position. I am, however, a pure vegetarian. My wife, who is from a non-vegetarian family, is not. Neither are my children.

Ramanuja Nayakar suddenly began chanting. When he stopped, he told me more about his life.

> I was once in the Communist Party, learned all its theories and taught them to the labourers. But the leaders gave me such trouble that I had to leave, even though I was a staunch party leader and union organiser. My disillusionment began when I noticed the hypocrisy of the leaders. During one conflict, they supported the capitalists. When I left the Party, I started chanting again. By chanting, you can transform even your enemies. Because I chanted, a Member of the Legislative Assembly who had given me trouble surrendered to the Lord after he had an accident.

Ramanuja Nayakar interrupted the conversation again by chanting, in a beautiful voice, one verse from Tirumaṅkai Āḻvār's *Tirukkuṟuntāṇṭakam*. When he finished, he elaborated on its meaning with great erudition.

The conversation turned to problems that Ramanuja Nayakar faced when teaching Tamil hymns at the temple.

> Both Brahmins and non-Brahmins, including boys and girls, are my students. I teach for free. Occasionally, they offer me gifts. The Brahmin priests are not too keen about

my activity. I think that this might be due to discrimination, or because the temple is becoming increasingly Vedic and therefore not so interested in the Tamil *Divyaprabandham*.

The Professor's Nostalgia for a Lost World

Dr A. Pandurangan, a retired professor emeritus of Tamil literature at Pondicherry University, was often my guide in Puducherry, thanks to a request by K. K. A. Venkatachari. We met Bhāgavata notables in the city and went on several car trips in the countryside, which led us to the traces of Rāmānuja Nāvalar, Bhuvanagiri and Nārāyaṇa Dāsar (discussed in Chapter 2). There was plenty of time for conversation on these journeys of discovery, and the professor's life story gradually unfolded.

> I am a ninth-generation Śrīvaiṣṇava. My children and grandchildren make eleven generations in all. The oldest ancestor in our lineage was named Āḻvār, after Nammāḻvār. He was from a small village called Maruthan Valvu, which is near Nammāḻvār's birthplace, Alvartirunagari in Tirunelveli district. My father left this village and migrated to a village called Subbulapuram in Madurai district, where he obtained a large tract of land for agriculture and brought many people from his previous village to help him open up the new fertile area.
>
> The men in my family maintained their Śrīvaiṣṇava identity by marrying only Śrīvaiṣṇava women, worshipping at the Narasiṁha Perumāḷ temple at Jambuliputtur, a small village nearby, and going on pilgrimage to places such as Srirangam. My grandfather, Ramaswami, was a trustee of the Narasiṁha-Perumāḷ temple and is remembered fondly by all. He used to stay in Srirangam for several months every year and also went during the Cittra festival to the Tirumaliruncolai temple near Madurai. Brahmin *ācārya*s from Srivilliputur visited his home and gave initiation to family members. I never met my grandfather, who was a staunch Śrīvaiṣṇava.

In my boyhood, an old relative taught me Periyāḻvār's *Tiruppaḷḷāṇṭu*. He did *bhajana*s and took me to visit nearby villages. Some of my other relatives would not accept food from this old relation's family, only from initiated Śrīvaiṣṇavas. As a result, the old man and I had to bring our own food and cook it there. These same relatives would not allow others into their home shrine. They were very fond of me, however, because my mother had died when I was only ten days old, and so they let me enter.

The family's faith was so strong that when the goddess Kālī's procession came down their street, they closed their doors because they refused to worship any deity who was not associated with Viṣṇu. I was especially impressed by an elderly widow in my family. She had no children and was extremely poor. She never complained and always refused help, saying that everything is God's grace and her only husband is Lord Mahārānī. This strong religious tradition virtually died out with my father, who was not interested in religion. Because of the family's wealth, my father, who was the eldest son, ignored the care of the lands. Other relatives helped out my grandfather, but then they siphoned away the wealth.

Because my family was very rich, it had close relations with local Brahmins and often gave them rice. In my boyhood, I ate in Brahmin homes. There was no conflict of purity rules because my own family, as 'staunch' Vaiṣṇavas, maintained these rules themselves.

Educated at the primary level in the local village school, I did my secondary school in Teni. Although I started in science, which gave me an interest in the scientific method, I did a B. A. in Madurai. At that time, Madurai College was controlled by Brahmins, mainly Śrīvaiṣṇava Ayyaṅkars, who were the teachers. Because I was a Vaiṣṇava, the Ayyaṅkars liked me. When they quoted *āḻvār* hymns, I knew them and was asked to recite them. When I was a student in Madras doing my M. A. in Tamil literature at President's College, I stayed in a non-Brahmin student hostel for one year. When the warden, a former Indian Oil officer, heard my name and recognised me as a Vaiṣṇava, he became very affectionate. He created a strong Vaiṣṇava influence in the hostel.

I stood first in my M. A. class, winning two gold medals. In 1956, I was forced to marry by my uncle, who had educated me, because he thought that he was going to die and wanted to fulfil his Hindu responsibility as my substitute father after my father had died, of arranging my marriage. I was married to my aunt's daughter. In 1961, I moved to Pondicherry, where I became a professor of Tamil literature.

My family had been Gandhians and Congress followers. My father and uncles wore only *khadi* cotton cloth, as I did before I became a professor. By that time, it was expensive and difficult to wash, and so I used it for a while only on ritual occasions.

Many of my fellow students had joined the Dravidar Kazhagam (DK) in the 1950s, when I was in high school in Teni. The DK spread like wildfire. Most young people were attracted to the speeches of its leaders. One of my uncles became a staunch DK member. He brought DK books to me. I was not attracted to them, especially after contempt for C. N. Annadurai, who broke away from Periyar's DK and started the DMK, became strong. One day, a DMK student attacked me, and nobody helped me. Almost all castes backed the DMK. By joining it, people were connecting with those in power. That was good for jobs. Some of those who joined these movements later returned to their religions.

When I was a student at the University of Madras, one of my teachers was Sangara Rajalu, a Telugu man. After being a student leader of the Communist Party of India, he became a staunch Vaiṣṇava and developed an interest in the *Divyaprabandham*.

After I came to Pondicherry, I joined a Vaiṣṇava *sabhā* with southern traditions—The Southern Acarya Sabai. It was headed by Rajagopalan, a Brahmin civil-supplies officer in Pondicherry. Although members were very fond of me and wanted me to be the secretary, I refused because it would be hard to obtain donations as a non-native in Pondicherry.

The *sabhā* tried to introduce the custom of Brahmins and non-Brahmins singing together in the main Perumāḷ temple. We were not allowed to chant in its inner sanctuary, only in the pillared hall of the first courtyard. We conducted Nammāḻvār's week-long celebration and arranged for endowments. The temple priests refused to give us *tīrtha* (sacred water). With its members disillusioned, the *sabhā* disbanded.

The names of my children and grandchildren are all Vaiṣṇava, which has helped to maintain their religious identity. No one received initiation in my generation because of my father's negative influence. Still, I decided to do it.

If they wanted initiation, Bhāgavatas went to any *ācārya* who was willing to perform it. I first considered going to Desikapillai, a Vaṭakalai *ācārya*. Then I thought about having initiation from a Srivilliputur *ācārya*, because that had been my family's tradition. The tradition had been lost by my father and brothers, and I could no longer trace our *ācārya* family. They had become mere priests. Other *ācārya*s did not want to initiate non-Brahmins. I thought also about going to Srirangam Narayana Jiyar, but he was not a real spiritual leader, merely the head of a *maṭha*. Because I believe that a guru should be above ordinary people, I wanted a very spiritual *ācārya*. I heard about the Vijawada *jīyar* in Andhra [Pandurangan was probably referring to Chinna Jeeyar Swami; I discuss him in Chapter 6], but it was too far away. Finally, I went to Varataa Ethiraja Jeeyar in Sriperumbudur and was deeply impressed by his affection. I had met him many years before and found him vigorous, smart, and the only one who has real compassion for non-Brahmins.

About ten years ago, my wife, my daughter and I were initiated by Varataa Ethiraja Jeeyar. He refused any *dakṣiṇa* (gift) for performing the ritual and said, 'If you insist, 4 annas (a few cents).' I gave him more anyway. When this *jīyar* receives a donation, he gives a receipt. He insists. Many Brahmins are against him, denying him all rights and honours. Processions in Sriperumbudur used to stop at his ashram. Now they refuse to do so. If you visit the *jīyar*, he always asks, 'Have you had any food?' Even if you say 'yes', he still prepares at least coffee. Other Brahmins won't cook or feed non-Brahmins with their own hands. I recently visited him in the hospital, after he fell and broke his hip.

I am vegetarian. My own relatives eat meat 'for good health'. These days, in the morning, I worship the *śālagrāma* stone and chant the *Tiruppāvai* and *Tiruppaḷḷāṇṭu* along with verses from the *Tiruvāymoḻi*, tasks that take me about an hour. I eat by 10 am. My children don't want to wait, because they must go to the office or have other things to do. My wife and daughter also don't chant, saying that their voices are not good enough.

Now I think a lot about the village of my childhood. My house there is more than 200 years old. It once had murals. One was of Krishna stealing the saris of *gopīs*. Another was of devotees offering fruits to the reclining Lord Raṅganātha. Yet another was of Nammāḻvār. I knew who these figures were only later in life. The walls have been whitewashed since then. I plan to restore them. I am now the only one who remembers these things. As the eldest son, I inherited the property. It is a huge house. Three to 400 people can sit in its courtyard. In the past, many people had their weddings there.

My own family tradition in my native village is now only for festivals and singing in the *rāmānuja kūṭam*. It is not very serious. As an elder who is trusted, I still remain in charge of many village affairs and return periodically. For the festival of the goddess Kālī, the deity who is important for the villagers, the festival ornaments are kept in my house. I am the custodian of them, even though they are not rich ornaments. I manage the revenues for the Kālī temple, even though I am a Vaiṣṇava. I levy the taxes for festivals and have increased the revenue. Four hundred participating couples pay Rs 100 and sometimes give offerings too. From these funds, I also give to needy people.

Speaking of caste and current politics, Pandurangan remarked that:

> My own caste, the Naidu, are no longer politically powerful, despite the fact that they once had high status as non-Brahmins. During Nayak rule, many Telugu Naidus entered Tamil Nadu as warriors and were rewarded with lands. Even though they claim a common Telugu identity, Naidus are not politically united because people from various places claim descent from different kings, and these then form sub-sects such as the Gauravas and Kamalas.
>
> Even though they are often rich landlords, Naidus have not managed to become a political force and belong to various political parties. By contrast, the Vanniyar and Kallar castes don't claim royal links; therefore, it is easier for them to unite politically. Now, there are two famous Naidus, Vijaya Kanth and Vaikō, who are developing political identities. Vaikō, for instance, has a big following with the MDMK [Marumalarchi Dravida Munnetra Kazhagam]. Although they attract Tamil youth across caste lines, their critics label them as Naidu politicians. There is also a Naidu political movement called Tirumali-nayaka. This is a cultural association. It has been established in various villages to mobilise Naidus.

Pandurangan's comments reflected the fluidity of non-Brahmin caste status and the importance of caste solidarity for political and economic goals. Most of my informants were not so explicit on this subject of the relation of caste support for politicians.

The Scholar, Teacher and Publisher

I met Aranga Perumal Ramanusan, a Naidu, on the outskirts of Puducherry. Once a mill worker, he gave up this job about twenty years ago and devoted himself to making the traditional knowledge of Śrīvaiṣṇavism accessible to everybody. That way, they could leave behind the rigorous and difficult Brahmanical scholarship. 'Not everyone, after all, can be an *ācārya*,' he joked. About himself, he said the following:

> I was initiated by the *jīyar* at Emperumāṉār Mutt in Tirukkoyilur.[7] I studied Sanskrit privately from a Brahmin pandit. Although there were Vedic schools in every temple, no non-Brahmins were admitted. I have a working knowledge of Sanskrit, enough to understand Maṇipravāḷam, the mixed language of Tamil and Sanskrit. I also did an M. A. in Tamil through a correspondence course. I want to translate all Maṇipravāḷa books into pure Tamil so that the common person has access to this knowledge. Because no one wants to finance the project, I must seek the resources myself. Unlike Western countries that fund the publication of Christian literature, India does not fund Hindu literature.
>
> I conduct classes for students and then send them to the Tirukkoyilur *jīyar* for initiation. After that, I teach them Teṉkalai works such as those by Piḷḷai Lokācārya and his brother Aḻakiya Maṇavāḷa Perumāḷ Nāyaṉār.
>
> I never act as a priest. Only Brahmins can be priests because that is what the Pañcarātra Āgamas prescribe. If someone doesn't know Sanskrit, then he can't pronounce the words correctly. I also don't give initiations. Only Brahmin *ācārya*s can perform *samāśrayaṇam*.

The introduction to one of his books says that:

> Araṅga Perumāḷ Rāmānuca Dāsar has published many works. Here, he is presenting a Meyyarivum that is based on the *Tolkāppiyam*, *Paripāṭal*, *Tirukkuṟal* and the *Divyaprabandham* as well as Sanskrit sources such as the Upaniṣads, Purāṇas and Itihāsas. He has written about many religious topics because his vocation is to serve the devotees (*aṭiyar*s). He writes neither to gain fame nor to become an *ācārya*. First, he learned the *sampradāya* from P. B. Annangaracariyar in Kanchipuram.[8] After that, he studied systematically with Antūrsvāmi (a Bhāgavata who knew the *sampradāya* works thoroughly). He studied Tamil and Sanskrit with many scholars. He has clear understanding and has instructed others to their entire satisfaction. The author himself says that he used to consult Tamil scholars at the French Institute of Indology, scholars such as T. V. Gopala Iyer (a Smarta

> Brahmin Advaitin scholar who is well-informed also about the *Divyaprabandham* and the *Rahasyatrayasāra*). Moreover, he studied with a Bhāgavata intellectual named Toppuswami[9] from southern Tamil Nadu. 'I am very humble,' he says, 'before such people.'

This Bhāgavata obviously understood his *kaiṅkarya* as publishing *sampradāya* works that would facilitate non-Brahmin understanding of the tradition.

The Epigrapher's Dream of Reform

I am to interview Dr G. Vijayavenugopal at his office at École Française d'Extrême-Orient (EFEO) in Puducherry. Scholars at this institute, which has a large collection of Indological books and palm-leaf manuscripts in its library, do research on the literature, archaeology, history, art history and epigraphy of Tamil Nadu. Dr Vijayavenugopal, a senior research fellow, is the epigrapher and historian here. After I questioned him about several of my own historical research interests—he is a great source of information—we started the interview.

> I was born in Trichi (Tiruchirappalli) into a Vaiṣṇava Telugu-speaking family. My great-grandfather had created a *rāmānuja kūṭam*, a charity that offers food, on Sattani Street, which my uncle's son maintains to this day. When I was very small, every morning at 5:00, my grandfather took all the boys in the family, dressed in silk *dhoti*s and with *nāmam*s on their foreheads, by horse and cart to the Srirangam temple for *pūjā*. After returning home, we did more *pūjā*. By 7:30, we had breakfast.
>
> Our ancestors were originally bangle sellers. An old mother goddess, Aṅkaḷa Parameśvarī (Pārvatī), is our family deity; this gives a clue to our ancient family tradition. I think that she was originally a jungle goddess (Koṟṟavai) of the chieftains in ancient times; warriors used to cut off their own heads for an offering to this goddess to ensure the king's victory. Goddesses like her were the original Dravidian deities. They were reinterpreted as

the pan-Indian goddess Durgā who was the protector of jungle forts. Later, they were linked with Śaiva myths, turning the mother goddess into the Śaiva goddess Pārvatī.

My grandfather did a B. A. degree at St. Joseph's College in Srirangam. The most prosperous non-Brahmin parents tried to get their children into this school; it was known for providing a good education. My grandfather was a stationmaster at Tiruchirappalli town station, division headquarters of the southern railroad. Most of his relatives were uneducated and got into the railroad system at various levels. My grandfather owned some fertile lands. One of his younger brothers was an administrative officer of the Srirangam temple. He was also a Trichi district cooperative bank director.

My father studied at St. Joseph's as well and specialised in chemistry and math. He then did a degree in teaching. He was the only non-Brahmin in this degree programme. Madras Medical College invited him to study there, but his grandmother didn't like this idea; 'You'll be a butcher,' she said, 'doing post-mortems.' Therefore, my father rejected the invitation to study medicine and became a high-school teacher.

My father's first wife died, and there were no children. His second wife, my mother, was born near Anantapur in what became known as Andhra Pradesh after the linguistic division of Madras Presidency into two states. My mother came alone to Trichi; her brothers stayed behind.

When it was time to go to school in Tiruvarur, where my father got a job, I was initiated into education by wearing religious marks, receiving a notebook and slate, going in procession with other children to the school and prostrating myself before the teacher. The teacher took my index finger and wrote the alphabet on the slate. Along with the other children, I received sweets.

Attracted to the Dravidian movement, my father was a member of the South Indian Welfare Association, later renamed the South Indian Liberal Foundation, which was a precursor to the Dravida Kazhagam (DK) and the Dravida Munnetra Kazhagam (DMK).

At the time, some non-Brahmin leaders were emerging and joined the Justice Party. Brahmins were advisors to the British and were IAS (Indian Administrative Service) officers. Therefore, the social structure, with power monopolised by the Brahmins, remained the same as under the former rulers. Rich and poor non-Brahmins were kept out of choice positions. Although my father was attracted to the Justice Party, he didn't join it because of its atheist position. By this time, my father was not going to the temple, which my grandfather had done. Still he had some piety.

My own wife is a Śaiva Brahmin. We were classmates and had a 'love marriage'. The Dravidian movement had given people new hope to get out of the caste system through inter-caste marriage. Therefore, my love marriage was backed by the new ideology.

This reform orientation was different from the International Congress Party. Congress preached democracy, yet allowed school hostels to be divided between Brahmins and non-Brahmins. Periyar broke away and formed his own movement (the Self-Respect Movement).[10] My father's younger sister's son was active in it. All party members wore black shirts. My cousin made me wear one and go to a Periyar lecture. One of my classmates, Nedumaran, was in the DMK and was a proponent of Tamil nationalism.

In 1949, when C. N. Annadurai left the DK to form a branch of the party in Madurai, which became the DMK, I became the DMK's official propaganda secretary and wrote the messages for billboards and pamphlets. When I was doing my M. A. in Tamil language and literature, my teacher T. P. Meenakshisundaram[11] belonged to the Indian National Congress Party. I stood first in his class. He tried to attract me and other students to Congress, but I was not interested.

My father taught M. Karunanidhi of the DMK, who became the Chief Minister of Tamil Nadu in 1969 when C. N. Annadurai, the DMK's founder, died.[12] My father helped the teachers to get better pensions by going with them to Karunanidhi's office. When Karunanidhi saw my father, his former teacher, he helped them.

I became a teacher because I wanted to be objective. When I did a paper in philosophy, comparing Advaita, Viśiṣṭādvaita and Vīraśaivism, I saw contradictions between their philosophies and their temple cultures. As intellectuals, philosophers were in an ivory tower. Through education, I wanted to make reforms. I still struggle in my heart between an anti-caste, socialist revolution and a religious philosophy. For instance, Mayawati, the Dalit Chief Minister of Uttar Pradesh, often[13] gave reservations to Brahmins. [That is, even though Mayawati, a Dalit, came to power, Brahmins have still managed to hold onto power through political alliances with Dalits.]

In my paper for the 2007 symposium, 'Sri Vaisnavism—Tomorrow', held at the University of Madras,[14] I argued that we must make everyone equal. The DMK denied God to get equality. But Periyar substituted a human political leader for God as the rallying point. People became devotees of Periyar or Gandhi. This is a religious phenomenon. It is also a family phenomenon. The leader is like the mother of children: 'I will take care of you'. In Śrīvaiṣṇavism, surrender or *prapatti* is absolute surrender. For women, this blends with their traditional chastity, that is, absolute surrender to their husbands. Therefore, this creates a beautiful conceptual matrix or ideological structure, which the leader can manipulate. People want a leader. If equalisation equals democratisation, then there will be no leader, and people won't be attracted. Even now, women can't get a ration card because they do not head their families. Therefore, we have a God-*darśana* structure and a family model of society.

Even though Periyar was an atheist, he remained a patron and trustee of a temple. This suggests that he was a hypocrite. I now vote according to the leader and have no party affiliation. Parties are all the same these days. I have no belief in the leadership.

I no longer do *pūjā*. My wife does her Brahmin *pūjā* by herself. I won't join. I am sometimes invited to give

> lectures because of my knowledge. I try to provide political ideas for a new path. Therefore, I don't follow the tradition. Vedic tradition merely protects the jobs of priests in the temples, and the only way the Sanskrit tradition is maintained today is by Brahmins knowing a few mantras. There is no real Vedic knowledge now. Brahmin priests, for example, sometimes do Āgamic rituals for the village goddess Mārīyammaṉ. And if they are asked, 'What is the source of these rituals?' they say the source is in an 'appendix' to the Āgamas, which implies a later and therefore non-authoritative addition, especially because it is about goddess worship.
>
> In the twelfth century, Rāmānuja attempted to convert non-Brahmins to Brahminism. After the fifteenth century, no non-Brahmin had an *ācārya* or formal initiation, *samāśrayaṇam*.[15] The twentieth-century figure Jayakanthan (b. 1934), who became a Marxist and a novelist,[16] wanted to convert all non-Brahmins to Brahminism. In their hearts, however, Brahmins still think that there is a radical difference. Non-Brahmins can't be upgraded. Brahmins make the (religious) law, and therefore they have to be the ones to change it. The poet Subramania Bharati, an Iyer Brahmin, initiated a Harijan.[17] This was a minor exception to the general caste ideology. Therefore, there is lots of rhetoric but no practice. Nevertheless, non-Brahmins played important roles. The non-Brahmin Kallars (weavers), for instance, protected the temple Alakarkōyil̲ against the Muslims.

In his symposium paper,[18] Vijayavenugopal argues that even before the twelfth century, inscriptions referring to donations to Viṣṇu temples always said that the Śrīvaiṣṇavas should protect them, even though Brahmins controlled the temple administration, rituals, and so forth. This, according to Vijayavenugopal, suggests a distinction between these two groups of Vaiṣṇavas—Brahmins and other Vaiṣṇavas—although Śrīvaiṣṇavas ideally are a casteless and classless society, staunch devotees of Viṣṇu, and respectful not only to humans but also to animals. Unfortunately, this broad concept of Śrīvaiṣṇavism was abandoned, he noted. The whole Vaiṣṇava tradition became:

> caste-centred (that is, Brahmin-centred) and logo-centred (that is, Sanskrit-centred). I feel that if we want to create a broad base to continue the Viṣṇu faith, this kind of exclusiveness has to be discarded and ways and means have to be found to restore this glorious tradition.[19]

Vijayavenugopal argues that he was not the first to call for reform. By the late thirteenth century, Piḷḷai Lokācārya and his younger brother Aḻakiya Maṇavāḷa Perumāḷ Nāyaṉār called for reform. Their works, Vijayavenugopal thinks, represent a Vaiṣṇava tradition that is casteless and classless, which must be distinguished from the Vedic tradition.

Vijayavenugopal offered examples of how these authors refute the Vedic-oriented objections to a casteless and classless tradition. For instance,

> these Śrīvaiṣṇava authors argue that the hymns of the *āḻvār*s are not inferior to the Vedas. Even though Nammāḻvār was a *śūdra*, his hymns are divine. There are no caste restrictions for *prapatti* because everyone who surrenders will reach the divine. Even animals have attained liberation. Brahmins who chide low-caste devotees will themselves become outcastes.
>
> Low castes who are pure and properly behaved should be worshipped by others. The devout are not *śūdra*s, but like Brahmins. Even earlier, Rāmānuja, who ate with low castes, thereby breaking the taboo on inter-dining, had endorsed this perspective by arguing that teaching Vedānta is not restricted to Brahmins.

After all these examples, Vijayavenugopal concluded:

> Unfortunately, this tradition was abandoned. How can it be revived? How are we to make people feel that they are Srīvaiṣṇavas and not identified with their castes? How are we to realise this in today's culture of reservations in the name of castes? A sincere effort should be made to achieve these Śrīvaiṣṇava ideals. True, it will be difficult in the field of religion and caste. Even so, it should be easy

> to open up Sanskrit and Tamil education by teaching the religious and philosophical texts to all Śrīvaiṣṇavas who want to study them. Here, the Śrīvaiṣṇava *maṭhas* have a role to play. Their activities should be broad-based.[20]

Vijayavenugopal's view of Śrīvaiṣṇava history was that there was once a golden age consisting of a casteless society, or at least leaders who believed in one. However, this declined over the centuries, despite periodic protests, and now, he argued, it has to be restored through reform.

The *Ācārya* Chosen by Lord Vēṅkaṭeśvara

In 1931, B. K. Rangachari wrote that:

> The Prabandhic movement of the Tengalais ... led to the rapid spread of Vaisnavism among all grades of people, and it became a popular creed. As a logical result of this movement several Non-Brahman castes, such as the Vanniyans, began to claim superiority, or at any rate, equality with the Sri Vaisnava Brahmans. This view was carried to such an extreme that certain Vanniyans took to the sacred thread, to the study of the Vedas and even to the establishment of temples and temple worship. Such a group of Vanniyans exists in Kumilam (Kumalam) village in South Arcot District .... So far, they have remained isolated and no mixture with Sri Vaisnava Brahmans has been affected. In spite of the theoretical views expressed by the Tengalai Brahmans, they have not mixed with them in any way.[21]

Kumalam is a Vanniyar (Nayakama) village. I met two priests there wearing *luṅgi*s and sacred threads, with their hair tied back in a knot. People addressed them as '*swami*'. The women of their families had diamond earrings, nose jewels, and gold bracelets; they were obviously well-off. One of the priests, Kannapiran Nadaswami, told me the history of the temple.

> My ancestor Ananta Nadaswami founded the temple. He used to visit Tirupati. According to both the family's

> tradition and the *purāṇa* about the village's temple,[22] Lord Vēṅkaṭeśvara appeared in a dream one night to him and said, 'Take the image of Vēṅkaṭeśvara that is in the Puṣkāraṇi temple tank and install it at a temple in your village.' The Lord himself then initiated Ananta Nadaswami and taught him the mantras.
>
> Our village is a substitute for Tirupati and thus has regional importance. People from other villages and even Chennai come here because of its sacred reputation. If they can't go to Tirupati for important rituals, they have them done here. The Tirupati influence is strong in Tamil villages. Members of all castes go there on pilgrimages. Sometimes, they walk there, which is over 200 kilometres from here. This is inspired in part by the fact that school children memorise an example of Tamil prose, written by a non-Brahmin, about a pilgrimage to Tirupati.

In the temple, I saw a 20-foot tall image of Lord Vēṅkaṭeśvara. It was coated in gold and adorned with many jewels. A statue of the family's ancestor, Ananta Nadaswami, was positioned before the Lord. The priest provided a leaflet about their Brahmotsava, which reveals that this festival is like those of major temples. They raise the flag at the beginning and lower it at the end. They take the *cakra* image to the tank, moreover, and everyone has a sacred bath. At the end, they perform twelve propitiations to compensate for any omissions during the festival. The chariot festival too is very popular at this place.

Kannapiran described the family's priestly roles.

> Four families act as priests for three months each. We wear sacred threads and call ourselves Banya Brahmins, that is, Brahmins who serve the Banyas (Vanniyars) or 'Brahmins among the Vanniyars'. Members of the Vanniyar priest families in this village are strictly vegetarian.

When I asked the village priests which Āgama tradition they followed for the temple rituals, they told me that they had Sanskrit texts written on palm leaves, and studied these before becoming priests. When I asked what kind of mantra they use, because this might identify the Āgama, they did not tell me.

In any case, the language of the *pūjā* combined Sanskrit and Tamil. Their language of conversation was colloquial, like that of Vanniyars in other villages.

Kannapiran continued with his oral history by saying that

> surrounding villages invite us to their temples to perform rituals, even though they are not Vaiṣṇava temples. We will conduct a *kumbha-abhiśekha* ritual or a *brahmotsava* for their *ammaṉ* (goddess) temple. Every twelve years, temples need this ritual to recharge their energy. Acting as Brahmin priests for the area is good business for the non-Brahmin priests of Kumanam village, but there is a big project in store. We need to renovate our own temple.

When I talked to a woman of a priestly family, I learned that it has matrimonial alliances only with the priests and cooks of the village. They never give their daughters in marriage to other families, although they accept girls for their sons from outside, if they are strict vegetarians, have had *samāśrayaṇam*, and follow the precepts according to family customs. A priest from their own family gives *samāśrayaṇam* and the rites of passage called *saṃskāras* to them.

I noticed that there are hardly any middle-aged men in the village. Those men probably have other jobs.

The Poet from Seliyamedu Village

The Puducherry network was active behind the scene, arranging people for me to meet. At some point, someone requested Kalladan[23] to take me to visit some Vaiṣṇava villages, including his own. By way of introduction, he told me his own story:

> I grew up in a village called Seliyamedu where my mother came from, and where my brother-in-law, K. Hariharane, still lives. After my primary education there, I went to Pondicherry for secondary school, as did many other children from this village. As a result, it is a well-educated village. I studied French at the Lycée Française and then

> worked for the government in personnel, tourism and information and publicity, becoming an under-secretary in general administration until I retired. I am a poet, following in the footsteps of my now deceased eldest brother, Vanidasan.
>
> Although I grew up in a Śrīvaiṣṇava family, I am not so interested in rituals and temples. I am not against prayer; however, I think it is more important to love others and be kind. For this reason, I am fond of the philosophy of Rāmaliṅga (1823–74), a great saint and poet from a village near Chidambaram.
>
> Considering that compassion is the only path to salvation and feeding the poor the highest form of worship, Rāmaliṅga set up a house to feed the needy in Vadalur, the Satya Dharma Salai. Against the caste system, Rāmaliṅga instituted the Samarasa Suddha Sanmarga Satya Sangam near Chennai. People of all castes could go, as long as they were vegetarians. His compassion extended to animals. Fire—represented by the fire in the stove that cooks food for the needy and a simple oil lamp that was to burn forever—is the only religious symbol he allowed.

I learned more about Kalladan from the Internet.[24] He has written more than eighteen books. These include short epics, collections of his poems, and a history of the *Tirukkuṛal*, for which he has won numerous government and literary awards.

Kalladan took me to his village, Seliyamedu. He said that most of the village is Naidu,[25] although there are also Reddiyars, Vanniyars, and Dalits. Originally, Naidus were Telugu speakers. Now, they have lost almost all of their Telugu. Their mother-tongue is really Tamil. By contrast, Reddiyars have maintained more Telugu.

After meeting his brother-in-law, Hariharane, we visited the Mathurakavi Alvar Sabha, which has been in this village for about fourteen years. (According to Kalladan, *sabhā*s are common in the districts around Puducherry; there are almost sixty of them.) Six men had gathered there to meet me. They described the *sabhā*'s activities. Aside from caring for the village temples, they raise funds and organise various religious activities.[26] They hold *bhajana*s, for instance, at which they sing folk songs about Krishna, Rāma, Tirumāl, and Keśava. And they chant the *Tiruppāvai*, using booklets for the words. On Saturday evening, the *bhajana* is combined with feeding about fifty people curd rice, tamarind rice, and dal. Everyone in the village comes. The *sabhā* organises festival celebrations for Krishna and Hanuman; the village has a temple for each. Villagers take the images in procession through the streets. They celebrate the festival of Ādipuram, too, and one for Āṇṭāḷ. During the month of Mārkaḻi, about thirty people gather in early morning to chant her *Tiruppāvai*.

Pilgrimage is a major activity for these villagers. Each year, a group of about fifty men take vows to walk barefoot to Tirupati, which is about 250 kilometres away. They return by bus. Others go to Tiruvahindrapuram each year. Occasionally, villagers go to Sriperumbudur, Cirkali, and Nanguneri (where the Vānamāmalai Mutt is located) in the far south. All have gone to Srirangam temple once or twice in their lifetimes.

The *sabhā* holds an annual conference. Bhāgavatas come from all over Tamil Nadu and Puducherry to hear lectures on the *Divyaprabandham* and other topics. These lectures are mainly by Bhāgavatas. As one *sabhā* member said, 'We are not against the Brahmins; if they talk nicely, we invite them and one or two come.' Finally, the *sabhā* offers food to the poor in times of heavy rains and famine; this is called *annadānam*, the gift of food.

The village's Vaiṣṇavas, they said, worship other gods as well. They go, for instance, to the Śiva temple and the Mārīyammaṉ temple. The latter is a recent phenomenon. They believe that all gods are one. Besides, worshipping more than one god helps to unite the village. The one couple that has had *samāśrayaṇam* from the *jīyar* of the Emperumāṉār Mutt in Tirukkoyilur, however, goes only to Vaiṣṇava temples. There is one Brahmin priest, a Śaiva, in the village. He does *pūjā*s in the morning and evening at the Śiva temple, as well as weddings and funerals.

When I asked members of the *sabhā* why they are Śrīvaiṣṇavas, they told me that it was the tradition of their ancestors. Alluding to the *Divyaprabandham*, one man liked the fact that pure Tamil is used. Another said that each god has special features. Rāma is famous for the bow, for instance, and Hanuman for sharp speech. On the topic of how to ensure a better future for Śrīvaiṣṇavism, one man commented that: 'We have enough hymns and don't need to seek other things; therefore, we need to preserve the tradition only by reading, understanding and propagating it.'

Sabhā members were at first reluctant to talk about their political affiliation. Finally, they went around the circle and named it: DMK, Congress, Congress, DMK, Congress, DMK. They were evenly split. Naidus are mainly in the DMK and Reddiyars mainly in Congress, they said, although some Naidus and some Vanniyars are also in Congress. Only during an election is there friction.

On the topic of their relations with Brahmins, they concurred that relations are good. 'Now,' one man commented, 'there is no enmity or misunderstanding.' Another said:

> And everyone mingles. When the Dravidian movement was strong in the mid-twentieth century, there was lots of antagonism. Besides, Brahmins used to do only religious affairs. Now, they have other occupations and are less pious. Non-Brahmins consider religion a matter of faith. Brahmins consider it a profession. Therefore, Brahmins are money-oriented. Today, if Brahmins concentrate just on religion, they will be poor. Only a few will belong to a rich temple and do well. Meanwhile, non-Brahmins are propagating the religion.

When I informed these villagers about the new programme in Chennai, training non-Brahmins to become priests in village temples, they became very excited. 'This is a good thing,' one said. 'It equalises society.'

These villagers were aware of some differences between Teṉkalai and Vaṭakalai sub-sects, beginning with the fact that their *nāmam*s are slightly different. Of the six people talking to me, five were Teṉkalai and one Vaṭakalai. One Teṉkalai reported: 'The Vaṭakalai Brahmins say that they alone are Brahmins; all Teṉkalais are non-Brahmins and therefore merely Bhāgavatas. Vaṭakalais often have the names Rāma and Krishna, moreover, whereas Teṉkalais use the name Bālāji.'

On the drive back to Puducherry, Kalladan and I discussed the function of the *sabhās*, which were prevalent everywhere I went. Many, he remarked, are combinations of men's clubs, charities and shared interests (which vary from religion to poetry). Judging from the number of older men I saw involved, the *sabhās* also offer purposeful activities for seniors.

Kalladan had mentioned that his older brother Vanidasan (1915–74) had been a famous poet. At first, he wrote about nature and love. Then, after joining Periyar and C. N. Annadurai, he wrote political poems, eventually publishing more than seventeen collections. He was honoured by the Tamil Nadu and French governments.[27]

The Conference Convener

Riding through the lush rice paddies southwest of Puducherry, I finally came to my destination for the day: the small village of Sambareddy Palayam in Cuddalore district.

I was greeted by Varadarajan Naidu, who was ninety-two, and his son, the village leader, V. Sampat Ramanuca Dasar.

Sampat commented that this agricultural village is in a very fertile area, on account of a vast irrigation system fed by the Perumal Lake. The fact that the lake takes its name from an important name of the Śrīvaiṣṇava God suggests a Śrīvaiṣṇava link with villages of the surrounding area. I soon learned that this is indeed a Śrīvaiṣṇava village. Remarked Sampat:

> These villagers are Telugu-speaking Naidu landowners, wearing the *nāmam* and marking their homes with it as well. They are totally vegetarian. Our village temple is dedicated to Rāma. Because we no longer have a Brahmin priest to perform *pūjā*, my family makes its own daily

IMAGE 4.1: V. Sampat Ramanuca Dasar in Sambareddy Palayam (Cuddalore district) holding a book with Rāmānuja's picture, published by Aranga Perumal Ramanusan.

Image credit: Author's collection.

> offerings. Beyond the village are the quarters of the Harijans who do hard labour in the rice paddies.

As I toured the village, someone remarked that the government wanted the village to integrate its Dalits, a proposal that the speaker did not like (judging from his grimace). Rejoining Sampat, I learned more about him.

> I received my *samāśrayaṇam* from the grandfather of the present *jīyar* of the Emperumāṉār Mutt in Tirukkoyilur. I am the secretary of the Sri Vakula Bhaskara Sabha, an organisation founded in 1937 and named for Nammāḻvār (Vakuḷa). It holds an annual conference, a day of learning on the birth-star of Nammāḻvār in the month of Vaikāśī. The organisation invites mainly non-Brahmin scholars to give lectures. People come from surrounding villages in a 30-mile radius. They also come from Puducherry, Cuddalore and Chidambaram. At one conference, we released a book called *True Knowledge about Mokṣa*,[28] which contains the text of Piḷḷai Lokācārya's *Arcirāti* and a commentary by Aranga Perumal Ramanucan Dasar, a Naidu intellectual from Pondicherry who knows both Sanskrit and Tamil. Its first page has a colour picture of Nammāḻvār and its last page one of Rāmānuja.

I had already interviewed Aranga Perumal Ramanucan Dasar, and found it intriguing to see support for his publishing activities in this small agricultural village.[29]

The Young Woman and her Internet Conversion

I met Dr Suganya Anandakichenin ('Suganya') in Puducherry, Vienna and Hamburg at several workshops of NETamil, a project funded by the European Union about the interaction of languages and cultures in Tamil Nadu.

At the time, Suganya was doing her Ph.D. in Hamburg on one of the *āḻvārs*, Kulacēkara, and so we shared many interests in Śrīvaiṣṇavism, especially its scripture, the *Divyaprabandham*. It was only after several years, however, that someone told me

IMAGE 4.2: Dr Suganya Anandakichenin, a Śrīvaiṣṇava scholar, at a workshop at École Française d'Extrême-Orient in Puducherry.

Image credit: Author's collection.

that she is a non-Brahmin whom I should interview. I did. Here is her story.

> I grew up in Pondicherry in a family of teachers (my father was the headmaster of a government school). I studied at the Elysée Française. At eighteen, I went to Paris where I did an M. A. in English and then started a Ph.D. in English literature. Because I was becoming interested in my own culture, I did not finish that degree. Rather, I did a Masters in Tamil at Institut National des Langues et Civilisations Orientales (INALCO), with a focus on modern Tamil short stories. I then started my Ph.D. with a focus on Śrīvaiṣṇavism. I wanted to write the thesis in English, and so I transferred to the University of Hamburg to work with the Tamil scholar Dr Eva Wilgen. While I was writing my thesis, entitled 'Kulacēkara Āḻvār and his Perumāḷ Tirumoḻi', I worked for the French Embassy school in Delhi. After I finished my Ph.D., I have been based in Puducherry at the École Française d'Extrême-Oriente (EFEO).
>
> I belong to the Yadava caste. From the names of my ancestors, it is obvious that about 100 years ago, the family had been Śrīvaiṣṇava, and some had had initiation. I have pictures of my great-great grandfather, with the family name Piḷḷai, with a *nāmam*. He was born in the French colony of Mauritius and became a trader. Our family has sometimes intermarried with the descendants of Anandaraṅgam Piḷḷai (1709–61), a famous trader who rose in the ranks of the French East India Company to become chief *dubhash* (an interpreter and provisioner of ships) of French India. He is famous for his diaries that describe eighteenth-century life in Pondicherry.
>
> My father's family were Vaṭakalais, my mother's Teṉkalais (her grandparents were from Tirukkurunkudi, which is a *divyadeśa*). It seems that this strong Śrīvaiṣṇava family identity faded. When I was growing up, no one in my household had been initiated.

Suganya's reference to Anandaraṅgam Piḷḷai reminded me that I had met one of his descendants and had a tour of the family mansion, now a heritage building in Puducherry. The conversation turned from the history of the family to Suganya's 'Internet conversion', as she put it.

> Since I was a teenager, I feared rebirth as a dog and searched for a way out of *saṁsāra*, the cycle of death and rebirth. I read many books on Advaita Vedānta. At that time, the Kanchi Śaṅkara 'pontiff' Chandrasekhara was very popular and had inspired my mother and then me to become vegetarian. Our household was like any other average Hindu household: we worshipped many deities, chanted hymns, performed vows and celebrated festivals. I began to study Sanskrit with a Śrīvaiṣṇava scholar.
>
> In 2005, when I was in Europe, I was exploring Śrīvaiṣṇavism on the Internet. I began to interact with Sri Ranga Sri, the publisher and scholar in Srirangam. He told me that *samāśrayaṇam* was the only way to achieve liberation and sent me to a site that answered many questions about liberation. Later, someone suggested that I contact Dr V. Sadagopan, a Vaṭakalai living in New York, who was the moderator of a Yahoo group. He told me that Rāmānuja promised *mokṣa*.
>
> Viṣṇu was always my personally chosen form of God (*iṣṭadevatā*) and I had been influenced by the television version of the *Rāmāyaṇa*. One of my aunt's colleagues was a Teṉkalai Brahmin *ācārya*. He didn't think that it was a good idea to have initiation because it would be very difficult to keep all the rules. Sadagopam convinced me, however, that it should be done, because even the desire for the ritual is installed in one's mind by the Divine Couple.
>
> In February 2005, I was in Paris. Because I was worried about the food rules and the fact that I could only worship Viṣṇu if I were initiated, I talked to my parents because initiation would add complications to our relationship in the future. Despite some initial opposition on their part, I decided to go ahead, worried that I could die before being initiated. My parents met Sriivan Sathakopa Sri Narayana Yatindra Mahadesikan, the forty-fifth *jīyar* of the Ahobila *maṭha*, to see if he were willing to perform the ritual. We fixed the auspicious time and place for it

> when I was still in Paris. It would be during the retreat season, when the 80-year-old *jīyar* was staying at a *maṭha* near Kumbakonam.
>
> After I returned from Paris, I went with my extended family there for *samāśrayaṇam* and the additional Vaṭakalai ritual. The *jīyar* was very flexible. He explained the importance of being vegetarian and then said that if I could not follow all the dietary restrictions, I could eat meat because ultimately it is the soul's liberation that is important, not what one eats. One should not worship another god, however, and not hurt another devotee. The day I was initiated, I received my *jīyar*'s sandals (*pādukas*), which he wears once and then gives to a disciple. The *pādukas* are now in our household shrine. I saw my *jīyar* just one more time before he died.
>
> At the time of my initiation, the *jīyar* chided my parents for not being Śrīvaiṣṇavas, because he knew that Yadavas have traditionally worshipped Viṣṇu, and therefore only I was being sensible. At first my father was indifferent to this goading; however, the next year both he and my mother were initiated.
>
> I don't chant all the verses of my *jīyar*'s lineage, just his. I have done several *kaiṅkaryas* or services; for instance, the day I was initiated, I did one. I have also visited many *divyadeśas*.

When I asked Suganya if she had experienced any discrimination as a non-Brahmin Śrīvaiṣṇava, she mentioned the following:

> Once at Srirangam, the *prasādam* was first given to Srirangam Brahmins, then other Brahmins and then only to non-Brahmins like myself. On another occasion, however, many people were waiting to enter the temple. For some reason, a Brahmin took me immediately into the sanctum all the way up to the deity. Perhaps it was because I looked wealthy and fair.

Colour-coding, as anthropologists have long warned, is a fallible guide to caste.

* * *

Before I arrived in Puducherry, I thought that one distinctive feature about Puducherry would be its French heritage. Coming from Quebec, the French part of Canada, I was curious how much French culture remained. From my everyday experience in the area, I encountered the proverbial *baguette* and *café au lait* for breakfast, and a few fine French restaurants in the colonial (and tourist) section of town, called 'White Town', along with architectural monuments such as Our Lady of the Immaculate Conception Cathedral, the wonderful colonial architecture, and a very active Alliance Française.

I found little French still spoken, except by the many French tourists attracted here, visiting French scholars, people who had worked for the French government, or those whose ancestors had had an important position in the French East India Company, and who had opted for French citizenship, yet continued to live in Puducherry. More to the point, there seemed to be no connection of the French heritage with Śrīvaiṣṇavism, except for some research by scholars on this religious tradition (such as the Vaṭakalai ṣcholar Varada Desikan and the epigraphist Vijayavenugopal, at the École Française d'Extrême-Oriente).

Aside from several Śrīvaiṣṇava temples in Puducherry and its outskirts, the hub for the general region—that extended beyond the Union Territory into Tamil Nadu proper—was the Emperumāṉār *maṭha* in Tirukkoyilur, which had non-Brahmin disciples from many castes, such as Vanniyars, Naidus, Reddiyars and Dalits. (I will discuss this *maṭha* in another chapter.)

Many Bhāgavatas, in Puducherry and its surrounding villages, whom I had interviewed, had been initiated by Srinivasa Ramanuja Jiyar of this *maṭha* (or, if they were elderly, by his father Tiruvenkata Ramanuja Jiyar). These disciples periodically visited their *jīyar* and maintained close relations. Śrīvaiṣṇavas had a special connection to places further away, such as Sriperumbudur. Dr Pandurangan, for instance, was the disciple of Varataa Ethiraja Jeeyar and periodically visited him at Sriperumbudur. Others wanted to visit Rāmānuja's birthplace at Sriperumbudur or the *samādhi* of Bhuvanagiri in a nearby field. Still others had a special connection with Tirumalai-Tirupati, despite the distance. Many had gone on pilgrimage there and one village, Kumanam, had established a local reputation as a Tirupati replica, as it were. The draw, therefore, seemed more towards the north rather than south to Srirangam, the other great Śrīvaiṣṇava centre. Nevertheless, many had gone on pilgrimage there too.

Speaking of sacred geographies reminds me of the one I discussed in Chapter 2, which was related to the late nineteenth-century non-Brahmin leaders Rāmānuja Nāvalar, Bhuvanagiri, and Nārāyaṇa Dāsar. As I noted in that context, there were temples and *samādhi*s connected with these figures: Nāvalar's to the north of Puducherry, Bhuvanagiri's near Cuddalore, and Nārāyana Dāsar's near Tirukkoyilur. Today, these are functioning as local temples. Although Bhuvanagiri's shrine was on the verge of historical oblivion, Nāvalar's shrine, where an annual festival is held in his honour, maintains some links with the past, and continues to serve as a local shrine.

Notes

1. See Chapter 2, section: 'A Forgotten Colonial History'. Besides a general conversion, one might undergo a further initiation ritual, *samāśrayaṇam* (see Chapter 1).

2. See Reddiyar, *Nalayira Divya Prabandham*.

3. Bharatidasan is the pen name (after his mentor, the poet Subramanya Bharathiyar) of Kanakasabai Subburathinam (1891–1964), who was born into a merchant family and wrote Tamil political and social poems, plays, and short stories. He was an important figure in the Dravidian Movement, his song to Goddess Tamil eventually becoming the state song of Pondicherry.

4. See 'Maraneri-nambi'.

5. This idea belongs to a later oral tradition, not Toṇṭaraṭippoṭi's verses. I have never seen it expressed in *sampradāya* works either.

6. See Chapter 2, section: 'A Forgotten Colonial History'.

7. See Chapter 1, section: 'A Sectarian Primer' (Religious Leadership) and Chapter 6, section: '*Jīyar*s and *Ācārya*s with Non-Brahmin Disciples'.

8. See Chapter 3, section: 'The Lawyer and his Service'.

9. See Appendix 6, section: 'Two Nadars on Discrimination'.

10. See Chapter 1, section: 'The Politics of Religion'.

11. T. P. Meenakshisundaram (1901–80) practised law and was an advocate at Madras High Court from 1923. Knowing many languages, he became professor of Tamil at Annamalai University and then Presidency Collage, Madras. After that, he was director of the Centre for Advanced Study in Dravidian Linguistics at Annamalai University, followed by administrative appointments. Author of many books on Tamil language and literature, he won the Sahitya Academy Award (1975) and Padma Bhushan (1976).

12. Karunanidhi was subsequently Chief Minister in 1971–74, 1989–91, 1996–2001 and 2006–10.

13. Mayawati has been Chief Minister of Uttar Pradesh four times, the last being 2007–12, and a member of the Rajya Sabha, the upper-house of Parliament, since 2012. In the 2019 election race, she expressed ambitions to be Prime Minister if the BJP did not win and her party formed an alliance with other parties to gain power.

14. Vijayavenugopal, 'Sri Vaisnavam-Tomorrow', 6–18.

15. Dr Vijayavenugopal might not have known about Bhuvanagiri and Ekāṅgi Svāmikaḷ in the late nineteenth century.

16. D. Jayakanthan, from an agriculturalist family in Cuddalore, South Arcot, had problems with his father, which led him to quit school at grade three. By twelve, he ran away from home and was brought up by an uncle who was inspired by both communism and the poetry of Subramanya Bharathi. Jayakanthan's mother then took him to a friend in Chennai, a member of the Communist Party of India (CPI), to see if he could provide a positive role model for her son. Jayakanthan worked in the CPI office as a lad and came to know many of the CPI leaders. One of them provided a Tamil tutor for his education (which facilitated his later literary success). When the CPI was marginalised by the DK and DMK and restrictions placed on it, Jayakanthan called them fascists and even publicly debated Periyar. All this forced him to turn to odd jobs for survival. As he reflected on his experiences, he became a writer, winning several prestigious awards, culminating in the Padma Bhushan in 2009. In his writings

and film scripts, he often portrays people on the margins of society and argues that a social stratum is defined by a person's behaviour, asking rhetorically, 'Why I am a Brahmin' (though born a non-Brahmin)? See 'Jayakanthan'.

17. He performed *upanayana* for a young Harijan, to turn him into a Brahmin. This was in line with his famous saying, 'there are only two castes in the world: One who is educated and one who is not'. See 'Subrmania Bharati'.

18. Vijayavenugopal, 'Sri Vaisnavam-Tomorrow', 6–18.

19. Ibid., 6–7.

20. Ibid., 17.

21. Rangachari, *Sri Vaishnava Brahmins*, 44.

22. I am told that there is a several hundred-year-old *sthala-purāṇa* that describes the temple and its history in more detail. I have not seen this text; my informants say, however, that a copy exists with Loka-nayakar-bania, who lives in a Chennai suburb.

23. This is his pen name; his real name is T. Janagiraman.

24. See 'Kalladan'.

25. Kalladan explained that these 'Naidus' are the same as Yādavas or shepherds.

26. Members pay membership fees of Rs 1,000, and now there is a Rs 50,000 fund. The interest is used for events. On special occasions, people give money (it costs about Rs 20,000 for a one-day conference).

27. See '*Vanidasan: Selected Poems*'. There are several critical studies in Tamil on him.

28. Its name is *Meyyaṟivum Vītupeṟum Mūlamum Uraium*.

29. See Chapter 4, section: 'The Scholar, Teacher and Publisher'.

five

Tales from Srirangam, Tanjavur and Beyond

K. K. A. Venkatachari arranged interviews for me at Srirangam with non-Brahmin gardeners and Sattadas, as well as one Brahmin *ācārya* with many non-Brahmin disciples, whom I will discuss in the next chapter. Having deep family connections at this famous temple, Venkatachari also arranged for my own private *darśana* of Lord Raṅganātha—something extremely rare for foreigners. I then understood how the sight of Raṅganātha had so thrilled Tiruppāṇ Āḻvār that he broke into ecstatic song: '... My God! His lovely dark body of unfading beauty strung with pearls and big dazzling gems fills my heart!' (*Amalaṉātipiraṉ* 9)[1].

The focus of my second trip was Tanjavur, both the city and the district. My guide was Dr B. M. Sundaram, the son of a famous Śaiva musician from this locale and a Śrīvaiṣṇava mother. We relived his family history. In addition, I interviewed several Bhāgavata musicians and *bhajana* singers. This gave me a better understanding of the link between non-Brahmin Śrīvaiṣṇavas and the musical world of Tyāgarāja and Maharashtrian *bhajana* traditions.

Gardeners for the Lord's Garlands

In Srirangam, I met C. Ramachandra, a Naidu, who received his *samāśrayaṇam* from a Vaṭakalai *jīyar*.[2] Ramachandra is a trustee of the Negamam Zamindar Charity, which helps educate Śrīvaiṣṇavas. He described the charity as follows.

> The charity was founded by the Zamindar Rama Krishna Naidu, my distant relative, who lived at the turn of the twentieth century and was from Negamam village near Coimbatore. In the 1870s, the Zamindar founded a garden called Tirunandavam at Srirangam near the Ammā Maṇṭapam by the Kaveri river.
>
> The Zamindar was close friends with an *ekāṅgi* named Maturakavi after the *āḻvār* who was Nammāḻvār's disciple. This *ekāṅgi* used to do *kaiṅkarya* by making garlands with flowers from this garden for Lord Raṅganātha and Tāyār (the goddess) in the Srirangam temple. In 1908, the Zamindar bought land at Srivilliputur and started another garden. The Zamindar had two wives, but no children. In 1915, he moved with his second wife to Srirangam, purchased a house and built a *rāmānuja kūṭam*. At this time, he set up a trust in his will to support the school established by Bhuvanagiri. Today, the trust is administered by Srirangam descendants of Negama Zamindar and his wife, some Chettiyars from Negamam village and some Srirangam Bhāgavatas.

A few days later, I visited the garden at Srirangam. Two gardeners, Sriman Ramanuja Dasar and Sriman Venkattaramanuja Dasar, showed me around. They told me that they were non-Brahmin *ekāṅgi*s who followed the example of Mathurakavi, the original gardener here. They described the religious significance of gardening.

> Gardening is called *puṣpa kaiṅkarya* (service with flowers) and refers back to the *āḻvār*s, who often mention worship with flowers in their poems. We chant the *Tiruppāvai* and other short *Divyaprabandham* works when picking the flowers. We make twelve garlands daily for Lord Raṅganātha and the goddess in the Srirangam temple

> and many more for the sixty festivals that occur annually there.[3]

For me, strolling through the garden and identifying flowers was a welcome respite from the hectic schedule of interviews. It also brought to life the many references in the works of the *ālvār*s about gardening as service to God.

Srirangam Sattadas Speak Up

In Srirangam, I went to a Śrīvaiṣṇava bookstore[4] to meet some Sattadas. One was K. P. Sundararajan, the supervisor of the Sattadas who serve in the Srirangam temple. As the senior Sattada, he carries the sceptre or silver stick in processions. This is what he told me:

> For nine generations, someone in my family has been honoured by the temple by being taken in procession on an elephant around the temple. Despite the honours, my family is very poor. We receive no salary from the temple. Rather, we serve there for the sake of tradition. I have four sons. Two are employed outside the temple (one in the government, another in an electrical company); the other two work in the temple. The family's specialty is making the garlands with leaves in the form of parrots for Vaikuṇṭha Ekādaśī and other special days. Two days of the year we carry the Lord on our shoulders; one is the procession on the first day of Brahmotsavam.
>
> Nalan Cakravarti Ayyangar at Alvartirunagari initiated me. Other Sattadas are initiated by the Vānamāmalai *jīyar* at Nanguneri or someone in the Parāśara Bhaṭṭar family in Srirangam.
>
> Today, Sattadas wear the sacred thread elsewhere, but not at Srirangam in the temple. Sattadas have no Sanskrit and no Veda. They chant only Tamil for their daily worship in the home shrine. They once had a *Divyaprabandham goṣṭhi* (a registered group in the temple for chanting), but not now because they don't have the sacred thread [this will be discussed in Chapter 7].

Sundararajan gave me his version of the history of Sattadas at Srirangam. This service, he claimed, began at the time of Rāmānuja. At that time, Sattadas stopped wearing the thread because Rāmānuja said that the daily rituals should be done without it. The next important figure was Kaṇṭātai Rāmānuja Ayyaṅkar.[5] He was an ascetic Sattada who served the temple and guarded the place, which is symbolised by an image of him with a knife at one of the entrances to the temple. He was with the deity from morning to night, even in processions. When the temple was closed, he was authorised to lock and unlock it.

I also met R. Andal. 'My native place is Madurai,' she told me, and with great animation, leapt into her life story.

> My grandfather had his own temple called Śrīnivāsa Perumāḷ Kōyiḻ in Koyilpatti, three hours from Madurai. It remained in the family. Then my father gave it away when he moved the family to Madurai to improve our opportunities by starting his own business selling sweets, crackers, and so forth. It was hard work. By the grace of God, he now has four savoury shops in Madurai. I am one of five children. Today, the business is in the hands of the kids. It is not doing so well. As a result of becoming business people, no one in my family is now a Sattada serving in a temple. Nevertheless, my father used to give monetary help to the temple. This was his *kaiṅkarya*.
>
> There are two types of Sattadas. Some speak Tamil and do *kaiṅkarya* in the temple. They are conservative and marry only within the community. The others speak Telugu, generally don't work in temples and go for better jobs. I am from the Telugu community. There are now thirty-six Sattada temple families in Tamil Nadu.
>
> I went to Madurai Kamaraj University and then did a B. A. by correspondence at Anna University in Tamil literature. In 1977, I married an engineer who is from a Sattada family in Salem. Some of my husband's relatives are still doing *kaiṅkarya*, making garlands and living on their temple incomes. My husband's family doesn't have deep knowledge of Śrīvaiṣṇava texts. Whereas my

father's family was 'orthodox' and ate only at home or inside Viṣṇu temples, my husband's family ate outside and went to other temples. My husband had no spiritual awareness. I inspired him to receive *samāśrayaṇam* from the Vāṇamāmalai *jīyar* in about 1990, and then I got all my husband's relatives, about 100 people in Salem, to do this. Now all the children receive *samāśrayaṇam* from the same *jīyar*.

My first daughter is in the United States working in information technology. Her husband Sudarshana is also from a Sattada family. My other daughter is doing her doctorate in homeopathy here in Tamil Nadu (Tambaram). My eldest son is studying in Anna University.

I have memorised some of the *āḻvār*s' hymns, and I am taking a post-graduate diploma in Śrīvaiṣṇavism. It was organised by A. Krishnamacarya at Srirangam. I have studied all the important Maṇipravāḷa texts with Ubhayavedānta Narasimhacharya, a *kōyiḻ vidvāṉ* (traditional temple scholar), and have learned recitation and interpretation in the traditional manner. I take classes for eight Brahmin ladies in the morning and eleven boys and girls in the evening. I do this in my home every day. My second daughter is doing a Śrīvaiṣṇava course by correspondence from Krishnamacharya.

Sometimes, I give public lectures on Śrīvaiṣṇavism, for example, on the greatness of the *ācārya*s and the greatness of Tiruppāṇ Āḻvār. On those occasions, I wear a nine-yard sari, which my mother and other Sattada women used to wear, just like the Ayyaṅkar (Brahmin) women. I am teaching my elder brother's daughter about the tradition. My eldest son sometimes gives spiritual talks in various places.

When a woman is pregnant, someone will come and chant daily, from the third month to the time of birth, the *Mumukṣupati*, *Ācārya Hṛdayam* and *Śrīvacana Bhūṣaṇam* so that the child in the womb will obtain wisdom. Now, my daughter in the United States is pregnant and is using a CD for the same purpose.

At this point, Andal broadened her discussion to community activities.

> Sattadas have an annual gathering in each district of Tamil Nadu. I give lectures for women at these, as do some men. The community has not had much inclination to learn about Śrīvaiṣṇavism, although slowly awareness and education are developing. When the community gathers, it holds discussions, arranges marriages and solicits funding for education. It holds competitions on the *Tiruppāvai* and hosts general oratory events as well as singing by children. It even holds fashion shows. When any of these functions begin, someone will chant some *āḻvār* verses from the dais. I am one of the few who does this.
>
> Sattadas attend an annual gathering in Tamil Nadu. It is organised by T. R. Parthasarathy and Raja Gopalan, who also put out a little journal in Triplicane. At this time, we exchange horoscopes for potential marriages and do charity work. The ladies wing is involved in a government self-employment programme.
>
> Although located mainly in south India, Sattadas have spread everywhere, both in India and abroad. The All India Sattada Srivaisnava Mahanatu brings them together. Narmada Devi, a Sattada who is a medical doctor in Ohio, collects donations for the community's uplift. Many donors outside India have good jobs. Here in India, many don't. Sattadas are not politically organised. They don't put pressure on the temples for better pay. They have no union. They just want to serve the temple so that it will develop.

The next day, I visited the Sattada Srivaisnava Matam; a sign calls it a *rāmānuja kūṭam*.[6] The Srirangam temple procession stops in front, to honour the Sattadas. This Sattada organisation has a president and vice-president and a priest named Gopala, who is also the priest for the Amma Mantapam, a place where various rituals for non-Brahmins are performed, and where Sattadas gather on Vaikuṇṭha Ekādaśi.

The Musicologist's Memories of Temple Music

On the Internet, one finds articles about, and interviews with, music *vidvāṉ* B. M. Sundaram. They include ones originally written for newspapers such as *The Hindu* and *The Indian Express*, or the music and dance magazine *Sruti*. According to his official biography, 'B.M. Sundaram is a leading historian of South Indian dance and music. Hailing from a traditional family of musicians that can be traced back over 40 generations, he has published extensively on the performance cultures and communities of South India.'[7]

When I first interviewed him, Sundaram, who was then over eighty, showed no signs of slowing down, as documented by the public record of his recent accomplishments. His personal story shows a different side to this musicologist, one that is germane to the theme of this book: discrimination. He belongs to the Icai Velala community. First, some background.

As explained by Davesh Soneji, the term *icai vēḷāla*—the cultivators of music—indicates a new *jāti*. As recorded in colonial census reports and ethnographies, Icai Velalas had described themselves as *vēḷāla*s, *piḷḷai*s, and *mutali*s. Traditionally, the elite of this group were female dancers (*devadāsī*s) and male musicians (and dance masters) who played the oboe-like *nāgasvaram* and *tavil* drum at the great temples of Śiva and Viṣṇu, as well as at marriages of elite castes. Some members of this community, however, had to eke out their living by combining these roles with other jobs.[8] As such, there were many sub-groups of varying status.

The next day, we visited Sundaram's home in Tanjavur. My questions about the paintings and photos on the wall brought forth memories from his childhood.

> My father had two wives. One had five daughters and one son. That son who became a famous musician was my half-brother. My mother also had five daughters, who all died, and one son—me. My father named me Sundaram, a Śaivite name. My mother was a Śrīvaiṣṇava from Tiruppernagar.

Pointing to a stunning picture of her, Sundaram commented:

> She was very fair, beautiful and cultured. My mother would teach us *Divyaprabandham* verses, my father *Tevāram* ones. People thought that she was an Ayyaṅkar, a Brahmin Śrīvaiṣṇava. She even spoke like one. I learned the Brahmin Ayyaṅkar speech from her. My mother had had *samāśrayaṇam*. She chanted devotional hymns in the morning, visited temples, and went on pilgrimages to Srirangam and Tirupati. She was not a *devadāsī* (a temple dancer), and nor was her mother. The family was connected with Śrīvaiṣṇava temples because the men were *nāgasvaram* players.[9] They played in the temple, for instance, after the priest recited the *suprabhātam* to awaken God in the morning.
>
> In the family, only my mother and I were vegetarian. My father, his first wife, and her children were all non-vegetarian. My mother wouldn't cook non-vegetarian food. Because my father had two wives, there were two households. When my father was with my mother, he would have one of his disciples bring food from the hotel. I didn't sit with my father for lunch, but with my mother. My father was very happy that I was vegetarian. He wanted me to fit into the Brahmin world.
>
> That was also why he wanted me to study Sanskrit as a second language and be able to recite religious verses. Once, when he was very young, a Brahmin had insulted him, saying, 'Don't talk to us. We are discussing important things in Sanskrit, which you don't know.' Because of this insult, my father wanted me to know Sanskrit. My mother didn't learn Sanskrit, yet she could recite religious verses. Her behaviour was just like that of the Brahmins. They told her, 'You are more Brahmin than we are!' Some priests would even let her go into their kitchen, where strict purity was maintained.
>
> I wore a *dhoti* like the Brahmins. My father did not. Brahmins used to call me 'Sundaram Iyer', Iyer being a Brahmin name. We have only Vedic rituals with Brahmin priests for weddings in my family. This has been a tradition from the time of our ancestors. Because of these

Brahmanical influences, many Brahmins to this day think that I am a Brahmin.

I think that all non-Brahmins should read Sanskrit and become vegetarian. It would be a positive influence and would help them control their senses and lead pure lives. When the body is pure, the mind becomes pure and service will increase. Discipline is important. The Brahmins' way of life is important because it teaches great discipline.

In Tamil University (Tanjavur), no Sanskrit is taught. But in Karnataka, there is a Muslim village on a hill, where everyone speaks only in Sanskrit. The government wants non-Brahmin priests. For that they need to be trained in rituals and Sanskrit.

Sundaram next described how his relatives had been connected with the Srirangam temple.

My mother's grandfather was a musician who played at the Srirangam temple. His wife called him a 'water buffalo', because he would go to the temple and spend the whole day bathing in the Kaveri river. Then, he would head for the toddy (liquor) shop before coming home. Another connection with Srirangam was my mother's sister's husband, who was a *nāgasvaram* player there.

Nāgasvaram musicians played during the daily *pūjā*s (at night, another musician would play the *vīṇā*). They also played during the temple processions, when one *nāgasvaram* and one *tavil* were mandatory, and at festivals, when they were engaged only for that occasion. Generally, there was only one family of musicians at a temple; they would receive rice, oil, and food from the temple. Even if offered more economic benefits elsewhere, they would stay there. Each temple had a particular musical tradition, although some compositions were played in most Vaiṣṇava temples. The temples were mainly interested in auspicious sounds, however, not composition. The only ritual honour given to the musicians was offering them the cloth that had been tied around the deity's head.

IMAGE 5.1: The Śrīvaiṣṇava wife of the *tavil* drummer Needamangalam Meenakshisundaram Pillai and mother of Dr B. M. Sundaram (former director of the music department, All India Radio, Puducherry).

Image credit: Author's collection.

> Musicians played also at weddings and auspicious social functions. Now cassettes have largely replaced live performances. The musicians have collaborated on these tapes.

Pointing to a small picture of his father with a large red *boṭṭu* (sacred forehead dot), Sundaram continued:

> My father, Needamangalam Meenakshisundaram Pillai, was dark-complexioned, a Śaiva, and a meat-eater. He learned how to play the *tavil* from his uncle. All the men in my father's family were *tavil* players. At the age of eight, my father was an accompanist. By the turn of the twentieth century, he was the most famous *tavil* player in south India and brought *tavil* playing to the stage. His fame was mainly in Tamil Nadu, because the *tavil* is a regional instrument.
>
> Because of The Madras Devadasis (Prevention of Dedication) Act of 1947, which made the tradition of female dancing at the temples illegal, the reputation of my community was in decline. This Act had criminalised professional dancer-courtesans. My father helped to improve its status by introducing the *tavil* and *nāgasvaram* to the concert stage. Unfortunately, he left few recordings.

On the way to Needamangalam, Sundaram's father's hometown, close to Mannargudi, Sundaram continued: 'My father put that village on the map because of his fame. That is why my father was sometimes called Needamangalam. I am the son of a great musician. Today there is mere learning. Before that, there was real education because of one's father's expertise.'

Thinking about his family, Sundaram told me more about his education, experiences at school, and desire to study music.

> I did my B. A. in Trichi (Tiruchirappalli) at St. Joseph's, which had about 1,600 students. It was very difficult to gain admission there because it was considered the best school. The priests kept a very strict discipline. If you were five minutes late, you had to pay twenty rupees. Although I wanted to study math and physics, my grades

were not high enough, and so I took economics and history. I liked history, not economics.

I was often teased for belonging to the Icai Velala community. When my mother would put powder on my face, my classmates would bully me, saying: 'Who earned the powder, your mother or your sister?' [The implication was that these professional dancing women earned their money as prostitutes.] I would reply: 'If you look like a Brahmin, then speak like a Brahmin.' Besides, in the past Brahmin men had sexual relations with the *devadāsī*s. If they had a child, it would be absorbed into the *devadāsī* community. Some Brahmin women were even attracted to the musician *vidvāṉ*s.

I used to hear my cousin being taught music and started to sing myself. Some people encouraged me to become a performer. My mother wanted me to be a tax collector. My father didn't want his sons to become musicians because, after the passing of the Devadasi Act, the reputation of our community had greatly declined. He thought that it would be impossible to have the same fame and respect in the future. Even now, people say behind my back that I 'belong to "that" community'.

The male musicians have fared better than the female dancers. In fact, now some *nāgasvaram* musicians don't want to give their girls in marriage to families that once had a *devadāsī* tradition because of the stigma. My mother would let me go to listen to music. My father would not allow even that.

I did odd jobs for Minakshi Sundaram Pillai, a famous dance master with the same name as my father. He arranged my marriage with his favourite student Balachandra, a great dancer who performed in elite homes in Tanjavur, but not in public because of the new stigma. She had never been initiated as a *devadāsī* because that tradition was on its way out. After our marriage in 1954, she decided not to perform again.

I didn't tell my friends about my marriage. They would think that I was not a real student. Once, I took my wife to a film in Trichi and ran into some classmates there. They thought that I was dating and went to my house to squeal. My wife was there, and my mother introduced her to them. My wife died just a few years later. I was devastated.

Another marriage was immediately arranged. My second wife, Lila, was educated and a badminton champion. She was the daughter of Janaki Ammal, a *devadāsī* who danced at the Prasanna Vēṅkaṭeśvara Perumāḷ temple in Tanjavur. A gentleman 'wanted Janaki'. Her father said, 'No. If you really want her, then marry her.' He did, and she stopped dancing from that day.

After my wedding, I decided to study music with M. Balamurali Krishna, who was in Vijayawada. My mother did not approve and threatened to give all the family property to my half-brother. Because she would not give me money to travel there, I collected funds from neighbours and went anyway. I arrived exhausted and dirty. Balamurali Krishna gave me a place to bathe, new clothes and a room. When he learned that I had been married only fourteen days earlier, however, he told me that my behaviour was bad and to go home. But after talking to my mother, he changed his mind and said that I was now to be his 'son'. I stayed with him for seven years, studying vocal music. Lila stayed with my mother.

Balamurali Krishna still performs and has a very melodious voice. He is more than merely a musical guru. There are many gurus in this world who will take money from their disciples, although few can remove trouble from their hearts. As the *Rāmāyaṇa* says, 'O my mind, please worship the feet that remove the sorrow of the common people.' He is still my guru, and we are in close communication.

My father died in 1949 on the day my stepbrother got married. My father wanted a traditional cross-cousin marriage for my stepbrother. This did not happen because the girl had a bad horoscope. It forecast that her mother-in-law would become a widow because of this marriage. Fourteen days after my father died, my elder brother picked up his drum and started to play. Within three concerts, he was famous, although he had had no formal training, and was paid a lot. Unfortunately, he became an alcoholic. He lived with his wife for only two months and then left her. Occasionally, my stepbrother would visit my mother, who was very fond of him. When his own mother died, he was in Ceylon and drunk. I had to perform all the death rituals for her.

In January 1963, my stepbrother was on his way back from Chennai where he had given a concert. Drinking heavily on the train, he fell down when disembarking in Tanjavur and died. He was only thirty-four. At 5:00 in the morning, someone brought the news to my mother. When she heard it, she fell down the stairs. After the fall, she became sickly. She made me promise never to play in public, that is, never to give concerts. I have kept that promise. She was then sixty. She died three months later. Just after my mother died, I went away with my guru, who was giving a concert in Mannargudi. It was decided that I had to stay with my wife Lila, who was still young and now alone. My mother had left all the property to me, despite vowing not to do so.

Once, my guru said that there were many vocalists but no researchers in the field of music. I should forget about a performance career because I could not expect money and fame. As a researcher, I could become famous and preserve our musical heritage. Then, my guru reminded me of the vow that I made to my mother not to be a performer. My guru knew that my research on music had begun in high school. On Saturdays and Sundays, I used to read manuscripts and books in the Sarasvati Mahal Library in Tanjavur. And so, I devoted myself to research on music.

I got my first job even before I went to St Joseph's. It was in 1951 at the All India Radio, Trichi station, which is one of eighty-three stations. I had a contract to sing and compose music. Sometime later, the director of All India Radio wanted me to be a composer on staff in Delhi and asked me to apply. I refused. The Pondicherry station started up, and my guru asked me to apply. This time, I did. There was a competition to select the music composer, which I won. In 1980, I was promoted to producer and as a government employee, I took care of an entire music

> department with all types of music. I had this job until I retired.

On 24 January 2011, we went to the Tyāgarāja festival, held every year since 1903 in Tiruvaiyaru, which is about half-an-hour by car from Tanjavur. 'The festival,' commented Sundaram, 'which usually attracts 20,000 people a day, both musicians and the general public, is of pan-Indian fame and is televised.' This day, the fourth in the five-day event, was very important because it commemorates the day on which Tyāgarāja attained enlightenment.

After watching the early morning worship on television, we headed for the *samādhi* where Tyāgarāja is buried, and where the crowds had gathered. The highlight was the singing of five compositions. According to Sundaram, the musicians sit in front of the *samādhi*-shrine, competing for the first row in order to be visible on television. Guests sit in a large tent to the side. An image of Tyāgarāja is ritually bathed. Usually, the *nāgasvaram* players start the music. This year, it was a very popular clarinet player.

Sundaram commented: 'Because of a dispute, I have taken a vow never to join the main festivities.' I waited outside the shrine, while Sundaram went for *darśana*. On the walls of the room where I waited were written some of Tyāgarāja's songs.

After we left the festival, Sundaram explained the relation between non-Brahmins and Brahmins in the music world. 'Brahmins are usually the vocalists, violinists, *mṛdaṅgam* players,[10] and *bhārata-nāṭyam* dancers. Those who belong to the Icai Velala community play the *tavil* and *nāgasvaram*. Because of the Devadasi Act, no women from our community now dance.' 'Why this division?' I asked, and Sundaram replied:

> In part, it is because the Brahmins don't have the technical skill to play the *tavil* and *nāgasvaram*, which necessitates a training traditionally found only in the Icai Velala community. The *tavil*, which is a very sensitive instrument, has no pitch, unlike the *mṛdangam* drum, and so the *tavil* artist must have mathematical prowess to create rhythmic variations throughout the performance.

> The *tavil* player accompanies the *nāgasvaram*, which is the main instrument, but takes the composition to greater heights and also performs a solo. Brahmins, moreover, view these instruments as polluting. Saliva ends up on the *nāgasvaram*, a wind instrument, and hands must touch the animal hides of the drums.
>
> In general, Brahmins view the Icai Velalas as low status and don't want to be associated with either them or their instruments. In fact, they have tried to keep Icai Velalas off the concert stage and relegated to *sabhā*s or local contexts that need auspicious music. As for the *devadāsī*s, any competition from them was completely removed by the Devadasi Act, which made their dancing illegal.

Sundaram pointed out that Tyāgarāja did not have this prejudice against non-Brahmin musicians. Even though he was a Telugu Brahmin, he had special relations with two Icai Velala *nāgasvaram* players: Swami Natham and Vedamswami Natham. They were probably his students. Sundaram continued his saga as follows:

> I think that the Icai Velala musical tradition will die out gradually. Because of their inferiority complex and their lack of guts to stand up to the Brahmins, they can't create their own association. Given these conditions, it would be a waste of time even to try. Because these musicians can't earn a living by playing only for *bhajana maṭam*s and *sabhā*s, Icai Velalas will lose their professional status. In the nineteenth and early twentieth century, Icai Velalas, or maybe Naidus, dominated musical performance. After that, there was a big decline. Today, non-Brahmin musicians search for other jobs. Many temples have stopped hiring *nāgasvaram* players or offer very poor pay. If they play at weddings, they get much more. Still, the non-Brahmin music tradition in general will fade.

As we walked the short distance from the Tyāgarāja *samādhi* to his family's own private temple, Sundaram reflected on his experience with the modern Brahmin control over the music world.

> In general, Brahmin-authored books avoid mention of Tyāgarāja's relations with non-Brahmins. The books on Tyāgarāja had been written by Brahmins, until I myself wrote one. Brahmins even now do not acknowledge my scholarship. Take the issue of where Tyāgarāja was born. They think that he was born in Tiruvarur. I have provided evidence to the contrary from manuscripts, compositions, old invitations to the festival, and logistics that it must have been in Tiruvaiyaru. For example, Tyāgarāja's father had been appointed by the Maharaja of Tanjavur to give daily lectures on the *Rāmāyaṇa;* therefore, he had to live a short distance from Tanjavur to travel back and forth. Tiruvarur is too far away.

We arrived at Sundaram's family temple. 'This temple was constructed by my mother's mother's father, who was Lakṣmaṇa Piḷḷai, a student of Tyāgarāja,' commented Sundaram.

> Once a year, all members of my family attend a festival here. Also, for any major event in the family, we go first to this temple. The deity is Aṅgala Parameśvarī. I don't know why my mother's family had this goddess shrine. They were considered Vaiṣṇavas who were connected with the Tiruppernagar temple, a Śrīvaiṣṇava *divyadeśa*. In fact, they were such strict Vaiṣṇavas that my mother's father, after returning late from the temple on Vaikuṇṭha Ekādaśī, would take so long putting on his *nāmam* that his wife would complain. She couldn't eat until he had eaten, and he wouldn't eat before putting on the *nāmam*. Maybe the family initially was a goddess family, but when Lakṣmana Pillai got a job as a *nāgasvaram* player at the Tiruppernagar temple, they became Vaiṣṇavas.[11]

The next day, Sundaram took me to a Naidu musician neighbourhood, the Mutthu Krishna Naidu colony,[12] which has about 100 houses. We located the house of Lakshmana Naidu, now an old man, whose family members had been *mṛdaṅgam* players for several generations. After introductions, he described his family's musical tradition.

> In the early twentieth century, my grandfather was the famous singer and *mṛdaṅgam* player Mutthu Krishnan, who had studied with well-known musicians.[13] The family was very wealthy at that time and had lots of land in Tanjavur. Although my grandfather himself had taught many Brahmins, they refused to acknowledge him when they in turn became famous. Over time, my family was marginalised from the music scene. I myself had a mental breakdown because of all this, and my son has had to take another job to keep going. He now teaches *mṛdaṅgam* only on the side for money or plays the *mṛdaṅgam* for other communities' *bhajanas*.
>
> My family has had a Śrīvaiṣṇava connection. Mutthu Krishnan received *samāśrayaṇam* from a Srirangam *ācārya*. Vēṅkaṭeśvara is the family's deity. Mutthu's son Virasami used to sing *Divyaprabandham* verses regularly, as did other members of the family. This tradition was given up by my time. I have not had *samāśrayaṇam*. But the family goes to the *maṭha* near the first lane of the neighbourhood. It is like a temple with its own Hanuman festival.

Lakshmana still wore a large *nāmam* on his forehead. Later, Sundaram suggested that this Naidu music tradition had been influenced by the Tyāgarāja tradition. 'Perhaps earlier generations were students of Tyāgarāja's disciples because Tyāgarāja's compositions were in their musical repertoire. Or perhaps it was the Telugu connection that attracted them to Tyāgarāja. Or his iconic status.' Hearing about these Naidu musicians reminded Sundaram of the difficult relations that Icai Velala musicians have had with Naidu musicians.

> Some Naidu musicians have discriminated against Icai Velalas. Nevertheless, some Icai Velalas have taken on the name Naidu, for example, Tirupati Narayana Swami Naidu, whose mother was a *devadāsī*. Many Naidus don't like their name being appropriated in this way. They call a man in the Icai Velala community the 'prostitute's son', even if his mother is married. When I hear this, I ask, 'Can you know for sure if your own wife is not a prostitute?'

Sundaram returned to this problem of prejudice against the Icai Velala community many times in the following days. The old insults that *devadāsīs* were prostitutes haunted him, even though he knew that they had been famous dancers and were wealthy and proud women outside the institution of marriage.

In the following days, we visited many *maṭhas* around Tanjavur. These belonged to the Maharashtrian Vaiṣṇava tradition that had come south with migrants after the establishment of Maratha rule in 1675. The new Maratha rulers enticed the Maharashtrian *kīrtaṅkars* (performers of songs about Rāma or Krishna[14]) to stay in their kingdom by offering them houses in Tanjavur, Mannargudi, and Konur. These houses became *maṭhas* and very popular places for worship and musical performances.[15] Between 1700 and 1830, the Marathi *kīrtana* tradition developed into performances with both devotional sermons and singing (*harikathās*), and performances with song, dance, and dramatic renditions of *purāṇic* stories accompanied by music. The Rāmadāsi *sampradāyas*[16] helped to popularise this movement.

Of relevance to me was how these *kīrtanas* and *harikathās* became an important part of the Śrīvaiṣṇava tradition, especially for non-Brahmins. The Śrīvaiṣṇava *ācāryas* and *jīyars* integrated their tradition into the *kīrtana* traditions of some Maharashtrian villages. Or the *kīrtaṅkars* integrated their *bhajanas* and *harikathā* performances into those of Tamil Śrīvaiṣṇava communities. 'The Śrīvaiṣṇava Empār Vijayarāghavacariar of Srirangam,'[17] said Sundaram, 'was the greatest *harikathā* performer.'

I saw also that the Śrīvaiṣṇava tradition and its link to the Maharashtrian *bhajana* tradition in some villages was in decline. One man said that his grandfather, father, and he had had *samāśrayaṇam*, but now that he was an old man, he had given up its required lifestyle because its orthodoxy was too demanding. Another said that his grandfather had sung *bhajanas* in street processions, although no one does that now. Young people refuse even to wear the *nāmam*.

One day, I went with Sundaram to Tirukkandiyur and interviewed Kulacekara Ramanuja Dasar. First, we visited his prosperous-looking house. Because he was not home, we went to his office near the court building. There, we encountered an imposing businessman with a big *nāmam* and a big moustache. After introductions, he began his life story.

> My parents and grandparents were Śrīvaiṣṇavas. When I joined the DK and then the DMK, I became an atheist and started to eat meat. I wanted to have a 'Member of the Legislative Assembly' seat. When I didn't obtain one, I reverted to Śrīvaiṣṇavism. My original name was Bhagavat Singh; I was initiated by Parasara Ranganatha Bhattar of Srirangam. He gave me the initiation name Kulacekara Ramanuja Dasar. Since then, I have been vegetarian. To be called a Bhāgavata, one must not only be vegetarian, but also wear the *nāmam* and have the conch and discus branded on the shoulders. Initiations for the non-Brahmins of this area are now done by the Vānamāmalai *jīyar* in Nanguneri, the Emperumāṉār Mutt *jīyar* in Tirukkoyilur, and Sri Chinna Jeeyar in Hyderabad.

Kulacekara was impeccably dressed because it was his birthday, and he was going to do *kaiṅkarya* in the form of feeding orphans. He added: 'I also do *kaiṅkarya* by feeding devotees three times a day during the twenty-five days of the Adhyayanotsavam festival and on Vaikuṇṭha Ekādaśī.' After showing us a carefully prepared ledger with the names and addresses of the Bhāgavatas he invites on these occasions, he remarked:

> There are 150 Bhāgavatas is this area. Brahmin Ayyaṅkars used to give classes on the 4,000 verses of the *Divyaprabandham* and on the *Śrīmad Bhāgavatam*. They no longer do this. They also used to come to do the death ritual (the *tirucūrṇa-paripalanam* or removing the power of the conch and discus branded on the shoulders). Although Dāsaris (non-Brahmin mendicants) could do it, the Ayyaṅkars did it in a more elaborate manner. Now, they rarely come, and so the death rituals are done by

> Bhāgavatas who have had *samāśrayaṇam*. The sixteenth day, when the ritual of *tirunārāyaṇa bali* is performed, is especially important. Some of Nammāḻvār's verses are chanted. Often a group of Bhāgavatas who know how to chant them will come from Srirangam. Alternatively, one Caturvedi Brahmin named Rajaraman Swamikal, who knows the 4,000 verses, will come and chant. He is planning to take 1,000 Bhāgavatas to all the northern sacred places, even the ones in Nepal.

Sundaram adds:

> Before the removal of the *mudrās*, non-Brahmins sit the dead person in a chair wearing a garland. Someone performs a *harikathā* for the crowd; the story mentions that everyone who hears this will go to heaven. Musicians who don't get many commissions do this for a fee. They are commissioned also to perform at weddings and other events such as those at temples.

After interviewing Kulacekara, we went to Ammapet.[18] The inhabitants of the Maharashtrian section of this village are silk weavers, who came to this region in the early Maratha period as part of a larger migration of Maharashtrians to all parts of India for the sari market. They are Vaiṣṇavas. Today, some have adopted high-status caste names, such as Iyer, Iyengar, and Chettiyar, and wear the sacred thread.

We found a Rāmaliṅga Swami *maṭha*. Inside, we saw a painting of him wearing a white robe, large *vibhūti*, and red dot. The *maṭha* is also used by the villagers for Śrīvaiṣṇava *bhajanas*. These begin with short *Divyaprabandham* works, such as Āṇṭāḷ's *Tiruppāvai* and Periyāḻvār's *Tirupallāṇṭu*, and end with Rāma and Krishna folk songs. These *bhajanas* occur on Saturdays, Ekādaśī days, and festival days.

I noticed at this Saurashtra *maṭha* that men wore the Vaṭakalai *nāmam*, which also adorned nearby houses. In fact, around Tanjavur, I saw more Vaṭakalai influence than Teṉkalai in non-Brahmin communities. The current leader of the *bhajanas*, who performs the rituals for them, wore a Vaṭakalai *nāmam*. I heard no discussion of specifically Vaṭakalai identity, however, and so these villagers probably knew little about sectarian differences. In any case, it was obvious that Śrīvaiṣṇava influence was declining in this village; only three people have had *samāśrayaṇam*.

The next day, we went to Ammaiyappan, a village very near Tiruvarur. We found the shrine, also a Vaṭakalai one. It features a large picture of Tyāgarāja and small pictures of *bhajana* processions.[19] At that moment, a small group of men carried Tyāgarāja's picture in a street procession. We followed them for a short distance.

On the way to Needamangalam, where Sundaram's father grew up, the conversation turned to politics and Sundaram's relation to Periyar. Sundaram began by saying:

> Periyar was a Tyāgarājarī Vaiṣṇava Naiyakar. Despite his avowed atheism, he would do his morning *pūjā* wearing the *nāmam*. When he came out of the *pūjā* room, he would wipe it away. When travelling away from home, he might have done mental *pūjā*. Periyar's chief agent was Ramanuja Iyengar, a Brahmin with a big *nāmam*. Periyar initially wanted to ignore caste, but he increasingly spoke out against Brahmins, at first mildly, as in 'If you boast as a Brahmin, be a Brahmin. Don't do other vocations. Just do the duties prescribed by the *śāstras* (religious texts).' Then the mild rebukes became harsh. When he was abusing Brahmins, Periyar admitted that 'without abusing Brahmins, I won't survive'. And then he would say, 'If you find a Brahmin, kill him. There is no god,' and 'Tamil is a savage king'. After repeating this many times, he would call his audience 'sheep'. Still they adored him.

Sundaram remembered a day in 1957. He was staying in a room at a cinema building on Mount Road in Chennai, next to Periyar's house.

> One day a cinema poster was plastered on Periyar's house. He was angry. Periyar's man came, demanding that the manager go to meet Periyar. The manager was not there, so he dragged me there instead. I was presented to Periyar, who was eating his breakfast. He demanded that

> the poster be removed. I said: 'I had nothing to do with the cinema. I was just renting a room in that building.' Periyar continued eating, not saying anything. Then he asked me if I were a Brahmin. I said, 'No.' Then he asked me why I was wearing Śiva's emblem, the *vibhūti*, on my forehead. I said, it is my family custom. My father wore it, and so did my brother. Next, Periyar asked me if I knew what each line meant, and I said, 'No.' He continued to ask me about the *vibhūti*, with questions such as: 'When should it be mixed with water?' I could see that he had considerable knowledge of these matters. Finally, he let me leave.
>
> Periyar was a hypocrite because he was the leader of the Justice Party, which had made atheism a cornerstone of its ideology, and yet he secretly practised Śrīvaiṣṇavism. He was politically expedient, moreover, because he said contradictory things such as, 'I oppose only Brahmanism, not Brahmins'. Still, he terrorised Brahmins enough to bring about social change. For that reason, we have to thank him.

Sundaram paused and then continued. 'Many Vaiṣṇavas were attracted to Periyar, but were also afraid of his atheism, and so they would remove their *nāmam* to hide their religious identity. I myself was never attracted to him.'[20] This prompted Sundaram to describe another incident with Periyar.

> Periyar's first wife had died. He then married into the *devadāsī* community. This is not widely known even today. There was a big difference in age between him and his second wife—he was seventy-seven and she was thirty—even though Periyar himself had preached against marriages with a big age difference. This wife's name was Mani-ammai. My family knew hers. Mani-ammai told me that she had been formally dedicated to a temple. One time, she had a big argument with Periyar. His driver, C. Cittrarasu, who later became a great orator, told me about the fight. Periyar had said to Mani-ammai: 'I have given you life. I have rescued you from prostitution.' She retorted, 'No, you are such an old man, you have not given me life; you married me out of your own interest!'

> My father was dead set against Periyar because he abused Brahmins. Brahmins, my father said, patronised our music and appreciated us. Therefore, we shouldn't abuse them. This perspective made many Brahmins see my father as both a great musician and a great man. In short, there has been a love-hate relationship between the Brahmins and the Icai Velala community.
>
> For me, the caste inclusion expressed by the *āḻvārs* and *nāyaṉmārs* is important. It makes the Brahmins appear hypocritical. It also makes the elite non-Brahmins appear hypocritical. They don't treat the Harijans very well.

Sundaram changed the topic and spoke more generally about Hinduism.

> To retain Hinduism, equality is good, but we shouldn't dilute the religion to globalise it. People are becoming too materialistic. Chandrasekhara, my guru, says that we should fly with two wings, the spiritual and the material. Now, however, with heavy materialism, there is no balance. This will cause us to fall and bring destruction.
>
> A devotee of Mahatma Gandhi, my father wore only *khadi* shirts and fasted, not taking even a drop of water, when Gandhi died. I myself met Gandhi when I went with my father to Delhi on 15 August 1947, Indian Independence Day. My father played for an hour with Gandhi present. I also used to know Dr Radhakrishnan when he was President of India. He had seen my father perform many times in Chennai, and called me the son of a great Vidvāṉ.

We were momentarily distracted from these reminiscences when Sundaram saw the village temple where his mother used to pray for a child. The conversation moved on. Because the topic had been political leaders, I asked him, 'Have you ever met Karunanidhi?' The answer was 'yes'.

> Karunanidhi is much older than I am. His mother is Anjukam Ammaiyar, from a *devadāsī* community in Tiruvarur district, where he grew up. He was at first a storywriter. He would come to Tanjavur and stay with my relatives. My mother-in-law's uncle was Karunanidhi's

> father-in-law. Karunanidhi joined Periyar and became a politician, and eventually Chief Minister.

As our trip together neared its end, Sundaram took a long look back.

> Chandrasekhara is my guru and my god. I met him first with my mother at his *maṭha* in Kumbakonam when I was eleven. I had been told how my mother had had five daughters, all of whom had died when young. Chandrasekhara had blessed her, saying, 'You will have a son'. I am that son.
>
> On 10 October 2006, my music guru M. Balamurali Krishna organised a birthday celebration for me. I was seventy-two. The party was held at Bharati Vidya Bhavan in the Mylapore section of Chennai. There were many famous people, including the director of All India Radio and TV Doordarshan from Delhi, the registrar of Tamil University, the scholar T. N. Ramachandran, famous musicians, relatives, and friends. Over the years, I have learned much from many great people. Sometimes, though, I think I made a mistake by not performing on the stage. Even now that I have achieved some fame, I have a hard time publishing my research. My most important works are still not published. I ask for no money, just a few complimentary copies.

* * *

Reflecting more generally on the region of Tiruchirappalli and Tanjavur that I had just visited, my thoughts began with Srirangam, called the 'capital' of Śrīvaiṣṇavism. Srirangam is famous, after all, because of its antiquity as a sacred place and impressive architecture, rituals, and festivals, the fact that all the *āḻvār*s had sung about it with the total number of verses amounting to more *āḻvār* verses about any other *divyadeśa* (Tirupati being second and the temples of Kanchipuram third), and the fact that it has been a main seat of the Śrīvaiṣṇava *sampradāya* from its earliest days.

Non-Brahmin connections with Srirangam mentioned to me ranged from a Zamindar trust's patronage of religious schools and gardens, to Sattada service in the temple, to the many non-Brahmin disciples living not only in the nearby city of Tiruchirappalli, but also villages throughout the greater Tanjavur region and beyond. As I found in other regions, there was a link between the religious centre and the villages, thanks to the proselytism of Srirangam *ācārya*s and *jīyar*s over the centuries, but that there was now little contact, making Śrīvaiṣṇava identity vulnerable in some villages.

I found that the second major focus for Śrīvaiṣṇava identity in the general vicinity is Tiruvaiyaru, where the *samādhi* of Tyāgarāja is located, and the annual festival associated with the famous composer is celebrated. The importance of Tyāgarāja for non-Brahmin Śrīvaiṣṇava identity, especially those who speak or identify with Telugu, cannot be overestimated. I had discovered that his devotional music formed the spiritual core of many religious *sabhā* events and processions throughout Tamil Nadu. It is therefore not surprising that devotees, not only from the surrounding villages but also from across Tamil Nadu, are attracted to his shrine. The importance of music for religious identity was highlighted in these interviews by B. M. Sundaram's life story and his family's connections with traditional music. The life story of Laksmana Naidu highlighted the importance of music too.

My research opportunities for interviews did not take me directly into the Madurai and Kanyakumari areas, which have their own Śrīvaiṣṇava *divyadeśa*s, such as Tirumaliruncolai, Srivilliputur, and Alvartirunagari, and a powerful *maṭha*, Vānamāmalai, the history and pervasive influence of which I have already described. But I did glimpse Śrīvaiṣṇava life in this area through the reminiscences of Dr Pandurangan, my own previous fieldwork on the *divyadeśa*s of the area, and my travels there with Sundaram and Davesh Soneji to study Maratha Vaiṣṇava influence.

Notes

1. Translation by Steven Hopkins, *Singing the Body of God,* 140. I have changed the format.

2. This was Periya Asramam Andavan Swamikal.

3. The Sattadas make the special garlands, such as one with an image of a parrot for festivals. The garlands on sale outside the temple are a commercial operation run by others. These are sold to worshippers, who offer them to the deity.

4. This bookstore is a hub of Śrīvaiṣṇava activity. It is run by A. Krishnamachariar, a retired senior officer from the Indian Oil Corporation, now involved in publishing new works about Śrīvaiṣṇavism and reissuing early editions. He himself edits the periodical *Panchajanyam*, publishes articles, and has authored several books on the history of the Srirangam temple.

5. This Sattada account reflects Sattada roles today and is somewhat different from the information in the inscriptions. See Chapter 1, section: 'Caste Conundrums' for a discussion of Śrīvaiṣṇavas' premodern views on caste.

6. It is located on Tiruveti Street in Srirangam.

7. His full biography appears in several places on the Internet, including the programme for an interdisciplinary symposium on Devadasi Dance at the Robert Gill Theatre, University of Toronto (9 June 2007), sponsored by InDance. For a list of Sundaram's publications, see Soneji, *Unfinished Gestures*, 292.

8. Soneji, *Unfinished Gestures*, 145.

9. *Nāgasvaram* literally means the sound of a *nāga* or snake. It is said that one end of this instrument looks like the head of a cobra and the mouthpiece like its tail.

10. This is the main drum that Brahmins play.

11. According to Soneji, 'Aṅgala Parameśvarī is a generic name, which refers to a deity, often a goddess, lying down; it is common for Hindus to have a goddess as the family (*kula*) or village (*grāma*) deity' (personal communication, January 2011). This could also explain Vijayavenugopal's family goddess.

12. It was located near the intersection of Pambatti Street and Abraham Pandit Road in Tanjavur.

13. These were Vaidya Naatha Iyer, Balakrishna Naidu, and Narayana Sami Naidu.

14. These performers wore a special long coat, cap, and bell-anklets for keeping the rhythm.

15. As B. M. Sundaram has written, these sites 'are derived from a Maharashtrian tradition of *kīrtana* or devotional songs that can be traced back to Sant Namdev (1268–1350) and Samartha Ramdoss Swami (1608–81)'. See Sundaram, 'Harikatha Kalakshepa'.

Maratta is the name for non-Brahmins; the phrase Tanjavur Maharashtrians refers only to Brahmins. When discussing this history, Soneji added: '*Kīrtana maṭam*s are householder *maṭams*—that is a hereditary, family tradition known as a musical *sampradāya*, which goes back to an ancestor who was a famous *kīrtaṅkar* in the early Maratha period and whose image is found in the home shrine' (personal communication, January 2011).

16. Rāmdās, a devotee of Lord Rāma, was a seventeenth-century Maharashtrian saint and the spiritual guru of the Maratha king Shivaji (this claim is now disputed). *Sampradāya*s carried on his spiritual tradition.

17. Born in 1909, in a family that traced its ancestors back to Empār, Rāmānuja's disciple, Vijayarāghavācāriar was trained in both traditional Śrīvaiṣṇava thought and in the *harikathā* style of performance, his most famous *harikathā* being about Tyāgarāja. In appreciation of his talent, he received the title 'Sangita Kalanidhi' from the Madras Music Academy.

18. This village is located about 16 kilometres from Tanjavur, on the road to Tiruvarur.

19. The Tyāgarāja and Śrīvaiṣṇava traditions had fused here.

20. In this case, Sundaram is different from others in his community. According to Soneji, 'Non-Brahmin assertion in Tamil Nadu, animated in large part by the Self-Respect Movement, allowed men from *devadāsī* backgrounds to participate in political spaces. Men from the *devadāsī* community were pivotal figures in Dravidian party politics in the middle of the twentieth century' (Soneji, *Unfinished Gestures*, 151).

six

Śrīvaiṣṇava Brahmin Voices

In my interviews with Bhāgavatas, the topic of Brahmins came up many times. Sometimes non-Brahmins viewed them negatively, sometimes positively, sometimes ambivalently. In this chapter, I begin with two Brahmins who lived during colonial times, and whose names had surfaced in my interviews and the biographies of the non-Brahmin leaders I discussed in Chapter 2. After this, I examine the field notes of Raymond Williams, who interviewed *ācārya*s and their relatives in 1988 and 1991 in order to detect changes that were occurring in their roles.[1] Presenting my own interviews, I search for further changes over the past twenty-five years. Finally, I compare my findings with the study of Tamil Brahmins by C. J. Fuller and Haripriya Narasimhan, published in 2014.[2]

Nineteenth-Century Radical Brahmins

When doing research for Chapter 2, I encountered memories or biographical details about two Śrīvaiṣṇava Brahmins who had lived in the late nineteenth century and been vanguards of social change. Their own radical actions—both initiated

Dalits—might have been inspired by religion, economics, or politics.

Sāttvika Ācārya

Sāttvika Ācārya lived in Tirumalicai (between Chennai and Sriperumbudur) in the late nineteenth century. When I visited Tirumalicai, a person who had ancestors related to Sāttvika[3] told me that in Sāttvika's time, a Dalit ascetic lived in a hamlet near Tirumalicai; after the ascetic's death, a small shrine for him was built there.

Sāttvika began doing initiations for Dalits. When other Brahmins objected, Sāttvika argued with them. He quoted Nammāḻvār's *Tiruvāymoḻi* 3.7.9, the now familiar verse about outcaste devotees being the paradigmatic preceptors.[4] He also told them the story about Rāmānuja allowing outcastes into the Melkote temple and supported this story by referring to Śrīvaiṣṇava works that denounce discrimination.[5]

Appalācāri Svāmi, Sāttvika's son, continued this tradition of initiating Dalits. His influence is still remembered. Śrīvaiṣṇava Dalits in a suburb of Chennai called Perambur received *samāśrayaṇam* from Sāttivka and his son. So too did the family of J. J. Thirunarayana Ramanuja Dasar (whom I discussed in Chapter 3).

I learned that someone else now does the ritual for those who want to have initiation; however, many Dalits are no longer interested in *samāśrayaṇam*. Still, if anyone were to ask, 'who are the disciples of Svāmi?', the Dalit disciples of Appalācāri would identify themselves and chant their Ācārya's lineage. A descendant of Sāttvika has a painting of him in his home shrine and still has all his books.

Ciṟupuliyūr

This *jīyar* belonged to a branch of the Kantāṭai Āṇṭāṉ family of Srirangam. This branch family once had a prominent role at the Kumbakonam temple.[6] A booklet published by the family[7] mentions that a non-Brahmin ruler named Pātrācāriya requested *samāśrayaṇam* from an *ācārya* of this family in the nineteenth century. 'Although a Teṉkalai (which means that he should have initiated him, given the sect's inclusive philosophy),' K. K. A. Venkatachari told me, 'the *ācārya* of this family refused initiation.' The ruler then went to a Vaṭakalai for initiation.

The next generation of this branch family produced three sons. One became an ascetic and was named after the town Cirupuliyur, where he lived. The family's biography tells his story only until he became an ascetic. It is possible that the family disowned him for encouraging non-Brahmins to perform *samāśrayaṇam* for non-Brahmins.[8] Remember, Ciṟupuliyūr was the *jīyar* who initiated (Kōyiḻ) Ekāṅgi Svāmikaḷ, who argued that non-Brahmins had the right to perform *samāśrayaṇam*. In addition, Ekāṅgi Svāmikaḷ might have initiated outcastes, because his *samādhi* in Chennai was located in an outcaste hamlet (see Chapters 2 and 3). For these reasons, Ciṟupuliyūr was probably a controversial figure in the eyes of his orthodox family and other Brahmins.

Ethnography from the Late Twentieth Century

We flash forward to the late twentieth century to learn about how the momentous changes of the non-Brahmin movement and Indian independence had affected the status and role of *ācārya*s.

In 1988 and 1991, Raymond Williams interviewed *ācārya*s who were encountering many challenges related to the maintenance of orthodoxy, education, economic support, and the religious ideal of inclusiveness.

Through his interviews, Williams learned about orthodox rules in manuals from earlier times. These focussed on daily routines in connection with food and hygiene (such as washing hands thirty-two times with a particular form of mud). Despite the fact that many Brahmins once followed this code of conduct, most had abandoned its rules by the time of Williams' interviews. Young Brahmins usually did not want to wear traditional dress, for instance, because that led to mockery in school or jobs. One *ācārya* said that wearing traditional dress and the *nāmam* marginalised him, except in Śrīvaiṣṇava circles during the performance of rituals.

The requirements of orthodoxy were especially strict for *ācārya*s. Informants from *ācārya* families told Williams that maintaining orthodoxy within the family made it difficult to arrange marriages for their sons. Young women now wanted refrigerators and other modern conveniences, and to watch movies, television shows, and videos. Even though it was prestigious to marry an *ācārya*, they did not want to maintain restrictions on food, such as not eating outside the home, or eating only food that orthodox Brahmins had prepared. Others disliked the fact that they could not continue to study in secular institutions or take jobs after marrying an *ācārya*. Moreover, future *ācārya*s were supposed to marry only daughters of *ācārya* families. That was becoming increasingly difficult because so few families were strictly following their *ācārya* traditions.

Another problem for *ācārya*s who needed to maintain orthodoxy was travel. In the past, they would not travel locally by car, much less go abroad. One person told Williams about his own family. When someone travelled abroad, all four of his children died 'in very mysterious circumstances'.[9]

Williams found that education presented a problem for *ācārya* families. Members of these families told him that disciples expected *ācārya*s to know both Sanskrit and Tamil and the Śrīvaiṣṇava scriptures. At the minimum, in order to take part in all the rituals and festivals, they had to recite from memory the 4,000 *āḻvār* verses, some Upaniṣadic passages and Sanskrit verses in praise of God, Rāmānuja, and other *ācārya*s. Moreover, they had to know the verses that constituted their own lineage of *ācārya*s.[10] They had to know the Maṇipravāḷa and Sanskrit commentaries on *sampradāya* works and how to perform the rituals associated with daily, monthly, and annual rituals. Most importantly, they had to be able to perform the *samāśrayaṇam* ritual.

Not knowing what the future had in store for the *ācārya* tradition, many *ācārya*s wanted their sons to benefit from both traditional and modern education. Because their fathers were living longer than ever, sons had to wait much longer to become *ācārya*s, and therefore needed gainful employment in the meantime (although only some jobs, such as teaching Sanskrit in a college, were considered appropriate). And families needed the income of the younger sons due to dwindling support from disciples.

It was hard for *ācārya* families to educate their sons in traditional lore. Many sent their sons to English-medium Hindu schools.[11] After returning from school and changing into traditional dress, sons went to the Brahmin elders to learn Sanskrit and the Vedas. Williams found that some sons said that they did not want to study any of these things. Rather, they wanted to study what would lead to good jobs in the modern world: computer science, engineering, chartered accountancy, or business. 'It was hard,' they said, 'to have both a classical Sanskrit education and a modern one.'[12] Considering these changes, Williams suggests in his fieldnotes that 'the more modern education young people receive, the further they go from traditional training and knowledge ... and so their religion becomes a kind of symbolic religiosity'.[13]

In the past, *ācārya* families had received lands, houses, and other endowments from rulers; they had also been supported by temples and their disciples, which gave them time for religious activities. Villagers were respectful to Brahmins and gave them rice and other produce from their fields.

Now *ācārya* families were facing serious economic problems. Besides daily maintenance and medical expenses for himself and his family, an *ācārya* faced the costs of major events such as sacred-thread ceremonies, weddings, events to honour the birthday of his ancestor, his own birthday and his own death—all of which demanded conspicuous display, in line with the special status of *ācārya*s. People reported that it was now more expensive to bring disciples together for functions because they wanted modern facilities. 'In olden days, they used to come and chant the *śloka*s free of charge, and they thought it was a service. Now the *ācārya* has to pay for the chanting plus provide food and other amenities'.[14] Although the incomes of *ācārya*s varied, one *ācārya* told Williams that at one time, ',we were starved for food, but we never complained'.[15]

People reported that traditional economic support for *ācārya*s had declined for various reasons. In some cases, *ācārya*s mismanaged these resources and major endowments declined, governments redistributed their land and the cost of farm workers rose. As one *ācārya* said, 'We have only disciples who are not very affluent and depend on salaries to maintain their own families. Many young people do not want to contribute to the support of another family, moreover, when they themselves have enormous economic stress in a competitive and increasingly commercialized society'.[16]

Williams learned that some *ācārya*s had begun charging disciples for their activities, or gave honours to them in return for a gift. Since the 1960s, some disciples had established trusts to support *ācārya*s and their families. These trusts kept track of disciples and collected dues from them, which regularised their contacts with the *ācārya*. They raised funds for special occasions too and helped with organisational activities. Some *ācārya*s had a personal secretary who did much of the correspondence and other work as service (*kaiṅkaryam*). In addition, the interest from trusts helped pay for expenses. 'It is clear,' said one disciple to Williams, 'that these organizations are the preserve of elderly retired persons. It gives them activity, and it fits the traditional pattern of devotion to religious matters in old age'.[17] Trusts often died out. There was another source of financial support on the horizon, said one person: wealthy Indians living abroad who visit India, re-establish contact with the family's *ācārya*, and have him perform their initiations. The *ācārya*s hoped their rituals would be reciprocated with gifts.

Williams' interviews reveal that Śrīvaiṣṇava Brahmins were aware of a decline. Of the seventy-four supposedly original *ācārya* families, only twenty or so still maintained the tradition. Some people feared that the institution would die out altogether. Fewer Brahmins than ever could recite the Vedas, for instance, and only a few chanted in the group at the end of religious processions. Even among Vaṭakalais, fewer than ever before knew the Vedas, aside from a few verses. One individual pointed out that there was a separate street in Kumbakonam for *ācārya*s, Iyengar (Ayyangar) Street, where about 100 *ācārya* families used to live. Only two *ācārya* families still lived there. The others had migrated to cities for secular jobs.

Another person commented that Brahmins now perform the rituals in perfunctory ways, not as a way of life. Still another said that *ācārya*s used to tour villages, visiting disciples, lecturing and instructing. 'Now,' he said, 'the *ācārya*s don't do these things. Disciples did. Only if *ācārya*s are invited for special occasions would they go.' 'The times have changed,' commented another informant, 'there is no fear of excommunication among Brahmins to enforce the tradition.'[18]

Williams' interviews provide an important insight into whether Śrīvaiṣṇavas, both Vaṭakalais and Teṉkalais, thought that their religion was once caste-inclusive, and whether it still was.

One Vaṭakalai informant challenged the claim that Rāmānuja had introduced a casteless Vaiṣṇavism. He also did not agree that Śrīvaiṣṇavas are a caste of servants, because they all serve each other. And he did not think that because everyone is a servant, everyone is equal. 'Rāmānuja never wrote anything in appreciation of *āḻvār*s' works,' this person said,

> and never wrote any commentary on the *āḻvār*s' songs. Rāmānuja maintained the Vedic tradition and accepted the caste system in total. All their (Teṉkalai) ideas were only in books. They were not practised in actual life. If they had been practised, Śrīvaiṣṇavism would have stood at the forefront as a model for the reformation of Hinduism. What really happened was that the Brahmin Śrīvaiṣṇavas never mingled with non-Brahmins.[19]

In addition, according to Williams' interviews, Brahmins also maintained positions of superiority based on control of knowledge. One of the people Williams interviewed commented, for instance, that only Brahmins attach *ubhaya vedānta* (or u. ve.) to their names and thus establish their attachment to bilingual status (that is, to Tamil and Sanskrit traditions). Because Bhāgavatas were not allowed to study the Vedas, they could not use the title. Another of his informants recalled that 'our forefathers used to teach those works only to a select few who were formally admitted to the fold of Śrīvaiṣṇavism. Thus, they guarded the works as a great treasure, which had to be preserved with utmost care.'[20] Yet another Brahmin commented that at one time, 'non-Brahmins were not allowed to listen to the Brahmin lectures'.[21]

Informants told Williams about the special honours that temples gave to visiting *ācārya*s, such as receiving the five *mudrā*s (emblems) at five places on the body, or being the first to receive *tīrtha* and *prasāda*. The temple would send oil to an *ācārya* at home for the birth of his first son (likely the future *ācārya*). And when an *ācārya* died, the temple would send fire from the temple kitchen for cremation rites.

Williams' fieldwork reveals other changes were afoot. More and more non-Brahmins were becoming knowledgeable about sectarian teachings and were giving discourses on religious topics. For this reason, Brahmins had to recognise this new reality, and so a compromise was developing. One non-Brahmin teacher, for example, took his disciples to Brahmin *ācārya*s for the formal initiation—the branding and mantras. He, the non-Brahmin teacher, sat nearby and gave instruction in the scriptures. In another case, the compromise included having a pious non-Brahmin participate, not just for his learning and popularity in non-Brahmin circles, but also because he was an important patron of festivals and other religious activities.

Therefore, Brahmin *ācārya*s were including non-Brahmin teachers in the initiation (*samāśrayaṇam*) ritual, albeit for different reasons. The *ācārya*s maintained as their exclusive role the initiation ritual and the teaching of the mantras. In other words, because in the past the *ācārya*s who were doing the initiations also had the role of introducing the treatises to be studied by the disciple—but often turned the actual teaching of them over to other Brahmin teachers as a kind of secondary, ongoing role—now some *ācārya*s were willing to recognise non-Brahmins in the role of teachers for their non-Brahmin disciples, and to include this recognition by having them present at the initiation ritual itself.

If, by the late twentieth century, Brahmins were sometimes willing to include non-Brahmins in their initiation rituals, the *ācārya*s still maintained distance from Dalits. One person told Williams that an *ācārya* would perform the ritual for Harijans at his house, although the Harijan must stay on the outside veranda. A non-Brahmin would transport the branding utensils from the *ācārya* inside to the Harijan outside and do the branding. Another person reported that *ācārya*s were not initiating Harijans 'because they can't go against society'. Some did not even like non-Brahmins initiating washermen at Srirangam, who were Harijans. As noted by one: 'Harijans give initiation to each other. They are cobblers.' Not all Brahmins held these positions. One told Williams: 'Harijans should be made Śrīvaiṣṇavas. If we say that all souls are equal, why should they be rejected?' Obviously, some Brahmins were ambivalent about who and what should be included in the religion.

*Jīyar*s and *Ācārya*s with Non-Brahmin Disciples

In the course of my own fieldwork, I had interviews with two Brahmin *jīyar*s and one *ācārya*: Varataa Ethiraja Jeeyar of Sriperumbudur, Srinivasa Ramanuja Jiyar of Tirukkoyilur, and Parasara Badri Narayana Bhattar of Srirangam. These interviews helped me understand the important and challenging role of *jīyar*s and *ācārya*s with many non-Brahmin disciples.

Varataa Ethiraja Jeeyar ('Ethiraja')[22]

Varataa Ethiraja Jeeyar (1927–2009) was the most radical of all the Śrīvaiṣṇava Brahmin leaders whom I interviewed. After hearing about him from J. N. B. Chakravarthi Ramanuja Dasar, N. D. Sabari Natchi, Sudarshana Acarya, A. Pandurangan, and others, I became curious about his support for Bhāgavatas, including Dalits, and women of all castes. So, I interviewed him at his *maṭha* in Sriperumbudur. It was the closing day of the festival that celebrates Rāmānuja's birth.

At his *maṭha*, which is directly across the street from the temple's pillared hall, Ethiraja greeted me. We entered a large room with many photos of the *maṭha*'s previous *jīyar*s and some of Ethiraja himself during his former service in the air force. This was where Ethiraja would sit on a throne to receive visitors. An adjoining room was more like a temple.[23] Here were large posters that featured Nammāḻvār, Āṇṭāḷ, Rāmānuja, and Maṇavāḷa Māmuni. Inserted into each was an oval picture of Ethiraja himself, with a temple *gopuram* in the background. Ethiraja, like many other *jīyar*s and Hindu gurus, was obviously entrepreneurial to attract disciples. He began to tell me about his life.

> I am a simple, humble officer who came to this post in Śrī Rāmānuja's birthplace after a thirty-two-year career as Flight Lieutenant V. Varadan. I was born in Sriperumbudur. My family is one of the seventy-four Brahmin *ācārya* families. My father was an *ācārya* and my sister's husband had become a *jīyar* in Tirupati. My elder brother was an *ācārya* at Kanchipuram. Both my father and brother were scholars. I was educated in Śrīvaiṣṇavism for fourteen years, studying both Sanskrit and Tamil texts. After that, I had English education and studied up to the tenth grade. I know Sanskrit, Tamil, Telugu and English.
>
> After my marriage at twenty-one, I joined the air force in 1948. Retiring in 1979, I returned to Sriperumbudur and became a deputy collector. I later resigned from that job. In 1983 at the age of fifty-six, deciding that I had completed all my worldly duties (working and supporting my

family), I took *saṃnyāsa*. As an ascetic, I then became the head of the Varadā Etirāja Jīyar Maṭha, which had been established several hundred years ago by the disciple of an important intellectual named Etirāja from Andhra, who settled in Sriperumbudur where he did service at the temple and founded the *maṭha*.

After taking *saṃnyāsa*, I no longer communicated with my wife and five children, all of whom are now educated professionals—English professor, chartered accountant, member of the air force, teacher and reserve-bank general manager—in Mumbai and elsewhere.

I have lived on my air-force pension and do not need to depend on my disciples, unlike other *jīyar*s. I discovered that most of the vast property of the Sriperumbudur temple had disappeared. This created considerable tension with other Brahmins. In 1983, I raised funds to improve the temple, adding new floors, renovating Rāmānuja's shrine, improving the temple tank and ordering a new temple chariot.

Śrī Rāmānuja preached spirituality to both the Paraiah (outcaste) and the Brahmin. Liberation is meant not only for the superior class of Brahmins, he said, but also for everyone. The door to liberation is open for all. Rāmānuja was daring in love and dauntless in war,[24] a menacing meteor and dreadful dragon introducing a combination of religion, philosophy and science. He began a social and religious revolution. The supreme commander invited everyone to come to the deity and said, 'Even if you are downtrodden, untouchable and uncivilised, if you are a devotee, come.' If one compares Śaṅkara to Rāmānuja, one must admit that the former had a great intellect. But Rāmānuja had a heart as wide as the universe.

I cling to the *āḻvār*s. Nammāḻvār was a *śūdra*, Kulacēkara a king, Tirumaṅkai a king and Tiruppāṇ an outcaste. Tirumaḻicai was brought up by non-Brahmins. The first three *āḻvār*s (Poykai, Pūta, and Pēy) were unborn. That is, they just appeared, and so their caste is unknown.[25] Nammāḻvār is the Lord Viṣṇu's lotus feet, a *śūdra*. We all bend and ritually take his feet on our head. If I go to Alvartirunagari, the birthplace of Nammāḻvār, I see the

> Brahmin Rāmānuja in statue-form sitting at the lotus feet of the *śūdra* Nammāḻvār.
>
> Only three *āḻvār*s were Brahmins. Here in Sriperumbudur, non-Brahmins—farmers, washermen, blacksmiths, goldsmiths, and temple sculptors—enter the temple. They play the cymbals, hold the sacred umbrellas and carry the statue of Rāmānuja on their shoulders in processions. They are all non-Brahmins. They all contribute their services with affection. Rāmānuja helped the outcastes, whom he called Tirukkulattār (those who belong to the sacred family), and allowed them temple entry. Today, a colony of Adidravidas (Dalits) near Sriperumbudur has the right to pull the chariot with Rāmānuja's image. I always have Adidravidas sit very close to me. I have given 30,000 initiations to them.

According to one account, Ethiraja had once become so concerned about Dalits converting to other religions that he placed advertisements in local newspapers, saying that he would initiate any Dalit.[26] That might help explain Ethiraja's spirit of inclusiveness, which is evident in his photo albums. He identified for me pictures of a Dalit priest in a Chennai temple and a High Court judge who had come from the Mudaliyar (Naidu) caste and held important positions in the Tamil Nadu and the Central governments.

I also saw pictures of several non-Brahmin Chettiyars and an Australian Jew who converted to Śrīvaiṣṇavism, was initiated by Ethiraja, and renamed Rama Ramanuja (now he also goes by Ram Sivan). There were many pictures of Rama Ramanuja juxtaposed with ones of Rāmānuja. Ethiraja told me that this Australian learned Sanskrit and Tamil, built a temple dedicated to Lord Śrīnivāsa, Rāmānuja, and Āṇṭāḷ in Sydney, and did *pūjā*s as well as weddings, funerals, and festival rituals.[27] Ethiraja called him an *ācārya* and a 'bachelor'. In addition, Ethiraja had pictures of four monks who belonged to the Ramakrishna Mission (a nineteenth-century monastic order, now worldwide, based on the teachings of Ramakrishna Paramahamsa) who had come to hear him speak, and a Swiss man who took initiation from him. Next, he showed me a silver chariot frame with inset pictures of a Christian couple. To one side were smaller insets of the woman when she was a young girl, with her Śrīvaisṇava father and grandfather.

Looking around the room, I noticed that Ethiraja had a picture of Chandrasekhara, the previous Kanchipuram Śaṅkarācārya, on his wall. To me, this was odd, because of the long-standing competition between Advaitins (who usually worship Śiva) and Vaiṣṇavas. So, I asked Ethiraja about the picture. He explained it as follows: 'When I was twenty, I knew this Śaṅkarācārya. I was in the air force at that time and was astonished when the Śaṅkarācārya predicted that I would be made an officer.' Ethiraja pointed out that Chandrasekhara was on the Vaiṣṇava side of Advaita, because he worshipped the Sudarśana Cakra.[28]

Next, Ethiraja described a poets' association that honoured him in April 2004. 'A booklet published by P. T. Radha, a poet and president of this association, called me "*vāḻum-irāmānucar*" (living Rāmānuja). The booklet contains poems in my honour, including some English ones.' When I asked Ethiraja if this title refers to him as an incarnation of Rāmānuja, he replied, 'No, though people can see Rāmānuja himself in me.' The following year, when I asked about this again, Ethiraja gave me a longer answer. 'Fifteen years ago, when I was the chief guest at a function to which representatives of various religions had been invited, an eighty-six-year-old Eastern Orthodox bishop from Trivandram embraced me, saying, "I have seen Rāmānuja".' 'But,' Ethiraja added, 'I do not rely on the praise of others.' When his disciples wrote to me after my visit in 2008, they also called Ethiraja '*vāḻum-irāmānucar*'.

On 26 September 2006, Ethiraja celebrated his eightieth birthday. He told me that the Adidravidas conducted a five-hour function in praise of him, and carried him in a procession on a palanquin. A booklet was published. Its cover has the three figures—Rāmānuja, Ethiraja, and Sudarshana Acarya—arranged vertically, from top to bottom. (This was the picture that I had seen on the huge poster at Sudarshana's ashram in Minjur.[29]) Ethiraja then said:

> No Brahmins came to the celebration, even though many non-Brahmins, including Adidravidas, did. I had taught Adidravidas some Sanskrit Vedic verses, Tamil Vedic (*Divyaprabandham*) verses, and other religious poems. Once, I had held an Adidravida seminar to tell them that they too could do *pūjā*; in fact, I said, they could do everything. I repeated that in writing. Years later, they showed me that they could recite all these poems at my birthday celebration. Local Brahmins do not like non-Brahmins reciting the *Divyaprabandham*. Rāmānuja is protecting me. Because the Brahmins are taking software jobs and other secular jobs, let the non-Brahmins take religious ones. If they begin by learning just a little, their learning will increase with time.

At this moment, some devotees entered the room for Ethiraja's blessing. He said to a little boy in Tamil, 'Become an engineer or a military officer.' Later, he gave me a sari. Accompanying me to the door with his walker, he became very emotional. He feared that his end was near. Besides heart surgery, he had just had an operation to repair a broken hip.

About a year later, I interviewed Ethiraja again. There was lots of activity on his veranda as we talked. Some were young male disciples who lived there with him. Others were village locals who had come for a visit. One man was an ascetic, already well into his three-hour morning ritual of chanting various hymns, along with the mantra *oṁ namo nārāyaṇāya*. He sat in the lotus position and applied *nāmam*s on his body, in the manner of ancient *nyāsa* (the practice of protecting and sacralising the body by adorning it with sacred emblems).

The ascetic was oblivious to my conversation with Ethiraja. When I asked Ethiraja what caste the ascetic was, Ethiraja's reply was evasive: 'He's not a Harijan, but like a *kṣatriya*'. He might have alluded to the identity of Vanniyars, who often describe themselves as *kṣatriya*s. Ethiraja told me that this man had come to him, wanting to become an ascetic. He was worried that only Brahmins could take *saṁnyāsa*. Ethiraja added: 'I replied that anyone can take it. I initiated him about nine years ago. This ascetic, who now moves from one Vaiṣṇava temple to another all over India, comes here periodically and stays for a while.'

My goal was to clarify some points from my previous interview. Who had helped to fund his temple renovations? Ethiraja told me that he had received money from both those Brahmins who perform death rituals[30] and non-Brahmins. 'Before, some Brahmins were stealing temple riches,' he muttered. 'Now it is the government people.'[31] What had his political identity been when he was young? 'As a student,' he replied, 'I followed Mahatma Gandhi who accepted everyone: Muslims, Christians, and Harijans. Therefore, I supported Congress and still do.' Why had he given the title *ācārya* to Sudarshana? 'It is because Sudarshana knows both Sanskrit and Tamil,' he replied. 'I watched him for four or five years. Then I gave him the title of *ācārya* "with Rāmānuja's blessings".'

As we talked, a large group of Ethiraja's disciples arrived. Pilgrims on their way to Tirupati, they came here first to see their *jīyar*. He gave them a calendar. At that moment, an Āṇṭāḷ procession passed by on the adjacent street. It was the day after her wedding to God was ritually re-enacted in the temple. 'The procession used to stop for ten minutes at my *maṭha*,' said Ethiraja, 'but the other Brahmins did not like this, and so they no longer stop.' Ethiraja connected my appearance that day with Āṇṭāḷ. I wasn't too sure what that meant, aside from a morphological similarity!

Through my interviews with Ethiraja, I now understood more about Sudharsana. Earlier, for instance, I had not been able to understand why Ethiraja had sent him to Chandrasekhara, the Kanchipuram Śaṅkarācārya, for education. Ethiraja's close friendship with Chandrasekhara explained everything. I realised also that Sudarshana's titles, Ācārya and Chinna Jīyar, came from Ethiraja. He had no respect for Brahmin control over these roles and was out to change the tradition by making non-Brahmins religious leaders, in order to spread the tradition throughout the villages. It was his deep affection for his disciples, more than theology and politics, that I found most striking. I remembered my interview with Dr Pandurangan, a retired university professor, who had told me about searching everywhere for an *ācārya* or *jīyar* to initiate him, and finding no one authentic until meeting Ethiraja.

In early 2009, several newspapers had reported that Ethiraja had petitioned the Madras High Court to provide armed police guards for the *maṭha*, claiming that it had 'vast movable and immovable properties and that it needed to be secured'.[32] He himself, 'due to old age and physical ailments ... needed security, because he might have to safeguard the interest of the *maṭha*'.[33] He claimed, moreover, that he had had armed guards between 1994 and 2006, which had then been subsequently withdrawn without explanation. The court dismissed his petition, saying that there 'was no material to substantiate ordering or withdrawal of security guards' in the past. Whatever the problem, Ethiraja obviously felt vulnerable.

Ethiraja died on 9 May 2009. A few hundred people came from nearby villages. It was not a huge gathering, because death rituals must proceed quickly. Govinda Etiraja Jiyar became the *maṭha*'s new *jīyar*, the appointment being decided by Brahmins associated with the *maṭha* in the past, after they considered *jīyar*s sympathetic to non-Brahmins. I was told that to ease the transition, they also created an organisation led by Ethiraja's disciples. Someone later posted a page in Ethiraja's honour on Facebook (where his official title is 'H. H. Varada Yatiraja Jeeyar Swami, the erstwhile Pontiff of the Yadugiri Yatiraja Mutt, Sriperumbudur'). The page shows a picture of Ethiraja (Yatiraja). In the background is the temple associated with the birthplace of Rāmānuja and a picture of Ethiraja on his throne, flanked by the Australian Rama Ramanuja Acharya and Sudarshana Acharya, along with pictures of Ethiraja with other disciples.

Srinivasa Ramanuja Jiyar

In a big audience hall, filled with many early photographs, I interviewed Srinivasa Ramanuja Jiyar, the twenty-fifth *jīyar*, at the Emperumāṉār Mutt in Tirukkoyilur. Many Bhāgavatas whom I interviewed had been initiated by him or by his father Tiruvenkata Ramanuja Jiyar, who was the *jīyar* from 1944–85. Raymond Williams had noted that 5,000–6,000 people would attend special events at this *maṭha* and that disciples lived all over Tamil Nadu and Andhra.[34] This is the *maṭha* that was once a *jīyar* tradition, consisting of members of a family who had taken *saṁnyāsa* and then changed to a householder tradition, which created the anomaly of a married *jīyar*. While I was there, Srinivasa and his wife greeted the many disciples who had come to pay their respects. He had so many visitors that day that I had little opportunity to discuss his personal life story. We talked mainly about the history of this *maṭha*, which I discuss elsewhere.

Srinivasa Ramanuja suggested one reason why the *maṭha* had so many local non-Brahmins: the surrounding district was agricultural lands, which some non-Brahmins owned and where other non-Brahmins were agricultural workers. Because the temple and *maṭha* had few resources, they needed the patronage of the local landowners, merchants, and labourers as well.

Parasara Badri Narayana Bhattar

I learned that Parasara Badri Narayana Bhattar (Badri here for short) of Srirangam had many Bhāgavata disciples, so I decided to meet him. Here is what he told me:

> Our family *ācārya* lineage goes back to Parāśara Bhaṭṭar, who was the son of Kūreśa, Rāmānuja's scribe, in the twelfth century. Today, there are three branches of the family. One lives next door. My grandfather used to perform the *samāśrayaṇams*, but he recently died. My father does them now because he is the eldest male.
>
> Despite my extensive education—I have B.Com., I.C.W.A., C.A., L.L.B., and Master of Foreign Trade degrees—I worked outside the religious context for only the three years that I needed to qualify as a chartered accountant. Now, I don't take outside jobs. My wife has

> an M.Sc. in Biotechnology. Before marriage, she worked for a major company (Jubilant Biosis) in Bangalore. After taking the company's exams, she qualified to go abroad, but married me instead. We have one child who is two years old, and can already do the hand gestures for rituals.
>
> It is difficult being an *ācārya* today. Although my family has disciples in the thousands, they don't accept financial responsibility for the *ācārya*'s family as disciples did in the past. They are ignorant about this tradition. And the *ācārya* can't say, 'Come, protect me' because an *ācārya* can't make demands. Therefore, I can't work outside—I do get some income, however, by tutoring students two or three hours a day in chartered accounting—and I can't ask disciples for help. As a result, we live very simply. I have not bought my wife a sari since we got married. Moreover, the family gets only a bit of temple *prasāda*.
>
> Śrīvaiṣṇava philosophy is the greatest philosophy. Its code of conduct is especially important. In the eleventh century, Yāmuna had disciples from all castes. Everyone is equal, he realised, because the souls of all people are equal. Caste differences are only on a person's surface. Ninety-five per cent of my family's disciples are non-Brahmins. My ancestors once went on a great *yātrā* (pilgrimage) to Andhra, Karnataka, and Odisha to spread Śrīvaiṣṇavism, which is why we have many disciples in those places. I myself give lectures in Tamil and Telugu. Today, very few in Srirangam chant the *Divyaprabandham* or Veda. Correcting problems here is more important than travelling about to meet disciples who always want me to visit.
>
> My main service is running the many activities of our trust. It manages *sampradāya* schools with about 700 students and gives scholarship money every year. These schools are now 60 per cent Brahmin and 40 per cent non-Brahmin. I think that it will quickly become 30 per cent Brahmin and 70 per cent non-Brahmin, especially now that non-Brahmins are becoming teachers.

I asked Badri whether there were tensions between Brahmins and non-Brahmins. 'Once one has full knowledge of the *sampradāya,*' he replies, 'one accepts the customs. One must keep the Rāmānuja tradition. If one follows one's own ideas, the tradition will collapse. Therefore, all people have duties according to the scriptures.' I asked: 'Will non-Brahmins still accept this position?' Badri followed this by asking another question: 'Do you accept God? Why?' He then answered it.

> Because God is there. God exists whether you accept him or not. Knowledge of God is based on the *pramāṇa*s (valid means of knowledge). Scripture equals truth. When a villager sees a gas stove for the first time, he sees that it is much faster than a wood fire. He also sees that it is lit by a match and thinks that if he puts the match to the cylinder itself, it will go even faster. A person who knows about gas, however, knows that this will cause an explosion. This is like Rāmānuja's manuals on proper conduct. If we don't accept them, we don't accept the scriptures fully. If one wants the benefits, one must follow correct procedures, not personal preferences. Truth is best. One must not accept just a part of a judgment. One must accept it all.

In other words, Badri argued firmly both for maintenance of tradition and supporting non-Brahmin disciples.

Chinna Jeeyar Swami

People often mentioned the name Chinna Jeeyar Swami, more formally known as Sri Tridandi Srimannarayana Ramanuja Chinna Jeeyar Swami (b. 1956), when the topic was Brahmin Teṉkalai *ācārya*s and *jīyar*s who had non-Brahmin disciples. He was born in Andhra Pradesh, near Rajahmundry, to a Tamil-speaking family. His grandfather, Tridandi Srimannarayana Ramanuja Jeeyar,[35] later called Pedda (chief/senior) Jeeyar, mentored him and he was educated by several scholars in Śrīvaiṣṇava Sanskrit and Tamil works and other Hindu scriptures. After taking *saṁnyāsa* when he was only twenty-three, he assumed leadership when H. H. Pedda Jeeyar Swamiji died in 1981, becoming the head of Srimad Ubhaya Vedantha Acharya Peetam, Nadigadapalem.

Chinna Jeeyar Swami founded the Jeeyar Educational Trust (JET), with branches in places such as Hyderabad, Chennai, and the United States, to help educate students in the Vedic tradition. His schools are open to everyone. In addition, he is known for his performance of Vedic rituals of peace and harmony, and religious discourses in simple language (he speaks several). He has performed thousands of *samāśrayaṇam*s. His understanding of *kaiṅkarya* includes modern social services, such as schools for tribals and homes for the elderly, orphans, handicapped, and destitute. Furthermore, he supports rural development, science and technology schools, as well as the introduction of computers for the study of the Vedas. His website showcases in a very precise fashion Chinna Jeeyar's many activities and what must be boundless energy. No wonder he has a worldwide reputation.

I tried to visit Chinna Jiyar at his *ashram* near the airport in Hyderabad, but he was away travelling to meet his many disciples. His disciples gave me a tour of the *ashram*.

More Reflections on Today's Tamil Brahmins

The guiding spirit behind the research of Raymond Williams (and for that matter, my own) was K. K. A. Venkatachari, who died in 2016. Venkatachari belonged to a Brahmin Teṉkalai *ācārya* family that traces its lineage back to Mutaliyāṇṭāṉ, Rāmānuja's nephew, at Srirangam in the twelfth century. That was thirty generations ago. Kōyiḻ Kantāṭai Āṇṭāṉ has been the family name since the time of Māṇavāḷa Māmuni. The family has a chart of the long lineage, which was prepared in the 1940s.

Venkatachari was educated in the Śrīvaiṣṇava tradition by his father (Appan Swami, also known as Tirumani Swami) and other *ācārya*s. In addition, Venkatachari earned advanced traditional degrees in Tamil, Sanskrit, and several other subjects, and a Ph.D. from the University of Utrecht in the Netherlands. His dissertation, which was published, is on

Maṇipravāḷa Śrīvaiṣṇava literature.[36] Here are his views on *ācārya*s and other Tamil Brahmins that I gathered through my conversations with him. Many echoed the points that had been made by the people whom Williams had interviewed twenty years before.

In the past, Venkatachari said, the *ācārya*s had their lands. Later, the government redistributed their lands, or their lands were no longer economically viable because of the need to pay high wages to workers.[37] Members of *ācārya* families and other Brahmins had to take jobs outside the villages. They no longer had time to proselytise in the villages. Therefore, many non-Brahmin Śrīvaiṣṇava families lost the tradition. The non-Brahmin Śrīvaiṣṇava movement became very weak. Adherents might have had links with the temples, despite the fact that they lacked the memory of the *āḻvār*s' hymns. They had no leader, no organisation. Yet, they remembered their identity as Śrīvaiṣṇavas belonging to a 'Perumāḷ kōyiḻ'.

'Many of the early *ācārya*s such as Rāmānuja,' he continued, 'were identified as Vaṭamāl because they came from the area around Sriperumbudur and Kanchipuram, which was north of Srirangam. Even today, Vaṭamāl is a sub-group of Smārta Brahmins following Śaṅkara.' At one time,

> there was no Smārta-Vaiṣṇava distinction. There is no early record, moreover, of Advaitins as Smārtas. That came later. In any case, up to the sixteenth century, the caste system was not very strong in south India. After that, the Smārtas interfered by putting down the Teṉkalais. As a result, some Śrīvaiṣṇava Brahmins headed towards Smārta traditions for status. Even today, Smārtas call Teṉkalai Brahmins Sattadas and therefore consider them non-Brahmins, but call themselves Brahmins.
>
> In Andhra, Ayyangars are also not considered Brahmins because they are not Smārtas. I personally experienced this. According to tradition, if you see a single Brahmin coming from the opposite direction, it is a bad omen [supposedly because only a single Brahmin priest does funeral rituals, which are inauspicious], and so you avoid

> them. The same thing occurs if two *śūdras* approach or one widow approaches, because these are also considered inauspicious situations and bad omens. When Brahmins approached me as a single Brahmin, people would not avoid me. When I challenged them, they said, 'you are not a Brahmin. Ayyangars are not Brahmins in Andhra. To Andhras of all castes, Ayyangars are Sattadas.'
>
> Back to history. In the late seventeenth century, the Vaṭakalais started separating out the non-Brahmins.[38] There is inscriptional evidence to this effect. At the beginning of the eighteenth century, there was a big influx of Brahmins from Andhra. They became the Vaṭakalai Tāttācāryas. They really hurt the Teṉkalais. During the colonial period, the British favoured the Smārtas and Vaṭakalais over the Teṉkalais. The Teṉkalais didn't get secular education and therefore lost out.

Venktachari might have been thinking about R. Rangachari's book, *The Sri Vaisnava Brahmans*,[39] which was published in 1931, because it is an example of the Vaṭakalai definition of their superior status. Since Rangachari thought that the real Śrīvaiṣṇava Brahmins were the Vaṭakalais, he emphasised that Rāmānuja and Vedānta Deśika were Smārtas, and that Vaṭakalai theology and customs are even today very similar to those of Smārta Brahmins. He also emphasised Sanskrit texts over the Tamil ones. The Tamil verses of the *āḻvārs* were only vehicles for spreading the Vedas. Rangachari harshly criticised many of the post-Rāmānuja *ācāryas* who would later be considered Teṉkalai. He glossed over their position of inclusivity, taking it to mean that there is no need to maintain caste, a position that was anathema to orthodox Brahmins. He argued that even Rāmānuja had upheld the need to maintain caste.

> To Rāmānuja, men who believed in Vishnu as the Supreme Being and followed the principles of Vaishavism were all Vaishnavites, and they were all equal in religious views and so are entitled to great respect. Nevertheless, Rāmānuja never interfered with the social order. In fact, he upheld and favoured the Varṇāśrama Dharma.[40]

Furthermore, Rangachari argued that under Teṉkalai leadership, 'non-observance of caste roles leads to social degradation and spiritual bankruptcy.'[41] Non-Brahmins caused such a decline of the religion that it was almost overtaken by Advaita, Jainism, and Śaivism, until rescued by Vedānta Deśika.[42] Rangachari also promoted orthodox Brahminism and Vaṭakalai arguments against Teṉkalai theology, non-Brahmin calls for social reform, and Tamil as the 'national' language, should a new country be forthcoming. In short, Venkatachari's comments on the Vaṭakalais reflected the Teṉkalai perception of marginalisation by them as articulated by Rangachari.

As for Venkatachari's views on non-Brahmins, I found that he was open to the idea that non-Brahmins could be *grantha ācāryas*, that is, the teachers of *sampradāya* works. Venkatachari did suggest a tradition of 'separate—presumably Brahmins and non-Brahmin Bhāgavatas—but equal'. He did not comment, however, on past conflicts or the special honours and privileges that temples gave to *ācāryas*, aside from mentioning that there had been court cases over the latter.

In one conversation, Venkatachari looked back over his life and commented:

> I was a rebel when I was young. For a while, I did not wear the Śrīvaiṣṇava *nāmam* or keep the Brahmin's tuft of hair. Once, I argued in a meeting for non-Brahmin participation. This created such controversy that the meeting ended. After that, I would not even stand with Brahmins in the temple. Today, I realise how vulnerable Śrīvaiṣṇavism is. We need reforms, we need non-Brahmin leaders. We also need to protect the tradition so that it does not disappear altogether. For this reason, I have tried to help Dasarathi, who is now an *ācārya* in my family, to protect the tradition. Because my family's *ācārya* role has been preserved, generation after generation since the twelfth century, it should not die out in this one.

Like Venkatachari, many Tamil Brahmins had lived through difficult times. During the non-Brahmin movement's heyday, they experienced threats of violence and sometimes actual violence. For over a century, they had been subjected to non-Brahmin critiques. They had experienced 250 years of bitter court cases to resolve disputes between Teṉkalais and Vaṭakalais. They had faced other court challenges from the government over matters such as allowing Dalits into the temples. When Brahmin Śrīvaiṣṇavas told stories about Śrīvaiṣṇava equality, they were upbraided for their own hypocrisy. Besides, Teṉkalai Brahmins had long had to face criticism, first from Smārtas and then from Vaṭakalais, over the fact that they had never even been Brahmins. In other words, they had been under identity siege, and they sometimes did not have the moral high ground.

Teṉkalai Brahmins knew, moreover, that there were no easy solutions to the conflicts that Śrīvaiṣṇavas faced. To be a religious leader, one had to have some distinguishing characteristics, but the *ācārya*s and *jīyar*s were gradually losing these. They knew that their own knowledge of the Vedas, *Divyaprabandham*, and other religious texts was waning. As they no longer controlled religious knowledge, most *ācārya*s clung to their right to perform *samāśrayaṇam*, which is linked in the hagiographies with Rāmānuja and salvation. Some clung to precedence and tradition, despite challenges from the Tamil Nadu government or the courts. As often happens in religious communities that face conflict, some leaders had maintained orthodoxy as the distinguishing characteristic of their special religious identity, and some had radically changed.

I found that occasionally, *ācārya*s even implied a hierarchy among the *ācārya*s themselves. This depended on whether they were initiation *ācārya*s or teaching *ācārya*s, whether they were well-educated or not, whether their families had maintained orthodoxy or not, whether they were of good character or not, whether they were wealthy and cosmopolitan or not, whether they spoke English or not, and whether they had only Brahmin disciples or not. The latter point is confirmed by K. Subramaniam, who notes that in some 'Tamil Brahmin communities, it is a serious matter for a Brahmin priest to have non-Brahmin clients even if this is done out of economic necessity'.[43]

As mentioned, I often encountered ambiguity in Brahmin views of non-Brahmins. One Brahmin told me, for instance, that 'non-Brahmins are not supposed to learn the Vedas and Sanskrit'. However, he also admired non-Brahmins who had such knowledge. Another described the relationship like this: 'there is a separate but equal philosophy; some non-Brahmins still give respect to Brahmins and engage Brahmins for the *pūjā*. This is the true spirit of non-Brahminism, not exclusion of Brahmins. When one says *dāsa* (servant) or *aṭiyeṉ* (I am [your humble] servant), it should come from the heart.'

Others were actively trying to bridge the gap. A retired newspaper editor, S. Ramanujam, for instance, started a *sabhā* called the Tirumal Atiyar Kulam to bring everyone together—Brahmins and non-Brahmins, men and women, Teṉkalai and Vaṭakalai. They would go in processions around the temple chanting verses from the *Divyaprabandham*, and then sit together for *bhajanas* and discourses by both non-Brahmins and Brahmins.[44] And I found that some families gave up the *ācārya* tradition altogether and moved into secular education, or compartmentalised their religious beliefs to cope with modernity.

In *Tamil Brahmans: The Making of a Middle-Class Caste*,[45] C. J. Fuller and Haripriya Narasimhan argue, on the basis of their interviews with Tamil Brahmins, that caste and a modern, upper-middle class orientation have fused for them. They explain this development as the result of maintaining or capitalising on some aspects of a secure traditional caste identity, in the sense of being vegetarians and guarding Sanskritic Hinduism, having wealth accumulated from former family positions as landlords or district administrators, and maintaining the value of education.

Fuller and Narasimhan further explain the development of a caste-class orientation as a willingness to adapt to new circumstances. This began with colonial English education, government administrative jobs, and reforms to improve the status of women, such as eliminating child marriage and seclusion, decreasing the hold of purity rules, and encouraging women's education, professional employment, and change of patriarchal marriage to a companionate model. After Indian independence, Tamil Brahmins pursued well-paying jobs such as engineering and information technology and participated in the market economy through investments and the housing market.

In addition, they fashioned a cultural identity as performers or connoisseurs of Carnatic music and *Bhārata Nāṭyam*. 'As Brahmin identity formed around the idea of classical music (and dance)', temple music and non-Brahmin temple musicians were 'deemed inferior'.[46] 'Music,' the authors continue, 'was never crucial for the cultural identity of non-Brahmans in the early twentieth century.' Rather, it belonged to the process of Sanskritisation for upward mobility.

That, I think, is an overstatement. Music was absolutely central to the Icai Velalas for it was their livelihood, gave them public status, and defined their cultural identity. It was important for Naidu musicians and their families, too, although it was probably not a Naidu caste identity marker, in the sense used by Fuller and Narasimhan. Finally, music—*bhajana*s, including Tyāgarāja songs—was certainly a sectarian marker for both Śrīvaiṣṇava non-Brahmins and Brahmins. In any case, many non-Brahmin Śrīvaiṣṇavas had practised Sanskritisation for centuries. This was not an accommodation to modernity.

Fuller and Narasimhan then comment that those Brahmins who remained in Tamil Nadu—a quarter had moved elsewhere in India or to other countries—skilfully avoided the political and economic problems created for them by the non-Brahmin movement. They avoided conflicts over reservations, moreover, by seeking employment in the private sector, especially with international companies. And they avoided the realm of politics altogether, unless it affected them directly, or they were Brahmin political leaders such as Jayalalithaa who held power by cultivating non-Brahmin support, especially that of the numerically dominant non-Brahmin castes.

When I compared the orientation of the Tamil Brahmins interviewed by Fuller and Narasimhan with the Tamil Teṉkalai Brahmins whom I interviewed, I found differences. Because my interest was in changes in religious identity as a component of caste identity, I found more Teṉkalai unease, sometimes even insecurity, over how to maintain identity and status in these changing times. Some wanted to maintain orthodoxy as a marker of Brahmin exceptionalism and religious leadership, and wanted to maintain control over religious roles and institutions, which was the basis for livelihood and status. However, there was also recognition that at least some members of their family had to have 'modern' education and jobs. I must add a warning here. My interviews were with those Tamil Brahmins still heavily identified with religious activities. Had I interviewed Teṉkalai Brahmins who had high-paying jobs in private industries, I might have found orientations closer to those described by Fuller and Narasimhan. It is also possible that the profile of Vaṭakalai Śrīvaiṣṇavas is closer to that of the Tamil Brahmins in the Fuller and Narasimhan case study.

* * *

In this chapter, I discussed two radical Brahmin *ācārya*s in the late nineteenth century, and then focussed on several ethnographies from the end of the twentieth century to detect changes that had occurred in Teṉkalai Brahmin—especially *ācārya*—lives. In my own interviews with several *jīyar*s and *ācārya*s, I found concern over how to handle the massive economic changes related to the huge scale of government reservations, and those related to their own financial support from temples and disciples.

Even though Teṉkalai Bhāgavatas have lived through a stressful period, there are signs that they are beginning to adapt to changes. They are introducing, for instance, English education and secular professions for their sons and daughters. Many are open to ways to improve relations with non-Brahmins. Some Brahmins told me that Brahmins should welcome non-Brahmins into the community as true equals, although it was not always clear exactly what equality meant. Only one, Ethiraja, focussed on the importance of initiating Dalits and destroying hierarchy.

Finally, from my interviews, I discovered very different views regarding whether only Brahmins could be *ācārya*s or *jīyar*s. Parasara Badri Narayana Bhattar stayed with the tradition that an *ācārya* had to belong to one of the seventy-four Brahmin families legitimated by Rāmānuja. By contrast, Ethiraja echoed the position of the non-Brahmins Bhuvanagiri and Ekāṅgi Svāmikaḷ, who lived from the mid-nineteenth century into the twentieth, that *anyone* could become an *ācārya* or *jīyar* and give *samāśrayaṇam*.

Another perspective on current relations between Brahmins and non-Brahmins can be gleaned from court cases. This takes us to the next chapter.

Notes

1. This discussion draws substantially from Raymond B. Williams' 'Srivaishnava Handwritten Field Notes', based on interviews that he conducted in 1988 and 1991. These are currently available in the Wabash College Lilly Library Archives (Crawfordsville, Indiana, USA). He kindly gave me access to this valuable raw data. I have avoided mentioning the names of his interviewees (unless this was someone whom I also interviewed) because I do not have informed consent from them. Rather, I have summarised his findings on various topics, occasionally including a quote that I present as anonymous.

2. See Fuller and Narasimhan, *Tamil Brahmins*.

3. In the course of our conversations, K. K. A. Venkatachari figured out that this was a branch of his own family.

4. See Chapter 6, section: '*Jīyar*s and *Ācārya*s with Non-Brahmin Disciples'.

5. A relative said that Sāttvika copied the *Vālmīki Rāmāyaṇa* on palm-leaves. In 1828, this family received a piece of land from the British. This was *vedamanyam* or tax-free land and was for a Vedic school for Brahmin students.

6. K. K. A. Venkatachari (personal communication, January 2008). According to him, the family lost control of the Kumbakonam temple and moved to Srirangam in the 1960s.

7. This family history was published in a commemoration volume on the sixty-first birthday celebration of Tiruvāḷi-aṇṇaṉ, which was attended by K. K. A. Venkatachari, who received a copy, which I consulted.

8. K. K. A. Venkatachari (personal communication, January 2008).

9. Williams, 'Srivaishnava Handwritten Field Notes'.

10. The *ācārya* may chant the hymns of the *āḻvār*s whose birthday is being celebrated.

11. Some *ācārya* families are keen to have their sons know English, in case they go for advanced education and professional jobs. Even if they become an *ācārya*, the ability to speak English attracts 'sophisticated followers'.

12. Williams, 'Srivaishnava Handwritten Field Notes'.

13. Ibid.

14. Ibid.

15. Ibid.

16. Ibid.

17. Ibid.

18. Ibid.

19. Ibid.

20. Ibid.

21. Ibid.

22. Shree Varataa Ethiraja Jeear is his transliteration of Śrī Varadā Etirāja Jīyar. Etirāja is derived from the Sanskrit *Yatirāja* (king of the ascetics, a title of Rāmānuja). I have added a 'y' in the word Jeear that appears in his name without diacritical marks, so that it aligns with a common popular transliteration.

23. After the morning procession, Rāmānuja's image is taken into the pillared hall opposite the temple, where it is kept on a swing and the milk bath (*abhiśekham*) is performed; after an evening procession, the image is returned to the temple.

24. He is probably referring to Rāmānuja's intellectual prowess and ability to defeat others in philosophical debates.

25. He is referring to stories about the *āḻvār*s in hagiographies, such as the *Divyasūricaritam* and *Guruparamparā Prabhāvam 6000*.

26. Mumme, 'Rules and Rhetoric', 131–32.

27. See his website 'Srimatham', www.srimatham.com (accessed 31 May 2019).

28. Sudarśana Cakra is Viṣṇu's disc-weapon or its personification.

29. See Chapter 3, section: 'The Almost *Ācārya* and his Cousins'.

30. These Brahmins are the ones with lowest status.

31. Ethiraja was a trustee of the Sriperumbudur temple, which was under the financial control of the Hindu Religious and Charitable Endowments Board. He must have had a dispute with them.

32. See 'Court Refuses Armed Guards for Jeeyar'.

33. See 'Court Dismisses Jeeyar's Petition'.

34. Williams, 'Srivaishnava Handwritten Field Notes'.

35. He was married and had children before becoming a *jīyar*. For these biographical details, see 'Chinna Jeeyar'.

36. See Venkatachari, *Maṇipravāḷa Literature*.

37. According to Venkatachari, 'Brahmins have been moving away from their traditional occupations. This has occurred for various reasons. For instance, in the 1940s and 1950s, there were approximately ten orthodox Brahmin families serving the temple at Sriperumbudur. They were satisfied receiving a full meal from the temple every day and dedicated themselves to temple service. Non-Brahmins such as the Sattadas were satisfied. If they got food for their families and some extra money, they were willing to work. This situation started to change in the late 1950s. After the 1990s, both Brahmins and non-Brahmins became more calculating and willing to offer their services for cash only; therefore, temples had to pay for their services. As a result, the temples supported fewer families' (personal communication, January 2011).

38. K. K. A. Venkatachari (personal communication, November 2009) gave the following example of how the Vaṭakalais emphasise the Vedic tradition. They would give the *sandhyā* rituals priority over the *pūjā* ones, which are done at the same time. The Teṉkalais overcame the conflict by doing the *sandhyā* ones a bit later. To substantiate his point, Venkatachari told a story set in Srirangam in the twelfth century. When Bhaṭṭar walks with the procession of Lord Raṅganātha to the banks of the Kaveri river, where the bathing ritual would be performed, one of his disciples informs him that the time for *sandhyā* had come. Because Bhaṭṭar was in the middle of his *kaiṅkarya* to the Lord, he says: 'I can perform *sandhyā* later'. With that he offers one more handful of water to the sun, asking God to excuse him for the delay. Therefore, Teṉkalais think that *kaiṅkarya* is more

important than the daily routines prescribed in the Gṛhyasūtras and that the Vedic rituals should be merged into *kaiṅkarya* ones. Consider my own experience at Bombay. Close to my residence, there was a Vedānta Deśika *sabhā*. Members would recite the *Divyaprabandham*. They invited me for this recitation. Those who participated were mainly Vaṭakalais. They would start the recitation, but would then disappear to perform *sandhyā* and then reappear. This was new to me.

39. *The Sri Vaishnava Brahmins* was a bulletin of the Madras Government Museum, Chennai.

40. Rangachari, *Sri Vaishnava Brahmins*, 15.

41. Ibid., 46.

42. Ibid., 38–39.

43. Subramaniam, 'Brahmin Priest of Tamil Nadu'.

44. Mumme, 'Rules and Rhetoric', 133.

45. See Fuller and Narasimhan, *Tamil Brahmins*.

46. See ibid., 201.

seven

Temple Politics and the Courts

Although the temple redistributive system—with roles sanctioned by precedent, common acknowledgement and chains of command—generally worked well for the medieval temple, it was a delicate system and conflicts could arise if boundaries were ignored or usurped. According to Arjun Appadurai, the king might have to intervene discreetly, but that was rare. By colonial times, however, the generally laissez-faire functioning of the temple was changing gradually through codification of what was deemed local rights and privileges, albeit now often arbitrary ones. The Teṉkalais gained the upper hand, even though the Vaṭakalais had attempted a takeover by manipulating the British predilection for rules, which enabled them to take control of the trusteeship and therefore the temple itself.[1]

As a result, factions in the temple developed over control of temple lands, people, and property. Conflicts ended up in the courts for resolution. Appadurai's careful study of the many legal cases related to the Parthasarathy temple in Madras is a case in point. Of interest here is his study of Teṉkalai legal and political manoeuvring that made them the undisputed power-brokers in that temple and solidified their sectarian identity (a strategy that, I would add, they pursued at many other temples, and usually successfully).

Appadurai's case study of the Parthasarathy temple also shows how the Teṉkalais themselves became factionalised into antagonistic Brahmin and non-Brahmin identities. Conflict usually focussed on non-Brahmin perceptions of discrimination, understood as dishonour (*avamāna*). In Appadurai's words: 'This term not only captures the sense of public degradation felt by the non-Brahmins but also tersely expresses their feeling that by manipulating the honors appropriate to non-Brahmins, Brahmins degrade them in the royal presence of the deity ....'[2]

One major conflict between Brahmin and non-Brahmin Teṉkalais occurred when some Brahmins attempted to remove non-Brahmin voting rights related to their role in temple administration by requiring a literacy test and a fee, a case that the non-Brahmins took to court, eventually lost,[3] and never regained.

Relations between non-Brahmins and Brahmins are now not as fierce as they had been at the height of the non-Brahmin movement. Still, court cases and a deep difference of opinion between the courts and the Government of Tamil Nadu, or the lower courts and the Supreme Court, mean that tensions can easily flare up.

In this chapter, I examine non-Brahmin accusations of unequal treatment in some of the major Brahmin-dominated temples, in connection with worship, chanting, and who can be a priest. I conclude with a discussion of a court case regarding access to the priesthood that went to the Supreme Court on this matter, and which was decided in 2015.

Equal Treatment in Worship?

Some Bhāgavatas told me that temple rights are not the same for Brahmin and non-Brahmin worshippers. There have been conflicts over which door non-Brahmins may use to enter the temple, where they may sit, and where and when they may receive *tīrtha*, *prasāda*, and the *śaṭakōpa*.

This has a long history. Consider the case at Parthasarathy temple in Chennai. Between 1944 and 1968, lower middle-class Naidus affiliated to the Nampillai Sabhā (which Appadurai characterises as small and lacking prestige[4]), along with other groups, protested acts of discrimination against non-Brahmin worshippers in the Parthasarathy temple. The government tried to address these concerns.

In 1959, the Hindu Religious and Charitable Endowments (HRCE) Act in Tamil Nadu set up a branch of the government for the administration and governance of public religious institutions, such as temples, *maṭha*s, and endowments, in a manner not to conflict with Article 26 of the Constitution (which stipulates that there can be social reforms of practices that are *not* religiously 'essential'). HRCE powers include registering institutions, protecting the health of pilgrims and worshippers, training of priests, inspecting property, appointing office-holders and servants, fixing fees for services, and suspending, removing, or dismissing trustees and priests for wrongdoing.

Many conflicts have been adjudicated by the HRCE Board. Nevertheless, there have been ongoing tensions. A conflict flared in 1964 when some Naidus complained that different vessels were used to distribute the sacred water to Brahmins and non-Brahmins, that Brahmins were given the sacred water and the *śaṭakōpa* first while everyone had to stand, but then the Brahmins sat down when the non-Brahmins received these, and that in any case, the *śaṭakōpa* was rarely offered to non-Brahmins. In this case,[5] the commissioner had held that there should be no discrimination between Brahmins and non-Brahmins regarding the distribution of *tīrtha* and the giving of the *śaṭakōpa*, and that they all, not only the Brahmins, should sit at this time and be served in the same way. The commissioner also held that ordinary Brahmins should not mix with the *adhyāpakā goṣṭhi*, which is the special registered group of

Brahmins who do the chanting and have the customary right to be served first.

In response, the Brahmin temple representatives claimed that non-Brahmin complaints amounted to undue sensitivity. Where there were privileges, these had existed 'by long established usage, and it is not correct to take objection to particular details in the light of new-fangled views'.[6] They gave examples of the privileges of Brahmin priests (*arcaka*s) and noted that special honours were based on meritorious service and gifts from ancestors, often recorded in inscriptions, which continue to be honoured by the temple. They argued, moreover, that some Brahmin ascetics and temple trustees had special rights.

The commissioner rejected these arguments, saying that the petitioners had rightly accepted some exceptions, such as the tradition of honours, but had argued that there was a more general problem because Brahmin and non-Brahmin *worshippers* were treated differently. The commissioner upheld Section 106 of the Madras Hindu Religious and Charitable Endowments Act 1959, which had said that 'there shall be no discrimination in the distribution of any Prasadam or Theertham in any religious institution on grounds only of caste, sex, place of birth or any of them'.[7]

Despite this decision, tensions were ongoing at the Parthasarathy temple and other temples as well. On 28 October 2014, for instance, there was a demonstration by Bhāgavatas outside the Varadarājasvāmi temple in Kanchipuram. This demonstration occurred in the wake of a long-simmering conflict over non-Brahmin claims of discrimination that had already gone to the Madras High Court. A verdict in 2008 had banned discrimination within the temple. According to the complainants, however, nothing had changed. Non-Brahmins were still prevented from entering Maṇavāla Māmuni's shrine through the main entrance and reciting the *Divyaprabandham* verses there. In addition, they were relegated to the back rows. This is a public temple, they argued, where everyone should be equal. Along with local non-Brahmin organisations, the protest was supported by the Tamil Nadu Untouchability Eradication Front, which was affiliated with the Communist Party of India, the Dravidar Kazhagam, the (Dalit) Viduthalai Chiruthaigal Katchi, and the Centre of Indian Trade Unions. Members of the local Brahmin *goṣṭhi* (chanting group) denied that non-Brahmins had been prevented from using the main entrance. As for who can chant the sacred verses in major Śrīvaiṣṇava temples, they argued that Brahmins had long had that right.[8]

Equal Treatment in Chanting?

One component of the case just discussed was the issue of who can chant in the temples. In one interview, a Brahmin told me that Brahmin Śrīvaiṣṇavas do not accept non-Brahmins in their *adhyāpakā goṣṭhi* (a group of Brahmin men who claim the right of chanting the *Divyaprabandham* within the temple).

It is quite clear that Brahmins have had the sole right to chant the Tamil hymns (the *Divyaprabandham*) in the major temples, at least in the twentieth century. In fact, they are often registered to do this as *adhyāpakā*s. There are *adhyāpakā* offices in many temples, moreover, and related honours and payments.

Still, a Brahmin monopoly on chanting in the major temples was not always the case. There was certainly a practice of non-Brahmins chanting *āḻvār* hymns at Rāmānuja's shrine within the Tirumalai temple in the fifteenth century, according to one inscription.[9] There is also evidence that non-Brahmins chanted in temple processions. The *Guruparamparā Prabhāvam 6000* describes, for instance, the procession at the time of Rāmānuja's death. There were 900 Śrīvaiṣṇavas without the *yajñopavīta* (the sacred thread)—this means that they were non-Brahmins—who were reciting the first 3,000 verses of the *Divyaprabandham*; those reciting the other 1,000 verses (the *Tiruvāymoḻi*), that is, the Brahmins, were reciting them with *tala*.[10] Despite the fact that this description is about the death of Rāmānuja who lived in the twelfth century, it too likely reflects a much later practice for temple processions. Just how late depends on one's dating of the *Guruparamparā Prabhāvam 6000*.[11]

Moreover, the *Kōyil Oluku*, the chronicle of the Srirangam temple (the current version is based on manuscripts compiled in 1803), says that Rāmānuja gave the (non-Brahmin) Sattadas the right to sit behind the Brahmins while reciting the *Divyaprabandham*. The Brahmins would recite the first two lines of a verse and the Sattadas the last two lines.[12] What is important here is that the practice existed at least at the time the *Kōyil Oluku* was compiled, if not before, and continued to 1942 when the Sattadas were prevented from chanting in the Srirangam temple 'by legal action'.[13] In short, precedent for Brahmin claims to the exclusive right to chant the *Divyaprabandham* in the temples was by no means found in all Śrīvaiṣṇava temples until the mid-twentieth century, and the fact that the tradition itself claims that Rāmānuja, its very figurehead of authority, had given these rights to Sattadas makes Brahmin claims to precedence for their exclusive rights ambiguous at the very least. The irony is that all the *ācārya*s have described the Tamil Veda (the *Divyaprapandham*) as the scripture for *śūdra*s and women, but they are not allowed to chant it in major temples.

There was also no chance for non-Brahmins to be part of the *Divyaprabandham* official chanting group (*goṣṭhi*) at the Parthasarathy temple in Madras. Codification had created many factions within the temple. Of interest here is a dispute between 1922 and 1925 pertaining to the *adhyāpakā*s, a dispute that was intertwined with a dispute between different factions of priests and which led to police intervention and court cases. We need not review the court cases here—Appadurai has done that—except to note that 'The detailed codification of their [the *adhyāpakā*s'] duties, perquisites, and honors by the court in this case has ever since been a major charter for the proud autonomy of this group and still is today.'[14]

And why were Tenkalai Brahmins, supposedly the supporters of inclusiveness, so keen on claiming the exclusive right to chant in temples such as Srirangam and Parthasarathy?

The fact that the Dravidian parties were asserting power in the 1930s—Periyar became head of the Justice Party in 1939—might have contributed to this Brahmanical attempt to marginalise non-Brahmin influence in the temples. Another reason might be that as their Vedic expertise waned, Brahmin desire for exclusive right to chant the Tamil scriptures increased (although they probably had had the exclusive temple right to chant Nammāḻvār's *Tiruvāymoḻi* through the sect's history). Besides, it is not incidental that the *adhyāpakā* rights included 'an immense list of paraphernalia, in terms of duties and honors'.[15]

So, what does this mean for today? A similar battle over non-Brahmins chanting in the sanctum has taken place in the Śaiva Nāṭarāja temple in Chidambaram, where a reclining image of the Vaiṣṇava God (Nārāyaṇa) is also located. In 2000, a non-Brahmin named Arumugasamy tried to sing verses from the Śaiva Tevāram and *Tiruvācakam* there. He was beaten up by the Brahmin Dikṣitar priests. This led to legal challenges and mass protest movements. Arumugasamy had argued that 'Reciting Tamil hymns in the temple in Tamil Nadu is our right', that too immediately in front of Lord Nāṭarāja.[16] After a government stay order, which made the Dikṣitars relent, Arumugasamy chanted before the God in 2008 with police protection. Since then, despite harassment by the Dikṣitars, he chanted the Tevāram before the deity every day to maintain his right to chant there, until a short illness followed by death in April 2017 made this impossible. After his death, his lawyer pleaded with other non-Brahmins for someone to carry on chanting in the area in front of Nāṭarāja's shrine, in order to protect this hard-won right for non-Brahmins to chant there.

We are reminded of Ramanuja Nayakar's saga told in Chapter 4, about his struggles with temple priests to chant the *Divyaprabandham* in a temple on the outskirts of Puducherry.

Equal Treatment in the Priesthood?

Opening the priesthood to non-Brahmins has been an issue in major Hindu temples in south India. Non-Brahmin village priests have always existed, but Brahmins have controlled the rituals and been the priests at the major Śrīvaiṣṇava temples, such as the *divyadeśas* located in Tamil Nadu.

The Tamil Nadu government has control over the training of priests, according to the Hindu Religious and Charitable Endowments Act of 1959. Therefore, it comes as no surprise that in 2006, the government issued the following order: 'Any person who is a Hindu and possessing the requisite qualification and training can be appointed as an *arcaka* (priest) in Hindu temples.'[17] That same year, some Brahmin *arcaka*s filed a petition that went eventually to the Supreme Court[18] to prevent this encroachment on what they considered their exclusive right to be temple priests. As they waited for the verdict, schools opened specifically to provide training for non-Brahmins to become priests, and thereby comply with the Tamil Nadu government order. This demanding training included how to perform rituals according to the Sanskrit Pañcarātra Āgama texts.

As I mentioned in Chapter 3, non-Brahmin students were being trained in the school that I visited in Chennai,[19] but it suddenly closed, and no one could tell me why. Did it have something to do with the pending Supreme Court decision? Were Śrīvaiṣṇava Brahmins at the Parthasarathy temple lobbying behind the scenes to stop these schools?

Stories about this contentious problem appeared periodically in the press, even in other countries. A 2012 article in the *Los Angeles Times*, for instance, tells the story of Kesavan, a Dalit, whose father and grandfather had performed rituals at a makeshift Dalit shrine. When Kesavan heard about the Tamil Nadu government's offer to train him as a Hindu priest, he took the course. He was never employed for four years, however, because of the court cases that have challenged this programme. He, along with fellow Dalit trainees, blamed the

IMAGE 7.1: Non-Brahmin students from the villages studying to be priests at a school near the Parthasarathy temple in Chennai before it was closed.

Image credit: Author's collection.

long delay on Brahmins, Hindu nationalists, and traditionalists who want to protect the caste system.

Dalits argued that the Constitution forbids discrimination on the basis of caste and, in any case, there is a need for priests in many of the state-run temples. 'The real problem isn't Dalit impurity or tradition,' they argued. 'Rather, it's that Brahmins don't want to share money or power .... Further upsetting tradition, the Dalit trainees want mantras and blessings to be said in the local Tamil language rather than ancient Sanskrit, which they believe further safeguards Brahmin power.'[20] In response, V. Jagannathan, general secretary of Chennai's Thamizhnadu Brahmin Association, said 'Dalits are not impure but they are not as pure as Brahmins,' adding that 'Dalits smoke, drink and wear dirty clothes'.[21]

Discrimination was not just by Brahmins. It was also by non-Brahmins. An article[22] points out that despite government attempts to make temples more inclusive, some village temples, even those that have non-Brahmin priests, do not allow Dalits to worship there. According to D. Ravikumar, a Member of the Legislative Assembly: 'If Brahmins are opposed to non-Brahmins staking claim to priesthood, the so-called backward classes are more fiercely opposed to yielding space for Dalits in the sacral realm.'[23]

During the long wait for a verdict on the Supreme Court case, the neighbouring state of Kerala began to introduce non-Brahmin priests. A website called 'The Modern Rationalist'—linked with the Periyar tradition, which had long backed the idea of equal access to priestly jobs—notes that in Kerala temples, non-Brahmin priests fill half of the vacancies. The website goes on to stipulate that the person applying for a priest's job should be a Malayali Hindu who has an elementary knowledge of *tantra-shastra*, Sanskrit, and the Brahmanical tradition, as well as a certificate from a Board-approved senior priest.[24]

In yet another article, Aravindan Neelakandan, a contributing editor at *Swarajya*, a monthly magazine and an online daily that calls itself 'liberal right of centre', suggests that Kerala has made greater progress than Tamil Nadu in ensuring equal access to the priesthood. Despite initial bitter battles over temple entry, 'traditionalists and reformers have converged successfully to bring the education and practice of temple rituals to the masses. It was not a sudden state-enforced imposition or a racial-binary based narrative that brought this change.'[25] He alludes to the fact that education and training for non-Brahmins came from the Vishva Hindu Sammelam, a branch of the Vishva Hindu Parishad (VHP) and the Rashtriya Swayamsevak Sangh (RSS) (organisations on the Hindu right that are ostensibly anti-caste), and the Board approval comes from the Kanchi Kamakoti Peetham. Neelakandan argues that unlike the political situation in Kerala, the 'DMK (the party in power in Tamil Nadu) was so anti-Hindu and anti-Brahmin, it has been incapable of working with them for reform'.[26]

This connection of making the priesthood accessible to everyone with the Hindu Right has also been noticed by Gilles Tarabout in his chapter 'Temple Priests and the Courts', in the book *Filing Religion: State, Hinduism, and the Courts of Law.*[27] He remarks that the RSS has supported schools to train non-Brahmins to be priests and argues that any non-Brahmin can become a Brahmin through initiation rituals.[28]

As Tarabout makes clear, many factors have been involved in the Kerala position that any Hindu who fulfils the requirements can be a priest in Hindu temples. These include the influence of nineteenth-century reform movements such as the Arya Samaj, the Brahmo Samaj, and the Ramakrishna Mission to eliminate the caste system, the gradual secularisation of religion through government involvement in the name of better administration (which can be traced back to the colonial period), the role of the courts to arbitrate temple conflicts, the development of the Hindu Religious Endowment Board in 1926 in Tamil Nadu, which influenced other states such as Kerala, and, after Independence, the State's duty to instigate Hindu religious reform.

In addition, Tarabout points to a number of court cases that have contributed to the idea that anyone can be a priest, as long as the person knows how to perform the rituals described in the texts correctly. Their qualification is based on education, not hereditary right (in other words: merit, not birth), and they are viewed as employees of the government. Even though Kerala has fully supported a priesthood not based on caste, comments Tarabout, there is an interesting twist to this idea: one becomes casteless by being transformed, through initiation and wearing the sacred thread, into a Brahmin, in a manner analogous to the Arya Samaj's rituals for reconverting Muslims and Christians back to Hinduism.

In any case, priest-training schools have been set up in Kerala, sometimes sponsored by particular castes such as the Ezhava (once outcastes), the Nayars, and others. Brahmins have managed the schools with government support and they have been the teachers. Students then apply for a job. There is a careful vetting process by the Travancore Devaswom Board or the Cochin Devaswom Board, with applications and interviews that are like an exam, with answers given a numerical figure and tallied with the final decision that is made by drawing lots in front of the deity's sanctum. Despite a few legal challenges, there has been a trend towards access to ritual education for anyone, which is breaking the Brahmin monopoly on the priesthood in many 'Brahmanical' temples in Kerala, even though the Boards pragmatically avoid placing low-caste priests in such temples. As a result, most of these new priests will probably find jobs in their own community temples.

Other states have tackled the issue of who can be a Hindu priest in ways similar to that of Kerala. By contrast, in Tamil Nadu, despite the government's desire to change the definition of who can be a priest, the government has only managed to abolish hereditary rights to the priesthood. Besides, there has been no willingness to create schools for non-Brahmin ritual training, or find sufficient teachers and students to make this a success, until recent times. Even then, those schools were suddenly abandoned the year before the Supreme Court judgment on who can be a priest was released.

According to an editorial in *The Hindu*, it is wrong to characterise the government's interest in temples as only a desire to appropriate their wealth, which it camouflages by calls for reforms. Ninety per cent of the temples it manages are small and have little property or wealth. Rather, the government's role has been to make sure that whatever resources temples have are administered properly for the public good, or to prevent 'unreasonable practices'. The example given was the government's intervention in 2008 to end the practice of preventing non-Brahmins from singing Tamil Śaivite devotional hymns near the sanctum at Chidambaram, an issue resolved out-of-court in favour of the non-Brahmins after an official stay order was issued.[29] As I have already mentioned, even with the court stay and a resolution out of court, this has been difficult to maintain and might collapse.

Underlying the issue of Teṉkalai Brahmins wanting to maintain control of the major temples in Tamil Nadu is the fact that control of the priesthood is one of the main ways of controlling the temple itself. This became more important as the government increasingly intervened in temple affairs. Concerns about state takeover of temple wealth are closely related.

The Supreme Court on Precedent

In December 2015, the Supreme Court of India finally ruled on the case about who can be a priest in Tamil Nadu, which had begun in 2006. To provide background for its decision, the Court reviewed two constitutional sections.[30] In Article 25, the Constitution protects a religion's 'essential features'[31] and in Article 26, it protects a religion's right to manage its religious affairs, albeit with a few exceptions within carefully defined limits: public order, morality and health, as well as social reforms of practices that are *not* religiously 'essential'. A key reform, for example, had been the Temple Entry Act of 1947, which made it illegal to prevent specific Hindu groups (such as Dalits) from entering public Hindu religious institutions.[32]

The Supreme Court ruled also that the focus must be on the 'denomination'. In the case of priests in many Tamil Nadu temples, that meant their identity as priests belonging to the tradition of the Śaiva Āgamas in the case of Śaivism, or the Pañcarātra, or Vaikhānasa Āgamas in the case of Vaiṣṇavism. The Court rejected the idea found in the Tamil Nadu Government Order of 2006 that any Hindu could be a priest (presumably in any temple), because that was too broad. For the same reason, it also rejected the idea that any Śaiva or Vaiṣṇava—a middle, but still too broad a category that only indicates worship of a particular deity (Śiva or Viṣṇu)—could be a priest in any Śaiva or Vaiṣṇava temple.

The Supreme Court examined whether it was an essential belief and practice for priests in these temples to belong to the temple's denomination and what 'belonging' meant to them. Āgamic priesthood, the Court held, is essential to the denomination. Members believe that priests maintain the purity of the image; if defiled, they must perform a purification ritual.[33] There is a precedent for this ruling, the Court further held, because maintenance of the image's purity had been the Āgamic practice for centuries.[34] In addition, members believe that their denominations had specific requirements for the priesthood.

The Court used the example that a Śaiva priest had to have *dīkṣā*, initiation in the Śaiva Āgama tradition. It did not mention that in the Pañcarātra tradition, only those with a certain initiation can be priests.[35] What the Court also left unsaid is the fact that there is a preceding tacit qualification for the Pañcarātra initiation: belonging to an endogamous Brahmin sub-caste from which members, and members only, can become the future Pañcarātra priests, assuming they have the special initiation for this and are selected. The Court ruled that as long as the Āgama does not *explicitly* deny someone the priesthood on the basis of caste, there is no conflict with the Constitution. Ironically, Śrīvaiṣṇava Āgama texts had originally emerged from an ancient inclusive Sātvata/ Bhāgavata orientation, which only later came under Brahmin control as Brahmins realised that the future would be in temple worship, not Vedic rituals.

At any rate, the Court concluded that entrance to the priesthood does not depend on caste because even Brahmins with higher status than priests, such as 'Pontifs and Acaryas', may not enter the sanctum. In other words, the Court held that '*dīkṣā*', which provides the necessary 'purity' to touch the image, is essential to this religion, that the Constitution protects the right of religious denominations to manage their own affairs, and that there have been many precedents for this opinion.[36]

Several years before the Supreme Court judgment, I had asked a Brahmin what he thought about the Chennai school to train non-Brahmin priests. He replied that

> custom, in particular temples under Brahmin control, will prevail legally because that has been the precedent, which the government has honoured in cases so far; non-Brahmin-controlled temples, including village ones, are another matter. They will be caste-inclusive, and therefore the government is training non-Brahmin priests for only these.

That limitation was never stipulated in the government order to allow any qualified Hindu to become a priest, which led in part to the legal challenge. This Brahmin certainly was right, however, about the legal recognition of precedence in the Brahmin-controlled temples. I could see from T. S. Ramaswamy's review of the Śrīvaiṣṇava court cases in Tamil Nadu and Andhra, and the previous judgments of the Supreme Court, that 'precedent' in a given temple has been the determining fact to resolve conflicts over priesthood.[37]

The importance that the Supreme Court has given to precedence or custom relates not only to the system of temple honours at the core of temple culture, but also the lower courts' role in adjudicating temple disputes in Tamil Nadu and other places in India for the past 200 years, when conflict sometimes turned violent and there was a need to maintain public order, a position that came to be recognised by the Constitution.[38] Some of the most difficult cases have been those between Teṉkalai and Vaṭakalai Śrīvaiṣṇavas in Tamil Nadu.

So just what is in store for non-Brahmin temples? Will they be allowed to introduce Āgamic worship performed by non-Brahmin priests (assuming that temples can find teachers to train non-Brahmins in Āgamic rituals) because these temples were always under the control of non-Brahmins and non-Brahmin priests? Āgamic ritual is attractive, especially for festivals. Because some non-Brahmins are attracted to Agamic-style elaborate temple rituals (I certainly witnessed this in Sudarshana's temple and elsewhere),[39] how will they cope with this issue of precedent? And what about Kerala, which had already made progress on the problem of non-Brahmin access to the priesthood? Would there be Brahmin challenges based on the Supreme Court judgment?

* * *

In this chapter, I have explored issues of discrimination against non-Brahmins in the temple context, and how these have become the subject of court cases beginning in colonial times. Although the Indian Constitution made provisions to address discrimination, this had effect mainly in reforms to allow Dalits entry into temples, the so-called temple entry acts.

In Tamil Nadu, the Hindu Religious and Charitable Endowments Department of the Government of Tamil Nadu addressed temple entry, along with other issues of discrimination in temples that affected worshippers. When disputes occasionally flared up, non-Brahmins and various civil society groups responded with legal cases or political agitation. What has been slower in coming, however, is the right to chant the *Divyaprabandham* before the deity in the major temples. Even though the conflict of non-Brahmin chanters with the Dikṣitar priests at the Nāṭarāja temple in Chidambaram was resolved in favour of non-Brahmin Śaivas and can be considered a precedent for Śrīvaiṣṇava temples as well, sounds of alarm have recently been raised that the gain at Chidambaram could easily be threatened.

The most problematic case to address non-Brahmin discrimination has been over access to the priesthood. Because the Supreme Court held in 2015 that precedent for access would be held on denominational precedents, this was a rebuke to non-Brahmin aspirations to be priests in major temples where Brahmins have held this role. It was also a rebuke to the Government of Tamil Nadu, which had facilitated schools to train both Brahmin and non-Brahmin priests in Āgamic rituals. In its wake, the Supreme Court decision has left several unresolved issues, which I discuss in Appendix 5. Since the Court has held that in future cases, the lower courts will have to make decisions on a case by case basis, which means temple by temple, the future looks litigious indeed.

Notes

1. Appadurai, *Worship and Conflict*, 146–99.
2. Ibid., 46.
3. See ibid., 209 and 201, for details of *Vijayaraghava Mudaliar* v. *Ranganadham Chetty* (C.S. 843 of 1919) High Court of Judicature at Madras, and *Viraraghavachariar* v. *Parthasarathy Iyengar* (C.S 527 of 1924) High Court of Judicature at Madras.
4. Ibid., 45. In Chapter 3, we encountered the Nampillai Sabhā (see section: 'The Lord's Proselytizer').
5. This case is known as 'Commissioner for Hindu Religious and Charitable Endowment Department and Representatives of the Sri Parthasarathiswamy Devasthanam', Madras-34, M.P. No. 6 of 1964.
6. 'Before the Commissioner'.
7. 'Before the Commissioner'.
8. See Rajasekaran, 'Recitation Row'.
9. See TTDES 2.68 (200-T.T.) of 1476. This inscription mentions the Sattina-Śrīvaiṣṇavas and the Sattada-Śrīvaiṣṇavas, who chant the works of the *āḻvārs* in the shrine of Uḍaiyavar [Rāmānuja]. The Sattinas have been described as Brahmins and, according to the *Kōyiḻ Oḻuku*, the Sattadas are Śūdras.

10. This passage was first pointed out to me by K. K. A. Venkatachari. See also Nagaswamy, *Ramanuja Myth and Reality*, 98 ff.

11. My own view is that it is largely a product of the seventeenth century. See Young, 'Development of the *Divyaprabandham*'.

12. See *Koil Olugu*, 89.

13. Lester, 'The Sāttāda Śrīvaiṣṇavas', 43. I have been unable to find further details about this 'legal action'.

14. Appadurai, *Worship and Conflict*, 207.

15. Ibid., 206.

16. See 'Man Who Fought for Thevaram No More'.

17. See 'Non-Brahmins Can Also Be Temple Priests'.

18. The legal case is 'Adi Saiva Sivachariyargal, Nala Sangam and Ors (petitioners) versus the Government of Tamil Nadu and ANR (respondents)'. In the Supreme Court of India Civil Original Jurisdiction Writ Petition (Civil) No. 354 of 2006 (http://www.viex.in).

19. See Chapter 3, section: 'The Maker of Village Priests'.

20. Magnier, 'Trained Priests from Lower Caste'.

21. Ibid.

22. Anand, 'Pujaris on the GO'.

23. Ibid.

24. See 'In Kerala Temples, Non-Brahmin Priests'.

25. Neelakandan, 'Tamil Temple Priests'.

26. Ibid.

27. Tarabout, 'Birth vs Merit'. In this chapter, Tarabout examines the court cases only until 2014, and therefore does not comment on the Supreme Court case on who can be a priest.

28. Tarabout, 'Birth vs Merit', 11, 17.

29. Srivathsan, 'Reforms in the House of God'.

30. These Constitutinal sections are:

'**25.** Freedom of conscience and free profession, practice and propagation of religion.—(1) Subject to public order, morality and health and to the other provisions of this Part, all persons are equally entitled to freedom of conscience and the right freely to profess, practise and propagate religion. (2) Nothing in this article shall affect the operation of any existing law or prevent the State from making any law—(a) regulating or restricting any economic, financial, political or other secular activity which may be associated with religious practices; (b) providing for social welfare and reform or the throwing open of Hindu religious institutions of a public character to all classes and sections of Hindus.

26. Freedom to manage religious affairs.—Subject to public order, morality and health, every religious denomination or any section thereof shall have the right—(a) to establish and maintain institutions for religious and charitable purposes; (b) to manage its own affairs in matters of religion; (c) own and acquire movable and immovable property; and (d) to administer such property in accordance with law'. 'The Constitution of India (As on 9th November, 2015), (New Delhi: Government of India, Ministry of Law and Justice (Legislative Department).' See 'Constitution'.

31. In a 1962 case, the Supreme Court had clarified that protection of religion included only the 'essential' features of religion, and the Court reiterated this point in 2015.

32. For an early history of temple-entry politics in Tamil Nadu, see Pillai, *Temple Entry*. The introduction is by E. V. Ramaswamy (Periyar), who had supported temple entry. The author was a retired High Court judge in Travancore, who had participated in the Self-Respect Movement.

33. According to Ramaswamy, it is incumbent on the priest to prevent pollution or defilement or desecration of the image, which can occur in many ways, including changing the rules by which it is worshipped, because this diminishes the Divine Spirit in the image, or even causes it to disappear. Should such a problem occur, the priest must perform purification ceremonies (Ramaswamy, *Judicial Solutions*, 129).

A distinction has been drawn between two contexts of untouchability: pollution of the temple by those deemed untouchable by caste Hindus and pollution of the image, or inner sanctum, by anyone without the proper Āgamic initiation. All Hindus have the right to worship in public temples (Constitution, Article 17); only *arcaka*s of a denominational kind have the right to do rituals in the temples, however, because only they can preserve the purity.

34. The concept of precedent is a difficult one, which explains the very different versions. Chidambaram Pillai argued that the Āgamas had been caste inclusive, because initiation alone counted for becoming a temple priest. 'An uninitiated Brahmin cannot even be a menial servant ... in a Hindu temple. A Chandala or Pariah can get initiated in much the same way as the Brahmin or any other' (Chidambaram Pillai, *Temple Entry*, 67). He recounts the low status

of temple priests in the eyes of orthodox Brahmins and the fact that most of the temples in Tamil Nadu started out as small village shrines with 'casteless' priests (who were *śūdra*s or outcastes in caste parlance); they were public temples and catered to all worshippers. In the distant past, orthodox Brahmins looked down on temples, although they gradually realised that temples would become more important due to the decline of public Vedic sacrifice. Therefore, they began to take over the temples. Chidambaram Pillai shows how this transition occurred, escalated during British rule, and was currently occurring (ibid., 67ff.).

It could be argued, however, that there are many Āgamas and that Āgamic beliefs themselves have undergone many changes since their inception over a millennium ago. The courts have acknowledged historical change in the context of precedent. It is probably for this reason that the Supreme Court has said that it must proceed on a case by case basis and not generalise.

35. By contrast, in the Vaikhānasa tradition, only those from families with hereditary rights can become priests, even though the Court in another case had already rejected the automatic hereditary right to priesthood, because it was the government's right to remove priests for wrongdoing or incompetence. See 'A.S. Narayana Deekshitulu vs. State of A.P. and others' (1996[9] Supreme Court Cases 548). T. S. Ramaswamy comments that 'the Supreme Court gave the finding that Sections 34 and 35 of A.P. Charitable and Hindu Religious Institutions and Endowments Act, 1987 abolishing hereditary rights of Archakas and other office holders are not violative of Articles 25 and 26 of the Constitution' (Ramaswamy, *Judicial Solutions*, 103).

36. The court had struck down a denomination's right to protect the hereditary succession of priests, arguing that this was a secular component. That was because kings had once removed priests for incompetence, bad behaviour, or unwillingness to maintain the temple's traditions. In other words, Arcakas are subject to the discipline and control of the authorities' (Ramaswamy, *Judicial Solutions*, 135).

37. For instance, in *Krishnasami Tatacharyar and others vs. Krishnamacharyar and others* (judgment 1 May 1882), members of the Teṉkalai and Vaṭakalai sects argued that the right at the Devarajaswami temple in Kanchipuram for the *adhyāpakā*s to recite the *āḻvār*s' verses existed from 'time immemorial', that only the mantrams of their sect be used at the beginning of the recitation,

and that they receive the honours and income that went along with this recitation (Ramaswamy, *Judicial Solutions*, 29). In this case, the Teṉkalais won—as they did in several similar cases, when the argument relied on precedent (ibid., 35–92).

38. See ibid., 20, for a review of these cases in Tamil Nadu and their judgments.

39. See Chapter 3, section: 'The Almost *Ācārya* and his Cousins'.

eight

Thinking about the Big Picture

Discussion of the 'big picture' must be framed, to some extent, by the fact that Śrīvaiṣṇava praxis and identity today have been shaped by the forces and interpretations of modernity. There are debates over whether modernity has a core definition, such as rationality and autonomy, or whether it is best understood by listing key components, such as industrialisation, science, technology, a market economy, urbanisation, the modern State, democracy, emancipation from exploitation, new collectivities, human rights, universal education, the rule of law, individualism, autonomy, the Internet, and secularism.

There are debates too over whether modernity indicates a degree of societal transformation through adaptation or deep structural change, whether it is transitional or permanent, whether the process is predetermined or not, whether it has universal features or varying responses, whether there are real modernities and mistaken ones, and whether modernity has been followed by late modernity and postmodernity as new phenomena, or whether such distinctions are only variations upon a theme. The analysis of the term extends to the role of historiography and other scholarly paradigms, such as functionalism, Marxism, or postmodernism.

An especially important debate for the focus of this book is: Is there one modernity defined by the West or several modernities, because those in other cultures are different?[1] According to Elsje Fourie, some scholars have argued that the theory of multiple modernities relies on an implicit notion of modernity, yet ignores or deconstructs any definition, essentialises civilisations to construct a claim of radical differences, and lacks any empirical methods to decide whether convergence is occurring.[2] In reply, advocates of multiple modernities have challenged the model of one modernity as a kind of evolutionary determinism and a Western moral superiority, based on ideas of progress that have not been tested over time.[3]

Many scholars accept the idea that some aspects of modernity are of Western origin and entered India with colonialism. These scholars point out, however, that their trajectories in India have been very different than in the West, because of interaction with India's distinct cultural and religious features. Others have argued that some of modernity's components have Indian origins as well, and so the phenomenon is not just derivative of the West but represents distinctive processes and configurations.

Anand Pandian's study of concepts of agrarian virtue, which help agrarian castes deal with the spiralling momentum of the computer *kālam* (the time of computers)[4] shows, for instance, that they go back to a precolonial inheritance in rural Tamil Nadu. Kaivan Munshi reminds us that caste has great tenacity today, given its deep roots in Indian history, and that affects the nature of modernity in India.[5]

In *Textures of Time*, Velcheru Narayana Rao, David Shulman, and Sanjay Subrahmanyam argue for an understanding of modernism between Western positivist historiography and postmodernism, where everything is just a discourse. They think that we need to do a better job of understanding what has happened in precolonial Indian history through a more sophisticated study of sources. This can reveal how historical events, political models, and indigenous concepts are embedded in multilayered texts. They argue that when one takes indigenous sources seriously (such as various Telugu literary genres and the history of bureaucracy), one finds a history from below, which provides clues to authorial intent and authority. Such an approach helps scholars decipher fact and fiction and reveals that an early form of modernity can be detected in south India from the late fifteenth or the early sixteenth century, characterised by 'a striking individualism, a new sense of the human body and its possibilities, a common political culture that cuts through the boundaries of collective ("religious") identities ... and so on'.[6]

Their case study for indigenous sources is one of Muslim-influenced bureaucracy (the *karṇam*). They do not mention the Persian, Turkish, and Renaissance influence on the Mughal and other Indian Muslim courts that were conduits of different traditions of historiography, not to mention incipient modernity. In other words, these Muslim traditions were already a cultural mix of outside and inside sources, which became even more complicated as they creatively interacted with south Indian cultures. That said, the authors offer an important challenge to theories of modernism's colonial origins and the simple Western hegemony that implies.

In his book *Tamil: A Biography*, David Shulman goes even further in the indigenous thesis. Drawing on his extensive knowledge of south Indian literatures, both general patterns and particular historical contexts, he argues that modernism is mainly an internal development that is organic and creative, gradual, continuous with its own past, complex and full of contradictions, not a mere colonial import. As such, it is not a 'shallow notion of reformist modernity that arrives as a result of the colonial regime'.[7] Shulman then analyses the intricate interplay of continuities and discontinuities that constitute the complexity of modernity: bureaucracy, cosmopolitanism, naturalism, realism, views of the self, Siddha iconoclasm, Deccanic secularism, and so on.

Satish Deshpande offers us a perceptive and nuanced take on this concept of multiple modernities that is particularly relevant to the topic of this book.

> ... modernization has been an omnibus-concept, a sort of summary description of epochal dimensions based on an underlying dichotomy between tradition and modernity. If there ever was a time when such an abstract, generalized dichotomy was conceptually useful, it is surely gone now.[8]

Deshpande, reminding us that there are now as many similarities as differences, warns us that using the frame of tradition versus modernity and judging a society by the teleological end of modernity, as defined by the West, and seeing any 'in-between-ness' as a failure because of the presupposition of modernity prevents us from understanding what is actually happening. Rather, we need to avoid generalisations and focus instead on the 'historicity of the present'.[9]

The oral histories of Śrīvaiṣṇavas presented here have provided a small window to a historicity of the present. They reveal how people—both non-Brahmins of many castes and Brahmins in Tamil Nadu—are experimenting with ways to achieve a coherence, or at least a secure and meaningful life that acknowledges the dynamic forces shaping their lives, as well as their own intentionality. For most of the people I interviewed, existential realities are not focussed on the mega-questions of identity, addressed by the theorists of multiple modernities—the importance of recognising something distinctive about being modern in India, as opposed to just being imitators of Western modernity, whatever that means. Rather, questions of identity play out in a more limited, albeit dynamic, process related to sect, caste, and political affiliation, or rejection of such identities, as the case may be.

With this backdrop in mind, I turn now to several major themes found in the interviews discussed in this book.

Non-Brahmin Śrīvaiṣṇavism

The interviews reveal many similarities, as well as different practices and understandings that constitute non-Brahmin Śrīvaiṣṇavism today on topics such as ritual, identity, initiation, status, access to religious leadership and religious competition in a saffron age. It is time to bring together the discrete points made in the interviews to see if any patterns can be detected to warrant the label Non-Brahmin Śrīvaiṣṇavism.

Religious Ritual

Bhāgavata religious lives have not been documented in scholarly literature. This study brings some of their traditions to the foreground.

Many of my informants described their daily *pūjā*s before their home shrine, which they did by themselves or with the whole family present. This daily worship included common Hindu acts of offering oil lamps (*āratī*), ringing a bell and presenting flowers, fruits, and cooked food to the deity.

Bhāgavatas also prayed or chanted, albeit in different ways. One person spoke of a simple prayer from the heart, others spoke of chanting short *āḻvār* works, such as Periyāḻvār's *Tiruppallāṇṭu* or a selection of Nammāḻvār's verses called *Kōyiḻ Tiruvāymoḻi*, often with the help of a printed book. For some people, the *Tiruppāvai* was the only scripture that they had memorised and chanted daily. Women were especially attracted to it, because it was a text composed by a young woman and about young women. Those who were initiated and had sufficient time in retirement chanted a daily selection of the *Divyaprabandham* verses, until the 4,000 were completed. So did one carpenter, despite the demands of a job and family. A few Bhāgavatas referred to meditation, breathing exercises, or yogic postures.

There was considerable variation among family members regarding their daily religious activities. Some retired men told me, for instance, that they spend much more time chanting and worshipping than their wives or children. Others said that their wives spent more time on religious rituals. Some parents mentioned that their children had too much schoolwork to chant or worship. And some said that they did more religious activities after initiation because that was required. Such differences seemed to be a function of personal interest or the amount of time they had, or whether they had had *samāśrayaṇam*.

Many Bhāgavatas mentioned communal worship at a *sabhā*. Some of these have histories stretching back to the late nineteenth century. According to Ramesh Bairy, '... non-Brahmin associations emerged in the colonial period as the primary articulator of the idea and the institution of caste and set the protocols of negotiation with the modern ethos and institutions.'[10] The *sabhā*s advanced and legitimised the projects of both elite individuals and communities. Whereas the main role of the *sabhā*s during the colonial period was Sanskritisation, Lloyd and Susanne Rudolph point out that after Independence, it has been political power and modernisation that combine birth (as caste or caste-cluster identity) and choice (as voluntary affiliation and support of the group) to increase a group's well-being and status through political advocacy.[11] Robert Hardgrave[12] puts the role of *sabhā*s like this: they have been the *modus vivendi* for caste adaptation to social, economic, and political change. New leaders from the lower and middle castes emerged from these local organisations. The leaders were the ones who had honed their oratory and leadership skills to become middlemen between the caste and the political establishments that control, at least in part, access to reservations, which facilitate access to education and good jobs. Scholars have discussed *sabhā*s mainly in the contexts of caste and politics, rarely in the context of religion.

I found *sabhā*s in both urban and village settings. They generally had an established meeting place, perhaps a local non-Brahmin temple, especially in the small villages, or a *rāmānuja kūṭam* or another building that had been built or endowed by a Śrīvaiṣṇava.

The focal point of the sacred space was usually a statue or picture of Krishna, Rāma, or Bālāji (Vēṅkaṭeśvara). Because the major Śrīvaiṣṇava temples, especially the *divyadeśa*s, are dominated ritually by Brahmin Āgamic priests, the *sabhā*s provide an alternative space for non-Brahmin Śrīvaiṣṇavas. These alternative spaces are important because some villages and city and suburban neighbourhoods do not have Vaiṣṇava temples. Ritual at the *sabhā*s—whether daily, weekly, or at festival times—is usually simple: the same offerings as in daily home worship. This may be followed by the singing of *bhajana*s, sometimes in street processions, or chanting *āḻvār* verses. The latter, however, did not seem as deeply rooted in the tradition as the *bhajana*s, especially the anonymous folk-style ones. Even though the *Divyaprabandham* verses are in Tamil, some devotees confessed that they found the metres difficult, which made it difficult to memorise and chant them. For this reason, they were taking classes to learn how to chant the *āḻvār* verses in the traditional manner.

The large or urban *sabhā*s have institutional structures with secretaries, treasurers, and so forth, along with leaders called *mudaliyar*s who know Śrīvaiṣṇavism and provide chanting, as well as discourses on topics that range from scriptural interpretation to theology. A leader might give a weekly discourse on Śrīvaiṣṇavism. The larger *sabhā*s also celebrate festivals throughout the year, such as the birthdays of the *āḻvār*s and *ācārya*s, especially those of important figures such as Nammāḻvār, Rāmānuja, or the *sabhā*'s founder. On these important occasions, all 4,000 verses might be chanted, usually by a local expert. Bhāgavatas often complained that chanting experts were not available for rituals. Some resorted to cassettes and videos.

Recitation of Āṇṭāḷ's *Tiruppāvai* was extremely popular, especially by groups in the month of Mārkaḻi (December–January). In some *sabhā*s, especially urban ones that have elaborate traditions, the *sabhā*-style worship might include Tyāgarāja or Maharashtrian *kīrtana*s and *harikathā*s. The deeply emotional music at these *sabhā* gatherings binds people together and creates a sense of community.

Occasionally, Bhāgavatas mentioned rites of passage, such as pregnancy rituals, weddings, and funerals, usually with reference to chanting verses from the *Divyaprabandham*. Recitation of Āṇṭāḷ's *Tiruppāvai* was auspicious at weddings and Nammāḻvār's verses about the postmortem journey of the soul to Vaikuṇṭha for funerals. One distinctive feature of non-Brahmin funerals was the removal of the Vaiṣṇava conch and discus emblems from the shoulders of those who had been branded when initiated.[13]

The Śrīvaiṣṇava ritual seemed fragile in many villages because infrastructure for the religion did not exist or was ad hoc, making it difficult to find priests or chanters or religious educators. People complained that the *yātrā*s of city-folk to bring Śrīvaiṣṇavism to the villages rarely brought lasting change. I did find the villages of Kumalam and Minjur to be vibrant centres of non-Brahmin Śrīvaiṣṇavism because they have a family-run temple or *ashram* with attractive rituals, festivals, *bhajana*s and food (even medicine and astrology, in one case), which draw people from neighbouring villages, if not the entire region. There is much more to learn about non-Brahmin religious practice, but these points gleaned from the interviews open the door to understanding Bhāgavata adaptations and innovations, which often straddle the worlds of personal, village, and urban life in the flux of a quickly changing society.

Identity, Initiation, and Status

Being strictly a devotee of the *one* god Viṣṇu, who has many names and forms, is a key tenet of Brahmanical *sampradāya* Śrīvaiṣṇavism. Nonetheless, I found that some Bhāgavatas in the villages still had strong links with local goddess worship, or occasionally worshipped other gods to promote village harmony. A few Bhāgavatas in the cities also did not hold to an exclusive Śrīvaiṣṇava identity. They told me that the various deities were only expressions of the one supreme god, and so there was no essential difference among Viṣṇu, Śiva, Kālī, and tribal deities or, for that matter, the Muslim or Christian deity. And one person argued in an Advaitin fashion that the 'gods' were simply aids for meditation and were ultimately an illusion. Some said that because Viṣṇu was the pervader, he was the true god within other gods. In other words, the boundaries defining Śrīvaiṣṇava identity were more porous for many non-Brahmins than they were for orthodox Brahmin Śrīvaiṣṇavas, although those Bhāgavatas who had had *samāśrayaṇam* were more concerned with sectarian boundary maintenance.

Nevertheless, many Bhāgavatas wore the Śrīvaiṣṇava emblem, the *nāmam*, on their foreheads, which identified them as Śrīvaiṣṇavas—and, depending on the shape, as belonging to the Teṉkalai or Vaṭakalai sub-sects—even though wearing the *nāmam* was going out of style in cities and modern workplaces. Although most Bhāgavatas freely described their identity as Śrīvaiṣṇava, they were aware of the differences between non-Brahmin religious practices in villages and *sabhā*s, and Brahmin-dominated temples such as the *divyadeśa*s.

Occasionally Bhāgavatas made a distinction between those who had had initiation (*samāśrayaṇam*) and those who had not. Non-Brahmins assumed that they had a choice over whether to be initiated. They knew some *ācārya*s or *jīyar*s who had performed it for non-Brahmins, and at least one Brahmin *jīyar* who had performed it for Dalits.[14] There was one case, however, in which access for a Dalit was blocked. She wanted to continue her family's tradition of *samāśrayaṇam* from a particular *ācārya* family connected to her family, but the *ācārya* in her generation, unlike his father and grandfather, would not initiate her and other members of her family. This is not surprising, given what we discovered about *ācārya*s in the nineteenth century requesting non-Brahmins to do the initiation rituals for Dalits, or what Williams reported several decades ago about some *ācārya*s being unwilling to initiate

Dalits, initiating them only on the veranda or having others handle the ritual implements.

In any case, most of my Bhāgavata informants considered the change in lifestyle required by *samāśrayaṇam* a serious commitment, one that could create complications for their families if some members continued to maintain other customs. Not all were interested in having initiation because this meant that they could no longer eat meat, which was their family tradition, or their own preference. In addition, Bhāgavatas commented that because of their jobs—carpenters, farmers, and lawyers all mentioned this—they did not have time for lengthy morning rituals and chants at home.

Some Bhāgavatas desired *samāśrayaṇam* precisely because it was associated with the status of Brahmanical lifestyle. This can be understood as an example of Sanskritisation. Many older Bhāgavatas, especially those from past elite non-Brahmin castes, whose families had had a tradition of *samāśrayaṇam*, proudly described their parents and grandparents as staunch Śrīvaiṣṇavas because they maintained strict vegetarianism and purity codes. Some had gone further by adopting Brahmanical dress, hairstyles, and even speech.[15] In one case, Sanskritisation had broken down the social barrier between a non-Brahmin's wealthy landlord family and the local Brahmins in the vicinity of Srivilliputur. A descendant of this family, who was my informant, told me why. The districts in this area had experienced little tension between non-Brahmins and Brahmins before Indian Independence because the landed communities such as Naidus and Reddiyars, and not Brahmins, wielded power in the villages. In several cases, non-Brahmins had been so staunch that Brahmins had accepted their purity and allowed them to eat with them.

There were Bhāgavatas who did not associate the lifestyle of those who took *samāśrayaṇam* with upward mobility. They considered it simply an expression of religious piety as good 'Śrīvaiṣṇavas', or the required behaviour mandated by their initiation. Still others, even one Dalit, openly admired the Brahmanical way of life for providing the values, learning, and discipline that would lead to prosperity in this world, and salvation after death.

However, one Vanniyar did not want initiation on principle because that would mean trying to be like a Brahmin by imitating the Śrīvaiṣṇava Brahmin lifestyle. He opined: 'Why would non-Brahmins want to be Brahmins after what Brahmins have done over the centuries to non-Brahmins?' Besides, status by imitating Brahmins was no longer necessary now that there were other ways to attain status, such as good jobs and roles in public life.

Access to Religious Leadership

Despite the Śrīvaiṣṇava theological message of inclusiveness, the key religious roles of *ācārya*s, *jīyar*s and priests remained Brahmin over the centuries. I was surprised to discover that this had been challenged at the turn of the twentieth century by non-Brahmin leaders, such as Rāmānuja Nāvalar, Bhuvanagiri, and Ekāṅgi Svāmikaḷ, who argued on the basis of their religion's professed inclusiveness that non-Brahmins could give *samāśrayaṇam*, which meant that they could be *ācārya*s and *jīyar*s.

These defiant acts made me curious about whether Bhāgavata Śrīvaiṣṇavas today hold the same views. I found that few Bhāgavatas, except for some in Puducherry and its environs, knew about this chapter of late-colonial, non-Brahmin history, despite their interest in equality and their knowledge of, or participation in, the non-Brahmin political movement. I was struck also by how many still supported the idea that only Brahmins should perform *samāśrayaṇam*.

One reason for accepting *samāśrayaṇam* only by a bona fide *ācārya* or *jīyar* was because *samāśrayaṇam* was popularly considered the key to salvation; it linked the devotee to the 'salvific' figure Rāmānuja (who had performed *prapatti* for everyone) through the *ācārya* as intermediary. Another reason was because their families had been connected to specific Brahmin *ācārya*s and *jīyar*s over several generations, and so these non-Brahmins had a stable and intimate link with them. Not everyone I interviewed agreed with this point of view. Some were critical of *ācārya*s and *jīyar*s because their lifestyles did not instantiate orthodox Brahmanical householder or ascetic norms of dress and behaviour, adequate knowledge of the Vedas, or financial accountability.

As described in Chapter 6, when Raymond Williams interviewed Śrīvaiṣṇavas several decades ago, he found that for some Brahmins and non-Brahmins, a compromise was emerging in connection with Bhāgavatas becoming *ācārya*s. As the tradition had already recognised two types of *ācārya*—those who gave *samāśrayaṇam* and those who taught and interpreted the *sampradāya* texts—some people thought that Brahmin *ācārya* families should continue to do the former, while non-Brahmins could do the latter.

Many Bhāgavatas since the mid-nineteenth century had been teaching the Tamil scripture and Śrīvaiṣṇava *sampradāya* works to other Bhāgavatas. This was becoming more common in the twentieth century, in fact, as non-Brahmins (as well as Brahmins) were rewriting Sanskrit and Maṇipravāḷa works in Tamil, along with exegetical aids. Bhāgavata religious leadership was based in part on the ability to give lectures on the works of the *āḻvār*s and *ācārya*s. Several Bhāgavatas, moreover, had done masters or doctoral degrees with dissertations in Tamil on Śrīvaiṣṇava topics. Others, with status as traditional scholars, were publishing their works or continuing the vibrant tradition of oral discourses.

The genie was out of the bottle, in other words. The status that non-Brahmin leaders gained through public discourses about Śrīvaiṣṇavism belonged to a more general context: new notions of the public square since colonial times, which made it accessible to non-Brahmin orators. The creation of non-Brahmin *sabhā*s too provided opportunities for Bhāgavatas to emerge as public figures, who comment on religion, caste, and politics. Unlike the *pulavar* orators of colonial times, with their patrons from closely knit networks, the prevailing pattern of Bhāgavata religious leadership today has been on a non-remunerative, voluntary basis, understood as service (*kaiṅkarya*) to the community, although indirectly it also provides status.

Nevertheless, it is interesting that most of those Bhāgavatas who gave lectures to their communities on religious topics did not describe themselves as *ācārya*s, even in the sense of *grantha ācārya*s or those who teach religious texts. Perhaps that was because they took non-Brahmin teachers for granted, at least within non-Brahmin circles. The one exception was Sudarshana Acarya, who had been given this title by a radical *jīyar* intent on destroying caste privilege and discrimination.

Despite such gains, non-Brahmin religious leaders knew that most Brahmins did not take their knowledge seriously, especially at prestigious universities. For this reason, they perceived the 2007 *Symposium on Sri Vaishnavism Tomorrow* at the Oriental Research Institute (University of Madras) in Chennai, which had non-Brahmin scholars and leaders at the podium, as a very significant event.

As for Bhāgavatas being trained in the *Āgama*s and serving as priests in major Śrīvaiṣṇava temples, I found my non-Brahmin informants to be generally supportive of, even excited by, this opportunity. Unfortunately, I did not have an opportunity to interview them again on this matter after the Supreme Court delivered its judgment in December 2015, which allowed 'denominations' to preserve their traditions in appointing priests, in effect making it impossible for non-Brahmins to become priests in temples with Āgamic rituals.

In this sense, Bhāgavatas were between a rock (lack of priests, whether Brahmin or non-Brahmin, for rituals in their homes and non-Brahmin temples) and a hard place (desire for more lucrative priestly roles and elaborate and 'prestigious' rituals). This raises the question: If non-Brahmins see that even Brahmin priests can no longer rely on patronage, or be employed in temples with good salaries, why would they bother to become priests? Of course, for poor villagers, any temple salary might be attractive. They might also hope (like poor Brahmin priests) to become priests in major temples with good salaries (comparatively speaking) and connections to wealthy people who hire priests for weddings and other home rituals.

As for Śrīvaiṣṇava Brahmins, they continued to support the tradition of Brahmin priests in major temples such as the *divyadeśa*s. After feeling besieged by the non-Brahmin movement for over a century and experiencing major changes in status and values, they clung to their temple traditions as an important marker of Brahmin identity and history. They were also fearful of government intrusion into the temple world, ostensibly in the name of reform and proper administration, but really, they feared, to obtain temple wealth and use it for government purposes. Because of such fears, the Central government tried to circumvent them by introducing a modern way to unlock temple wealth, so that it could be used for society's benefit. In 2015, Prime Minister Narendra Modi introduced a scheme with incentives to monetise an estimated 22,000 tons of gold, worth about one trillion USD, which is lying idle in households and religious establishments. The government recognised that the decision-making power would remain with each temple or individual, but hoped that when the gold and silver were melted down, the parties could earn interest on their holdings. Temples, for instance, could use the income for humanitarian services such as hospitals. Modi's proposal had a 'lukewarm' response.[16]

Religious Competition in a Saffron Age

Despite occasional tensions, most non-Brahmin and Brahmin Śrīvaiṣṇavas share the view that Śrīvaiṣṇavism needs to be protected from the more popular Śaivism, just as Hinduism needs to be protected against proselytism by other religions. From what I could see, there has been little attempt in Tamil Nadu to bring the major sects together. In Karnataka, some Brahmins tried to consolidate a general Brahmin identity through the concept of the equality of the great sectarian traditions, represented by Śaṅkara, Mādhva, and Rāmānuja (in order to create a united front against the state-aided non-Brahmin attack).[17] I did not see sectarian collaboration in Tamil Nadu, aside from occasional, locally organised joint *Tiruppāvai* and *Tiruvempāvai* recitations that cross Śrīvaiṣṇava, Śaiva, and Smārta boundaries. If anything, the government-organised non-sectarian Pongal festival, which celebrates the season's first rice, has become the important quasi-religious way to create pan-Tamil unity.

Some *ācārya*s had told Williams that there had been a revival in Hinduism in the 1950s. In part, this was a response to the decline of the non-Brahmin movement, both its atheism and its criticism of Brahmin leaders. A new Brahmin willingness to bridge the gap between Brahmins and non-Brahmins was symbolised by the Śaṅkarācārya. Reports Williams,

> The Śaṅkarācārya started touring all over South India by foot (before he was carried by a non-Brahmin). He had probably noticed the non-Brahmin political slogan 'why should we carry Brahmins?'. When he was in his late seventies, the Śaṅkarācārya still walked about by holding onto a cycle rickshaw for support. He had a major impact on both Brahmins and non-Brahmins.[18]

However, my informants were less optimistic about a Hindu revival today. One of them put it this way:

> In my village, there is Muslim and Christian influence. There are many Christian conversions. One Harijan, whose son had become a Christian, approached me, asking me to stop this. Christians get funds from the West. Muslims get money from some Arab countries that are oil rich. Muslims are not proselytising like Christians; there are fewer conversions to Islam. Therefore, Christianity is the real problem here.
>
> When there is intermarriage, Christians pressure Hindus to convert. Forty or fifty years ago, for instance, a Brahmin boy, whose father was a schoolteacher in Sriperumbudur, wanted to marry a Christian. The boy was taken to the village where the girl was living, converted, and then the wedding took place. Boys or girls

> from poor families want to marry Christians so that their economic status improves. Nowadays, boys who want to go to the Gulf for work often convert to Islam in order to get a job there.

The Śrīvaiṣṇavas in Ekangipuram, the former outcaste hamlet (discussed in Chapter 3), worried about conversions to Christianity and Islam. In fact, this worry was expressed to me many times by various castes, in many places. 'Both Brahmins and non-Brahmins as Hindus and Śrīvaiṣṇavas are concerned about this,' one person confided.

> We need to awaken the masses to their own religious tradition and help them understand the religion through the Tamil hymns of the *āḻvār*s. Then they become attracted to Hinduism. The Śaivas, too, are attracting people back to Hinduism through the hymns of the *nāyaṉmār*s (the medieval Śaiva poet-saints). Today, many Hindu organisations are addressing the problem of conversion to other religions. They come with evidence and statistics of conversion. They give lectures and publish articles about this problem.

Occasionally, views on conversion became more political. I was told that today,

> only Hindus are not allowed to talk about the problem of conversion because of the need to protect minorities. The BJP is called communal, but not the Muslim league or Christian associations. When the BJP [Bharatiya Janata Party] and RSS [Rashtriya Swayamsevak Sangh] wanted to raise this problem in public, other parties such as Congress branded them as 'communal'. In 1948, when an RSS person killed Mahatma Gandhi, the party was banned by Nehru and others in the government. For twenty years, any connection with the RSS was considered taboo. In recent decades, the RSS has presented its views through the BJP.
>
> Hindus have been compelled, for instance, to take birth control, but not Muslims and Christians. It is not right to give political importance to the minorities, for example, giving reservations for Muslims. Two states—Uttar

> Pradesh and Bihar—will have Muslim majorities in the next twenty years.

After these strong words (a common litany of woes), this individual added: 'There is no connection of non-Brahmin Śrīvaiṣṇava organisations and the BJP and the RSS. The Bhāgavata *sabhā*s are completely religious.' The implication was that the BJP and the RSS are merely political, although both are famous for their strong Hindu sympathies, referred to by critics as 'Hindutva' or 'Saffronisation' (a synecdoche, in which the colour of ascetics' robes signifies Hinduism itself). Still, no one had explicitly mentioned to me connections with a pan-Indian party or organisation on the right of the political spectrum. When political identities were discussed, they were with the regional DMK and AIADMK parties and the Congress. Even though I found it hard to detect BJP or RSS affiliations, I do not rule these out because it is well-known that these national Hindu parties have tried to create alliances with parties in Tamil Nadu, and the Tamil parties have connections with *sabhā*s in many communities. Perhaps a study focussed on the politics internal to temples would have revealed more influence, but that was beyond the scope of my research.

In any case, one could argue that Hindu proselytism to counter that of other religions—Christianity, say, or Islam—might help to create Hindu unity, and this in turn might contribute to Saffronisation. In short, there seems to be a kind of threat hierarchy for many Bhāgavatas: first Christianity, then Śaivism, and then Islam. This helps to explain why non-Brahmin leaders have been trying to stem the proselytism of other religions by giving discourses and leading processions in villages, creating new village *sabhā*s that are connected to larger *sabhā* networks, and publishing books to teach Bhāgavatas about their religion.

It is no wonder that Hindutva organisations and political parties see processions (and the larger-scale *yātrā*s) as key to defining political space, proselytising their message, and binding Hindus into a sense of national community. As we have seen in this study of Śrīvaiṣṇavism in Tamil Nadu, they have a ready-made platform for politicising religion at the local level that only needs to be tapped and slightly re-oriented. It remains to be seen if south Indian Hindu sects, which have a sense of vulnerability, will provide fertile ground for sacralising the nation-space as, in Deshpande's terms, 'the Nehruvian nation-space shaped by an economic geography for the elites declines'.[19]

Religion and Caste

Since colonial times, non-Brahmin caste networks have helped to move castes into new industrial, trade, and business jobs that provide economic security as well as social mobility by connecting ancestral villages in rural areas to urban ones.[20] My informants in the cities moved freely between outskirt villages, some now suburbs, and cities such as Chennai, Puducherry, Tanjavur, and Tiruchirappalli. They were highly mobile and connected to other places through intersecting networks of religious, social, and political kinds. Young people in the villages were often working in nearby towns and cities, which created another fluidity, thanks to modern transportation and communication. The division of city and village is no longer sharply demarcated, but caste networks are still important.

Arranged marriage within a caste or sub-caste cluster remains key to maintaining these functional networks. It is striking that there have been very few inter-caste marriages in India as a whole (about 11 per cent), and Tamil Nadu has second to the lowest rate at about 3 per cent,[21] despite government monetary incentive programmes to eliminate caste conflict through inter-marriage.[22]

The continued importance of caste identity and networks helps explain why Śrīvaiṣṇava identity continues to have such a strong caste orientation. Religious identity in turn helps the maintenance of caste identity. Religious rituals, for instance, create identification with the caste from childhood and generate horizontal social bonding. Caste identity is framed, moreover, by a larger religious orientation that gives meaning and purpose to life, culminating in salvation, and this intimately links caste and destiny.

The fact that members of a caste or sub-caste network gather from across the region for special 'conferences' or 'functions', and that these are framed by religious rituals and chanting, also helps to maintain the loyalty of individuals to their caste. And the fact that major Śrīvaiṣṇava temples have caste-based *maṭha*s that serve their members with lodging or food, especially at festival times, further bolsters network caste solidarity, as does the fact that marriages are arranged at such times of communal gathering.

In addition, the Śrīvaiṣṇava concept of service to others, or *kaiṅkarya*, enhances mutual support by making it key to religious identity, and by fostering a religious ethos of humility, trust, and charity that is essential for ideas of community. The *rāmānuja kūṭams* have been an especially important institution in this regard. The tradition of feeding devotees, for instance, helps those affected by poverty. Because members of the caste are honoured for their service to the community, definition of this status within the group serves to bond people horizontally, yet still satisfy the desire for recognition, if not status. And when *sabhā*s honour those who serve the community, pride in religious and caste identity grows.

The traditional Śrīvaiṣṇava concept of service has expanded in the modern period to include secular notions of social service. Remember Sudarshana in Chapter 3 who offered devotees traditional medicine when they visited his ashram. The key example of social service in a Śrīvaiṣṇava context is the concept of *kaiṅkarya* as social service in the many enterprises of Tirupati, the wealthiest Indian temple and a pan-Indian pilgrimage centre heavily influenced by Śrīvaiṣṇavas. It sponsors hospitals, orphanages, universities, and so forth. Chinna Jeeyar Swami's creation of schools for tribals and homes for the elderly, orphans, handicapped, and destitute reflects this modern social service orientation as does, on a smaller scale, the Srimaan Trust, run by Parasara

Badri Narayana Bhattar at Srirangam, which provides food, medicine, clothes, and so forth for the needy.

Do we find differences in how Tamil Brahmins and non-Brahmins adapt to modernities? When I compared Fuller and Narasimhan's analysis of Tamil Brahmins with my analysis of Tamil non-Brahmin Śrīvaiṣṇavas, I found both similarities and differences.

I found similarities between Brahmins and non-Brahmins from elite backgrounds within their castes. Many of my informants belonged to families that had privileged positions within their castes several generations ago—Naidu landlords, Vaiśya businessmen, Dubash traders or military men, and lawyers during the Raj. Even for those from lower economic echelons, there were early twentieth-century union leaders, small landowners, and workers in key industries such as the southern railroad. These jobs gave them economic security and status that facilitated their family's upward mobility in post-Independence India. Like the Tamil Brahmins, many had changed from village agrarian life to urban life in Chennai, Puducherry, Tanjavur, and Tiruchirappalli, which demanded of them adaptation to aspects of modernity. Just as caste has remained endogamous for many Tamil Brahmins, so it has for Tamil non-Brahmins, mergers of sub-castes notwithstanding.

There are differences as well. Let me try to list them.

First, non-Brahmins had a slower start into new modern identities, given the much lower rates of education and government jobs in the colonial period. For them, the major impetus for change, both mindset and opportunity, came from the non-Brahmin movement and subsequent Dravidian parties. And it was focussed, by and large, on education in Tamil rather than English, even though many of my interviewees were conversant in English. Still, most of my non-Brahmin informants were optimistic about their own futures. After all, they were lawyers, doctors, professors, academic researchers, government bureaucrats, businessmen, and radio hosts, the elite of their own caste groups. Society had certainly changed for them. Behind these 'success' stories, one encounters modern print culture and education in Tamil, which has led to many opportunities for further education and good jobs. The two exceptions were the two young Nadar men who told me that because of corruption, they would never obtain jobs as university professors, because of the need to pay large amounts of money to secure such a position (see Appendix 6).

Second, my informants did not represent their castes or caste clusters in the same way as the Tamil Brahmins. The people I interviewed are the elite among their own caste groups, after all, and not the norm. This is not to downplay the significance of their accomplishments for their communities. They have been important models for upward mobility, and many have worked hard to help other members of their group succeed in these new circumstances. Even though they are the elite of their castes, most belong to the middle or lower-middle class in economic terms, not the upper-middle class, which was the group that Fuller and Narasimhan studied.

Third, there were differences in cultural identities. Fuller and Narasimhan found that defining cultural identity through appreciation of Brahminised forms of music and dance had become important for Tamil Brahmins. By contrast, I found that one non-Brahmin caste, the Icai Velalas, had always had music at the core of its self-definition; for others, it was more a traditional family identity, as with some professional Naidu musicians, than a caste identity per se.

In any case, being music connoisseurs was not a *new* caste identity for non-Brahmin castes. Perhaps this was because many people did not live in the city core, because they were not upper-middle class, or because they perceived Brahmin domination of these arts today on the concert stage. It could be, too, that their energies were focussed on identity through their religious caste or caste cluster organisations. Of course, it could also be that my questions were mainly about religious, caste, and political identities, not ones focussed on the arts.

Be that as it may, I found that sometimes caste identity emerged in the foreground, sometimes non-Brahmin identity, sometimes Śrīvaiṣṇava identity, and sometimes Hindu identity. Castes have exhibited enormous tenacity as well as adaptations to modernity.[23] Social scientists focus on the latter. Christophe Jaffrelot, for instance, summarises[24] the interaction of religion, caste, and politics and attributes the crux of the transformation to colonial policies, especially the census, which instigated castes to organise themselves in caste associations for leverage to improve their rank and access to reservations, the associations in turn becoming mutual-aid societies with schools, hostels, and cooperative movements. An important change was the unification of sub-caste groups by using one name in the census. This unification broke the barriers of endogamy among these groups, created 'non-hierarchical social imaginaires', and provided an egalitarian alternative identity, which was cultural, historical, collective, and capable of questioning social hierarchies.

According to Kaivan Munshi, the 'aggregate evidence indicates that there has been some convergence in education, occupations, income and access to public resources across caste groups in the decades after independence'.[25] He thinks that this has resulted from both affirmative action and caste-based networks that seek out opportunities. He admits, however, that 'it will be many generations before income and consumption are equalized across caste groups'.[26] Based on comparative data from other developing countries, Munshi concludes that traditional economic networks (in this context, caste-based ones) will disappear when a modern market economy is in place. In other words, he abides by a modernisation thesis, albeit a very slow one.

It is impossible to predict the future. In my view, despite major changes, caste still is tenacious. It will probably continue to exist as long as it serves a valuable function.

Women's Changing Roles

Like many non-Brahmin men, non-Brahmin women were also Periyar's followers; they proudly declared 'themselves atheists and insisted on secular burial rituals for themselves'.[27] It is important to see how the lives of non-Brahmin Śrīvaiṣṇava women have changed since Periyar's time.

As I stipulated in Chapter 1, my research did not extend into women's domestic world and the dynamics and ambiguities of their devotional activities with reference to male authority and caste status.

However, I did encounter non-Brahmin Śrīvaiṣṇava women who were housewives, caring for young children or their extended families, and although I met women still conforming to conservative norms for women, I was struck by how many non-Brahmin women from many castes I met during my interviews were working women. For instance, one had a B.Com. degree and was working as a medical transcriptionist; another, the daughter of a female teacher, was a purchase officer for the Corporation of Madras; another was the director of a major Chennai company; and one was an academic researcher, contributing her expertise in languages and Śrīvaiṣṇavism to international projects. I was told about wives who were medical doctors, a sister who was a nurse, and daughters planning to be physicians or engineers. Some women were extending their education through post-graduate diplomas and correspondence courses. However, former *devadāsis* and their daughters were struggling with downward mobility, if not debilitating poverty, because of the Madras Devadasis (Prevention of Dedication) Act of 1947, which had made their traditional profession illegal.

These were changing times for Śrīvaiṣṇava women. On several occasions, I lectured at M. O. P. Vaishnav College for Women in Chennai. Although people told me that for many young women, college education functioned more as a marriage credential than a stepping stone to further education and a career, the young women I spoke to were intellectually curious and seemed to take their education seriously. Who knows what would happen after marriage? Would they be like the Brahmin women in *ācārya* families, who gave up further education or careers to abide by traditional norms of *strīdharma*, which were still a mark of status in some circles? Or would they be teachers, lawyers, engineers, and doctors? I would bet on the latter.

In this context, we should remember that in many non-Brahmin castes, women have always worked outside the home, and that the system of south Indian cross-cousin marriage maintained important kinship ties for women close at hand, which gave them emotional support after marriage. Munshi has found that lower-caste girls, whose mothers have labour jobs outside the home, are more likely to pursue educational and job opportunities. He thinks, however, that their opportunities increase if they are freed from the constraints of arranged marriage to maintain the caste's network. With inter-marriage, their income level increases, as does the education of their children.[28]

I also encountered some *ācārya*s who were conflicted about women's roles. *Acārya*s wanted educated brides, even though many also wanted them to stay at home after marriage. Others feared the rising divorce rate that would create problems for the arranged marriage system. These views, I suspect, kept some Teṉkalai Brahmin women from staking out new identities and moving into the more lucrative jobs that would give them upper-middle class standing, although some certainly did.

I was struck by the fact that most of the Bhāgavata men who argued so strongly for non-Brahmin priests as an issue of justice did not raise the question of whether women should also be priests. Despite the fact that the Tamil Nadu government ordinance of 2006 uses the gender-neutral language of 'person', it was only young men who attended the Chennai school for training priests (because male priests had always been the tradition in Vaiṣṇava temples).

Regardless, the Supreme Court's ruling that the priesthood should be based on precedent, which for Śrīvaiṣṇava priests is the Pañcarātra Āgama (with its custom of a male priesthood), has reinforced the priesthood as a male enclave in Śrīvaiṣṇavism. The argument of precedent has allowed the Court to circumvent engaging with common arguments about why women should not be priests, such as women's impurity when menstruating, or the impropriety of a woman receiving gifts from a man who is not her husband (priests sometimes receive such gifts), or the seemingly 'adulterous' act of performing rituals symbolising the bonding between the client and the priest, which in this case would be between a woman and an unrelated man, and scandalous in orthodox eyes.

I suspect that women priests, at least in the near future, will continue to be found mainly at some goddess shrines that have an established tradition of female priests, such as Melmaruvatur, about 80 kilometres from Chennai, where female priests perform *pūjā* to the goddess Ādi Paraśakti and female devotees, dressed in red to symbolise the blood that flows through everyone, visit the temple even when menstruating.

That said, the role of non-Brahmin Śrīvaiṣṇava women as religious teachers and chanters has been gaining momentum. Non-Brahmin women are teaching other women and children verses from the *Divyaprabandham*, or leading the chanting in *sabhā*s. In addition, they are giving public discourses on religious topics. Likewise, *sabhā*s are inspiring non-Brahmin women to take up leadership roles and become active in the women's wing of some of the large Śrīvaiṣṇava *sabhā* organisations. *Sabhā*s are important, moreover, for women's family interests and networks. District and pan-Tamil Nadu conferences are times, for example, when women facilitate the process of arranging marriages. Śrīvaiṣṇava women's religious expertise and oratory skills reach even beyond the *sabhā* context. I attended a public lecture by a Sattada woman, a medical doctor by profession, who had attracted a large crowd to hear her discourses on one of the Hindu epics.

Besides the fact that these are changing times with women on the ascendant, some non-Brahmin men recognise that support of women is important if caste networks, the locus of male economic and political power, are to be maintained. But they also keep decision-making power largely in their control, unless it pertains to the interests of just women.

Religion, Democracy, and Hindutva

Religion and politics in Tamil Nadu have been intertwined in various ways. This is particularly true for the elderly Bhāgavatas whom I interviewed, who had lived through the turbulent politics in the late-colonial period and had been influenced by Gandhi and Periyar.

One Bhāgavata thought that his understanding of Śrīvaiṣṇavism and his Gandhian/Congress affiliations came together in terms of equality. He had been a member of a group that promoted chanting of the *Divyaprabandham* by both Brahmins and non-Brahmins. He had also chosen to be initiated by a Brahmin who radically supported all non-Brahmins, including Dalits. Nevertheless, he implied that most Brahmins would have to mend their ways and develop real affection for non-Brahmins. Another Bhāgavata—who had been influenced by his father, a disciple of Bhuvanagiri, who worked for equality in the late nineteenth and early twentieth century—had supported the DK for a while. When he detected hypocrisy and grew disillusioned, however, he returned to Śrīvaiṣṇavism and worked to ensure that its message of equality was put into practice. Still another person had been a communist and union leader. He returned to religion when he detected double standards.

Someone else found an affinity between his Śrīvaiṣṇava views of equality and Periyar's sense of equality. His subsequent participation in the DMK, which he thought did not live up to its own ideal of equality, led to cynicism and rejection of both its atheism and political orientation. This person found in the *āḻvār*s the ideal of a casteless and classless society. Since it had not changed society sufficiently, he saw the need for reform today, even though he did not think there was much hope for it. Either Brahmins would have to change, he suggested, or schools would have to teach non-Brahmins both Sanskrit and Tamil religious literature.

Many Bhāgavatas themselves pointed to a detection of DMK hypocrisy as the reason for their return to religion after the heyday of Periyar's movement. Of course, it is also possible that the waning of Periyar's fierce atheism had paved the way for a return to religion, as had the turbulence of modern life. Those who returned to Śrīvaiṣṇavism after participating in the non-Brahmin movement belonged, moreover, to non-Brahmin families with a strong Śrīvaiṣṇava family history, and probably had never lost their deep religious orientation. Furthermore, it is possible that as these Bhāgavatas aged, they thought about religion more often.

Rajadurai and Geeta, in a 2017 interview for *Forward Press*, explain the massive return to religion as follows. Although Periyar 'interrupted, powerfully and with intellectual and social verve, a longer history of religiosity, that does not mean that this history was stood on its head. Its logic persists to this day.'[29] It was State power, whether that of Napoleonic France or the Soviet Union, they point out, that dislodged religion, 'not rational persuasion or consistent civil opposition'.

At any rate, one thing is very clear. All of my Bhāgavata informants thought that the twelfth-century Śrīvaiṣṇava savant Rāmānuja was the egalitarian par excellence. One person after another told me stories about Rāmānuja's affection for non-Brahmins and his activist stance against the caste system. He had introduced the distribution of food supplies to anyone who came to the temple, for instance, without any restriction. He had approached a non-Brahmin, Tirukaccinampi, to be his teacher. Rāmānuja had become an ascetic, moreover, after his wife's failure to treat a non-Brahmin properly. And he made the recitation of the sacred syllable *om* available to everyone.

Many of these stories come not from what we know textually about Rāmānuja as the erudite author of the commentaries on the *Brahmasūtra* or *Gītā*; rather, they come from hagiographies written centuries later about his life. Nevertheless, this view of Rāmānuja's critique of the caste system underscores the idea that God is gracious, salvation *in this life* is available to everyone, and religion is based in a community of devotees who respect and serve all members. The hagiographic images of Rāmānuja have been religious touchstones, as it were, of the non-Brahmin political impulse for equality that has swept Tamil Nadu since the late nineteenth century and provided a foundation for equality within democracy after Indian Independence.

Another thing is very clear. The fact that the *āḻvār*s came from many castes is central to non-Brahmins' identification with Śrīvaiṣṇavism. Stories about the *āḻvār*s were more popular, in fact, than the *āḻvār* verses collected as the *Divyaprabandham*, judging from how often people told these stories to me with great delight. That said, the *Divyaprabandham* as *Tamil* scripture—the Tamil Veda—is core to Bhāgavata identity as well. And the caste-inclusive rhetoric found in many Śrīvaiṣṇava works remains significant in Bhāgavatas' view of 'real' religion, inspiring them to read anachronistically the idea of a casteless society into Śrīvaiṣṇava *sampradāya* views on inclusiveness and equality; but this seems to be a romanticised ideal that has little to do with removing caste identities. Despite the religious impulse for equality and identification with new political movements for equality, caste identities have remained. Desire for equality did not inspire inter-caste marriages in the past, nor, it seems, even in the present. I did encounter a description of one such marriage in my interviews—a man who had married a woman from another caste during the time when both were members of the DMK. Moreover, for many Śrīvaiṣṇavas, caste and caste networks have continued to have functional importance, from welfare nets to political clout.

Non-Brahmins today think that the problem of discrimination lies with certain Brahmins, not with the inclusive theology of the early *ācārya*s. Some Brahmins, they said, no longer follow the rules of orthodoxy and therefore are 'not real Brahmins', or some Brahmins have abused their power over the centuries, which is why there is a non-Brahmin movement today. Because this view of Rāmānuja as reformer is at the heart of Bhāgavata religiosity, many of my informants viewed Brahmin support for caste hierarchy in all its manifestations over the centuries as a sign of moral decline.

Turning to the big picture of the relation of religion to democracy, I find Lucia Michelutti makes an important point: since the Constitution has linked 'rights to collectivities rather than to individuals, the Constitution made categories like caste, tribe, religion, and ethnicity open to endless political manipulation'.[30] She notes that, paradoxically, political use of the categories caste and religion 'is deepening democracy among all sectors of society, and in particular among the marginalized'.[31] Religion, Michelutti argues, is not an epiphenomenon of this process, or something to be ignored as mere tradition standing in the way of democracy and modernity, but rather provides values and practices that energise popular politics and caste populism.

My findings agree in part with Michelutti's view that the values and practices of democracy become embedded in particular cultural and social practices, and in the process become entrenched in the consciousness of ordinary people. A problem exists, however, with her theory of the vernacularisation of democracy. It implies that it owes its origin just to the West, and ignores the deep roots of Indian concepts of equality and service that contribute to modern ideas. As such, the idea of vernacularisation is too top-down to adequately characterise the dynamic interaction of religion and politics. This calls for a history on the ground and, to use Deshpande's phrase once again, a history of the present to reveal just how Indian democracy has a distinctive character, whether one is focussed on India in general, or on Tamil Nadu in particular.

Religion, Caste and Vote-bank Politics

Vote banks are organised by caste. In Indian democracy, a numerically dominant caste, which will be spread over a wide area in a political constituency, will have an electoral advantage if members are organised through existing networks, *sabhās*, and especially middle-men who link the caste to a party in order to deliver votes. When the candidate wins, s/he will reciprocate by fulfilling promises. Reciprocity between a dominant caste and a political party must be based on trust and cooperation, moreover, so that their power alliance can move beyond a particular election.

In Tamil Nadu, the three politically dominant castes are the Tevars (about 26 per cent of the population), Vanniyars (about 18 per cent), and Gounders (about 14 per cent). These gained power in the rural areas after land reforms in the 1950s, when land was transferred from absentee Brahmin landlords to lower-caste independent cultivators. They became better-off than 'lower castes in the upper caste dominated village',[32] because after the reforms they had better land and they gradually obtained better education. With the growth of Other Backward Classes (OBC) power after implementation in 1990 of the Mandal Commission Report, which expanded reservations to this cluster of middle castes, they gained further access to education, jobs, services, and other resources. In this context, it is important to remember that many Vanniyars are Śrīvaiṣṇava.

The only other group with a large population is the Dalits, who constitute 21 per cent of the population (and 25.55 per cent of households in rural Tamil Nadu),[33] which means that if they become politically organised, Dalits can challenge the other numerically powerful castes, unless they align. Perhaps this is why Tamil Nadu stands third in the nation for crimes against Dalits, and the conviction rates for crimes against Dalits is the lowest in the country at 12.5 per cent (compared to 46.5 per cent in Rajasthan and 54.1 per cent in Uttar Pradesh).[34] In this context, one remembers headlines such as 'Dalit Student Hacked to Death for Intercaste Marriage in Tamil Nadu'.[35]

The subject of 'vote-bank' politics was occasionally mentioned in my interviews by those who criticised the dominant castes for such practices and the power that accrued. It was never mentioned by the Vanniyars, who formed the second largest caste in Tamil Nadu. Whenever I asked about political connections with a *sabhā*, in fact, I was assured that it had nothing to do with politics. Does this mean that members of the dominant caste preferred not to expose this link to an outsider, a link which we know is strong from other sources?

Continuity and Change, Tamil-style

Several events between 2015 and 2018 dramatically illustrate how Śrīvaiṣṇavism, caste, and politics have remained intertwined. In 2013, Sruthisagar Yamunan, president of the DMK, interviewed M. Karunanidhi,[36] then at the ripe age of ninety-one. Yamunan asked him why he—the very custodian of Periyar's legacy, an avowed atheist and anti-Brahmin—was planning to script a television series on 'Saint Ramanuja' for the Tamil channel Kalaignar.[37] Karunanidhi replied:

> I know that Ramanuja is one among the great men who engineered revolutions in religion. When a request was made that I narrate those incidents, which sowed the seeds of change, to the people to nourish their thinking, I came forward and took it up. But because I am writing about a part of his life, it does not mean I have accepted his theistic idea or given up my atheistic, self-respect ideology.[38]

When Yamunan pressed him further by asking why leaders like him held a high opinion about Rāmānuja, a Brahmin, Karunanidhi suggested that it was because Rāmānuja treated all faiths and the oppressed classes equally, 'with respect and without discrimination'. (He did not add that Periyar had belonged to an elite Śrīvaiṣṇava non-Brahmin family, but had, from childhood, turned against his family's religious background.) As for the fact that Rāmānuja was a Brahmin, Karunanidhi implied that it was Rāmānuja's reforms that were important, not his caste. Besides, other Brahmins such as Rajaji (C. Rajapogalachari) 'have mingled with our thoughts'.

Yamunan next asked whether the television series would destroy the popular view that the DMK criticises Hinduism, to which Karunanidhi replied that '90 percent of those in the DMK belong to the religion you mentioned. However, we are against fundamentalist activities of a few who claim to be the protectors of Hinduism'.[39] Pushed again by the interviewer about whether Rāmānuja's followers have implemented his reforms, Karunanidhi noted that Rāmānuja's reforms did not lead to major changes but, given his times (the twelfth century), his reforms 'did create awareness to an extent'. When Yamunan queried, 'Why did the DMK not recognize Rāmānuja or his reforms when it was in power?' Karunanidhi replied:

> It is true we did not recognize him individually when we were in power. But we did function in a manner that recognized his social reforms. For example, the Government Order allowing persons of all communities to become priests; release of several books such as Tamil Aagama Noolgal, Tamilil Vazhipadu, Tamilil Velvi, Tamil Potri; coaching centres for training in Divya Prabandham (Vaishnavite bhakthi poems) in areas where Dalits, Tribals and Backward Class people lived etc. There is a long list of such achievements under the DMK's rule.[40]

In October of that year, the media was offering further evidence of a shift from DMK's radical atheism to religious tolerance.[41] M. K. Stalin, Karunanidhi's son and president of the DMK, had visited the Śrīvaiṣṇava *divyadeśa* Tirukkottiyur just before the 2016 Assembly Elections. (According to some hagiographies, Tirukkottiyur is where Rāmānuja had travelled seventeen times to learn the sacred mantra *oṁ namo nārāyaṇāya* from a sage, but was continually rejected by the sage until Rāmānuja had eliminated his egoism. On the eighteenth visit, he received the mantra. Although the sage instructed him to keep it secret, Rāmānuja climbed to the top of the temple tower and shouted it out for all villagers to hear, rationalising his action by saying that it would help them attain salvation.)

When asked about his visit to the temple, Stalin said that it was not to personally pray, but rather to visit the place where the series on Rāmānuja was being broadcast. Later, Stalin echoed on his blog Karunanidhi's recent comment that 90 per cent of DMK members were Hindus and that the DMK government had spent money on temples in Tamil Nadu. The matter of the DMK's new tolerance of Hinduism was being debated on blogs. One person speculated that by appearing supportive of Hinduism, a door would be open for a DMK–BJP alliance. Another suggested that it was necessary for the party's popularity because its competitor, the AIADMK, accepted religion and temples and had the support of the dominant castes (eight Tevars and eight Gounders were in the AIADMK cabinet at the time). Because the DMK had been viewed as anti-Tevar, it came as no surprise that Stalin had begun to promote Tevars in his party. Here, too, we find continuity—religion remaining important, say—but also change, represented by the DMK's repositioning itself on the sensitive issue of religion when out of power.

Just as DMK leaders who had long championed atheism and anti-Brahminism in the Periyar tradition were softening their rhetoric against religion, tensions involving religion, caste, and politics were escalating. These began when Jayalalithaa died on 5 December 2016. In the immediate aftermath, old tensions between non-Brahmins and Brahmins flared over what was to be done with her body. As already mentioned, Jayalalithaa was a Vaṭakalai Śrīvaiṣṇava Brahmin. She often wore the Śrīvaiṣṇava (Vaṭakalai) *nāmam* on her forehead and prayed regularly. But unlike the tradition of cremation for Śrīvaiṣṇava Brahmins, Jayalalithaa was buried. The papers hotly debated this fact.

The Indian Express mentioned that one reason given for why the Tamil Nadu government buried her next to MGR's memorial on Marina Beach was that

> she was not an Iyengar for us ... she was beyond any caste or religious identity. Even most ... Dravidian leaders, including Periyar, Anna Durai and MGR, were all buried ....[42]

Another reason for burial was that it made it possible to have a memorial. One person offered the view that Sasikala, who had been Jayalalithaa's close friend and foster sister, and who was planning to take over the government, did not want Jayalalithaa's relative Deepa Jayakumar—the only blood relative in line for performing the death ritual—to be in the spotlight, fearing that she was a potential rival for the role of Chief Minister.[43] I would add: burial had long been common for some Hindus. Ascetics, for instance, were buried because cremation rituals were household ones, done by a son with a Vedic fire, which ascetics who had renounced household life could not do. In the ancient Dravidian world as well, heroes would be buried and the place marked by a 'hero' stone. In modern times, saints and political heroes have been buried, honoured, and even worshipped at *samādhi*s. Elsewhere, some *samādhi*s such as that of Gandhi contain only the ashes after the body had been cremated.

The *Huffington Post*[44] reported that after the burial, Jayalalithaa's relatives in Srirangapatna in Karnataka, who were miffed at not being consulted about the burial, gave her a traditional Vedic cremation on the banks of the Kaveri river. If you are wondering how you can have a cremation without a body, Hindu ritual already had a script for such situations: one uses an effigy. One blogger said that a cloth doll represented Jayalalithaa. Another blogger offered the Vedic ritual details, saying that the body was represented by traditional *darbha* grass, and that Vedic chants 'recreated' the body.[45] Whatever the case, the ashes of the cremated effigy were then immersed in the Kaveri. Some people attributed the different decisions regarding burial or cremation made by politicians and her family to the law of karma. Be that as it may, continuity and change coexisted to keep everyone satisfied. One can always find strategies in ancient Hindu texts to resolve such conflicts.

There is more to tell in the ongoing saga about religion and politics in Indian democracy. After Jayalalithaa's death, it seemed that Sasikala would replace her as Chief Minister of Tamil Nadu. Because she was a Tevar, she would maintain the AIADMK's important alliance with the numerically dominant Tevar caste. Then O. Panneerselvan, also a Tevar and acting Chief Minister after her death, who had been supporting Sasikala, turned against her in February 2017 and allied with E. K. Palaniswami from the Gounder caste, the third largest one in Tamil Nadu.

Just after that, the Supreme Court finally settled a 21-year-old case of corruption against Sasikala and ruled that she could not contest elections for ten years. In the wake of this verdict, she nominated Palaniswamy as leader and he became Chief Minister later that month, and his new ally O. Panneerselvan became Deputy Chief Minister of Tamil Nadu and Convenor of the AIADMK. This alliance brought together the first and third of Tamil Nadu's most dominant castes—the Tevars and the Gounders. It comes as no surprise that later that year, the Vanniyar, the second most powerful caste which had been left out in the alliance, was pushing for more cabinet posts.

These political manoeuvers reverberated in Delhi. All-India parties such as the Congress and the BJP needed alliances with Tamil Nadu parties to maintain their own power. This was why Rahul Gandhi had been reaching out to the AIADMK during Jayalalithaa's illness and to the Party after her death, even though his Congress Party supposedly had an alliance with the DMK. The BJP was also jockeying for a connection.

In this case, Dr Vasudevan Maitreyan was a key link. He had been a former MP in the Rajya Sabha (Council of States or Upper House of the Indian Parliament), representing the AIADMK. Like Jayalalithaa, he is a Vaṭakalai Śrīvaiṣṇava Brahmin. When Jayalalithaa was alive, he acted as her representative to Prime Minister Modi. This ended in 2014, when he fell out of favour with her. No doubt sensing an opportunity for a political comeback, Maitreyan immediately headed to O. Panneerselvam's residence within an hour of the acting Chief Minister's change of allegiance from Sasikala to Palaniswamy.

This provided the BJP with a back door into the AIADMK, because Maitreyan had belonged to the RSS and then the BJP from 1990–99, serving first as general secretary, then vice-president, and finally president of the Tamil Nadu unit, before quitting to join the AIADMK. Many political commentators noted that his long-standing saffron sympathies might connect the AIADMK and the BJP. At the very least, Maitreyan's Delhi connections, developed during his tenure in the Upper House of Parliament, could prove valuable. In any case, Maitreyan's influence would continue a Brahmin presence close to the dominant party alliance in Tamil Nadu, and that would be of interest to Brahmins within the BJP, who were promoting Hindutva through political alliances with dominant castes.

The saga goes on. H. Raja, another Tamil Brahmin, who was the BJP national general secretary, threatened on his Facebook account in March 2018 that Periyar's statue in Tamil Nadu should be destroyed like Lenin's had been in Tripura, just after the BJP won an election that ousted the CPI(M) state government. M. K. Stalin immediately warned that no one should dare touch E. V. R.'s statue. Nevertheless, a local BJP member and his Communist friend vandalised a Periyar statue. The next day, the BJP Coimbatore office was petrol-bombed and some Brahmins attacked near the Parthasarathy temple in Triplicane (Chennai), and their sacred threads cut off. (They might have been Śrīvaiṣṇavas who live around that temple.)

In a home ministry advisory, Prime Minister Modi said that he disapproved of the vandalism of the Lenin and Periyar statues and ordered that such statues be protected elsewhere. Other BJP party members echoed the Prime Minister, adding that anyone engaging in such actions would be disciplined. Gradually, tensions subsided.

Then, on 7 August 2018, Karunanidhi died at the age of ninety-four. Condolences poured in from all parts of India, hailing him as a deep-rooted mass leader with a firm moral compass, especially for social welfare but also for opposing the Emergency, a moderniser intent on developing IT, a brilliant party organiser, a masterful speaker who could draw on an extensive knowledge of ancient Tamil literature, and a literary figure who wrote poetry, novels, essays, and a daily column in the DMK's newspaper.

Almost immediately, a conflict broke out over a request for permission from the AIADMK-led state government to build a memorial on Marina Beach next to Annadurai, a request that was refused and immediately taken by the DMK to the Madras High Court, which quickly ruled in the DMK's favour.

In the meantime, the Central government announced that there would be a full state funeral and plans were made for an official day of mourning, when government offices and educational institutions would be closed.

Within a week of the funeral, the nation's newspapers were offering more nuanced analyses of Karunanidhi's legacy, noting his shadowy nepotism (like that of Jayalalithaa for her clan), but also his capacity for subtle compromise. They were also at work, taking stock of where Tamil Nadu's politics were headed. Some argued that the DMK might be in a good position to win the next election (2021), thanks to a pre-arranged succession through Karunanidhi's son M. K. Stalin and the lack of charisma and pettiness (the rejection of the memorial request) of the current AIADMK leadership. But others saw a political vacuum that could be exploited by outside parties such as the BJP or Congress, and still others prophesised a challenge to Stalin's leadership by M. K. Alagiri, Stalin's brother.

The deaths of Jayalalithaa and Karunanidhi within a year of each other signalled the end of an era. It makes sense to draw our discussion to a close.

Final Thoughts

Even though I found some patterns when considering particular themes that emerged from an analysis of my interviews with Bhāgavatas, I am aware that these patterns can change very quickly. Tamil society is rife with stress and ferment, partly because of its history and partly because of its many collisions and collaborations with aspects of modernity, however conceived.

Another whole book could be written, for instance, with a focus on non-Brahmin Śrīvaiṣṇava youth and how the Internet is transforming their view of reality. In 2016, *The Times of India* was reporting, for instance, that 'Tamil Nadu has the highest number of broadband subscribers in the country'.[46] As I was doing my research, I could see that the Internet was also transforming religion. Some *ācārya*s and *jīyar*s (or their supporters, if they were not computer literate) were communicating with disciples through the Internet to arrange events, solicit donations, and promote pilgrimages to all the *divyadeśa*s in Tamil Nadu, or even to remote ones in the Himalayas. A Śrīvaiṣṇava publisher and bookstore had a large Internet presence. Devotees in the diaspora were connecting through the Internet with their *ācārya*s and fellow Śrīvaiṣṇavas in Tamil Nadu.

I often found relevant Śrīvaiṣṇava sites during my research. Some were dedicated to making *sampradāya* works available online, others to explaining intricate details of doctrines or rituals, and still others to recounting Teṉkalai and Vaṭakalai histories. Many of these sites were managed by retired Brahmins. Some were by non-Brahmins who were facilitating their caste's connectivity through e-magazines or blogs. The major temples and *maṭha*s had their sites, which included the schedules for daily worship and festivals. And the Government of Tamil Nadu had its own sites to promote temple tourism, or the activities of the Hindu Religious and Charitable Endowments, including all their activities to improve non-Brahmin religious lives.

These are by no means the only kind of sites for the topics discussed in this book. On *Quora*, a California-based question-and-answer platform started by former Facebook executives, for instance, one finds the question, 'Why is there hate for Brahmins in Tamil Nadu?'[47] It is difficult to know whether those who answered are digital nerds in the diaspora or Tamil Nadu.

Nonetheless, they do reveal a range of views. Periyar was ignorant, hypocritical, and attracted non-Brahmins with his message of contempt. The British were anti-Brahmin. The British divided the Brahmins and non-Brahmins. There were so few Brahmins, they could easily be victimised. Many Tamils who are famous have been Brahmins. Brahmins do not live up to the true meaning of being a Brahmin, which is devotion to the supreme. Brahmins by culture were docile and could not fight back. Since there were only Brahmins and *śūdra*s in the society, there were no other *varṇa*s to mediate the poles.

Brahmins were flexible, adapted to new conditions and became successful, which made non-Brahmins jealous. Brahmins were the first to learn English and so were successful. Brahmins look and speak differently, and so they could be easily identified for victimisation. Non-Brahmins have an inferiority complex. 'Othering' Brahmins avoids dealing with real social issues. Films have made fun of Brahmins.

The bloggers drew on their knowledge of history and their own experiences in their comments. Some thought the problem of hating Brahmins had largely disappeared, especially if Brahmins had non-Brahmin friends and avoided arrogance. Others thought that Brahmins were still experiencing discrimination.

Another question on *Quora* was about the position of Śrīvaiṣṇavism on the caste system. Two answers are given. One argues that Śrīvaiṣṇavism focusses on *varṇa*, not caste, and argues that Śrīvaiṣṇavas should observe the duties of their *varṇa*, per the authority of Rāmānuja. There is no discrimination in Śrīvaiṣṇavism because there is no hierarchy in the original conception of *varṇa* (hierarchy came later), and because there is a means to attain salvation for each *varṇa*. Thus, there is no discrimination, although there are distinctions in the duties and type of path towards salvation.[48] Put otherwise, there is unity in diversity. The other answer is similar; it says that Rāmānuja and other preceptors did not rank the *varṇa*s, that everyone is equal because of God's unconditional grace and love, and because everyone can have *samāśrayaṇam*, can attain salvation, and has equal opportunity to do good.[49] Thus, Bhāgavata identity transcends caste identity.

Quora[50] even had a question on the significance behind doing *samāśrayaṇam*. Answers included definitions of identity (worshipping only the supreme deity Nārāyaṇa, being branded on the shoulders, and wearing the *nāmam*); eligibility for formal worship; devotion to one's own *ācārya*, the mantras he taught, and access to salvation through his link back to Rāmānuja, who sought liberation for everyone; and attainment of supreme heaven at the end of this very life.

Juli Gittinger reminds us that the Internet is a site for more general discussions of Hinduism.

> Theoretically, Hinduism would seem to have a natural affinity towards electronic media; the lack of central institutional authority allows for more participatory discourse, the diversity of Hinduism as practiced 'on the ground' should allow for more variations to be promoted and accepted on the web.[51]

The web, she suggests, is also a domain where religion 'becomes abstracted, simplified, westernized, or distorted'.[52] Hinduism might be imaged as the 'world of Vivekananda, ashrams, colorful gods and goddesses, exotic music, and incense-laden ritual'.[53] Or it can be politicised. Her case study of the latter is the BJP, which has a team of 100 IT and social media experts, and skilfully uses social media and cyber-activism. The 'electronic public sphere', Gittinger observes, 'is a theater in which "Hindu" (identity) and "Hinduism" (religion, culture, political ideology) is contested openly'.[54] Online communities are formed. Some Facebook pages have rules to define belonging: no secularists, Marxists, or even those who accept religious pluralism.

I cannot go further into this new reality, which has had only scant research, except to say that it bears watching whether it enhances inclusiveness in the public sphere and how it shapes future understandings of Hinduism and its relation to the state, not to mention Śrīvaiṣṇavism's relation to the Tamil Nadu government and to Tamil political parties, as well as national ones such as the BJP and the Congress.

Come what may, it is evident that religion, caste, and politics remain closely connected in Tamil Nadu and India as a whole. As Monika Wohlrab-Sahr and Marian Burchardt argue,[55] secularity should be distinguished from secularism (the ideologically desired absence of religion). It should be understood empirically as the separation of State and religion, be it for individual freedom, balancing religious diversity, promoting economic and social progress, or creating the independence of institutional domains. There are multiple secularities, related to specific cultural histories and the problems the society is facing.

The prevailing model in Tamil Nadu, I think, has been economic and social progress. Politicians have engaged in a reform of Hinduism, from making it possible for Dalits to enter temples, to ensuring that temples are financially accountable, to attempts to open temple jobs to any qualified Hindu. This model of progress is certainly in play with other national models, such as balancing religious diversity (the Congress party model) or asserting Hinduism's primacy (the BJP model).

Many questions remain. Were the threats to Periyar's statue that led to counter-attacks on Brahmins in Triplicane simply flare-ups or signs of ongoing deep tension? And what about the BJP inroads into Tamil politics? What about the theories that features of modernity and secularity will eventually converge on the Western model? Will problems of survival or fundamentalism take hold, making other histories possible? Is there a new form of Tamil nationalism developing as a pushback to Telugus in positions of power?[56] Will Mother Tamil have new political incarnations?

Clearly, the interviews in this book and our case study of Śrīvaiṣṇavism reveal that we must do a better job of documenting and reflecting on history from below and the history of the present to capture how religion, caste, and politics are intimately connected and shape the flow of events. Ultimately, careful tracking of societal trends, including religious ones, with large-scale surveys and listening carefully to the voices of ordinary people, including women and youth belonging to various religions and castes, will provide the best insights into what the future might hold.

Whatever the future, I hope this study introduces the rich traditions of Śrīvaiṣṇavism as it interacts with changing caste and political identities. At the very least, I hope it contributes to a better understanding of Śrīvaiṣṇava Bhāgavatas today, who have gone through turbulent transformations and deserve to be heard as they forge new religious roles to make Śrīvaiṣṇavism accessible, attractive, and valuable to ordinary people.

Notes

1. Although those arguing for modernity and those for postmodernity were once far apart, the theories have been converging in recent years (Fourie, 'Multiple Modernities', 22–26).

2. Fourie, 'Multiple Modernities', 22–26.

3. I think the scholarly debates over one or multiple modernities would benefit from engagement with the anthropologist Bruce Trigger's methodological reflections on whether the development of early civilisations is similar or different, which has some analogies, strange though that might seem, with the matter at hand (Trigger, *Understanding Early Civilizations*, 3–39, 653–85).

4. Pandian, *Crooked Stalks*, 224.

5. Munshi, 'Caste and the Indian Economy'.

6. Narayana Rao, et al., *Textures of Time*.

7. Shulman, *Tamil: A Biography*, 250. Shulman looks on the modern period of Tamil history with nostalgia for what has been lost: the rich world of literature, mainly the cosmopolitan, occasionally even universal, orientation of a linguistically heterogenous society with its interlocking cultural contexts. This was a world in which literati—whether in the courts, temples, or *maṭha*s—marked their age with creativity of both composition and commentary. He warns us against superimposing a modern agenda of Tamil nationalism on the past, when the north was only rarely devalued, Sanskrit and Tamil were not antitheses, and there was a prevailing symbiosis of Brahmins and non-Brahmins. He bemoans, moreover, the role of the colonial regime with its shallow, impoverished views on reforms, and denounces the stridency and identity politics that erupted in the modern period. Although this is Shulman's general assessment of the impact of modernity, he also notes that there existed some long-standing tensions between Brahmins and non-Brahmins, created by Brahmin privilege and power, related to their high level of education and lavish royal land grants.

I do not think that this does justice to the problem of injustice. The non-Brahmins of Shulman's history were mainly Vellalas, especially Śaiva Vellalas—non-Brahmins who belonged to *pulavar* literati circles, especially in their own *maṭha*s.

Even though Shulman's lens of Brahmin–non-Brahmin symbiosis has revealed intricacies of Tamil literary history, it has hidden a key component of non-Brahmin feeling of discrimination: the case of Śrīvaiṣṇavism. The exclusion of Śrīvaiṣṇava non-Brahmins from centres of literary and religious expertise was made worse because they did not have their own *maṭha*-centres of learning, including Sanskrit learning and *pulavar* literary culture. Shulman's focus also hides the anger of non-Brahmins, such as the agriculturalists who toiled, sometimes in conditions of slavery, for the elites, be they Brahmins or Vellala non-Brahmins.

Finally, when Shulman locates the indigenous roots of concepts of egalitarianism, iconoclasm, scepticism, and rationalism in Siddha antinomianism, Tantra and Jaffna Sri Lankan neo-Śaivism, I think he neglects to mention one of the most basic of human desires: the right to be treated as equal, at least in the sense of human dignity or equal opportunity. That, after all, is what much of the modern world is all about, and it will have to find its place in any description of modern Tamil Nadu. Shulman himself points in this direction when he observes that Tamil literature is now portraying formerly marginalised groups, such as the agriculturalists and caste heroes. But, I would add, the sense of marginalisation and injustice could occur at the very core of the culture: the temple world.

The promise and power of the non-Brahmin movement was strident and disruptive, yes, and had its own injustices, but it occurred for very important reasons that should not be overshadowed by an appreciation of a cosmopolitan past, however rich and complicated that might have been.

8. Deshpande, *Contemporary India*, 41.

9. Ibid., 4.

10. Bairy, *Being Brahmin*, 203.

11. See Rudolph and Rudolph, *Modernity of Tradition*.

12. Hardgrave, *Nadars*, 199.

13. For non-Brahmin Śrīvaiṣṇava ritual practices of death, see Young, 'Triumph Over Death', 389–96. Ritual removal of the *mudrās* (brand marks of conch and discus) by ablution is a custom only for non-Brahmin Śrīvaiṣṇavas (K. K. A. Venkatachari, personal communication, 2007).

14. In 1988, Raymond Williams stated that there were many untouchable Śrīvaiṣṇavas in the region around Madurai and Chidambaram. They received their initiation from non-Brahmin preceptors. See Williams, 'Śrīvaiṣṇava Handwritten Field Notes'. I would add that the initiation in the Chidambaram area might be attributed to Bhuvanagiri and his disciples.

15. According to R. K. Kshirsagar, 'Some of the Dalit leaders also thought that by following the Brahmanic manners ... they would be able to elevate themselves to the higher position in the caste hierarchy' (Kshirsagar, *Dalit Movement*, 408).

16. See 'Gold-rich Temples'.

17. Bairy, *Being Brahmin*, 186.

18. Williams, 'Śrīvaiṣṇava Handwritten Fieldnotes'.

19. Deshpande, *Contemporary India*, 82.

20. Munshi, 'Caste and the Indian Economy', 2.

21. Kavitha, 'Inter-caste Marriage'.

22. Ibid.

23. Although the topic of urbanisation was not addressed per se by my informants, it has certainly been a factor in the massive changes underway, from the growth of Madras as a metropolis in the nineteenth century to the mega-city that it had become by the twenty-first. The move of people from villages to towns and cities has begun to disrupt the spatial constraints of hegemonic caste norms, although not without serious challenges. Urban geographers, for instance, have found that upper castes have controlled the real estate in choice areas of Chennai to maintain upper-caste domination in these areas (see Auclair, *Ville* à *Vendre*, 28–51).

24. Jeffrelot, *Religion, Caste and Politics in India*.

25. Munshi, 'Caste and the Indian Economy', 2.

26. Ibid., 60.

27. Rajadurai and Geetha, 'Periyar's Ideals',

28. Munshi, 'Caste and the Indian Economy', 45, 61.

29. Rajadurai and Geeta, 'Periyar's Ideals'.

30. Michelutti, *The Vernacularization of Democracy*, 6.

31. Ibid.

32. Muralidharan, 'Caste Over Tamil Pride'.

33. 'It's Now Dalits vs. Non-Dalits in Tamil Nadu'.

34. Ibid.

35. Marszal, '"Untouchable" Who Married Upper-caste Girl Hacked to Death on Busy Indian Street'.

36. Yamunan, 'DMK against Fundamentalists, not Hindus'.

37. This series, consisting of 433 episodes, was aired from 1 July 2015 to 27 January 2017. The 'historical soap' had the highest rating of a Tamil series at that time. See 'Ramanujar (TV series)'.

38. Yamunan, 'DMK against Fundamentalists, not Hindus'.

39. Ibid.

40. Ibid.
41. Ramanathan, 'A Historic Debate'.
42. Janardhanan, 'Jayalalithaa Was Buried'.
43. *Quora*, 'Why was Jayalalitha buried but not cremated as per Hindu tradition?' Available at www.quora.com, paraphrase of Abhijeet Kothari (accessed 25 February 2018).
44. Hebbar, 'Jayalalithaa's Relatives Perform Her "Cremation"'.
45. *Quora*, 'Why was Jayalalitha buried but not cremated as per Hindu tradition?' Available at www.quora.com, paraphrase of K. S. Kiran (accessed 25 February 2018).
46. Prabhakar, 'At 14.9 mn, Tamil Nadu Has Highest Broadband Subscribers in Country'.
47. *Quora*. 'Why is There Hate for Brahmins in Tamil Nadu?', Available at www.quora.com (accessed 9 June 2019).
48. Paraphrase of Ramanuja Dasan, *Quora*. 'What is the position of Sri Vaishnavism on caste system?' Available at www.quora.com (accessed 9 June 2019).
49. Paraphrase of Manik, *Quora*, 'What is the position of Sri Vaishnavism on caste system?' Available at www.quora.com (accessed 9 June 2019).
50. *Quora*. 'What is the significance behind doing Samasrayanam?' Available at www.quora.com (accessed 9 June 2019).
51. Gittinger, *Contesting Hinduism*, 22.
52. Ibid.
53. Ibid., 177.
54. Ibid., 76.
55. Wohlrab-Sahr and Burchardt, 'Multiple Secularities'.
56. As one of my informants said: 'Telugus now "rule" Tamil Nadu. EVR [Periyar], MGR and Jayalalithaa were all Telugus. Even many professors in Tamil departments are Telugus. In the cinema, most actors are Telugu, even though they use Tamil medium. In short, Telugus, who hide their caste name, are ruling and plan to divide and conquer. A movement to encourage Tamil power called "Naam Tamilar Iyakkam" is growing through Internet information and connections.'

It remains to be seen how this might affect many people in Tamil Nadu, whose ancestors' mother-tongue was Telugu, but who themselves have lost knowledge of Telugu and have become Tamils by speech, culture, and long history.

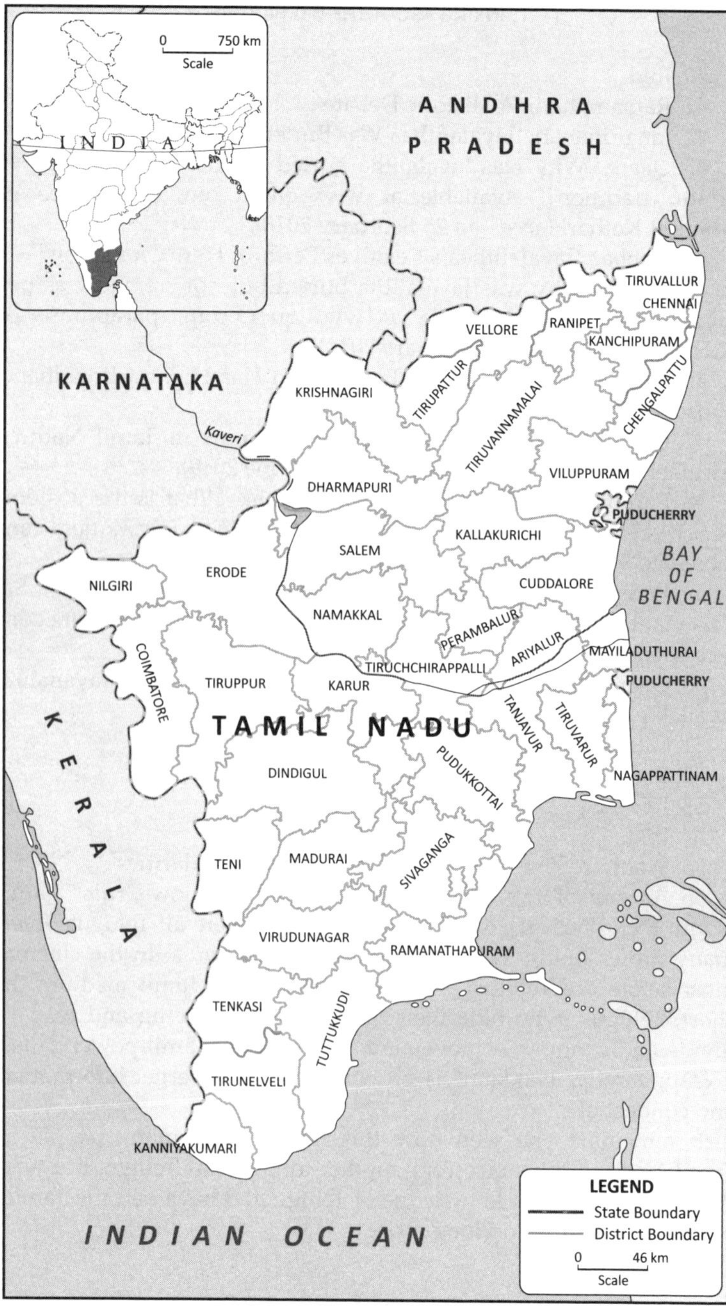

Map showing 38 districts of Tamil Nadu

Appendix 1

Location of Places Mentioned in Interviews

Places (with variant modern spellings) are located in the relevant district (2020) of Tamil Nadu, moving generally clockwise from northeast to the south and northwest. A more precise location of these places can be found by searching for the village name on the Internet or the name plus the word 'map'. Otherwise, one can search for the district and then for the place. One can also find maps of the 108 *divyadeśa*s on the Internet.

♠ Indicates a *divyadeśa* (a place mentioned by an *āḻvār*), an *āḻvār* birthplace and/or a major *maṭha*.
* Indicates site of an interview.
Otherwise the list includes places mentioned in the interviews or analysis. Some sites are in neighbouring states.

Chennai and Beyond

Tiruvallur District

* Athipet (Ambattur)
* Minjur

Ponneri
♠* Tirumalicai

Chennai District

* Alwarpet
* Ekangipuram (Ayanavaram)
* George Town (Muthialpet)
* Mount Road (Anna Salai)

Mylapore (Mayilaappoor)
Perambur
* Tambaram
♠* Triplicane (Thiruvallikeni)

Ranipet District
Walajahpet

Vellore District
Pallikonda
Vellore

Tirupattur District
Ambur

Kanchipuram District
♠* Kanchipuram
Melmaruvatur
* Nariyampakkam
♠* Sriperumbudur

Chengalpattu District
Chengalpattu
♠ Madurantakam
Mahabalipuram
Paranur
Tirumani

Tiruvannamalai District
Arani

Puducherry and Beyond

Union Territory

* Eppakkam
* Puducherry
* Seliyamedu (Seliamedu)

Viluppuram District

* Kottaimedu
* Kumalam
  Nallan Pillai Perral
♠* Tirukkoyilur (Tirukoilur)
* Virapandi (Veerapandi)

Kallakurichi District

  Kallakurichi
* Kottaimedu
♠* Tirukkoyilur (Tirukoilur)

Cuddalore District

* Bhuvanagiri
♠* Chidambaram
  Cuddalore
  Manjakuppam (Cuddalore city)
  Panruti (Pannuruti)
♠ Srimushnam
♠* Tiruvahindrapuram (Thiruvahindrapuram)

Srirangam, Tanjavur and Beyond

Tiruvarur District (Thiruvaroor)

  Ammaiyappan
♠* Mannargudi
  Needamangalam (Nidamangalam)
♠* Cirkali (Sirkali)

Thanjavur District

- Kumbakonam
- ♠* Tanjavur (Thanjavur)
- ♠* Tiruppernagar (Thirupper Nagar)
- Tiruvaiyaru (Thiruvaiyaru)
- ♠* Tirukkandiyur (Thirukkandiyur)
- * Ammapet (Ammapettai)

Tiruchirappalli District

- ♠* Srirangam

Karur District

- * Koyampalli
- Jambuli

Madurai District

- Subbulapuram
- ♠ Tirumaliruncolai (Thirumaliruncholai)

Virudhunagar District

- ♠ Srivilliputur (Srivilliputhur)

Ramanathapuram District

- Ramnad (Ramanathapuram)

Thoothikudi District (Tuticorin, Tutukuti)

- Maruthan Valvu (Maruthan Valvoo)
- * Thoothukudi
- ♠ Tirukkurunkudi(Thirukkurungudi)
- ♠ Alvartirunagari
- Koyilpatti (Kovilpatti)

Tirunelveli District

- ♠ Nanguneri
- Karaiyiruppu
- ♠* Tirukkurunkuti (Thirukkurungudi)

Kanyakumari District

- Swamithope
- Nagerkoil (Nagercoil)

Theni district
Teni (Theni)

Erode District
Erode

Salem district
Salem

Beyond Tamil Nadu

Andhra

Nadigaddapalem
Nellur (Nellore)
♠* Tirumalai-Tirupati

Telangana

Hyderabad

Karnataka (previously Mysore)

Melkote (Melukote)
Srirangapatna

Kerala

♠ Trivandrum (Thiruvananthapuram) (Travancore)
Kalati (Kalady)

Appendix 2

*Āḻvār*s and Early *Ācārya*s

*Āḻvār*s (seventh–ninth century)

Poykai
Pūta
Pēy
Tirumaḻicai
Periyāḻvār
Āṇṭāḷ
Kulacēkara
Nammāḻvār
Toṇṭaraṭippoṭi
Tirumaṅkai
Tiruppāṉ
Madhurakavi

Early *Ācārya*s (tenth–fifteenth century)

Tenth century	Nāthamuni
Eleventh century	Yāmuna
Twelfth century	Rāmānuja
Twelfth century	Empār

Twelfth century	Mutaliyāṇṭāṉ
Twelfth century	Piḷḷāṉ
Twelfth century	Kūreśa (Kūrattāḻvāṉ)
Twelfth century	Parāśara Bhaṭṭar
Thirteenth century	Nañjīyar
Thirteenth century	Nampiḷḷai
Thirteenth century	Periyavāccāṉ Piḷḷai
Thirteenth century	Vaṭakku Tiruvīti Piḷḷai
Thirteenth–fourteenth century	Piḷḷai Lokācārya
Thirteenth–fourteenth century	Aḻakīya Maṇavāḷa Perumāḷ Nāyaṉār
Fourteenth century	Vedānta Deśika
Fourteenth–fifteenth century	Maṇavāḷa Māmuni

Appendix 3

Changing Definitions of Caste

As Nicholas Dirks has argued, we must separate the earlier caste system from the influence of colonial thought. The latter assumed that caste was a pervasive, totalising, and uniform system. He reminds us that before the colonial period, caste was not the key category or symbol of Indian civilisation, not even a system; it was merely one expression among many of social identities. Others included 'temple communities, territorial groups, lineage segments, family units, royal retinues, warrior sub-castes, "little" kingdoms, occupational reference groups, agricultural or trading associations, devotionally conceived networks and sectarian communities ...'.[1]

Dirks points out that the British observed, described, enumerated, and portrayed caste in the eighteenth and early nineteenth century. Despite exotic or stereotypical features, this picture still reflected the diversity of life and occupation. Change was coming. The Tirunelveli Census of 1823 posited and ranked eight general categories: 'Brahmans, Ksatriyas, Sudras connected to the religious establishment, Sudras of different denominations, "Muhamedans", "Christians of different castes", inferior Sudras, and the low castes (or untouchables).'[2]

Dirks notes that this list blends Manu's concept of *varṇa* with revenue classifications.

The rebellion of 1857, continues Dirks, was interpreted by the Raj as its failure to understand Indian culture (especially the caste system, but also religious and other customs), and not British complicity in troubling economic and political policies. As a result, ethnography in Madras under the leadership of Edgar Thurston between 1885 and 1908 led to the collection of data on physical measurements (anthropometry), as well as marriage customs, death rituals, evil eyes, and a host of other topics. More importantly, it led to district manuals and gazetteers that included all kinds of information about castes and customs, including some about Śrīvaiṣṇava practices and conflicts.

Under the leadership of H. H. Risley (1851–1911), an attempt had been made to organise the groups by *varṇa*. In 1881, the question of size was formalised (100,000 or more). Ten years later, use of *varṇa* was replaced by occupation. However, as the Census of 1901 (which he was in charge of) itself admitted, it was difficult to classify castes in this way, and it would be 'better to enumerate a few of the castes, which, from numbers or for any other reason, are of most importance in several provinces'.[3] The census used a classification by occupation, yet even then had to comment that many groups no longer followed the occupation their caste title suggested.

Gazetteers from the late nineteenth century show that even the *śūdra*s were hierarchically organised. The elite *śūdra*s in Tamil Nadu were the Vellalars, often landowners, village revenue collectors, and businessmen.[4] They lived mainly in the districts of North Arcot, Coimbatore, Salem, and Tinnevelly, and came to prominence under British rule 'by ousting [some of] their Telugu counterparts, the Kapu or Reddiyar cultivators, who had previously migrated into the area'.[5] They often imitated orthodox Brahmin religious customs such as vegetarianism and daily ablutions. The Naidus, especially the Balija Naidus, a subdivision of the Kapu, were a Telugu

Vaiṣṇava Vellalar group, whereas most Tamil Vellalars were Śaivas.

Below the Vellalars, in the early twentieth century, were other cultivating *śūdra* castes such as the Vanniyars in northern Tamil Nadu, southern Andhra, and Mysore (Karnataka), and around cities such as Madras, Kanchipuram, Chengalpattu, and Pondicherry. One of the largest caste groups in Tamil country, the Vanniyars, many of whom were agriculturalists, considered themselves descendants of the vassal chiefs of Pallava, Cēṟa, Cōḻa, Vijayanagara, and other past rulers. Some evidence backs up this claim.[6] Alternatively, they claimed to be baniyas (*vaiśya*s), a twice-born group according to the *varṇa* classification.

It was the low-ranking and impoverished untouchables, however, who performed the arduous labour of cultivation such as weeding, transplanting, and harvesting. In south India, they were the servants, even slaves, of landowning masters, both Brahmins and elite non-Brahmins.

The Census of 1901 emphasised ranking, supposedly as understood by the castes themselves in each locale, although actually as understood by Brahmins and therefore based on gradations of purity and impurity. There had been protests against rankings—the Vanniyars had already petitioned to be counted as *kṣatriya*s in the 1871 census[7]—but now many groups sent in petitions to claim the status of a twice-born *varṇa*. Every caste had its own story about its origin and its own view of hierarchy, in which it was on top. The former outcastes, for instance, claimed to be the original (*ādi*) inhabitants of the southern land: the Adidravidas.

Even after the government eliminated ranking from later censuses, agitation continued. So did the notions of pure and impure as the organising principles of caste.[8] A 1906 British gazetteer's description of Tanjavur, for instance, notes that

> Brahmans wear the sacred thread, have *gotrams*, and their touch or their presence in another's house, so far from polluting, confers honour. Their own sanctity is so sensitive that the approach of a Paraiyan, Pallan

> or Chakkiliyan ... [outcastes or a rank above] ... or his presence in the Brahman street, pollutes them .... On the other hand, these castes strongly object to the entrance of a Brahman into their quarters, believing that harm will result to them therefrom. The upper non-Brahman castes generally only pollute them by touch, by entry into their kitchens, or by seeing their food in the course of preparation or after it has been cooked.[9]

The author remarks that this description would be characteristic even in the eighteenth and nineteenth centuries and in some other areas of Tamil Nadu.

In 1901, Thurston published his *Castes and Tribes of Southern India*. As he soon realised, the identity of castes in Tamil Nadu was a tangled tale because of the myriad subdivisions (the *jāti*s or exclusive groups into which people are born, intermarry, and inter-dine) and because of the overlapping titles that had become surnames, a situation that arose partly because of group attempts at upward mobility by changing their caste name to that of one with higher status.

A Pillai, for instance, often called himself a Vellalar. In North and South Arcot districts, Tamil Vellalars called themselves Mudaliyars. Around Kanchipuram, however, weavers used the same name. The title Nayakar and its variant Naicker, which means 'leader' in Telugu, was used by people who speak Telugu, such as the Balija Naidus,[10] as well as by the (traditionally) lower-ranked Vanniyars. As for the Vanniyars, they sometimes used names such as Varma, Pillai, Reddiyar, and Padayachi (army chief).

Classifying and ranking castes were such difficult tasks that the British eliminated both from the 1931 census. Nonetheless, argues Dirks, caste became the central category for understanding Indian society; in addition, it established a pan-Indian system that relied on the Dharmaśāstras. Many modern scholars—notably Louis Dumont[11]—inherited this mindset, Dirks observes, and read it into the past as a pan-Indian system, even though many anthropologists disagreed.[12]

After Independence, the Indian Constitution (1950)[13]—with considerable input from Dr B. R. Ambedkar, a Dalit educated at Columbia University in New York and a leader of the Dalits—addressed the problem of social injustice by calling for liberty, equality, and fraternity in its Preamble and special provisions to minimise inequalities in income, status, facilities, and opportunities with special attention to the Scheduled Castes and Scheduled Tribes. In addition, the Constitution made provision for the reservation of seats in the Central and state governments for ten years to improve the status and well-being of these groups. Further, commissions were to report on progress, and lists of Scheduled Castes and Scheduled Tribes were to be created. This did not solve the problem, however. From the 1960s, there was considerable violence, for example, against Dalits in rural areas.

In 1982, an amendment to the Constitution stipulated specific quotas in public-sector and government-aided universities: 15 per cent for Scheduled Castes and 7.5 per cent for Scheduled Tribes for five years. The amendment was then to be reviewed (it has been routinely extended since then). 'Efforts to contain the political organization of depressed classes have continued to the present day,' says Dirks, 'but it is ironic that the very upper-caste non-Brahman groups who contested Brahman privilege were the ones who sought to keep the depressed classes in their ritual position of inferiority and subservience.'[14]

In the wake of the study of the plight of other groups by the Mandal Commission[15] and enormous political mobilisation of the groups themselves to be classified as 'backward', the Central government in 1990 declared that Other Backward Castes, an administrative term used originally by the Raj for the 3,000 sub-castes of Hindus who had suffered discrimination, would be given 27 per cent of government positions.

The early reservation policies for Scheduled Castes and Scheduled Tribes had been generally accepted throughout India, including by the elite, as a way to end the well-known discriminatory abuses of the caste system, and so there had not been major protest to the Constitution's provisions. The introduction of 27 per cent reservations for the Other Backward Castes in the wake of the Mandal report, however, was another matter, for the so-called Forward Castes sensed that their opportunities would be dramatically curtailed. Protests erupted on the streets, with some students burning themselves alive in protest. This did not happen in Tamil Nadu, however, because the Forward Castes were only 13 per cent compared to about 36 per cent elsewhere in India.

The Supreme Court of India subsequently ruled that reservations cannot exceed 50 per cent of the 'vacancies' in public institutions—even if the total number of competing candidates from the designated groups went above that number. In 1992, it also tried to prevent abuse of the reservation system in a ruling called the Mandal Judgment, which said that reservation for Backward Classes was valid, provided that the socially advanced persons or sections of this group, the 'creamy layer'—those who were no longer disadvantaged because of their parents' or their own type of jobs, such as doctors, lawyers, IT specialists, and so forth—were excluded.

Like many other state governments, the Tamil Nadu government has had aggressive reservation policies in public institutions, which means that it has ignored the Supreme Court's stipulation that reservations cannot go over 50 per cent of the vacancies. In fact, Tamil Nadu has the highest percentage of reservations at 69 per cent now that Andhra (which had 83.3 per cent) has been divided into two states (Andhra Pradesh and Telangana).

Tamil Nadu has ignored the Supreme Court's ruling on the reservations. A challenge to Tamil Nadu's 69 per cent quota by two students—who had been denied admission to a public medical school despite having high scores—went to the country's Supreme Court, which then requested the Tamil Nadu government to justify its high percentage. The Tamil Nadu government did so, saying that the population of the Scheduled Castes, Scheduled Tribes, and Other Backward Castes was really 87 per cent, and so the special treatment was justified in this extraordinary situation. In 2014, however, the Supreme Court said that a meritorious candidate coming within the cut-off mark of 50 per cent reservation cannot be denied the right of admission.

The debates on reservations continue: What groups are to be included, in what percentage, and for what opportunity? Some of these debates, for instance, are about reservations for women, others about promotions, and still others about whether new categories should be introduced.

Notes

1. Dirks, *Castes of Mind*, 13.

2. Ibid., 119–120.

3. Dirks, *Castes of Mind*, 203, quoting Henry Waterfield, *Memorandum on the Census of British India of 1871–72* (London: H. M. Stationery Office, 1875).

4. Hemingway, '*Tanjore*', 82.

5. Irschick, *Politics and Social Conflict*, 6–7.

6. See Thurston, *Castes and Tribes*, for details of these claims and his view of possible historical substantiation.

7. In 1833, they had gone to court in Pondicherry to prove that they should be recognised as *kṣatriya*s (Rudolph, *Modernity of Tradition*, 51–52).

8. Additional sources of agitation, though of vague origin, were the many conflicts between the right-hand and left-hand groups. See Dirks, *Castes of Mind*, 76, and Appadurai, 'Right and Left'.

According to Pamela Price, by the end of the nineteenth century, right-hand and left-hand conflicts had been replaced by ones between castes or religious groups over honours in temples, churches, festivals, and processions (Price, 'Acting in Public', 50).

9. Hemingway, *Tanjore*, 80.

10. See 'Balija' for details of origin and *jāti*s within this group.

11. Bryan Pfaffenberger tries to make sense of these differing descriptions (one suggests a replica of the classic model, the other challenges it with regional differences). First, he argues that caste ranking in the north does follow the classic model, and even in the Dravidian south, groups 'use the language and the ideology of those

scriptures to conceptualize their social relations', despite regional variations (Pfaffenberger, *Caste in Tamil Culture*, 8). Second, he suggests that *śūdra* domination has persisted in the south because the power of the dominant caste in its village has been so pervasive and so adept that the dominated have found it necessary to accept their status, even though they see no justification for it in the religious notions of rightful domination that can be found in the Dharmaśāstras (ibid., 10–11). See also Seshadri, *Social Change*. The fact that these dominant *śūdra* castes acknowledge the Brahmin's superiority and consider the untouchables impure is further evidence, Pfaffenberger argues, that the classic model is the underlying one (ibid., 13–14).

12. These anthropologists opined that a textual and structural analysis does not do justice to the complexity of *varṇa* and *jāti* configurations in various regions. The organising principle of hierarchy need not be pure versus impure, the resultant hierarchies are often very different from the model and, in any case, the hierarchies are not static but dynamic.

13. See Articles 15, 16, 17, 38, 46, 330, 332, 334, 340, 341, 342, 366 (sections 24 and 25).

14. Dirks, *Castes of Mind*, 241.

15. The Mandal Commission was established in 1979 by the Janata Party then in power to identify the backward groups on the basis of eleven indicators to determine which groups should receive affirmative action; it submitted its report the following year.

Appendix 4

The Colonial Cauldron of Anti-Brahmanism

Ferment in the colonial period created a powerful mix of forces that would eventually culminate in the non-Brahmin movement. One commonality among these forces was anti-Brahmanism.

Already in the nineteenth century, non-Brahmins had begun to protest exclusionary caste practices[1] in Madras Presidency. This new self-consciousness was abetted by missionary critiques of the abuse, superstition, hypocrisy, and cunning of Brahmin priests. One of the first to adopt anti-Brahminism was Abbé J. A. Dubois (1765–1848). In *Hindu Manners, Customs, and Ceremonies* (1806), he praised Jains on the one hand and criticised Brahmins on the other. A more scholarly basis for anti-Brahminism was the concept of the Dravidian. In *A Comparative Grammar of the Dravidian or South Indian Family of Languages* (1856), Rev. Robert Caldwell (1814–91) showed through linguistic and other methods that Tamil belonged to a family of languages that he called Dravidian. Caldwell then extended the concept of Dravidian to include culture and religion. He contrasted that with Aryan culture and religion, that is, Brahmanical culture and Advaita Vedānta, especially its modern version, known as neo-Vedānta. The word *drāviḍa* provided an umbrella for political mobilisation. Caldwell appealed to non-Brahmin sentiments by pointing out that Brahmins had lumped the Dravidians together as *śūdra*s at the bottom of the caste system. In this spirit, S. Sundaram Piḷḷai (1855–97), a Vellalar, wrote: 'The Veḷḷālas who form the flower of the Dravidian race, have now so far forgotten their nationality as to habitually think and speak of themselves as Śūdras ....'[2]

A contemporary of Caldwell was George Pope (1820–1907). Since he had translated Dubois' work from French to English, he echoed Dubois' praise of Jainism, noting that its *Nālaṭi-Nāṉūṟu* was so popular among the Vellalar that it was called the 'Veḷḷāḷa-Vetham'. He goes on to champion south Indian Śaivism as the pre-Aryan religion of south India and the guardian of Tamil poetry.[3] (As the translator of Maṇikkavācakar's *Tiruvācakam*, written in the ninth century, he had developed an interest in Śaiva religious poetry.)

Śaiva non-Brahmins promoted this anti-Brahmin view in the Tamil weekly *Oru Paisa Tamilan*. Numbers and solidarity gave them power. They began to re-think history. The result was a renaissance in the scholarship on Tamil literature, history and Śaivism. Many elite Tamil non-Brahmins rallied around this idea of Śaivism, especially Śaiva Siddhānta, as the original Tamil religion.

They took their inspiration also from Āṟumuka Nāvalar (1822–79), a Tamil-speaking Vellalar from Jaffna, Sri Lanka, where the landowning Vellalars dominated the caste hierarchy. He was instrumental in promoting a Śaiva religious identity and using the printing press to popularise his ideas.

Elite Śaiva non-Brahmins have long had leadership roles in Śaiva Siddhānta. The thirteenth-century Meykaṇḍar, who was a Vellalar, for instance, was its first preceptor. He wrote the seminal *Śivajñānabodham*. Several later Śaiva monasteries had non-Brahmin leaders since the sixteenth century and Tamil libraries that became centres of Tamil learning.

As Śaiva Siddhānta had accorded great importance to the Sanskrit Śaiva Āgamas, some non-Brahmins had access to Sanskrit and its literature.[4] Other Śaiva leaders wanted to promote only Tamil. Maraimalai Atikal (Maṟaimalai Adigal; 1876–1950), educated in Tamil literature, for instance, wanted to rid Tamil of Sanskrit vocabulary and influence. He started the 'Pure Tamil' movement. In this way, elite Śaiva non-Brahmins used the ideas of the missionary Orientalists and their promotion of Tamil language, culture and religion for their own purposes.[5] According to the *Tanjore Gazetteer*, there were many more Śaiva Vellalars than Śrīvaiṣṇava Vellalars.[6]

V. Geetha and S. V. Rajadurai note that these developments provoked confrontations with Brahmins who did not appreciate rebukes and challenges to their authority. Despite being willing to accept some reforms in order to stop non-Brahmin conversions to other religions, some Brahmins mocked non-Brahmin aspirations. More specifically, they ridiculed the idea that non-Brahmins could create a common identity out of divergent castes and castigated elite non-Brahmins for their treatment of outcastes.[7]

After the Mutiny of 1857, when the British government began to administer its territories directly instead of indirectly through the East India Company, the government promised equality and religious freedom for everyone. This new policy made education, the legal system and the press theoretically available to all. The government passed a special Marriage Act in 1872, moreover, so that a person of any caste or religion could legally marry someone of any other caste or religion. It secularised wells, too, so that they would no longer be designated as polluted or pure.

Secularisation speeded up with the advent of new markets, garrisons, schools, public meeting halls, libraries, and courts. The government's authority was to rely on reason. Since this meant supporting merit over status by birth, remaining indifferent to matters of religion such as purity and pollution, and promoting the rights of all, non-Brahmins were attracted to the British values of equality.[8]

Furthermore, Madras Presidency needed alliances with the large landowners—which included the non-Brahmin Vellalars in Tamil districts, the Balija Naidus in both Telugu and Tamil districts, and the Kammas and Reddiyars in Telugu country—to facilitate tax collection in the villages. They wanted to curtail the Brahmins' growing power in administrative jobs, moreover, which Brahmins easily obtained thanks to their long history of learning. In 1901, Tamil Brahmins were 17.88 per cent literate, Balija Naidus .98 per cent, Vellalars .19 per cent, and Reddiyars .04 per cent.[9] A similar situation existed for government jobs. In Madras, Brahmins had 80 per cent of them; elite non-Brahmins had only 20 per cent.[10] Brahmins, some of whom were large landowners, did not want opportunities to expand for non-Brahmins who far outnumbered them, for fear of competition.[11]

The advent of change for Dalits is a different story. In the eighteenth century and the first half of the nineteenth, many saw their lives improving, especially those who served in the armies of the Mughals and their allies, Marathas, and then the British East India Company. The Dravidian thesis was very appealing to Dalits who had long suffered under the authority of Brahmins and elite non-Brahmins who endorsed the caste hierarchy. Now the outcastes were claiming to have been the original Tamil inhabitants; the Brahmins, they said, were merely Aryan invaders. With this insight, they renamed themselves Adidravidas, the original Dravidians.

One major development was the abolition of slavery. According to Eugene Irschick,[12] Paraiyars (untouchables) and Pallis were bonded labourers for landowners, or those who had hereditary rights to the produce. These groups often became economically indebted to their employers. Despite insurrections, their lot was compelled into virtual slavery, sometimes enforced by violence. By the mid-nineteenth century, the British noticed the contradiction between their noble values and their ignoble actions. They had legitimated the Raj, after all, on moral grounds: a rule that relied on justice and fairness. This meant the elimination of master-slave relationships. In 1843, Act V made slavery illegal in India. In

1860, the Indian Penal Code (Act 45) instituted a fine and up to seven years' imprisonment for anyone dealing in slaves.

The practice of slavery changed very slowly. By the late nineteenth century, British utopian thinkers were still upbraiding colonial administrators in India for the continuing slavery and for increasing poverty. Several famines exacerbated the situation. Dalits were moving about, moreover, to escape indebtedness. Under pressure to collect taxes and trying to avoid reprimands from the mother country, colonial administrators had to improve the lot of these groups, including their status.

In Chengalpattu, for instance, colonial administrators began to give the Dalits free house sites and allowed them to record houses as their own property. This enabled the magistrates to praise Dalits as loyal and sedentary.[13] Besides this, there was the emergence of organised labour. Becoming aware of their political and social rights, Dalits were beginning to protest their ritual status as impure. Colonial administrators used some of the Orientalist research produced by Christian missionaries to upgrade the status of Dalits.

Some Hindu intellectuals began to publish articles on the problems that Dalits faced. Shri Kasi Viswanatha Mudaliar (1806–71), a Brahmo Samaji, propagated Ram Mohan Roy's critique of caste in Madras. In 1870, an organisation[14] was founded in Madras 'to raise the consciousness' of the Dalits. The Dalit John Rathinam started the popular magazine *Dravidian Pandian* in 1885. The next year, he started a school and then, in 1899, a hostel for Dalits in Madras. In 1889, Pandit C. Iyodhi Dass (1845–1914), an important leader of the Dalits in Tamil Nadu, and some theosophists[15] started several schools for Dalits. In the 1890s, the Adi-Dravida Mahajan Sabha[16] petitioned the government in Madras for agrarian reforms and lower test standards for admission to some medical schools. In 1893, Shri R. Srinivasan started a magazine, *Paraiyan*, to awaken Dalits in Madras, and in 1902, Colonel Olcott published *Poor Pariah*, which argued that long ago, the Pariahs (an Anglicisation of Paṟaiyars) had been Buddhists.

Those Dalits who were unable to change their material conditions either started their own sects or, more often, converted to other religions. Pandit C. Iyodhi Dass converted to Buddhism. Many others converted to Christianity, becoming members of groups such as the Society for the Propagation of the Gospel, the London Missionary Society, the Madurai Church Council, or the Tamil Evangelical Lutheran Church.[17] Dalits often represented half or more of the converts.[18] Christianity offered material incentives (mass conversions often occurring during or just after famines[19]), and educational and social ones as well. By the late nineteenth century, therefore, life was changing for some Dalits.[20]

Although these forces during colonial times were often conflicting, some began to coalesce as the non-Brahmin movement developed organisational structures. But the tensions between Dalits and 'caste' non-Brahmins would remain a political issue long after Indian Independence.

Notes

1. Hemingway, *Tanjore*, 80.

2. Ravindran, 'Discourses of Empowerment', 71.

3. According to Kamil Zvelebil, G. U. Pope's first Tamil teacher was Rāmānuja Kavirayar (c. 1785–1853) from Ramnad, a famous scholar. From his name, it is clear that he obviously belonged to a Śrīvaiṣṇava family. He also had Miron Winslow (1789–1864) and several other Orientalists for his students (Zvelebil, *Tamil Literature*, 238). Given this close Śrīvaiṣṇava connection, it is odd that the Orientalists focussed on Śaivism and not Śrīvaiṣṇavism. Another early figure was Gopāla Kṛṣṇa Piḷḷai (1827–1900) from Tirunelveli. In his village (Karaiyiruppu), he studied Tamil grammar, literature and Sanskrit under the guidance of his father, who was well-versed in these subjects and *Kambaṉ Rāmāyaṇam*. Gopāla Kṛṣṇa Piḷḷai was initiated by Āṇṭāṉ Svāmi of Srirangam and learned Śrīvaiṣṇava texts from him. Very pious, he would wear his *nāmam*, do *pūjā* at his home shrine, and read the *Kambaṉ Rāmāyaṇam* daily. He was appointed by Bishop Robert Caldwell as a Tamil teacher in the village of Sayarpuram (where the Society for the Propagation of the Gospel was influential).

Gopāla Kṛṣṇa Piḷḷai converted to Christianity and changed his name to Henry Alfred Krishna Pillai. Eventually, he became a Tamil pandit at Presidency College in Madras. His most famous work is his *Rākṣanya Yātrikam* (1984), which retells in Maṇipravāḷam John Bunyan's *Pilgrim's Progress*.

4. Dominic Goodall refers to 'the apparently partly non-brahmin spiritual lineage leading to Rāmanātha in eleventh-century Tiruvārūr' (Goodall, 'Saiddhāntika paddhatis', 186). He points out that names which end in *deva* might be initiatory names for *kṣatriyas*, as is stated in other texts, and that this might mean that 'some of the initiates of this lineage, including perhaps Rāmanātha, were non-Brahmin' (p. 194).

5. Ravindran, 'Discourses of Empowerment', 79.

6. Hemingway, *Tanjore*, 81.

7. Geetha and Rajadurai, *Non-Brahmin Millennium*, 37.

8. Ibid., 50–51.

9. Irschick, *Politics and Social Conflict*, 17. 'According to the 1871 census, in Chingleput District, by far the largest proportion of the inhabitants were Vellalas. They amounted to 62% of the population, while the pariayars were 24.3% and the pallis 19%.' Brahmins were only 3.6 per cent (Irschick, *Dialogue and History*, 100).

10. Irschick, *Politics and Social Conflict*, 13.

11. Irschick points out that Tamil Brahmins seldom discussed reform (unlike the Telugu Brahmin Virasalingam in Andhra, which argued for equality). A few Marathi-speaking Brahmins, such as K. Srinivasa Rao and R. Raghunath Rao, were reform-minded. Tamil Brahmins in Madras were more interested in a revival of Hinduism and joined groups such as the Hindu Sabha (Irschick, *Politics and Social Conflict*, 24–25). Seshadri (*Srivaishnavism and Social Change*, 113) argues that from the medieval period, Telugu-speaking Andhras had greater tolerance and inclusion vis-à-vis outcastes than did people in the Tamil country.

12. Irschick, *Dialogue and History*, 3ff.

13. Ibid., 191ff.

14. Called the Hindu Sreyobhi Vardhini Sabha, it was founded by Shri Kokkonda Venkata Ratnam Panthulu.

15. These were Colonel Olcott, Mary Balbare and Annie Besant.

16. This was later called the Pariah Mahajan Sabha.

17. Kent, *Converting Women*, 16–18.

18. See Kshirsagar, *Dalit Movement*. See also Kent, *Converting Women*, 17 for statistics on Christian conversions.

19. Kent, *Converting Women*, 45.

20. See Radhakrishnan, 'Backward Classes'.

Appendix 5

Śrīvaiṣṇavism's Future?

It is hard to predict what Śrīvaiṣṇavism might be like in another twenty years. Conceivably, this could go in several directions.

One direction is a general decline of Śrīvaiṣṇavism. The reasons that made it a minority sectarian tradition in Tamil Nadu throughout its history might contribute to such a decline. A few reasons, however, are new. People told me, for instance, that Śrīvaiṣṇavism demanded too much of people. 'The dress of Tamils has changed,' said K. K. A. Venkatachari.

> Men once had long hair; then they started to cut their hair. Tamil scholars once wore traditional dress; then they adopted Western dress. Because Western dress is not allowed in Vaiṣṇava temples, devotees can enter the temple only up to a particular point. Śaiva temples are more liberal; one can go in any dress, and so they are more popular.

Initiation necessitates vegetarianism, moreover. Many people, even Brahmins, however, are no longer vegetarian or never were.

Many among even those Bhāgavatas who admired the Brahmanical lifestyle noted that this lifestyle had declined in their own family traditions since the days of their grandparents, albeit for various reasons: moving away from Srirangam, for instance, or a father who was profligate and irreligious, or attraction to Periyar's anti-Brahminism, or the demands of modern jobs. There is no guarantee that a family's religious identity will continue into the next generation and after, especially if the forces of secularisation take hold—so far there are few indications of that—or other religions or Hindu sects attract more converts. Even the traditional signs of Brahmin status are disappearing, except in some pockets of orthodoxy.

In addition, villagers complained that they could *not* find Brahmin or even non-Brahmin priests to perform the rites of passage, such as marriages and funerals. They also could not find people to chant verses from the *Divyaprabandham* on these occasions. Nor could they find Brahmin or non-Brahmin priests to officiate at their village temples. Now that the Supreme Court has rejected the idea that temples must accept non-Brahmin priests who have the required expertise, the problem of finding priests to serve the many temples is not being addressed. This too might contribute to the decline of the sect in its incarnations as Teṉkalai and Vaṭakalai.

Some people noted that despite the fact that Śrīvaiṣṇavas have travelled about to spread the religion in the villages, the influence is usually short-lived. Others noted that *sabhās*, charities and trusts come and go, that temples, *maṭhas* and *sabhās* are mismanaged, that patronage that had supported non-Brahmin musical families has dried up, and that conversions are attracting people away from their traditional religion. Even though there are signs of a new vitality on Śrīvaiṣṇava Internet sites, these seem to attract mainly Brahmins who enjoy sharing their erudition on the tradition. True, people point out that there is also growth in tourist pilgrimage and many new temples are being built, a sign of improving economic conditions in the country. But is that enough?

Śrīvaiṣṇavism's precarious existence can be attributed not only to having passed through a century of turbulent times and transformations, but also to a general lack of institutional structures that speak for the sect as a whole. This is true even for the Teṉkalai and Vaṭakalai subsects. Indeed, the major institution in Tamil Nadu that addresses issues related to religion might be the Hindu Religious and Charitable Endowments Department, an arm of the government. Its influence could grow if the Teṉkalai and Vaṭakalai orientations weaken.

There are other possibilities for the future of Śrīvaiṣṇavism. One is the status quo, with the locus of non-Brahmin Śrīvaiṣṇavism based in caste *sabhā*s, which might periodically join cause with other *sabhā*s. At least at this caste level there are deep roots for identity and continuity to counter the negative offshoots of modernity, such as hyper-individualism, consumerism and anxiety.

Another possibility is the formation of 'new non-Brahmin denominations', perhaps a new Śrīvaiṣṇava reform tradition that furthers the original caste-inclusive message of early *bhakti* religion, the verses of the *āḻvār*s, and the works of some of the early *ācārya*s. That in turn would necessitate turning the rhetoric about sectarian unity into social reality. Such a tradition would need the composition of a new *Āgama*, called, for instance, the Śrīvaiṣṇava Reform *Āgama*, which would be written in Tamil for easy accessibility and again emphasise the ancient inclusive aspect of the religion. Such a movement would need to create its own traditions of precedent, moreover, with a clear record of its traditions and government registration of its priests, chanters of the *Divyaprabandham*, and so forth, so that there would be no denominational and legal confusion in the future.

Most religions have had histories of reform movements that result in new institutions, so this trajectory is not inconceivable. At the moment, however, it is hard to imagine such a development in Tamil Nadu. The non-Brahmin identification as Śrīvaiṣṇava seems to operate mainly at the caste/sub-caste-cluster level, and not at the collective non-Brahmin level. Non-Brahmins, moreover, continue to have their own hierarchies of discrimination. More importantly, a new denomination would need a visionary leader, one who knows Śrīvaiṣṇava history, theology and languages and can promote and defend the new movement and inspire people to join it. It would need schools to train priests and *ācāryas* from any caste, at least for the temples in its network. It would need to build new temples as well, which would need patrons, and it would need to make the Śrīvaiṣṇava reform tradition a vibrant religion for many existing village temples and the new ones being built. This is a tall order.

Perhaps people will decide that a more realistic scenario would be for reform to take place within Śrīvaiṣṇavism itself, first by reintegrating the Teṉkalai and Vaṭakalai subsects, and then by reforming the existing Śrīvaiṣṇava temples, *maṭhas*, and other institutions. Even if the priesthood in many temples remains functionally a Brahmin preserve because of the Supreme Court's position on 'precedent', people might try to ensure that each temple does a better job treating all worshippers equally. They might argue that a step forward would be to unite Śrīvaiṣṇavas by having temples invite non-Brahmin *goṣṭhis* to form, be registered in the temple and chant near the sanctum at certain times; or better yet, to create additional new 'registered' *goṣṭhis* that would have both non-Brahmin and Brahmin chanters. The *Divyaprabandham*, after all, is at the heart of Bhāgavata identity and to be excluded from chanting near the sanctum of major temples does not bode well for the long-term viability of Śrīvaiṣṇavism, especially given the strong competition with Śaivism and other Hindu sects on the one hand, and the possibility of increased secularisation on the other.

In addition, Śrīvaiṣṇavas might propose more internal temple committees consisting of both Brahmins and non-Brahmins to address complaints of discrimination, and work towards improving relations before conflicts end up in court. If problems are addressed internally, the government would have less reason to interfere in temple affairs and a reconciliation between castes might begin to occur, especially if behaviour is carefully monitored and court challenges remain an option.

Moreover, *ācārya*s and *jīyar*s with a large number of non-Brahmin disciples and close connections to major temples might take the initiative in building Śrīvaiṣṇavism as a community of devotees that moves beyond rhetoric towards social solidarity for justice. Teaching non-Brahmin and Brahmin youth together would be important. Significantly, some *ācārya*s and *jīyar*s, especially those with many non-Brahmin disciples, are already doing this.

K. K. A. Venkatachari was quite adamant that the religion's future was in the hands of Bhāgavata Śrīvaiṣṇavas.

> Three per cent of the people are Brahmins in South India and of these, only 1 per cent are Śrīvaiṣṇava Brahmins. If we do not accept the non-Brahmin Śrīvaiṣṇavas today, we have a very small group. Therefore, we need to include them. In any case, this is the Teṉkalai tradition. Anti-Brahminism has now died out because the Brahmins no longer are a force to be reckoned with, although there are still tensions.

That said, it is up to non-Brahmins to decide for themselves what they want for the future. They have other options and they would need to be convinced that the Brahmin domination of the past would not be reinstituted.

There is one other scenario for how Śrīvaiṣṇavism might evolve in the future, and that is by being reshaped by the Sangh Parivar, the Hindu nationalist organisations such as the Rashtriya Swayamsevak Sangh (RSS) and its affiliated political party, the Bharatiya Janata Party (BJP). One can see that the Sangh Parivar already has developed strategies that could respond to problems faced by Śrīvaiṣṇavism: (*i*) by the building or renewal of village temples with village involvement; (*ii*) through an ideology of caste inclusiveness, with temple committees comprising representatives of various castes and educational institutions that teach everyone; (*iii*) through social services in the form of charities; (*iv*) by networking through pilgrimage tourism, print media and social media; and (*v*) through an appeal to a Hindu identity, with common enemies being Christianity and Islam. Given Tamil Nadu's strong sectarian traditions and the lingering effects of the non-Brahmin movement, the organisations of the Sangh Parivar might work at first *within* the sectarian traditions in this region to build its sense of Hindu community.

The fact that Tamil Nadu's political parties, even the DMK, have been increasingly willing to appeal to people's religious interests, as have the national parties, suggests that a possible scenario could be greater collusion of politics and religion, not less. Is the fact that the Sangh Parivar has made deep inroads into other regions in India, despite many spirited contestations, a sign of things to come in Tamil Nadu? Sceptics will point to the fact that in the 2019 national elections, the BJP did not fare well in south India. In Tamil Nadu, for instance, the AIADMK–BJP alliance (with Vanniyar support) lost heavily (thirty-seven of thirty-eight Lok Sabha seats went to the DMK led by Stalin, Karunanidhi's son, which had an alliance with Congress and the support of minorities, a breakaway party from the AIADMK, and the CPI, in addition to its traditional base).

At this point, it seems there is no clear way out of the turbulence that has characterised the past several centuries.

Appendix 6

Two Nadars on Discrimination

At a Tamil workshop in Puducherry, I met two researchers with PhDs, T. Rajarethinam Chettikulam and M. Prabhakaran. After I gave a talk on my project on non-Brahmins, they told me how their experience differed from my description. They were from the Kanyakumari district, the southernmost part of Tamil Nadu, which borders the modern state of Kerala (about 60 per cent of Nadars speak Malayalam). Although they are not Śrīvaiṣṇavas, they are a kind of Vaiṣṇava that has links with Śrīvaiṣṇavism. For instance, the personal form of the supreme is Viṣṇu-Nārāyaṇ, who is also called Perumāḷ. Despite the risk of digression, I think the history of discrimination against this low-caste Vaiṣṇava community and its reaction is an important example of how some Tamil Vaiṣṇavas reacted to discrimination in one region of Tamil Nadu that is related to, and yet very different from, the Śrīvaiṣṇava case.

Rajarethinam and Prabhakaran discussed how, in the nineteenth century, the Nadars had been subjected to discrimination by Brahmins (both Tamil Brahmins and Kerala Nambudiri Brahmins), as well as by Nayars, Kuruppas and Vellalars. Nadars were not allowed into the Travancore

(Trivandrum) Padmanabhasvami temple (a *divyadeśa*). Nadar low status (they were traditionally ranked just above the Dalits[1]) was visually obvious, moreover, because their women were not allowed to wear sari blouses, men could not wear the turbans called *vastram*, a kind of cloth tied around the head, and Nadars could use only coconut leaves for their hut roofs. To make matters worse, the government had taxed them for these customs, which they were not even allowed to change. They had to pay a special tax, moreover, when their young girls attained puberty. All this led to the 'Upper Cloth Controversy' (whether Nadar women could cover their breasts like upper-caste women). Christian missionaries were the first to address the Nadars' problems, but then used this support to convert many to Christianity. They attracted Nadars by allowing the women to wear blouses, the men turbans, and so forth. In addition, they developed quasi-ethnographic accounts of converts to help other missionaries. This provoked a pushback from the Nadars.[2]

The two young Nadar men, Rajarethinam and Prabhakaran, told me about a new religion[3]—summarised as One Caste, One Religion, One Clan, One World, One God—that had started in the nineteenth century with the Nadars in south India, and which had then spread to other castes and regions. It is called Ayyāvaḻi, which means 'path of the father'. According to its scriptures,[4] the father is Viṣṇu-Nārāyaṇa, a personal form of The Ekam, the One (which is formless and absolute).[5] Viṣṇu-Nārāyaṇa remains in the sea, but is himself incarnated in Vaikuṇṭar[6] in order to destroy illusion (*māyā*) after a final judgement.[7] Vaikuṇṭar becomes the supreme deity who will usher in the new age, the Dharmayuga.

Over time, variants of this theology developed that looked more like other Hindu sects, and for some followers, Ayyāvaḻi came to resemble a polytheistic village religion, although followers commonly wore on their foreheads a flame-shaped *nāmam* rising from a lotus and celebrate the holy day called Ayya Vaikuṇṭa Avatāram, the day of Vaikuṇṭar's incarnation.

My informants told me more about Vaikuṇṭar's life (ca. 1809–51 CE) from the hagiographies about him.

> When Ayya Vaikundar was born in a town near Kanyakumari, his parents named him Muṭisūṭum Perumāḷ because the family worshipped this deity, probably on account of the influence of the Padmanabham temple in Travancore. When the government heard the name of the infant, they sent soldiers to prevent the parents from using this name. He was then called Muttukuṭṭi, meaning the pearl that is the newborn calf.
>
> Muttukuṭṭi had some kind of a disease, and so his parents took him to Tirucendur, a Murukaṉ temple. According to tradition, he went into the sea to bathe before going to the temple. After three days deep in the ocean, he emerged with a glorious light and, after three days, declared that he was the incarnation of Perumāḷ. This account probably had both Vaiṣṇava (Nārāyaṇa is associated with the ocean) and Christian influence.
>
> Followers of Muttu—now called Ayya Vaikuṇṭar—worship the 'formless form of God'. In the temple room, there is a stool, a *vēl* [spear] and a dhoti cloth. People face the spear with folded hands. A leader of the community chants from the sacred book, and the congregation repeats a communal prayer, a tradition that might have Christian influence too. Prayers have integrated various names of God, such as Śiva. For worship, men won't wear shirts, although they do wear turbans and a *nāmam*, which is a white vertical line symbolising fire or freedom.

Vaikuṇṭar had disciples called Gurus, who helped him and proselytised the new religion. One named Podukutty was the manager of the main temple in Swamithoppu (where Vaikuṇṭar's *samādhi* is located), a role that was continued by his descendants. As the religion spread, there developed seven sacred places called *pathi*s; in addition, thousands of simple shrines were built by poor village people. Elderly village men led the simple rituals and the congregation in chanting. Everything was spoken or read only in Tamil.

Vaikuṇṭar instituted many social reforms to destroy the pernicious hold of the caste system. He had his followers wear the forbidden clothing, he had them refuse to pay penalty taxes or work without wages. And he encouraged them to undergo purification to eliminate meat-eating (at least a few days a week; he himself was vegetarian), toddy-drinking and tobacco-chewing. To break down the purity-pollution mentality, he designated a village well in Swamithope as the temple's *tīrtha*; all castes could draw water for bathing and drinking, unlike other wells that could not be used by the lower castes. Its water supposedly had curative properties and prepared one for life in the paradise of Dharma Yuga. (Vaikuṇṭar was known as a miracle worker.)

Moreover, Vaikuṇṭar encouraged his followers to have meals with outcastes and to serve the festival food with their own hands. The religion operated an orphanage, an old-age home, and a charity that provided food for the needy. It promoted literacy and economic development, from agriculture to businesses and small-scale industries, in order to help eliminate the negative image of Nadars as toddy-tappers. Ethical principles included charity, tolerance, love, and peace.

In the nineteenth century, Christian missionaries expressed concern over the growing popularity of Ayya Vaikuṇṭar, denouncing the movement as demonic and a threat to the spread of Christianity.

After Indian independence, the Nadar situation improved, especially when Kamaraj, a Nadar, became Chief Minister.[8] Although today Nadars are ranked as Other Backward Castes (OBC), they have achieved considerable upward mobility through education, economic development and astute political organisation.

This was evident in the two young Nadar men from uneducated families (albeit with good labour jobs) whom I was interviewing. Both were the only ones in their villages to pursue higher education—thanks in one case to a youth spent in libraries and in the other, to an inspiring teacher—obtaining PhD degrees from the University of Kerala. Even though they now had academic research jobs, they were sceptical about ever having a professor's job because of the need to pay a huge amount of money just to obtain a post. They both admitted that they vote for individuals, not for parties, which are often corrupt. They admired the former Nadar Chief Minister of Tamil Nadu, Kamaraj.

The accounts provided by the two Nadars about growing up in Kanyakumari where their caste had experienced extreme discrimination by the Kerala elites, which had inspired the creation of a new Vaiṣṇava sect, has similarities with the Śrīvaiṣṇava story. The new religion Ayyāvaḻi emphasised equality and inclusiveness, and promoted social service. Of course, the fact that its members were based largely in one caste made it easier to create cohesiveness. Its religious leadership was Nadar, and it avoided a formal priesthood. It will be interesting to see if any of the Śrīvaiṣṇava castes whose religious identities function mainly at the caste level within their own caste *sabhās* will develop a Nadar-like independent orientation in the future, or whether the time for such a religious reform dispensation is over now that many political rights and educational and economic opportunities are increasing.

Notes

1. They were not allowed to enter Hindu temples. They supported the Self-Respect and the Justice parties.
2. Schröder, 'No Religion, But Ritual', 131–60.
3. Others call it a reform movement within Hinduism. See Ponnu, *Vaikunda Swamigal*; Bergunder, et al., *Ritual, Caste and Religion*; Hardgrave, *Nadars*. See also 'Ayyavazhi' and 'Nadan (Nadar subcaste)'.
4. There are two scriptures that are in Tamil. The primary one is the *Akilathirattu Ammanai* (*Akilattīraṭṭu Ammāṉai*), said to have been told by Lord Nārāyaṇa to Lakṣmī, his consort, which consists of 15,000 Tamil verses. The secondary one is the Arul Nool (*Aruḷ Nūl*), which contains prayers, hymns, rituals, prophesy, and accounts of Vaikuṇṭar's life.

5. The creation story explains how The Ekam gives rise to Śiva and Śakti, the Trimūrti, the other deities, and the universe. Śiva and Brahmā give Viṣṇu all their power, which makes him the supreme power in the Kali Yuga.

6. The Ekam and all other deities, including those of other religions in the Kali Yuga, are also incarnated in Vaikuṇṭar.

7. Viṣṇu-Nārāyaṇa must incarnate to destroy Kaliyaṉ because Kaliyaṉ had obtained a boon comprising the power of all the deities, which included Viṣṇu-Nārāyaṇa's own power, and this power had become the power of *māyā*.

8. See Chapter 1, section: 'Politics of Religion'.

Bibliography

Primary Sources, Works in Tamil and Dictionaries

Aḻakiyamaṇavāḷa-rāmānuja-ekaṅki-svāmikaḷ, 1968. *Śrīvaiṣṇava Tīpikai*, 2 Parts. Madras: K. Nārāyaṇa Reṭṭiyar.

Aṟumukaṉ, K., 1984 [1966]. *Tirunārāyaṇatāca Suvāmikaḷ Varalāṟu*. Vīrapparaṇṭi: Nārāyaṇatāca Cuvāmikaḷ Tēvattānam.

Inscriptions of Sadasivaraya's Time: From 1541 to 1547, 1998, V. Vijayaraghavacharya (trans. and ed.), Tirumala Tirupati Devasthanams Inscriptions, Vol. V. Tirupati: Tirumala Tirupati Devasthanams.

Irātākiruṭṭiṇaṉ, M. [Pāvalar Maṇī Cittaṉ]. 'Vaiṇavattiṉ Etirkālam', in *Symposium on Sri Vaishnavism Tomorrow*, 62–71. Chennai: Bysani Madhavachetty's Charity Fund.

Kauvintarājalu Nāyuṭu, 2003. *Puvaṇakiri Śrīmat Aḻakiya Maṇavāḷa Rāmānuja Ekāṅki Suvāmikaḷ* by Kuṭalū.

Keśava, A. M., n.d. *Vaiṇava*. Madras: P. V. Kannappa Mudaliar.

Kiruṣṇasvāmi Ayyaṅkār, S. (ed.), 1975 [1968]. Piṉpaḻakiya Perumāḷ Cīyar, *Ārāyirappaṭi Kuruparamparāpirapāvam* [*Guruparamparāprabāvam 6000*]. Tirucci: Śrīnivāsam Accakam.

Koil Olugu, 1961, V. N. Hari Rao (trans. and ed.). Madras: Rochouse and Sons.

Kṛṣṇa Piḷḷai, Gōpāla, 1892. *Ācārya-hṛdaya-sāra-saṅgraham*. Chennai: Kalaratnākara Press.

Monier-Williams, Monier, 1963 [1899]. *Sanskrit-English Dictionary*. Oxford: Clarendon Press.

Nālāyira Tivya Prapantam, 2005 [2002], Vol. 2. Mumbai: Sri Bhagwat Ramanuja Siddantha Prachar Sabha.

Pāṇḍuraṅgaṉ, A., 2007. 'Nālaikku Śrīvaiṣṇavam', in *Symposium on Sri Vaishnavism Tomorrow*, 19–34. Chennai: Bysani Madhavachetty's Charity Fund.

Purushothama Naidu, B. R., 1970. *Śrī Vacaṉa Pūshaṇam* (with the commentary of Maṇavāḷa Māmunikaḷ). Cuddalore: T. K. Narayanasami Naidu.

_____., n.d. *Śrīrāmāyaṇam Pācurappaṭi* (*Rāmāyaṇa* as found in the [*āḻvārs*'] verses). Chennai: Manavar Manram.

_____ (ed.), 1951–59. *Tiruvāymoḻi Īṭiṉ Tamiḷ Ākkam*, 10 vols. Madras: University of Madras.

Rāmānuja Dāsar, Lokanātha, 1930. *Kōyiḷ Aḻakiya Maṇavāḷa Rāmānuja Ekāṅgi Svāmikaḷ Vaibhavam*. Kalati.

Rāmānuja Nāvalar, A. V., 1869. *Patmottara Purāṇam* (trans. into Tamil). Madras. Available at http://books.google.ca/books?id.

_____, 1891. *Tiruccitirakuṇapurāṇam* (trans. into Tamil). Chennai: Śriniketana Mutrakṣaracalai, K. R. Sundaram Iyer, Memorial Library. Available at https://www.yur/user/musicademy) (accessed 23 January 2015).

_____, 1968. *Vairakkiya Curiyotayam*. Pannurutti: Ramanuja Navalar Svamigal Sabhai. Available at http://nationallibrary.gov.in/showdetails.php[?id=376178 (accessed 20 June 2016).

Ramasamy, A., 1969. *Tamil Nattil Gandhi*. Madurai: Gandhi Smarak Nidhi.

Reddiyar, K. Venkataswami (ed.), 1981, *Nalayira Divya Prabandham*. Madras: Tiruvenkattan Tirmunram.

Śrīśaṇḍīlya-viśiṣṭa-parama-dharma-śāstra (with Hindi commentary), 1930. Kanchipuram: Sri Prativadibhayankara Matha.

Tivya Vaipava Caṅkrakam [*Divya Vaibhava Saṅgraha*] (about Putuvai Vilakṣaṇa Kavi), A. V. Irāmānuja Nāvalar Svāmikaḷ, collected by K. Nārāyaṇa Reṭṭiyar, 1972. Paṇṇuruṭṭi: Irāmānuja Nāvalar Svāmikaḷ Capaiyār (Sabhā) Veḷiyiṭṭalu.

Tamil Lexicon, 1982—83, 6 vols. Madras: Madras University Press.

Tātācāriyar, Akṉihōtram Irāmānuca, 1973. *Vālaṟṟil piranta vaiṇavam* (*The Vaiṣṇavism Born of History*). Kumbakonam: Sri Sarangapani Devasthanam.

Secondary Sources

'Achievements in the Field of Percussive Arts over 50 Years (1947–97)'. *MusicResearchLibrary.NetPeriodicals*. Available at http://archive.org/stream/MusicRes-Periodicals/PAC-Souvenir (accessed 16 December 2014).

Ahimohanan, A. S. 'Ayya Vaikundar: A Different Revolutionist and Social Reformer'. Trivandrum: Nadar Family Welfare Centre. Available at www.ayyavaikundar.org (accessed 28 March 2016).

'A. K. C. Natarajan'. *Wikipedia*. Available at http://en.wikipedia.org/wiki/A._K._C._Natarajan (accessed 6 June 2012).

'Alarmel Valli'. *Wikipedia*. Available at http://en.wikipedia.org/wiki/Alarmelvalli (accessed 15 March 2015).

Ambalavanar, Devadarshan Niranjan, 2006. 'Arumuga Navalar and the Construction of a Caiva Public in Colonial Jaffna'. Ph.D. dissertation, Harvard University.

Anand, S., 2006. 'Pujaris on the GO: TN Can Now Have Non-Brahmin Priests; Will Caste Hindus Agree?' *Outlook: The Magazine*, Tamil Nadu, 12 June. Available at http://www.outlookindia.com/article/Pujaris-On-The-Go (accessed 3 September 2015).

Appadurai, Arjun, 1974. 'Right and Left-Hand Castes in South India'. *Indian Economic and Social History Review* 11: 216–59.

____, 1977. 'Kings, Sects and Temples in South India, 1350–1700 A.D'. *Indian Economic and Social History Review* 14 (1): 47–73.

____, 1987. 'The Past as a Scarce Resource', in George W. Spencer (ed.), *Temples, Kings, and Peasants: Perceptions of South India's Past*, 196–221. Madras: New Era Publications.

____, 2007. *Worship and Conflict under Colonial Rule: A South Indian Case*, Cambridge South Asian Studies. Cambridge: Cambridge University Press.

Auclair, Christine, 1998. *Ville à Vendre: Voie libérale et privatization du secteur de l'habitat à Chennai (Inde)*. Pondichéry: Institut Français de Pondichéry.

'Ayyavazhi'. *Wikipedia*. Available at https://en.wikipedia.org/wiki/Ayyavazhi (accessed 28 March 2016).

Bairy, Ramesh, 2010. *Being Brahmin, Being Modern: Exploring the Lives of Caste Today*. New Delhi: Routledge.

'Balija', *Wikipedia*. Available at http://en.wikipedia.org/wiki/Balija (accessed 17 May 2016).

Bate, B., 2013. *Tamil Oratory and the Dravidian Aesthetic: Democratic Practice in South India*. New York: Columbia University Press.

Bergunder, Michael, Heiko Frese and Ulrike Schroder, 2011. *Ritual, Caste and Religion in Colonial South India*. New Delhi: Primus Books.

Brimmes, Niels, 1999. *Constructing the Colonial Encounter: Right and Left-Hand Castes in Early Colonial South India*. London: Psychology Press.

Carman, John B., 1974. *The Theology of Rāmānuja: An Essay in Interreligious Understanding*. New Haven: Yale University Press.

Carman, John, and Vasudha Narayanan, 1989. *The Tamil Veda: Piḷḷa<u>n</u>'s Interpretation of the Tiruvāymoḻi*. Chicago: University of Chicago Press.

Chhibber, Pradeep, and Sandeep Shastri, 2014. *Religious Practice and Democracy in India*. Cambridge: Cambridge University Press.

Chidambaram Pillai, P., 2008. *Right of Temple Entry: A Critical Analysis*. Chennai: MJP Publishers.

'Chinna Jeeyar', 2016. *Wikipedia*. Available at https://en.wikipedia.org/wiki/Chinna_Jeeyar (accessed 26 January 2016).

Clooney, Francis X., 1996. *Seeing Through Texts: Doing Theology among the Śrīvaiṣṇavas of South India*. Albany: State University of New York.

_____, 2002. 'Fierce Words: Repositionings of Caste and Devotion in Traditional Śrīvaiṣṇava Hindu Ethics'. *Journal of Religious Ethics* 30 (3): 399–419.

'The Constitution of India (Full Text)', 2017. *National Portal of India*. Available at http://www.india.gov.in (accessed 21 January 2017).

Dalmia, Vasudha, 1995. *Representing Hinduism: The Construction of Religious Traditions and National Identity*. Thousand Oaks, CA: Sage Publications.

Das, Kumudini, et al., 2010. 'Inter-caste Marriage in India: Has it Really Changed Over Time?' European Population Conference, Vienna, 1–4 September. Available at epc2010.princeton.edu/papers/100157.

Deshpande, Satish, 2003. *Contemporary India: A Sociological View*. New Delhi: Viking.

_____, 2013. 'Caste and Castelesness: Towards a Biography of the "General Category"'. *Economic and Political Weekly* XLVIII (15).

_____, 2018. 'Srinivas, M. N. (1916–99)', in Hilary Callan (ed.), *The International Encyclopedia of Anthropology*. Hoboken, New Jersey: John Wiley & Sons.

Dirks, Nicholas B., 2001. *Castes of Mind: Colonialism and the Making of Modern India*. Princeton: Princeton University Press.

Ebeling, Sascha, 2010. *Colonizing the Realm of Words: The Transformation of Tamil Literature in Nineteenth-Century South India*. Albany: State University of New York Press.

Fourie, Elsje, 2012. 'A Future for the Theory of Multiple Modernities: Insights from the New Modernization Theory'. *Social Science Information* 51 (1): 52–69.

Francis, W., 1906. *Madras District Gazetteers: South Arcot*. Chennai: Addison & Co.

Fuller, C. J., and Haripriya Narasimhan, 2014. *Tamil Brahmans: The Making of a Middle-class Caste*. Chicago: The University of Chicago Press.

'Fundamentals of Oral History: Texas Preservation Guidelines', Texas Historical Commission. Available at www.thc.state.tx.us/public/upload/publications/OralHistory.pdf (accessed 1 January 2016).

Geetha, V., and S. V. Rajadurai, 1999. *Towards a Non-Brahmin Millennium: From Iyothee Thass to Periyar*. Calcutta: Samya.

Gittinger, Juli L., 2015. 'Contesting Hinduism in the Electronic Public Sphere'. Ph.D. Dissertation, McGill University.

The Economic Times, 2015. 'Gold-rich Temples Weigh Monetisation Scheme, But "Melting" a Dampener', 20 December. Available at http://economictimes.indiatimes.com (accessed 19 February 2018).

Goodall, Dominic, 2014. 'Saiddhāntika paddhatis 1. On Rāmanātha, the Earliest Southern Author of the Śaivasiddhānta of Whom Works Survive, and on Eleventh-century Revisions of the *Somaśambhupaddhati*', in Marzenna Czerniak-Dorzdzowicz and Ewa Debicka-Borek (eds), *Cracow Indological Studies: Tantric Traditions in Theory and Practice*, 169–202. Ksiegarnia Akademika.

Hancock, Mary E., 1995. 'The Dilemmas of Domesticity: Possessional and Devotional Experience Among Urban Smārta Women', in Lindsey Harlin and Paul B. Courtright (eds), *From the Margins of Hindu Marriage: Essays on Gender, Religion, and Culture*, 66–91. New York: Oxford University Press, rev. edn.

Hardgrave, Robert L., 1969. *The Nadars of Tamilnad: The Political Culture of a Community in Change*. Berkeley: University of California Press.

Hardy, Friedhelm, 1978. 'The Tamil Veda of a Śūdra Saint: The Śrīvaiṣṇava Interpretation of Nammāḻvār', in G. Krishna (ed.), *Contributions to South Asian Studies*, Vol. 1, 29–87. Delhi: Oxford University Press.

Hardy, Friedhelm, 1983. *Viraha-Bhakti: The Early History of Kṛṣṇa Devotion in South India*. Delhi: Oxford University Press.

Hari Rao, V. N., 1976. *History of Srirangam Temple*. Tirupati: Sri Venkateswara University Press.

Hebbar, Prajakta, 2018. 'Jayalalithaa's Relatives Perform Her "Cremation" to Ensure She Attains Moksha'. *HuffPost*. Available at http:/www.huffingtonpost.in/2016/12/13/jayalalithaas-relatives-perform-her-cremation-to-ensure-she-a_a_21627450/ (accessed 20 March 2018).

Hemingway, F. R., 1906. *Tanjore*, Madras District Gazetteers. Madras: Superintendent, Government Press.

Hinde, Robert A., 2010 [1999]. *Why Gods Persist: A Scientific Approach to Religion*. London: Routledge.

The Hindu, 2009. 'Court Dismisses Jeeyar's Petition', 6 May. Available at http://www.thehindu.com/todays-paper/tp-national/tp-tamilnadu/court-dismisses-jeeyars-petition/article276599.ece (accessed 3 June 2016).

——, 2014. '69% Quota: SC Notice to Tamil Nadu', 6 November. Available at http://www.thehindu.com/todays-paper/tp-national/69-quota=sc (accessed 25 September 2015).

——, 2015. 'It's Now Dalits vs. Non-Dalits in Tamil Nadu'. 5 July. Available at

http://www.thehindu.com/news/national/tamil-nadu/its-now-dalits-vs-nondalits/article7386958.ece (accessed 3 April 2018).

Hindustan Times, 2015. 'Non-Brahmins Can Also Be Temple Priests, says SC', New Delhi, 16 December. Available at www.hinustantimes.com/India/non-brahmins-can-also-be-temple-priests (accessed 14 May 2016).

Hopkins, Steven Paul, 2002. *Singing the Body of God: The Hymns of Vedāntadeśika in their South Indian Tradition*. Oxford: Oxford University Press.

Hudson, D. Dennis, 1992. 'Winning Souls for Siva: Arumuga Navalar's Transmission of the Saiva Religion', in Raymond Bradbury Williams (ed.), *The Sacred Thread: Modern Transmissions of Hindu Traditions in India and Abroad*, 23–51. Chambersburg, PA: Anima Publication.

——, 1995. 'Tamil Hindu Responses to Protestants: Nineteenth Century Literati in Jaffna and Tinnevelly', in Steven Kaplan (ed.), *Indigenous Responses to Western Christianity*, 95–123, New York: New York University Press.

The Indian Express, 2017. 'Man Who Fought for Thevaram No More', 29 April. Available at www.newindianexpress.com/states/tamil-nadu/2017/apr/09/man-who-fought-fir-tgevaran-b-more-1591692.html (accessed 4 December 2017).

Irschick, Eugene F., 1969. *Politics and Social Conflict in South India: The Non-Brahman Movement and Tamil Separatism, 1916–1929*. Berkeley: University of California Press.

____, 1994. *Dialogue and History: Constructing South India 1795–1895*. Berkeley: University of California Press.

Jaffrelot, Christophe, 2010. *Religion, Caste and Politics in India*. Oxford: Oxford University Press.

Janardhanan, Arun, 2016. 'Jayalalithaa Was Buried: This Could Be Why', *The Indian Express*, 7 December. Available at http:/www.indianexpress.com (accessed 27 March 2018).

'Jayakanthan', *Wikipedia*. Available at https://en.wikipedia.org/wiki/Jayakanthan (accessed 3 June 2016).

'Kalladan', 2016. *Geocities.ws*. Available at www.geocities.ws/kalladan (accessed 4 August 2016).

Kavitha, S. S., 2007. 'Inter-caste Marriage Scheme Not a Hit'. *The Hindu*, 27 December. Available at

http://www.thehindu.com/todays-paper/tp-tamilnadu/inter-cas-caste-marriage-scheme-not-a hit/article14902415.ece (accessed 6 November 2017).

Kent, Eliza F., 2004. *Converting Women: Gender and Christianity in Colonial South India*. New York: Oxford University Press.

Krishnamurthy, R., 1979. *The Saints of the Cauvery Delta*. New Delhi: Concept Publishing.

Krishnasvami Aiyankar, S., 1941. *A History of Tirupati*, Vol. 2. Madras: Tirumalai-Tirupati Devastanam Committee.

Kshirsagar, R. K., 1994. *Dalit Movement in India and its Leaders* (1857–1956). New Delhi: M. D. Publications.

Leopold, Simon Robert, 1984. *Spiritual Aspects of Indian Music*. Delhi: Sundeep Prakashan.

Lester, Robert C., 1994. 'The Sāttāda Śrīvaiṣṇavas'. *Journal of the American Oriental Society* 114 (1): 39–53.

Magnier, Mark, 2012. 'In India, Trained Priests from Lower Caste Still Awaiting Jobs'. *Los Angeles Times*, 1 October. Available at http://articles.latimes.com/2012/0ct/01/world/la-fg-india-caste-(accessed 7 March 2015).

Maraneri-nambi, 2013. SrivaishNavaguruparamparai. Available at guruparamparai.wordpress.com/2013/03/02/maraneri-nambi (accessed 9 May 2015).

Marius-Gnanou, Kamala, 2010. 'Nouvelles activitées économiques et dynamique métropolitaine: Le cas de la périphérie Sud de Chennai'. *Ann. Géo.* 671–72: 28–51.

Marszal, Andrew, 2016. '"Untouchable" Who Married Upper-caste Girl Hacked to Death on Busy Indian Street'. *The Telegraph*, 14 March. Available at https://www.telegraph.co.uk.

McCann, Erin, 2016. 'Defining Identity: Language, Religion and Caste in Piḷḷai Lokācārya's *Śrīvacana Bhūṣaṇam*'. Ph.D. thesis, McGill University.

Michelutti, Lucia, 2009. *The Vernacularization of Democracy: Politics, Caste, and Religion in India*. New Delhi: Routledge.

Mitchell, Lisa, 2009. *Language, Emotion, and Politics in South India: The Making of a Mother Tongue*. Bloomingdale: Indiana University Press.

The Modern Rationalist, 2012. 'In Kerala Temples, Non-Brahmin Priests are Appointed in 50% of Vacancies', 13 April. Attributed to *The Times of India*, 12 March 2012. Available at http://www.new.modernrationalist.com/...in-kerala-temples-non-brahmin-priests-are-appointed-in-modernrationalist.com (accessed 16 March 2016).

Mumme, Patricia Y., 1993. 'Rules and Rhetoric: Caste Observance in Śrīvaiṣṇava Doctrine and Practice'. *Journal of Vaiṣṇava Studies* 2 (1): 113–38.

———, 2009 [1988]. *The Śrīvaiṣṇava Theological Dispute: Maṇavāḷamāmuni and Vedānta Deśika*. Madras: New Era Publications.

Munshi, Kaivan, 2017. 'Caste and the Indian Economy', Cambridge Working Papers in Economics 1759. Cambridge: Faculty of Economics, University of Cambridge. Available at https://ideas.repec.org/p/cam/camdae/1759.html.

Muralidharan, Ravitha, 2016. 'Caste Over Tamil Pride'. *Outlook: The Magazine*, 19 December. Available at https://www.outlookindia.com/magazine/story/caste-over-tamil-pride/298250 (accessed 21 March 2018).

'Nadan (Nadar subcaste)'. *Wikipedia*. Available at https://en.wikipedia.org/wiki/Nadan_(Nadar_subcaste) (accessed 25 March 2016).

Nagaswamy, R., 2008. *Ramanuja Myth and Reality: A Critical Study of Ramanuja's Life and Works*. Chennai: Tamil Arts Academy.

Narayana Rao, Velcheru, David Shulman and Sanjay Subrahmanyam, 2002. *Textures of Time: Writing History in South India 1600–1800*. New York City: Other Press.

Narayanan, Vasudha, 1990. 'Renunciation in Saffron and White Robes', in Austin B. Creel and Vasudha Narayanan (eds), *Monastic Life in the Christian and Hindu Traditions*, 161–83. Lewiston, NY: Edwin Mellen Press.

____, 1994. *The Vernacular Veda: Revelation, Recitation, and Ritual*. Columbia: University of South Carolina Press.

____, 2005. 'The Life and Lyrics of Tiruppan Alvar', in Eleanor Zellior and Rohini Mokashi Punekar (eds), *Untouchable Saints: An Indian Phenomenon*, 55–80. New Delhi: Manohar.

Narayanan, Venu Raza, 2007. 'Sri Vaisnavism Tomorrow', in *Symposium on Sri Vaishnavam Tomorrow*, 109–12. Chennai: Bysani Madhavachetty's Charity Fund.

Neelakandan, Aravindan, 2015. 'Tamil Temple Priests: Supreme Court Should be Applauded for Its Verdict'. 17 December. Available at swarjyamag.com/politics/tamil-temple-priests (accessed 17 January 2016).

Olivelle, Patrick, 1997. *Rules and Regulations of Brahmanical Asceticism: Yatidharmasamuccaya of Yādava Prakāśa*. Albany: State University of New York.

____, 2011. *Ascetics and Brahmins: Studies in Ideologies and Institutions*, Cultural, Historical and Textual Studies of South Asian Religions Series. London: Anthem Press.

Pandian, Anand, 2009. *Crooked Stalks: Cultivating Virtue in South India*. Durham: Duke University Press.

Pandian, M. S. S., 2003. *Brahmin and Non-Brahmin: Genealogies of the Tamil Political Present*. New Delhi: Permanent Black.

Pettukola, Gnaneshwar B., 2007. 'Is Sri Vaishnavism for Vaishnavites Only' in *Symposium on Sri Vaishnavam Tomorrow*, 72–82. Chennai: Bysani Madhavachetty's Charity Fund.

____, 'Are We Different', 'Towards Reconciling the Soteriologies of the Tenkalais and the Vadakalais', 'Thiruvaimozhiyil Saaranagathi', 'Is Sri Vaishnavism for Vaishnavites Only'. *Neovaishnavism Blogspot*. Available at http://neovaishnavism.blogspot.ca (accessed 15 May 2015).

Pfaffenberger, Bryan, 1982. *Caste in Tamil Culture: The Religious Foundations of Sudra Domination in Tamil Sri Lanka*. Syracuse: Maxwell School of Foreign and Comparative Studies.

Pillai, P. Chidambaram, 2008. *Right of Temple Entry*. New Delhi: MJP Publishers.

Ponnu, R, 2000. *Vaikunda Swamigal and the Struggle for Social Equality in South India*. Madurai: Ram Publishers.

Prabhakar, Siddharth, 2016. 'At 14.9 mn, Tamil Nadu Has Highest Broadband Subscribers in Country'. *The Times of India*, 22 August. Available at https://timesofindia.indiatimes.com/city/chennai/broadbannd-subscribers-in-country/articleshowprint/53802348.cms (accessed 10 April 2018).

Prentiss, Karen Pechilis, 1999. *The Embodiment of Bhakti*. Oxford: Oxford University Press.

Price, Pamela G., 2000. 'Acting in Public versus Forming a Public: Conflict Processing and Political Mobilization in Nineteenth Century South India', in Keith E. Yandell and John J. Paul (eds), *Religion and Public Culture: Encounters and Identities in Modern South India*, 27–55. London: Curzon.

Quora. 'Why is There Hate for Brahmins in Tamil Nadu?' Posted on 10 May 2018, 6 February 2018, 20 October 2017, 9 March 2017. Available at https://www.quora.com/Why-is-there-hate-for Brahmins-in-Tamil-Nadu (accessed 18 May 2018).

——, 2016. 'Why was Jayalalitha Buried But Not Cremated As Per Hindu Tradition?' 6 December. Available at https://www.quora.com/Why-was-Jayalalitha-buried-but-not-cremated-as-per-Hindu-tradition (accessed 25 February 2018).

——, 2017. 'What is the position of Sri Vaishnavism on caste system?' Posted on 7 November. Available at https://www.quora.com/What-is-the-position-of-Sri-Vaishnavism-on-caste-system (accessed 18 May 2018).

——. 'What is the significance behind doing Samasrayanam?' Posted on 23 November 2016, 16 February 2017, 5 August 2017. Available at https://www.quora.com/what-is-the-significance-behind-doing-Samasrayanam? (accessed 18 May 2018).

Radhakrishnan, P., 1990. 'Backward Classes in Tamil Nadu: 1872–1988'. *Economic and Political Weekly* 25 (10): 509–13; 515–20.

Rajadurai, S. V., and V. Geetha., 2017. 'Periyar's Ideals and Today's Tamil Nadu'. *Forward Press* 3. Available at https://www.forwardpress.in?2017/01/periyars-ideals-and-todays-tamil-nadu/.

Rajasekaran, Ilangovan, 2014. 'Recitation Row', *Frontline*, 28 November. Available at www.frontline.in/the-nation/recitation-row (accessed 31 May 2016).

Raman, K. V., 1975. *Sri Varadarajaswami Temple, Kanchi: A Study of its History, Art and Architecture*. New Delhi: Shakti Malik Abhinav Publications.

Raman, Srilata, 2005. '*Samāśrayaṇam* in Śrīvaiṣṇavism', in Jörg Gengnage, Ute Hüsken and Srilata Raman (eds), *Words and Deeds: Hindu and Buddhist Rituals in South Asia*, 91–114. Vienna: Harrasowitz.

____, 2007a. *Self-Surrender (Prapatti) to God in Śrīvaiṣṇavism: Tamil Cats and Sanskrit Monkeys*. New York: Routledge.

____, 2007b. 'Initiation and Conversion in Medieval South India: Pañcasaṁskāra as Historical Practice in the *Śrīvaiṣṇava* Hagiographical Literature', in Gerhard Oberhammer and Marion Rastelli (eds), *The Relationship between Viśiṣṭādvaita and Pañcarātra*, 263–86. Vienna: Austrian Academy of Sciences.

____, 2010. '"Religion", Religious Identity and the Frustrations of Modernity'. *Religions of South Asia* 4 (2): 213–19.

____, 2011. 'Tamil, Vaidika and *Vaiṣṇava*: Kiruṣṇacuvāmi Aiyaṅkar, Irāmānuja Tātacāriyar and Modern Tamil Literary History'. *Journal of Indian Philosophy* 39: 647–76.

____, forthcoming 'Tamil V*aiṣṇava*s, The Vedas and the Demands of Modernity', in Vasudha Dalmia and Martin Fuchs (eds), *Multiplicities and Monoliths: Religious Transformation in India, 1800–2000*. Oxford: Oxford University Press.

Ramanathan, S., 2015. 'A Historic Debate is Afoot in the Dravidian Movement: Is DMK Trying to Project a "Pro-Hindu" Image?' *The NEWS Minute*, 15 October. Available at http://www.thenewsminute.com/article/historic-debate-afoot-dravidian-movement-dmk-trying-project-'pro-hindu'-image-35172 (accessed 13 February 2018).

Ramanuja, T. Bhasya, 2005. 'Are the *maṭha*s essential?' in T. Ramanuja Bhasya (ed.), *Tirumāmakaḷ*. Chennai.

'Ramanujar (TV series)'. *Wikipedia*. Available at https://en.wikipedia.org/wiki?Ramanuja_(TV_series) (accessed 4 February 2018).

Ramaswamy, Sumathi, 1997. *Passions of the Tongue: Language Devotion in Tamil India, 1891–1970*. Berkeley: University of California Press.

Ramaswamy, T. S., 2003. *Judicial Solutions for Temple Disputes: A Critical Analysis*. Chennai.

Rangachari, Bahadur K., 2000 [1931]. *The Sri Vaishnava Brahmins*. Bulletin of the Madras Government Museum. Chennai: The Commissioner of Museums, Government Museum.

Ravindran, V., 2000. 'Discourses of Empowerment: Missionary Orientalism in the Development of Dravidian Nationalism', in Timothy Brook and Andre Schmid (eds), *Nation Work: Asian Elites and National Identities*, 51–82. Ann Arbor: University of Michigan Press.

Reddiyar, K. Venkataswami, 1981. *Nalayira Divya Prabandham*. Madras: Tiruvenkattan Tirmunram.

Rudolph, Lloyd, and Susanne Rudolph, 1967. *The Modernity of Tradition: Political Development in India*. Chicago: University of Chicago Press.

The Rules and Regulations of Bysani Madhava Chetty's Charity Fund, 1977. Madras: Madhava Chetty's Charity.

Schmitthenner, Peter L., 2001. *Telugu Resurgence: C. P. Brown and Cultural Consolidation in Nineteenth-century South India*. New Delhi: Manohar.

Schröder, Ulrike, 2011. 'No Religion, But Ritual? Robert Caldwell and the Tinnevelly Shanars', in Michael Bergunder, Heiko Frese and Ulrike Schöder (eds), *Ritual, Caste and Religion in Colonial South India*, 131–60. Delhi: Primus.

Seshadri, Kandadai, 1998. *Srivaishnavism and Social Change*. Calcutta: K. P. Bagchi and Co.

Shulman, David, 2016. *Tamil: A Biography*. Cambridge, MA: Belknap Press.

Soneji, Davesh, 2012. *Unfinished Gestures: Devadāsīs, Memory, and Modernity in South India*. Chicago: University of Chicago Press.

Spratt, P., 1970. *D.M.K. in Power*. Bombay: Nachiketa.

Srinivas, M. N., 1962. *Caste in Modern India: and Other Essays*. New York: Asia Publishing House.

'Sriperumbudur Sanskrit College'. Available at http://sanskritcollege.in/samvardhini.html (accessed 9 January 2018).

Srivathsan, A., 2014. 'Reforms in the House of God'. *The Hindu*. 13 January. Available at https://www.thehindu.com/opinion/op-ed/reforms-in-the-house-of-god/article5570711.ece (accessed 22 March 2016).

Stein, Burton, 1965. 'Coromandel Trade in Medieval India', in John Parker (ed.), *Merchants and Scholars: Essays in the History of*

Exploration and Trade, 47–62. Minneapolis: University of Minnesota Press.

Steinschneider, Eric, 2016. 'Beyond the Warring Sects: Universalism, Dissent, and Canon in Tamil Śaivism, ca. 1675–1994'. Ph.D. thesis, University of Toronto.

'Subramania Bharati'. *Wikipedia*. Available at en.wikipedia.org?wiki?subramania_bharati (accessed 3 June 2016).

Subramaniam, Kuppu, 1974. *Brahmin Priest of Tamil Nadu*. New Delhi: Wiley Eastern.

Sundaram, B. M., 2011. 'Harikatha Kalakshepa'. *Narthkai*, 15 March. Available at www.narthaki.com/info/articles/art294.html (accessed 16 May 2014).

Tarabout, Gilles, 2016. 'Birth vs Merit: Kerala Temple Priests and the Courts', in Daniela Berti, Gilles Tarabout and Raphael Voix (eds), *Filing Religion: State, Hinduism, and the Courts of Law*, 3–33. Oxford: Oxford University Press.

Tatachar, D. Ramaswamy, 1937. *The Vanamammalai Temple and Mutt*. Tinnevelly.

Thurston, Edgar, 1909, assisted by K. Rangachari. *Castes and Tribes of Southern India*. Madras: Government Press. Available at http://openlibrary.org (accessed 10 January 2015).

The Times of India, 2009. 'Court Refuses Armed Guards for Jeeyar', Chennai, 5 May. Available at http://timesofindia.indiatimes.com/city/chennai/Court-refuses-armed-guards-for-Jeeyar/articleshow/4484179.cms (accessed 3 June 2016).

Trigger, Bruce G., 2003. *Understanding Early Civilizations: A Comparative Study*. Cambridge: Cambridge University Press.

Upadhyay, Surya Prakash, 2013. 'Sanskritization at Large: Cultural Changes in Contempoary India'. *Indian Anthropologist* 43 (2): 1–44.

Vaithees, V. Ravi, 2016. *Religion, Caste and Nation in South India: Maraimalai Adigal, the Neo-Saivite Movement and Tamil Nationalism*. Oxford: Oxford University Press.

Vanidasan: Selected Poems Translated into English, 2001, Pondicherry Institute of Linguistics and Culture (ed.). Pondicherry: Pondicherry Institute of Linguistics and Culture. Digitized by the University of Michigan, 15 May 2008.

Veeramani, K., 1992. *Periyar on Women's Rights*. Madras: Emerald.

Venkatachari, K. K. A, 1978. *The Maṇipravāḷa Literature of the Śrīvaiṣṇava Ācāryas*. Bombay: Anantacharya Research Institute.

Venkatesan, Archana, 2010. *The Secret Garland: Āṇṭāḷ's Tiruppāvai and Nācciyār Tirumoḻi*. Oxford: Oxford University Press.

Venkatesan, Archana, and Crispin Branfoot, 2016. *In Āṇṭāḷ's Garden: Śrīvilliputtūr*. Mumbai: Marg Foundation.

Vijayavenugopal, G., 2007. 'Sri Vaisnavam-Tomorrow', in *Symposium on Sri Vaishnavam Tomorrow*, 6–18. Chennai: Bysani Madhava Chetty's Charity Fund.

Viraraghavacharya, T. K. T., 1962. *History of Tirupati (The Tiruvengadam Temple)*. Tirupati: Tirumala-Tirupati Devasthanams.

Vishwanatha, Rupa, 2014. *The Pariah Problem: Caste, Religion, and the Social in Modern India*. New York: Columbia University Press.

Waghorne, Joanne Punzo, 1985. *Images of Dharma: The Epic World of C. Rajagopalachari*. Delhi: Chanakya.

Williams, Raymond B., 1988, 1991. 'Śrīvaiṣṇava Handwritten Field Notes'. Wabash College Lilly Library Archives: Crawfordsville, Indiana, USA.

Wohlrab-Sahr, Monika, and Marian Burchardt, 2012. 'Multiple Secularities: Toward a Cultural Sociology of Secular Modernities'. *Comparative Sociology* 11: 875–909.

Yamunan, Sruthisagar, 2015. 'DMK Against Fundamentalists, Not Hindus'. *The Hindu*, Chennai. 4 April. Available at www.thehindu.com/news/interviews-with-dmk-chiefm.../article7068535.ece (accessed 3 April 2018).

Young, Katherine K., 1978. 'Beloved Places (*ukantaruḷiṉanilaṅkaḷ*): The Correlation of Topography and Theology in the Śrīvaiṣṇava Tradition of South India'. Ph.D. thesis, McGill University.

——, 1983. 'Dying for *Bhukti* and *Mukti*: The Śrīvaiṣṇava Theology of Liberation as a Triumph Over Death'. *Studies in Religion (Sciences Religieuses)* 12 (4): 389–96.

——, 1995. 'Theology Does Help Women's Liberation: Śrīvaiṣṇavism, A Hindu Case Study'. *Journal of Vaiṣṇava Studies* 3 (4): 173–232.

——, 2002. 'Om, the Vedas, and the Status of Women with Special Reference to Śrīvaiṣṇavism', in Laurie L. Patton (ed.), *Jewels of Authority: Women and Textual Tradition in Hindu India*, 84–121. Oxford: Oxford University Press.

——, 2007. 'Brāhmaṇas, Pāñcarātrins, and the Formation of Śrīvaiṣṇavism', in Gerhard Oberhammer and Marion Rastelli (eds), *The Relationship between Viśiṣṭādvaita and Pañcarātra*, 179–262. Vienna: Austrian Academy of Science.

Young, Katherine K., 2009. 'Fate Hangs on a Particle: The Hermeneutics of *Bhagavadgītā* 9:32–33'. *The Journal of Hindu Studies* 2 (2): 229–41.

____, 2014. 'Śrīvaiṣṇava Topoi: Constructing a South Indian Sect through Place', in Valérie Gillet (ed.), *Mapping the Chronology of Bhakti: Milestones, Stepping Stones, and Stumbling Stones*, 335–64. Pondicherry: Publications de École française d'Extrême Orient.

____, forthcoming (a). 'Who is the Āḻvārs' Supreme God?', in Marcus Schmücker (ed.), *Changing Forms and the Becoming of a Deity in Indian Religious Traditions: The God Viṣṇu-Nārāyaṇa*, Studies in Hinduism V. Beitrage zur Kultur-und Geistesgeschichte Asiens Nr. Vienna: Press of the Austrian Academy of Sciences.

____, forthcoming (b). 'Development of the *Divyaprabandham*: A New Approach to Śrīvaiṣṇava History'.

Zvelebil, Kamil, 1974. *Tamil Literature*. Vienna: Otto Harrassowitz Verlag.

Index